THE ADDICTION RECOVERY HANDBOOK

*Understanding Addiction and Culture, Stabilizing
Chaos, and Creating a Prosperous Human Spirit
(Including a theist and an atheist path for recovery.)*

Richard W. Clark

*The world is large enough for different beliefs and yet small enough
that acceptance and respect are necessary for us to live in harmony.*

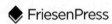 FriesenPress

Suite 300 - 990 Fort St
Victoria, BC, V8V 3K2
Canada

www.friesenpress.com

ISBN
978-1-5255-6826-8 (Hardcover)
978-1-5255-6827-5 (Paperback)
978-1-5255-6828-2 (eBook)

1. SELF-HELP, SUBSTANCE ABUSE & ADDICTIONS

2. SELF-HELP, TWELVE-STEP PROGRAMS

Distributed to the trade by The Ingram Book Company

Reviews

You may think this a long review, but the books by Richard Clark are important. Being an alcoholic, forty years of drinking, now fifteen years in recovery, I was ready to give up on trying to help drug addicts. I didn't understand them or their addictions. Then I read Richard Clark's book *Spiritual Transformation* and read this book *The Addiction Recovery Handbook*.

Richard has an analytic mind, the ability to write well and the generosity and willingness to share his hard-earned knowledge, insights and experience regarding addiction. Upon reading the book *Alcoholics Anonymous*, I understood that alcoholism was a spiritual malady and recovery depended upon a spiritual solution. Richard explains that in detail.

If you want his insight of thirty-six years of experience in addictions counselling and therapy and the insight of forty years of studying and analyzing the spiritual remedy for addictions found in twelve-step programs – read this book. If you want an understanding of addictive behaviour in life verses spiritual behaviour in life and an understanding of the confusion caused by the treatment of symptoms of addiction versus the cause of addiction – read this book. If you want to understand the ubiquitous nature of addictions in our post-industrial globalized societies or to understand why treatment centres have such dismal long-term success or high first year relapse rates – read this book. If you want to understand how an atheist can recover as effectively from addiction in a spiritual life as a theist – read this book. If you want to know more about what is going on in addiction, addiction treatment or twelve-step programs – read this book.

If you are looking for an easy read, or a pill or therapy, that will cure addictions quickly and without a great deal of work by the addict or their helpers or society, don't read this book.

. R.T. Wood

I read Richard Clark's earlier book *Spiritual Transformation* which is an extraordinary document... I learned more about the twelve steps in reading (and re-reading) that book than in thirty years of AA meetings. It methodically destroys commonly held but erroneous beliefs that keeps people shackled to lives of misery and despair. This book, *The Addiction Recovery Handbook*, is another extraordinary work by Mr. Clark. He has shaken up some commonly held, but erroneous, beliefs as to where the solutions lay in our current addictions crises. It is a very interesting read with some very astute observations. Both books are a challenging read but well worth the time and effort.

Tim M. Perritt

Other books by Richard W. Clark:

Spiritual Transformation
An In-depth Examination of Addictions… Third Edition
Friesen Press, 2017
Available at Amazon and www.friesenpress.com/bookstore
(softcover 606 pages)

Addictions and Getting Recovered
The Myths and Realities of Twelve Step Programs
Trafford Publishing, 2004 (out of print)
(softcover, 438 pages)
Being Edited and updated.
Third Edition will available late in 2020.

Permission – University of Alberta

The author is greatly indebted to Jim Hackler, formerly of the University of Alberta, Sara Dorow, Chair of the Department of Sociology, and Lesley Cormack, Dean, Faculty of Arts, University of Alberta (Edmonton). They were kind and generous in giving me permission to reprint Prof. Hackler's paper, *The Reduction of Violent Crime and Equality for Women, Discussion Paper 18*. This is reprinted in full at Appendix I.

Permission – Alcoholics Anonymous

The author is also greatly indebted to Alcoholics Anonymous World Services, Inc., for their generous permission to quote at length from their published material. The material quoted and excerpted from *Alcoholics Anonymous, Twelve Steps and Twelve Traditions*, and other material they hold copyright on is used with permission of Alcoholics Anonymous World Services, Inc. Permission to use this material does not mean or imply that AA has reviewed or approved the contents of this work, nor does it mean or imply that AA agrees with the views expressed herein. Alcoholics Anonymous is a program of recovery from alcoholism only; use of their material in connection with programs and activities which are patterned after AA, but which address other problems, or in any other non-AA context, does not imply otherwise.

Dedication

The person most responsible for influencing me into this writing requested to remain anonymous. Our meetings and conversations early in 2019 about addiction and treatment offered me new insights and left me with no doubt that this writing was overdue and is necessary. In truth, I would not have taken this to publication had it not been for my discussions with her. I know she did not intend that influence and had no idea this book would happen. She will probably be surprised by this dedication. It feels a little strange and incomplete to say thank you while she remains anonymous. This book is dedicated to her.

Acknowledgements

Encouraging and supporting me in my work and writing have been Tim Perritt, Mike Guthro, Ken Ramkeesoon, and Terry Wood. There are many others too numerous to list. It is interesting that a few people, in their disapproving criticism of my work and seminars, have helped me to understand that I have to be more outspoken.

In my own personal endeavours, there are two Buddhist monks and two spiritual advisors who wished anonymity, and several professionals I have consulted with. They have been, over four decades, significant influences. Thank you to them, distant in my past but not forgotten. I end by thanking all the students and clients I have had the pleasure of knowing. They trusted me by exposing their fears and chaos which allowed me to aid them such as I could.

Respect & Dignity

Readers may encounter ideas they disagree with. My intent is neither to insult people, nor to persuade them to reject what they believe or cherish. I am putting to words the reality I see around me, and offering alternatives to people who are foundering, confused, or dissatisfied in their pilgrimage out of addiction. The world is large enough for different beliefs, and yet small enough that acceptance and respect are necessary for us to live in harmony.

Regarding Citations and Quotations

I refer to other authors and to people who are successful or famous in various fields of endeavor. By quoting them, or referring to their ideas, I do not mean to imply that they agree with or endorse the views I offer in this book; and, I may not necessarily agree with everything they say. Regardless of this, I wish to express my gratitude to all of them for provoking and challenging and teaching me. The observations I make throughout this book are entirely my own.

Kind regards to all...
Richard Clark
White Rock, BC
May 2020

Richard W. Clark

This book cannot be read the way people ordinarily read books in this day and age. In some respects, its readers will have to work their way through each page and even each single sentence the hard way. This was done deliberately; it is the only way this book can become what it is intended to be for the reader. Simply reading it through is as good as not reading it at all. The spiritual truths it contains must be experienced; that is the only way they can be of value.

Rudolf Steiner [1]

The world is not a 'prison house,' but a kind of spiritual kindergarten where millions of bewildered infants are trying to spell 'God' with the wrong blocks.

Edwin Arlington Robinson [2]

Our unique talents or devotion may not be witnessed or appreciated on a grand scale, but the magic of the human condition is that we all harbor greatness.

Richard W. Clark [3]

We shall find that every important philosophical reformation, after a time of too highly strained metaphysical dogmatism or unsatisfying skepticism, has been begun by some [person] who saw the necessity of looking deeper into the mental constitution.

Croom Robertson [4]

1   Rudolf Steiner, Theosophy, The Introduction, 3ʳᵈ edition, Anthroposophic Press, 1994.

2   Edwin Arlington Robinson, Edwin Arlington Robinson, Selected Poems, Penguin Classics, 1997, p. xx.

3   Richard W. Clark, Spiritual Transformation, An In-depth Examination of Addictions, Third Edition, Friesen Press, 2017, footnote, Chapter 10.

4   As cited in Buddhist Manual of Psychological Ethics, Caroline A.F. Rhys Davids, 1900. Emphasis added by Rhys Davids. George Croom Robertson was a Scottish philosopher (1842-1892). His principle works were Elements of Philosophy and Elements of Psychology.

From the editor to the author:

Your thesis is the 1939 Twelve Step Program [model] is anachronistic and needs to be revised to reflect changing religious/non-religious demographics and address modern social challenges... Your analysis traces addiction as a "social enemy," a bias that has impeded effective treatment. You make a strong argument for all addiction being rooted in social and cultural causes, and your concept of *dukkha* lays the emotional source in our modern collective and individual dislocation of values, ethics, and morality. A demoralized and addicted culture is trying to fix the addiction problem, with diminished chances of success. Your justification for making needed changes to recovery treatment is "because of its attachment to religious morality, the interference of politics, associations to crime, and the historical demeaning of character."

Further to your argument, in a growing population not inclined to the notion of God-forgiveness, you make a strong point that this aspect of [traditional] treatment creates social alienation of atheists from treatment and contributes to relapse. While you don't advocate abandoning the Twelve Steps, you suggest that it become a more inclusive "spiritual" approach, one that applies the tools of psychology and education. "A model of adult education regarding addictions, relationships, culture, and the psychology of the steps... is more proximate to what needs to be achieved in recovery today." This rightfully bestows a form of empowerment to addicts to become the expert in control of their own recovery by whatever means are most appropriate. Your emphasis on recognizing the behaviours and identifying emotional responses provides a guide to communication skills, self-recognition, and self-treatment. You've written a thorough and effective tool to replace the God-forgiveness model.

Your emphasis on humility is profound: "Humility requires that the fundamental prerequisite to all interaction be a sincere belief in equality. To interact with anything other than this is evidence of racism, elitism, sexism, assuming privilege, etc., and fails to honor the universal truth of apparent unity that underlies all categorizations of life."

January 2020

Table of Contents

Preface

After hearing some well-considered observations from friends and readers it was suggested that I first explain what this book is about. Here is my attempt at explanation...

This isn't just about junkies and drunks. It's an overview of addiction as it has been seen in our history, reflected in the human condition, perceived in this society, condemned by religion, dismissed by cultural prejudices, influenced by commerce and politics, and what recovery might look like. There is ample research to say that alcoholism is the most destructive addiction world-wide, with the most visible, destructive consequences. But there is mounting evidence to demonstrate that it is not the most prolific addiction, nor is alcohol the most easily accessible in comparison to other addiction concerns.

In examining addiction, from the Temperance Movement through the opium commerce in the 1800s, a century of politics, changing culture, and prolific technology (and many other concerns), I can only say by way of introduction: It is complicated, very complicated. Most of us don't really understand alcoholism, the oldest variety of addiction, never mind the dozens of other ways addiction shows up, many with cultural approval. That, and the hundred-and-sixty-three opinions about treatment, makes writing about it seem disjointed or fragmented and appear repetitious. That is the nature of the subject.

My own experience, over forty years, is exactly that, understanding addiction is disjointed and circular. As soon as I thought I had it figured out some other influence would be discovered. In 2020, too many of us are focused on the wrong symptoms and ignore history, the complex contributing causes, and the abysmal ineffectiveness of what we now call treatment. I write about many concerns that are usually spoken of as separate from addiction, or separate from each other, or not spoken of at all.

Equally important is: This is not a condemnation of people who use recreational drugs or alcohol, buy lottery tickets, spend money, enjoy sex, watch TV, or exercise in some manner of a responsible lifestyle. One critical issue in understanding addiction, or classifying some concern as addictive or not, is whether or not there are life-damaging consequences subsequent to the behaviour. This is explained in some detail later in the book.

1

In a random order, I discuss the social views of drunkenness in the middle ages, conflict resolution, the Plague, parenting, childhood development, relationships, portable bedrooms, counsellors, doctors and psychiatry, the Temperance Movement, Narcotics Anonymous, cultural criminals, chaos in religious beliefs, communications, abuse, and adult education. There's also discussion of The Oxford Groups, laudanum, sex, opium, Buddhism, speakeasies, the Suffragettes, atheists, deists, Alcoholics Anonymous, the DEA, repetitive inadequacy, patriarchy and parallelism. There's still more on Prohibition, addiction symptoms and treatment, illness vs. disease, gangsters, the opium trade of the mid-1800s, spirituality, flappers, Victorian poetry, Protestant Christianity, Vietnam, and probably a dozen more topics. These are all at least mentioned in passing and are connected, either directly or indirectly, to an understanding of addiction and recovery.

Addiction is like a bad rainstorm. It's as if people are standing in a rainstorm and nobody knows when it started to rain or that they are all wet. I guess that's what this is about, it's pouring out there, the streets are flooded, we are all wet, and nobody knows how to get dry. Society is left in fear and dread, fumbling in inefficiency.

In a *Time Magazine Special Edition* 'The Science of Addiction' October 2019, pg. 24, Chris Anderson (now a compulsive-gambling counsellor) said of himself there are two types of people in his life, *"those who want to talk to me because they know that I get it, and those who want to avoid me like the plague because they know that I get it."* The majority of people in my life are of the second type.

I am left feeling grateful for the people who have supported me over the years in my heterodox views of addiction. I think Mr. Eliot summed it up best regarding society...

"The hubbub of a marching band going nowhere. The drum is beaten but the procession does not advance."   T.S. Eliot, *The Sacred Wood.*

I would suggest we're going backwards, never mind not advancing.

Introduction

"I must ask the reader to forgive me for having ventured to say in these few pages so much that [may be] new and perhaps hard to understand. I expose myself to [your] critical judgment because I feel it is the duty of one who goes their own way to inform society what they find on their voyage of discovery... The criticism of individual contemporaries will not decide the truth or falsity of [these] discoveries, [that is left to] future generations."

Carl Jung, *Two Essays in Analytical Psychology*

These next two brief quotes are taken from *The Idea of the World*, Bernardo Kastrup, iff/John Hunt Publishing Ltd., 2019. They set the stage, as it were, to understand more of what and how I write.

"Peer-review can be a prejudiced process that stifles valid non-mainstream views whilst overlooking significant faults in mainstream arguments... As an author whose ideas systematically defy the mainstream, I had doubts about whether [my book] would receive an impartial hearing. And indeed, often [I don't]." And, *"...peer review can also be constructive , insofar as it provides penetrating criticisms that help sharpen one's arguments."* (p. 7)

"Some repetition of content occurs across the chapters. Some readers may consider this annoying, but I think it has a positive side effect: it provides a regular recapitulation of key ideas and context throughout the book, helping the reader keep track of the overarching argument line." (p. 9)

To write about addiction and understand it is complicated. This book ended up covering more territory I originally intended. Our society, meaning everyone in it, including people with addiction and those that endeavor to assist in its resolution, have been attempting to objectify addiction(s) as a disease of sorts since about 1985. I.e. I have a broken leg; I have cancer; I have addiction, let's treat that. However, that objective and much too simplified model of disease makes it impossible to achieve recovery. An addiction is a malady or an illness, yes, but not a disease, and it cannot be objectified.

Social perceptions of gross drunkenness are embedded within the society and era they are particular to. From about 1600 CE habitual drunks were seen as a rather rare self-destructive nuisance. From about 1835 onward, in the United States, drunkenness or drinking to any degree became particularly personal because of the Protestant-religious views that drinkers were moral sinners. And, from 1920 to 1933, during US Prohibition, alcoholics were both morally degenerate and criminals for public drinking. It's been more confusing since 1939. There's more about this in Chapter 8.

Drug addicts have had quite different social stereotypes and labels to contend with. Up to about 1945 they were a minor nuisance and minor criminal. From about 1953 to 1970 it was confusing to categorize drug users, but they were still more or less minor criminals and trouble-makers. After 1973 they became serious criminals and a social enemy. In the last few decades, from about 1975, social labels for drug addicts have been ill, criminal, social enemy, morally deviant, irresponsible, and corrupt, all at the same time. I also speak to sex, gambling, religion, exercise, television, shopping, and various other addictions throughout the book. Social perceptions of them have changed, too.

Whether you think you have an addiction or not, all of this social chaos affects everyone. There are different styles of addiction which may or may not have social approval. At a different level, the extended consequences of addiction promote damage to the environment.

There are certainly religious and social-political reasons for these changing views. This is what makes understanding the history of alcoholism, addiction, and what we offer as "treatment," so important. We must know what has happened in history and use that knowledge in addressing the epidemic we are now ineffectively dealing with. All of this is extremely personal because of its effect on personality, its existing attachment to religious morality, the interference of politics, associations to crime, and the historical demeaning of character.

Addiction is personality, not an aspect of it, and affects all of an addict's perceptions, values, and thought structure. Addiction and treatment can never be objective. We cannot approach addiction like we are healing cancer or diabetes. An addict cannot separate themselves from their addiction; they cannot say: "This is me and *that* is my addiction." The addict is the illness. This is why, eventually, the addict must be taught how to become come the managing director of their recovery and manage their own healing (explained later, at footnote 46).

How we defend personal freedom against religious oppression and tolerate the intrusion of self-righteous politics and religion into personal morality, *and* how these institutions demand compliant behaviour, are historically significant. Religious morality and its legendary condemnation of addicts, alcoholics, different religions, alternative lifestyles, and choice in morality, have been present throughout history. They are still present in 2020.

There is strength in numbers so religious opinion appears strong but only because it's loud and there's a lot of them—a lot of believers and a lot of loud opinions, not because they are authentic or valid. Religion cannot adequately justify itself or its claims to truth regarding God or morality. There's a definite and increasing fragility to their influence. People with addiction are dying because of this.

In the end, the more we objectify addiction the less any treatment is effective. The label of deviant behaviour, whether it's obsessive-compulsive disorder, mania, dual disorder, depression, or addiction, is that it is an illness, not a disease. But today, the recovery sentence "I am sick not crazy," carries more the implication of disease than illness and is the life raft for addicts against social ostracism. Addiction is an illness-phenomenon related to culture and should be viewed as such.

Society attempts to separate itself from the addicts and alcoholics contained within it. People who drink, drug, gamble, or use pornography or prostitutes whether you are one or buy one, to any degree of social disruption, puts society's self-perception of moral righteousness in jeopardy. This is like the parent who refuses to associate with a disobedient child. The rejection of the child is a major part of the problem, not the disobedience. The social rejection of "certain types of addicts" is a major part of the problem. It keeps society "separate" from the addicts they condemn and innocent of all responsibility. Addicts are not separate, and culture is not innocent.

I write about all of this in this book and suggest what I hope are more effective points of view. I do hope there is enough information to shift our understanding of what we are up against with addiction.

Who is this book for?

I started out writing about the needs of people in recovery. To explain myself, that expanded into discussions of society, culture, doctors, therapists, counsellors, other professionals, theories of adult education, childhood development, clients in treatment, twelve-step participants, the AA steps, theism, deism, atheism, humanism, and some history on addictions. I wanted to ensure that I didn't fall into the trap of only offering a half-measure, which is a caution about recovery from *Alcoholics Anonymous*: "half measures availed us nothing," p. 58.

I have been asked, "Who is this book really for?" It is really for all the people in the groups listed above. It was suggested, by one of the early readers, that I write two books, one for professionals/counsellors and one for addicts. That didn't sit well with me. I was also advised if I was going to do this, it had better be thorough.

There is far too much misinformation "out there" about addiction, too much moral suspicion against addicts (in recovery or not), too much irresponsibility everywhere. There are too many people who meddle with personal opinions and make things worse, and too much chaos. Besides all of that, in a spiritual world, what's in this book applies to everyone. Why? Everyone is affected by addiction, even those that aren't addicts, and most of us are addicts to some minor or major degree (explained later).

I decided to make this for everyone. There are several reasons for this, not the least of which is that, from what I have seen, many people in the category of helper or those in recovery, are themselves subject to low-grade, culturally approved addiction. These must be, at the least, looked at and considered along with the prevailing but incorrect view that an addict or alcoholic is one because they use drugs or drink alcohol heavily. I decided to weave the information in this book back and forth between the needs of everyone, without being specific to which group the writing applies. Although, at times, that will be obvious.

The drastic changes in all areas of culture require, through education, how we view the addiction epidemic we live in. Addictions are an epidemic, worse than any plague in the dark ages. This is explained in Chapter 8. But first, we must understand the nuance of addiction outlined in Chapter 3. Explanations of the requirements of recovery are the remaining chapters. So, this is for clients, new-comers, members of self-help groups, the general public, twelve-step members, counsellors, doctors, professionals, spiritual advisors, therapists, teachers, family, friends, theists, deists, atheists, humanists, and whoever else is just curious. (Did I leave anyone out?)

Most, and I do mean most of the people I have interviewed, from highly trained professionals to people in early recovery, well-educated or not, have thoughts, feelings, beliefs, and values that are conflicted. In that inner, chaotic state of mind, they're expected to drag themselves through an ineffective 1939 recovery process. Or, from counsellors and doctors, we expect professionals to have the competence to direct resolution in others when they have the disloca-tion in themselves.

From a spiritual point of view, everyone is entitled to know everything in this book. Read it with a view to achieve what understanding you need and appreci-ate what applies to you. Leave the rest. Remember whatever doesn't apply to you will be meaningful to someone else, and everyone has a part to play.

> "Oh God, that men should put an enemy in their mouths to steal away their brains. That we should, with joy, pleasance, revel, and applause, transform ourselves into beasts!"
>
> Cassio, from *Othello*, Act II, Sc. III,
> Wm. Shakespeare, c. 1603

Readers may encounter ideas they disagree with. My intent is not to insult people, not to offend them, and not to persuade them to reject what they believe or cherish. I am putting to words the reality I see around me. What I write here is what I see and believe regarding addiction, history, culture, and transformation. We have to recover from this culture as much as anything else.

I am offering alternatives to people who are foundering, confused, or dissat-isfied in their pilgrimage out of addictions, which may be the most subversive and destructive issue facing all of society: Addiction. There are people who feel alienated because of all the God-forgiveness talk that is insidious in self-help meetings. The recovery world is large enough for different beliefs, and yet small enough that acceptance and respect are necessary for both recovery and living in harmony.

The actual dynamics of addiction require that people be spiritual to recover from them (explained later). But that can be spiritual either in psychology without religion or God, or spiritual with God-beliefs.

It must be taken into account, and not forgotten, that new people in recovery are living in delusion, defiance, denial, blind to the depth of their illness, don't understand what their addiction implies, don't know the two categories of symptoms of it, exist in broken relationships, are cynical to a noticeable degree, embody repetitive inadequacy, and are significantly dishonest and suspicious. They live with no authentic sense of what is killing them or their spirit. To demand or expect they trust anything in early recovery invites more chaos, as does too many intrusive questions. Being "spiritual" is a verb and whether humanist, atheist, theist, agnostic, or deist, that will only be available after a few years of personal effort. It is always a very slow process to acquire spiritual values and be able to act on them.

There is a need for change in the understanding of addiction, its complex origins, and treatment. It is also important to include information about the historical background of the modern social issue of addiction. What is the history of addiction (and recovery) that leads to the mess we are in today? What is addiction? What are the symptoms of it? What does "being recovered" or being spiritual mean? How does anyone get there?

Many of us need to be made aware of several concerns that are not usually spoken of in treatment or in twelve-step meetings. This will provide stable options and avenues, through knowledge, for becoming recovered. This is to assist people who are confused and dying from addictions, and there are a lot of us. All of this is spoken of in this book.

R.D. Laing offered that *"it's a very zany, peculiar field that we're talking about if we go beyond its public presentation."* In a video-taped interview he said, *"Even though our behaviour is not criminal—we are not breaking the law in terms of how we conduct ourselves—our state of mind is considered undesirable and should be put a stop to... The single word would be suffering, suffering and confusion... misery, consternation, bewilderment, constantly bewilderment, dreadful hellish states of mind that people get into by their fear. People are afraid of other people... afraid of other human beings."* [5]

---

5   Mr. Laing's comment, *"It's a very zany, peculiar field that we're talking about if we go beyond its public presentation."* was on psychiatry, taken from *R.D. Laing, The Man and His Ideas*, by Richard I. Evans, E.P. Dutton & Co. 1976. That is very applicable observation on addictions treatment: zany and peculiar. Here we will go underneath addiction's public presentation. It is much more how we treat people than how we treat their addiction. The second longer quote is taken from a YouTube interview; search R.D. Laing.

I see this as one part of the problem in addiction—the addict's fear of other people promotes lying, manipulation, and self-destructive behaviour. Many of us, addict or not, are as terrified of people, love, honesty, and true commitment to another as we are afraid of death. The uninformed general public are terrified of addicts and hold them in low regard.

This book is intended only as an introduction to addictions treatment and recovery; an entry level awareness. Only the basics are presented here, which limits the scope of what I write about. So... for what it's worth, read this carefully and have some awareness of what's discussed. It is best read the first time from beginning to end. Try not to flip around because many insights are dependent upon information that precedes them.

What May be Confusing

This is generally directed to clients or residents in treatment centers, to people in the usual collection of twelve-step programs, and the professionals, sponsors, and advisors who assist them. In my view, most people are confused about addictions, the categories of symptoms and, within the majority of the population, there are silent and unresolved prejudices against addicts. As is explained later, there's also a significant portion of the population living with socially approved, subtle addictions. All of this must be examined, especially each addict's deeply ingrained prejudice against themselves.

Ours is an era of anxiety, fear, and startling change in culture. People begin their recovery in emotional and mental chaos, feeling ashamed and afraid. Self-criticism, self-rejection, and repetitive inadequacy are prevalent in their personality. What is best for chaotic, anxious people to encounter is a stable and confident environment as their recovery experience. It must never be demanding of immediate trust or require intrusive exercises for the first few months after abstinence is achieved. The treatment environment that sees the best chance of recovery from any addiction is one that is calm, organized, focuses on addictions education with quiet, patient interventions that change attitudes and self-perceptions. God, atheism, humanism, higher powers, or spirituality should be very quiet, sideline conversations for a long time; months for sure and tailored to the needs and level of each individual. This type of non-intrusive stability is essential.

Much of this information is for counsellors and those working in the recovery industry. Many professionals, physicians of all categories, religious authorities, certainly therapists, counsellors and sponsors, lack knowledge about the drastic changes in the types of addiction. Abstinence not-available addiction (process and behaviour, sex and relationship addiction) and culturally approved addictions are now more prevalent than alcohol or drug addictions. [6] From what I

---

6   Sponsors and various "old-timers" in the usual arena of twelve-step programs are in need of more

have seen, many people including those in the category of helper, are themselves subject to low-grade, culturally-approved addictions. It is a culturally prevailing view, but incorrect, that an addict is one because they use drugs, drink alcohol very heavily, buy prostitutes, or gamble a lot.

All of this makes any traditional model of treatment less effective. "Mild" addictions are rarely seen as harmful because they are socially acceptable, and these addicts are socially functional. This is the principle bar to a spiritual life for people in mediocre recovery—their reluctance to challenge socially-approved addictions. This is examined in some detail later. Any socially-approved addict is reluctant to challenge any low-grade addiction which reluctance is, itself, symptomatic and related to the psychology of addiction. The defeating mindset of concealment being safer than disclosure is what makes Chris Anderson's comment, in the preface, substantively true: hiding from exposure.

Certainly, this book may be for sponsors or spiritual advisors who are lost in the enormous changes in various twelve-step programs, themselves unsure of what to do. Altogether too many people are involved in culturally approved addictive behaviour (see Chapter 3) which makes all of this muddy and confusing.

There are also drastic changes in religious perspectives which affect, and should modify, how we do or don't continue to embrace the 1939 model of recovery (more later). We are in an epidemic of addiction, much worse in both magnitude and consequence than any plague in the late middle ages (more in Chapter 8).

For clients, newcomers, twelve-step members, counsellors, professionals, family, lovers, and friends, there is often a real frustration. "That person (or group) doesn't understand what I, we, or you, need here." And, from traditional twelve-step sponsors, "Why don't they just surrender to the God-thing in the twelve steps and do what they are told?" The needs of any one group are often seen as conflicted with the needs of other groups. But those needs are in fact often mirrors of each other. [7], [8]

I decided to weave the information back and forth between the needs of everyone: counsellors, doctors, directors of programs, sponsors, spiritual advisors, clients, newcomers, old-timers, believers and non-believers, family, and interested outsiders. Yes, it is principally for people in recovery and those who work with them, but from a more spiritual point of view, everything in this book

---

knowledge about alternatives beyond the traditional God-Forgiveness model. Their clinging to old ideas defeats this.

7   Unmet recovery needs usually arise from misunderstandings about the illness (as opposed to moral failure), what recovery requires, and the imposition of non-essential demands.

8   It is no longer surprising to me that many people, from newcomers to professionals to religious types, when in doubt or fear, make up theories about addiction and inject them into "treatment." These theories have not been proven effective or valid, but they suit their vanity or seem convenient to conceal their lack of insight.

applies to everyone. Read this with a view to achieve what understanding you need and appreciate what applies to you. Leave the rest.

I have been told many times, by a wide range of people, that my approach to addictions and recovery is quite unique. I have also been told, more than once, I am a maverick and can easily alienate people. Both are true. As a result, a few times I have been invited to present seminars at treatment centers and within a few weeks had my seminars cancelled. The record for cancellation, at two centres, was after only two seminars. This is a very typical way my teaching was terminated:

> "...*a fundamental disagreement in addictions philosophy from a seminar presenter has created ongoing confusion and conflict for both clients and staff.*" [9]

It is interesting to me that after decades of treatment and decades of psychological analysis, some people still think this is a philosophy; there shouldn't be a philosophy. There is no philosophy about diabetes. If addiction is claimed to be an illness (or disease) there is no philosophy to be presented but a psychology to be understood. Many counselling or executive staff have been insecure about what I present, usually because it disagrees with their quasi-religious beliefs about God and they become entrenched in defensiveness. There are exceptions of course, not all staff react that way. What I believe about the psychology of addiction, and some of the historical influences, are reflected in what I teach about culture, relationships, sex, psychology, spirituality, religion, culturally approved addictions, and self-help recovery. Well, here is my addictions "philosophy" in a book.

This is a basic outline of how I understand addiction and approach recovery therefrom. Self-destructive psychology, spirituality, relationships, sex, and culture are addressed in a more all-encompassing approach than the book *Alcoholics Anonymous* and its God-forgiveness model. This is the result of my near forty years of work in this field. As was written by Thomas Merton:

> "*We owe a definite homage to the reality around us, and we are obliged, at certain times, to say what things are and to give them their right names and to lay open our thought about them to the [people] we live with.*" [10]

In the time of Bill Wilson, principle author of *Alcoholics Anonymous*, the Christian orientation presented in that book and in meetings of that era were the only course available to them. What has become evident since then is there are other options. Addictions "treatment" is often-times sadly out of date as regards

---

9   An edited representation from personal communications received by the author.

10   Thomas Merton, *No Man is and Island*, Shambala Publications Inc., p. 200.

the needs of individual addicts-alcoholics in this culture. Far too many people are lost in the imposed religious perspectives of recovery that arose in 1939. It is a significant and unnecessary roadblock for most of the people in recovery today. [11]

Our cultural environment of 2020, and its contribution to addiction, is a modern-day catastrophe. Society's very dislocated structure with technology, convenience, greed, celebrity worship, and disposability, are primary causes of addiction. Yet, in this addicted culture is where we are trying to fix it. We are rescuing people from a fire that we started and telling them to live in a burning building.

Since AA's origin there are new and dramatically different cultural changes to employment, education, sexuality, some drugs now legal, designer drugs and opiates illegal, unstable relationships, socially approved addictions, abstinence not-available addictions, family disintegration, and much higher levels of stress. There's the loud voice of big pharma companies advertising drugs on television creating hypochondria. Some doctors create addiction by prescription and then patients walk across the street to another doctor to be treated for addiction.

There's the influential voice of formerly silent minorities, increased immigration, globalization of business, the modernity of this culture, stress, exposure to different religions, the drastic increase in atheism, and gender equality. All of these are strong contributing factors to the rise in addictions. These altogether create an extremely different recovery population than in the 1940s. I do not intend to criticize them but to appreciate their influence in recovery.

These observations are made to point out how recovery programs, professionals, treatment, and the public, must incorporate all of this into their offerings of assistance. They cannot, with success, demand from new people in this different culture compliance with the Christian God-forgiveness model from 1939. [12] It is also apparent that spirituality and humility, which are essential to recovery, are misunderstood as religious dogma.

---

11   Reduced religious influence is a problem for some people in society and for religious organizations. For contemporary recovery meetings and treatment, the decrease of a God-perspective can be a source of recovery chaos (Who and what do I believe?), desperation and confusion for some (Where do I go now?), and a sense of relief for others (I'm relieved I don't have to believe, but now what do I do?). Any external emotional chaos, or any chaos for that matter, is a serious detriment to recovery, to education and therapy, and in the long-term to a spiritual lifestyle. At the same time, the atheists or humanists in treatment and recovery are reasonably expected to rise to near fifty percent of the general population in the next ten years. That must be taken into account, and at the same time, it is also important for the remaining group of religious theists or deists to have their views respected in their recovery. (More on this later.)

12   Forgiveness is optional, which is dependent on a person's perspective of "illness." I know this will generate some controversy with some people, but it has proven viable. See Chapter 8 in this book and 'Contracts and Forgiveness' in *Spiritual Transformation, Third Edition*, Richard W Clark, pp. 332 – 352.

There are areas wherein formal treatment or self-help recovery groups fall far short of effective intervention. They lack accurate and needed information on sex, the dynamics of the illness itself, addiction's cancerous-like influence on relationships and sexuality, or the popularity of abstinence not-available addictions. Nor do they usually incorporate any alternative to the God-focused perspective as regards spirituality.

Increased effectiveness regarding all of this can be accomplished by well-presented education, not general education but adult education. Factual information about addiction (both personal and cultural), successful self-restraint (in Chapter 3), options for a spiritual lifestyle, addiction symptoms, its disruption of relationships—intimate, social, and professional—and the specific needs of clients in short-term intensive treatment, must be understood.

What is often left unstated is the culpability of some sponsors, groups, programs, and culture. Far too often, in the face of externally imposed chaos or outdated treatment, the client or newcomer is left subconsciously desperate and gets blamed for a lack of effort or a having superficial commitment. [13]

The helpers, whether lay persons or professionals, may be well-intended, no doubt there, but good intentions do not lower the relapse or increase the recovery rate. I have worked with many care-givers who were acting out in socially approved addictions, themselves being angry, belligerent, or patronizing and non-accepting of a client's unique needs. This is often insight-related and as helpers acquire new knowledge and develop an inner-directed sensitivity, they become more compassionate.

Some counsellors (and sponsors) expect their clients should simply agree with any counsellor-imposed agenda. In a camouflaged way this really means, "Do what you are told by me and be like me, and you will be okay." When I have consulted as a supervisor to counsellors, what has often been apparent is they approached "counselling" with the underlying premise their job was to get the client to think and believe like themselves, the counsellor, then all would be well. This is indoctrination not treatment.

---

13   In the introduction to *Alcoholics Anonymous* a recovery rate of fifty percent immediately and twenty-five percent after a few relapses is reported. Treatment, in any disguise today, is almost unilaterally reported to be in the area of five percent successful. That original seventy-five percent AA success figure from the 1940s only confirms that the original AA program was in-line with the American-Christian culture of that era. That success does not mean those people then were more committed than people today. A 1939 recovery model was effective in the 1940s because there was a very close social parallel between that 1940 Christian culture and the Christian perspective presented in the early AA program. People in recovery in that era of AA were preaching to the choir. It is not effective in 2020 because that 1939 close parallel between society and AA no longer exists. This is why any back-to-basics program in AA is only marginally effective. Back to basics only works if we can also go back to that parallel Christian culture (unless you are already a committed Christian; then it sometimes works). For at least seventy or eighty percent of members it won't.

Many treatment centers, and certainly most sponsors, reside in a hardline, cookie-cutter mentality—every addict must address their addiction in the same way. Demanding compliance is fatal to an eventual spiritual lifestyle. [14]
What comes to light is...

(a) a reluctance for some people to embrace personal change within themselves or to resolve socially approved addictions,

(b) a reluctance for some professionals, sponsors, etc. to embrace any change in their perspectives of addiction, or to understand how to address the increasing cultural approval of addiction, ·

(c) a reluctance to implement change to addictions treatment whether step-work or professional intervention, and to advance the necessary related education for all concerned; and,

(d) for counsellors, themselves in recovery, insisting what worked for them must work for others.

Any helper at any level can only take a new person to a recovery-point just short of where the helper is. Should the helper be involved in secret addictions, culturally approved addictions, or a dominance model of helping, this energy will slow down or defeat any treatment or recovery. Part of this handbook is to bring to light these concerns. [15]

Have no doubt that a well-trained and competent counsellor who can balance an in-depth psychology protocol, with an understanding of this addictions-based culture, knows both psychological and social symptoms of addiction, and their opposite—spiritual principles, *and* can appreciate the psychology of the original steps (with or without a higher power) as the transformation strategy, is actually worth their weight in gold. That's a lot, but in 2020, this level of awareness and ability is necessary.

Here, I will repeat myself. The needs of everyone in society overlap and are interrelated in relation to addiction. I do not separate them into special groups in this writing. It is the reader who must decide on what information applies to themselves and what to do with the information presented here.

---

14 What is poorly understood is that whatever is the new person's initial exposure to recovery, whether that be stable, chaotic, rigid, old-fashioned, intrusive, God-based or not, responsible, not responsible, punitive to family, meeting unique individual needs or not—whatever that first exposure is becomes embedded as the recovery standard and influences all that follows.

15 Participants are usually well informed about a twelve-step program and society now regularly embraces recovery jargon. This, by itself, has become routinely inadequate for abstinence not-available addictions or the horrendously complex issues of sexuality, polyaddictions, integrated addictions, culture, and dual diagnosis.

Rights & Responsibility [16]

It is important that you understand these before reading further. This brief explanation is regarding your rights in personal relationships and, with that, your one responsibility. These rights should be present in all personal relationships *and* be evident in your every-day life. There are four. These will help with the observation of Bill Wilson regarding Step Eight noted in An Approach to Relationship in Chapter 2. These will also help addressing abuse in relationships as listed in Chapter 4.

You have the right to say "No."
You have the right to confidentiality.
You have the right to your dignity and respect.
You have the right to ask questions or disagree.
You have a responsibility to respect these in others. [17]

(1) You have the right to say "No" without fear of malicious or punitive consequence. This includes your right to limit your participation in activities where others demand of you more than you would care to give. If you decline an invitation to participate or limit what you do or say, there should be no other-imposed harmful consequence like being ridiculed, teased, or ostracized. People should receive respect for their personal choices not rejection or punishment.

(2) You have the right to expect confidentiality in intimate relationships; what you say or do will be kept appropriately or respectfully private. Gossip is always a betrayal of trust. Many of us think confidentiality is limited to the legislated obligation of privileged information like therapists and lawyers. Confidentiality goes far beyond that and doesn't automatically mean keeping secrets. Confidentiality, often subtly demanded by abusive people, cannot masquerade as a device to conceal reprehensible behaviour. To offer confidentiality is to offer respect and to create trust in personal relationships.

(3) You have the right to your dignity and respect. These are crucial to intimacy and spirituality. You should be treated with respect and

---

16   Rights are explained in more detail in *Spiritual Transformation*, cited earlier.

17   There are some exceptions in the areas of law and commerce, or in relation to children and their parents. This is principally to help negotiate the path from dysfunctional, abusive relationships (see the types of abuse in Chapter 4), or those that embody unequal influence or privilege which are never emotionally intimate, to healthy, spiritual relationships that are intimate. Please keep this in context. Over the years a few people have asked to reproduce this list large size, framed, to hang up. That is okay provided you have included Richard W. Clark and this book title as the source. Reproduction of this list cannot be for resale, only for limited personal use.

consideration—not knowingly be shamed or humiliated, maligned, or misrepresented through sarcasm, criticism, inuendo or patronizing behaviour. Being able to maintain our dignity throughout recovery and in our lives is crucial.

(4) You have the right to question or respectfully challenge anything that happens in relation to yourself or to those under your legitimate care. This can be particularly tense when questioning some cultural authority figure. We all have the right to understand what's happening around us, and to exit a situation or declare our opposition if we disagree. We have the right to understand what's going on in relation to ourselves. There may be other consequences to asking assertive questions but the consequences of saying nothing may be greater.

Attendant to these rights, your one responsibility is to ensure other people receive these rights from you. People must have access to these rights, and you should not deny these to others through power, criticism, debate, concealment, or punishment. We are each responsible to ensure that other people have these rights when they are in relationship with ourselves.

Without these rights we cannot be in an emotionally safe or intimate relationship. Without them, all relationships are power struggles and promote disrespect, anxiety, and conflict. When there is no access to rights and no acceptance of responsibility there is no intimacy or safety and in that, there can be no recovery. [18]

---

18   In *Spiritual Transformation*, rights are explained in the experiential chain of rights, freedoms, and values, in that order. Some of this is related to Virginia Satir's work.

Chapter 1

Some Background and Culture

Five important things that must be stressed in treatment or in recovery efforts, are: (i) an understanding of how culture is probably the most significant contributor to the increase in addictions (Chapter 8); (ii) knowing the actual dynamics of both categories of symptoms in an addiction illness. It is not a moral deficit (Chapters 3 and 8), but is still thought of that way, and neither is addiction a disease; it's an illness. Addicts and those who assist them in recovery, actually everyone, has to be clear about this. (iii) Alcoholism, drug, gambling or sex addiction, and other behaviour addictions have remarkably different histories which influence how we view and address them. (iv) Believing in God and prayer are optional opinions; and (v), this is a lifestyle change as much as anything and long-term participation in after-care support is required.

What is rarely taken into account in discussions of drunkenness or drug use are the views of culture. Interpretations changed according to religious and political undercurrents. In order to set the stage for what follows, here is a very brief outline of addiction through history. There is more detail throughout the book.

From near 1600 CE, drunkenness (as we understand it today) was comparatively rare and seen as a nuisance. Drug addiction was virtually non-existent in Europe. After 1750 or so, drunkenness was more common and seen as irresponsible behaviour. Drug addiction was hardly noticed. Near 1835 in the US, drunkenness became viewed as Protestant-religious moral corruption. Although not thought to be important, after 1850 opiates were easily available in laudanum. In Europe, England, and in the larger centers of the US, laudanum use was generally ignored because the users were mostly women. It wasn't blatant and so wasn't of serious concern to society.

Then, near 1875 the name for habitual drunkenness changed to alcoholism. Even with a new medical-sounding name, it was still viewed as being an irresponsible degenerate and very much viewed as a Christian moral problem. Alcoholics (formerly called nasty drunkards) were viewed as sinners and moral degenerates.

Opiate use was increasing through laudanum, principally used by women. For women, opiates had become an easily available solution to various problems like "the vapors," melancholy, "hysteria," cramps, depression, pain, headaches, anxiety, chaotic emotions, etc. Laudanum was easily available. Opium dens, after

16

1890, were also common in larger cities and frequented by the select few addicts who could afford them.

In 1920 alcoholics became law breakers on two fronts. First was the enforcement of drunk driving laws in Canada, the US, and the United Kingdom. And, in 1920, in the US, Prohibition appeared. Alcoholics, in addition to being morally corrupt, now had the opportunity to be social criminals because they drank. In that same era, after 1917, laudanum was no longer easily available. It had been severely restricted by federal law. An estimated ten percent of upper, middle-class women in larger cities lost their drug supply. After 1917 street-drug addicts were still rare—a nuisance and a minor side-line for law enforcement. Yes, it's complicated, but it is all related.

Then in 1933, alcoholics lost their social-criminal status in the US. Prohibition was repealed. Alcoholics were no longer criminals for drinking. They were criminals for impaired driving (rarely enforced) and still morally corrupt—religious views of sinner still prevailed.

A few years later Alcoholics Anonymous begins. Soon after 1939, alcoholics were no longer hopeless moral trouble-makers. *Alcoholics Anonymous*, the book, offered a mild parallel to a Protestant Christian semi-religious movement and began to show some success in rehabilitation: from sin to respectability. Drunks were now, in a formal way called "alcoholics" and ill with a malady called alcoholism… but still morally corrupt. This was a variation on the sinner views of The Oxford Group.

Drug addicts, who remained segregated from alcoholics, were a minor criminal nuisance until the early 1940s. Organized crime, born in Prohibition, was losing money with the repeal of prohibition. Illicit alcohol was no longer a part of their criminal purview. Gangsters, who had become somewhat organized, saw profit in drugs—principally heroin. Heroin sales were targeted for other criminals, low-income urban males, prostitutes, non-white neighborhoods, "low-life" petty criminals, and similar street-types. Cocaine became prominent later.

As an important aside to that, in the later 1940s, gambling in Cuba and shortly after in Nevada, and in Atlantic city, became a major source of criminal income. The "free-wheeling" aura of the 1920s was recreated in gambling centers. There was an organized, easy access to sex, drugs, adrenalin highs from gambling, and social defiance for the financially elite, and all generally ignored by law enforcement.

In the 1950s, with the advent of Narcotics Anonymous following thirteen years after AA, in 1953 drug addicts started to shift from being moral degenerate/criminals to being ill. They were still a moderate social nuisance. Alcoholics, much larger in number, were certainly ill as presented in AA, but were still viewed as morally irresponsible sinners (providing they didn't drive). Drug addicts were both moral degenerates and criminals. In the early 1970s everything changed. Drug addicts lost their hard-earned and newly-won illness status gained through NA. "Junkies" became hard-core, social-enemy criminals via The War on Drugs. Both addicts and alcoholics were morally suspicious, socially shunned, and still are. There's more in Chapter 8.

Side note: Worthy of reflection was the change in society's views of photographs. In the 1950s and 60s, there were pictures of naked women which were called pictures of naked women. Whether a person carried a view of religious sexual morals or was a libertarian, these were either shameful smut or just naked women. After 1975, however, these became pornography. Then came pictures of naked men, also called pornography. Apparently, other art and statues were exempt of this categorization. In pointing this out, I am only advocating for the awareness of cultural and political agendas and careful reflection. Society, especially in addiction and sexual expression, is never innocent of subtle forms of persecution. Now, back to addiction...

From about 1990 we have new, obvious social addictions like online sex, internet surfing, internet gambling, relationship and sex addiction in dating sites, spending, shopping, food, television, romance, body image, exercise, social media, technology, and celebrity worship. These, collectively, are the prominent addictions of society and are generally abstinence not-available. These are remarkably different from alcohol or drug addiction and require new intervention strategies (more later).

To ever-increasing percentages, addiction has always been around as a phenomenon of society, just perceived differently in different eras. From about 1980, for the first time in 500 years, alcohol and drug addiction were co-opted by the medical community. They were classified as an objective medical disease. That is not an improvement and creates all manner of problems (more on this later).

It has come about in recent decades that addictions treatment, with the influence of culture, medicine, psychology, technology, and psychiatry, has gone far beyond the traditional 1939 approach of the Protestant-Christian representation found in *Alcoholics Anonymous*. That focus was presented in the early decades of meetings and continues to this day. With the more complex social and associated medical issues we face in 2020, and with the phenomenal increase in culturally approved, abstinence not-available addiction, *and* the great increase in atheism-humanism, *and* the less-than-efficient medical views, changes in the traditional manner of treatment are overdue. This change is being undertaken in some centers but really should be more prevalent.

What has been left out of discussions regarding treatment (and never spoken of within twelve step meetings) is the culture of the 1930s and those addiction demographics changed drastically from then to 1970. By 1970 the culture of 1939 no longer existed. Moreover, twelve-step meetings drastically changed again in the mid 1980s. Their social structure and demographics were significantly different. But what is routinely offered within most recovery programs, and still subtly demanded within AA itself (including NA and all the others), is the basic Christian God-forgiveness model. That has not really changed since 1939. [19]

---

19   1939 is the year the book *Alcoholics Anonymous* was published.

Our society now has a widespread, seriously extensive presence of behaviour, distraction, and abstinence not-available addictions. These are often culturally approved (see Chapter 3). And, there's a significant increase in humanism, atheism, and being agnostic. These factors make it ever more necessary that recovery programs have to change. Many programs, whether formal treatment or self-help, have largely not changed to accommodate this new culture. [20]

There is the recent proliferation of no-god groups for atheists and agnostics with hundreds of groups spread across North America. Along with the presence of these humanist-atheist groups, we now have the influence of cultural changes regarding religion, stress, sexuality, the internet, the increase of abstinence not-available addictions, the easy availability of gambling, the propaganda and horrors around harm reduction, the immigration of non-Christian religions, and notable changes in age and gender demographics (especially since 1985). We are left with substantial chaos in any traditional form of treatment that may have been generally effective prior to 1975. Treatment and self-help and similar programs have not kept abreast of social changes or individual needs. In most areas all of this chaos has been ignored or unaddressed.

They have not been ignored out of indifference. What I see has happened is in two parts. (i) These social changes have been so rapid and drastic since about 1980 that many people, both addicts and helpers, have simply not known what to do and struggled along in some old facsimile of helping. (ii) People have not been presented with any viable alternative to what they have been offered. Cultural attitudes can change very quickly; treatment bureaucracies change very slowly. Twelve-step meetings are a defiant bureaucracy, as are medical interventions and most treatment programs.

The people involved, from service providers and counselors to sponsors, clients, and newcomers are unclear of what to do with all of this. They may quietly realize what is being offered doesn't work but have no alternative. They have left treatment interventions and protocols generally unmodified from the 1939 God-forgiveness model. There has been nothing available to change to, so they stayed the same.

Cultural chaos, onward from about 1890, has always contributed to addiction. More recently, the drastic changes since 1980 have largely defeated traditional recovery efforts. This needs to be explored and understood. At the minimum, this would be to examine the influence of religious violence and reactionary righteousness, the dismaying contradiction between increased education and reduced literacy, significantly increased atheism, social greed, the emotional isolation and irresponsibility inherent in technology, celebrity worship, obsessions with fitness and beauty, mass marketing, and the internet. Other influences are the cruel shift to people being disposable, part of which generates the abuse of harm reduction

---

20   There are now a few centers that are incorporating psychology and various insight programs that do not include God. This is to their credit. Abstinence or successful restraint are necessary. God isn't necessary for everyone.

(see Chapter 8), culturally approved addictions, and the continuous demonizing of addicts. A few other things, apparently innocuous to addictions like international travel, the tourist industry, a global market, cross-cultural marriage, and immigration are a sideline concern to all of this. Addictions recovery and treatment programs must respond accordingly and adjust out of the 1939 traditional AA paradigm. [21]

As much as some of this is being addressed in some quarters, there should be more adult education for clients and staff. Education is the key to change (more later). This is complicated, but it is hoped there is enough information in this book to open the door to awareness, and to encourage curiosity about new, long-range alternatives to accomplish stable recovery.

Regarding twelve-step programs, a factor that is quite frightening to many of the established members in these God-oriented programs is the terrifying possibility of the influence of the irreligious—atheists, humanists, and agnostics. I have witnessed their fear and defiance to the no-God participant time-and-again for over thirty years. They invoke the *Alcoholics Anonymous* chapter "To Agnostics" as the authority to insist on a God belief. Irreligious-humanists will soon be at forty-five percent of the adult population (see graph below). My own considered and personal estimate is close to fifty percent of the population before 2030.

There is a serious need for an effective educational approach to treatment—a more psychological approach rooted in fact. This is possible. To those who adhere to the older AA approach it will require an open-mindedness than is not presently evident. [22]

Religious Cultural Change

Religious and Irreligious in Canada

There are major changes in the beliefs of North American culture. These are significantly different from the decade that accompanied the inception of Alcoholics Anonymous. Old statistics that I have viewed from the 1920s and 30s suggest one or two percent of people declared their atheism at a public level. Humanism, only generally known to philosophers until the 1960s or so, was not discussed at all. Here are reports from StatsCan as of 2011, ten years ago:

21　My observation is that addictions treatment must now respond to these cultural and global changes and go far beyond the presentation in *Alcoholics Anonymous*.

22　The available alternative is to be spiritual in a committed style of personal psychology. That is described in some detail in Chapter 7. This would not require religion or a belief in God-higher power or even the inference of these.

- 23.9 percent of adult Canadians are irreligious, meaning atheist, agnostic, or humanist. This embraces a psychology that rejects religion and God. Within that noted 23.9 percent (4.9 million Canadians) there were:
  - 1.9 million atheists
  - 1.8 million agnostics
  - 1.2 million humanists

Of the approximately 21 million Canadians who offered census information:

- 9.8 million believed religion does more harm than good (47%),
- 13.44 million declared religion provides more questions than it answers (64%),
- 11.98 million declared religion as unimportant (57%).

These are significant numbers in a country that has a population of thirty-seven million and a long, established history of Christianity in its society and government. These numbers demonstrate a drastic increase from any earlier census. The chart shows a gradual increase from 1971 to 1991 of about four percent. Next are western provincial rates of increase of the irreligious from 1991 to 2011 from four or five percent to near twenty-four percent. That's about a five-hundred percent increase over twenty years. In the ten years 2001 to 2011 there was a ten percent increase across western Canada (Manitoba, Saskatchewan, Alberta, British Columbia, Yukon, and NWT). Altogether, this is a major shift in culture and has profound consequences. [23]

Percent of Canadians: Atheist, Agnostic, Humanist

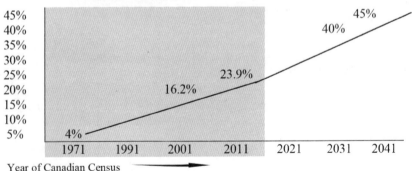

Year of Canadian Census

Figures in the clear panel (2021 - 2041) are projected over the next twenty years at an increase of irreligious-humanists at about ten percent per decade in

---

23   These figures are readily available from the Statistics Canada website.

western Canada (the approximate rate over the last three decades). Through general on-line information, these percentages are consistent with what is reported in the US, although the USA is slightly lower by approximately 3 percent. It is also slightly lower in Eastern Canada. As an aside, overall, I believe that the percentage for atheists-humanists in Canada in 2011 is under reported.

There were 4.9 million Canadians who declared themselves irreligious. There were 9.8 million who believe religion does more harm than good. There is certainly inclusion of the 4.9 in the 9.8 group. That leaves us with a strong suggestion that over four million people in Canada, who may believe in God, also believe religion is harmful (about 24 percent). This was strangely reflected in a survey in Ontario in 2011, noted below. It revealed an interesting and puzzling dynamic.

- 1,129 adults were polled in a separate survey in Ontario.
- of those who declared themselves as Catholic, 30 percent do not believe in God.
- of those who declared themselves as Protestant, 28 percent do not believe in God.

It stands to common sense that, by definition, if you are Catholic or Protestant you would be expected to believe in some Christian version of God which is a part of their mandate. But, thirty percent of these two groups, within the general population of Christian-religious folks, don't believe in God. It does sit as a puzzle how a person can claim to be Catholic or Protestant and reject their definition of a Christian God to claim atheism. Granted, this is very general, but it is worthy of careful reflection. People are fascinating. [24]

If we follow the federal census information of 2011, about seventy percent of Canadians are believers in religion in many different forms. If we take that percentage and apply it to Ontario, then the Ontario survey is generally confirmed—about thirty percent of the entire Christian faith do not believe in God.

So that leaves us with these many different groups within Canada, mostly based on Christianity:

- Religious people who believe in God.

- Religious people who do not believe in God (religious atheists).

- Religious people who believe religion causes more harm than good.

---

[24] I am not a statistician. The numbers and graph aren't perfect but are quite accurate and worthy of special notice. As regards "Christian atheists," they are alive and well. "One who denies God but at the same time asserts the excellence of Christian values and the incomparable virtue of evangelical morality." From *In Defense of Atheism*, Michel Onfray, Penguin Canada, p. 56.

- Religious people who believe that religion provokes more questions than it answers.

- Non-religious people who believe religion causes more harm than good.

- Non-religious people who believe that religion provokes more questions than it answers.

- Non-religious people who believe in a Higher Power but are not religious (deist).

- Non-religious people who do not believe in God (atheist).

- People who believe that nothing can be known about God or its existence or non-existence; claiming neither faith nor disbelief (agnostic). [25]

- People who don't know what to believe; just old-fashioned confused and avoid the whole mess.

Mix into this people from other cultures and religions who are not Christian and have a completely different concept of religious tradition. This culture is in a major chaotic transition. Confused yet?

This is presented here because of the implications for any traditional AA recovery program or treatment which is styled after the Protestant-Christian God-forgiveness model. This chaos has a detrimental effect in understanding the concepts of spirituality and the nature of illness. Forgiveness, whether a religious or a social politic, will take this entire recovery game out of the illness model which was initially presented by Mr. Wilson in 1939 (more on this later).

Inference and Innuendo

Aside from those atheist percentages, within our English or French language in Canada, and certainly within the USA, our language is itself heavily indoctrinated with Christian religious innuendo and inference. An unexamined part of our language used in treatment and recovery embodies the ideas of religion and God in our everyday communication.

The dynamic of religious inference is always at play in the use of the word God or higher power. It is the same with using the words salvation, redemption, sin, Christmas, spiritual, atonement, pilgrim, forgiveness, charity, and miracle. This

---

25 Agnostic is a word coined by Mathew Arnold (1822-1888), an English poet and cultural critic of industrialism. As a result of the cultural and religious uncertainty in England subsequent to the published work of Charles Darwin (and several others c. 1855) Mr. Arnold wrote a poem, *Dover Beach* (pub. 1867). It speaks to a religious, cultural uncertainty that was quite pervasive in England at that time.

unexamined inference of religious-language is the ocean we swim in. Anyone may claim their use of the word God or miracle does not imply a traditional Christian perspective, but it does. Our language and culture, and several federally imposed statutory holidays, are so heavily indoctrinated in Christianity that a disrespectful mandate exists. The full array of non-Christian Canadian citizens, including the present thirty percent of the irreligious, are politically forced to participate in a religion that isn't of their choosing. This goes unexamined. [26]

Up to about the year 2000 the presence of atheists was known and tolerated within AA. There were very few admitted ones and they were quiet about it. Now they are not so quiet, and they are socially ostracized. The increase of the irreligious is a fact that traditional AA-style addictions treatment, recovery, and culture must now contend with. This is evident in the simple graph (above) that shows their rapid rate of increase. As I have seen in programs and treatment, this drastic change is often left unaddressed and actually contributes to relapse. It cannot continue to be ignored.

While considering this, know there are five strong criteria to suggest that the category of the irreligious will increase more rapidly over the next decade, not ten percent but probably closer to fifteen percent. A reasonable projection is that by 2030 at least forty-five percent of the population will be irreligious, and possibly fifty percent. The five criteria that will stimulate more rapid change are:

(i)   The more religious of the god-believers/theists are often over sixty years old. Their absence from religion through attrition (illness and death) will be a significant influence.

(ii) Science and physics are more and more capturing the minds of people. Religion or God will become of less and less influence or relevance. This attitude will increase.

(iii) Addictions are increasing, especially to culturally approved abstinence not-available addictions. For any abstinence not-available addiction successful self-restraint can be quite confusing to sort out and should be approached carefully. (More on this later.) People of this era with these addictions will examine their psychology more than their relationship with God.

(iv) The awareness of historical religious corruption will increase. The abuses, unearned wealth, lack of charity; their tax-free status, religious wars and conflict, religious terrorism, persecution of cultures and other religions, sexism, racism, and criminal complicity in hiding abusers and terrorists, will become more exposed. This will increase the numbers of category (ii). [27]

---

26   This concept is admirably addressed in *The Christian Delusion*, ed. John W. Loftus, Prometheus Books, 2010, at p. 33.

27   This is evident in the popularity of books by Michel Onfray, Christopher Hitchens, Peter Boghossian, Peter Watson, Matthew Kneale, John W. Loftus, and many other writers about atheism. There is also the film *Religulous*, Bill Maher, writer, and produced by Larry Charles, 2008. Athe-

(v) The irreligious are speaking out more. Humanists and atheists are out of hiding, which makes the more-timid non-believers more outspoken about their non-belief.

Addictions Treatment and The AA Model

What this means for traditional AA-based (God-oriented) treatment is that presently at least thirty percent of members of twelve-step groups, or clients in treatment centers, are irreligious. Within a few years, it will be upwards of forty-five or fifty percent. These people will resist any "God or religious" focused program and pretend or pay lip-service to remain included in treatment. They quietly sense they need treatment but must endure the imposition of finding God. Nothing is ever made peaceful by righteousness.

If clients don't believe there is a god, what's presented in any traditional program (whether professional treatment or self-help recovery) will not be taken seriously. They won't feel supported or respected. If there is no suggested alternative, atheists won't participate sincerely. There can be no personal investment in recovery if their beliefs are not respected. The irreligious will keep their disagreement a secret and create an impression management scheme. [28] AA-Grapevine Publishing recognized this in 2018. They published a recovery book for atheists and agnostics. [29]

The psychology within the AA literature is quite profound. Sidestep around God and praying and understand the steps present a process of personal change in the only sequence it can be (psychologically) successful and authentic. This demonstrates a valid structure for psychological change, but an in-depth analysis of that intrusive psychology is not relevant here. What is briefly explained later is, AA offers outside of God, day-to-day sobriety, understanding addiction as an illness not a disease or moral deficit, identifying that help is required and seeking that, identifying inner emotional turmoil, allowing internal healing, being honest, never blaming, and taking responsibility. Next is externalizing that responsibility into making amends in relationships and community on a moment by moment basis. That creates new and stable relationships. And lastly,

---

ism and disapproval of religion have now become social forces to contend with.

28 Impression Management: Investing energy and conscious effort into making oneself appear as one is not. I.e.: A god-believer when you're not. A heterosexual when you're not. Accepting and tolerant when you're not. It's a devious self-advertising campaign designed to conceal shame, character defects, or aspects of personality that might well meet with social sanction. All "unacceptable" aspects of personality are concealed by creating a false impression. This is a significant manipulation strategy and should be carefully examined.

29 *Under One Tent – Recovery for Atheists and Agnostics*, an AA-Grapevine publication, 2018. One of the recurring themes mentioned throughout that book is the intolerance received by atheists from believers (in a program that declares acceptance as significant).

to commit to insightful understanding through frequent meditation. It works, with or without God or prayer.

What must be born in mind is that a valid healing psychology is buried underneath a lot of Christian, religious rhetoric that represents the American, patriarchal culture of 1939. In meetings today people more and more read "around" the God parts. Certainly, there are those people of a strong Christian bent that declare God as essential, some with conviction, others without conviction (hoping it's true), but proclaim God as a required truth anyway. For both atheists and believers, underneath any adamant declarations about the existence or non-existence of God, God is still an opinion.

Feminism declares that God may be a Her not a Him (yet another opinion). Some alcoholics won't read any AA literature and they still stay sober. There are No-God recovery groups all over North America. The Washingtonians, c. 1845, were successful, possibly more than AA in their early decades, and they were generally secular. That group fell apart because of politics not because of ineffectiveness in establishing personal recovery.

Some people see God as an unnecessary or harmful fiction, others see God as essential, and both types stay sober (and both types relapse). The historical philosophy of God as the only higher power is being abandoned. There are many atheists in twelve-step meetings who hide their atheism to avoid social ostracism. Many god-oriented members are disgruntled by atheism, which is palpable in some meetings. [I have been verbally attacked and argued with many times for speaking such heresy in recovery meetings and seminars.] Other God-believers claim strong faith but secretly can only hope it's true. Social rejection of the irreligious within meetings, although usually silent, is real and tangible. [30]

Everything, to this point, shows a definite but unexamined general chaos and despair in modern culture and desperation in recovery. Everyone (and no one) is responsible. What must be learned is (a) the significant contribution that culture is making to the drastic rise in addictions; and (b), the significant need for many to step around God and religion in recovery. [31] What we must come to terms with is, (i) in the treatment of addiction, we are not treating an illness, a disease *or* addiction, we are treating people; and (ii), addiction is never an issue of God-deficiency. [32]

---

30 In Bill Wilson's writing, cofounder of Alcoholics Anonymous, *The Best of Bill*, and in *Language of the Heart*, he makes observations in the early 1960s that are worthy of note. One of them is his reflection about how many recoveries were scared away by Christian dogmatism and righteousness (my words).

31 A point to remember is desperation is always a destructive reason to force yourself into some belief system that doesn't sit right. To be repeatedly told some version of God is your only option is certainly untrue and will be either disrespectful or abusive. This is something that very few people are willing to discuss.

32 Treating something like diabetes or diarrhea is focused on that specific illness—treat the disease. Fair enough. Addiction is a mind-set of self-destruction and severe relationship alienation. This

The Solution

In terms that are overly simplified, the education that I propose throughout this book is required because of the two clusters of symptoms—social and psychological, the misdirection in modern recovery, the never-discussed horrific relapse rate, and the ever-decreasing importance of God. That requires the need to examine the influencing chaos of culture and culturally approved addiction. Altogether, this makes necessary:

- Entry-level education. For recovery, this is more effective than therapy. A well-grounded education regarding the aspects of addiction, culture, and relationships, is first. This must be dependable and authentic. People first have to know what they are up against—know their enemy. Then the steps are completed as psychology, and after that, if necessary, a proper course of trauma reduction and therapy can be initiated. (The involvement of God, or not, is a decision of personal opinion that comes much later.)

- The classic 1939 AA process is only for those who eventually choose to believe in God. This belief and the AA-historical suggestion of the God-Forgiveness model is a personal choice. It is not required, it's optional.

- For humanists, atheists, and other non-believers, again a personal opinion, there are very successful, dependable alternatives within psychology. This involves a different understanding of the twelve steps with the same end result (more later).

The twelve steps are always the specific path. What is determined by the individual is whether these are from a deist or an atheist point of view.

- For new people, if they are unsure of what to believe, no indoctrination should occur. Don't impose anything. Say nothing about theist, deist, atheist, or agnostic. Eventually they will choose whichever path of opinion they want.

- Becoming spiritual is the process out of addiction, not god-believing or atheism.

- A person can be spiritual through psychology and not believe in religion or God. Being spiritual, outlined in the five spiritual principles (Chapter 7),

---

culture is alienation personified. We cannot treat addiction as a disease; it isn't one. At one level we must learn to educate culture, at another level we "treat" the entire person for an illness that is incredibly unique among other illnesses and singularly peculiar to each person, and an extension of the culture they have experienced, again exclusive to them. Very few people have come to understand this. (Footnote 46 relates.)

27

regardless of your beliefs, is achievable by completing the steps as a path of psychology.

Everything appears to be pointing to the dislocation in culture as the major contributing factor to the increase in addictions. Bruce Alexander calls this modernity (briefly explained and cited later). Everyone is, to some degree, responsible for this but no one should be blamed. It is true and worthy of respect that Bill Wilson *et al* patched together the twelve steps in a way that has stood the test of three generations. However, Mr. Wilson's 1939 culture is gone. This culture's increasing humanist-atheist membership, and radical change in addiction, requires change to that older process.

We (a very generic we) have to be entering the arena of psychology as treatment with reality-in-education and personal responsibility as the primary approach. As it says in the 1939 version of How It Works, we cannot cling to old ideas and expect any progress. [33] A well-grounded adult education, as the introduction to all recovery, is the principle focus that we must use to unravel this Gordian Knot.

---

33   Letting go of old ideas, a statement in How It Works (p. 58 *Alcoholics Anonymous*) has no restrictions attached to it. We are now at the stage where some old ideas from *Alcoholics Anonymous* must be let go of and the influence of culture and society must be examined. An excellent read about old ideas and changing them is found in *Being Wrong, Adventures in the Margin of Error* by Kathryn Schulz, HarperCollins, ECCO Paperback, 2011.

Chapter 2

A Change in Focus

"If you think education is expensive, try ignorance." [34]

What we fail to take into consideration is the book *Alcoholics Anonymous* (written in 1938, published in 1939) is now eighty-one years old. It represents one perspective of <u>one</u> addiction, alcoholism, from an almost ancient civilization—a different culture.

There were radically different principles for work and recreation. Attitudes in society were also drastically different than they are today. Protestant religion ruled the country. Homosexuals were not welcome in society, neither were drug addicts (and in some areas neither are welcome today). There were different cultural beliefs about women and children and dramatically different sexual values. In 1934 thirty percent of the work force was unemployed and twenty percent of the people were dependent on government social programs.

In 1939, AA catered to a sociologically restricted membership—no Muslims, few Jews, no declared atheists, no persons of colour, no Aboriginal-first nations, and no alcoholics that were not extremely desperate. Moderate alcoholics need not apply. The AA guidelines carried an imposed Christian religious view, there were no women for the first four years, and no young people for decades. That process was designed principally for white, American males, over thirty years old, who were definitely Christian. God was a He, the culture was patriarchal, and it was alcohol only.

As we study the book *Alcoholics Anonymous*, and the literature that arises consistent with it, it can only allow us to be familiar with 1939. All we can learn is the very limited psychology of that decade, their perceptions of alcohol addiction, and the religious-social structure of that era. Some of it may be transferable into 2020 but considering the very drastic changes to culture and society, much of that old perspective is notably outdated. It can never go farther than making us conversant with what was believed in 1939. This is clearly demonstrated within the chapters To Agnostics and More About Alcoholism in that book.

Today, without exposing the essential psychological truths in the AA book, new members must sift through the rubble of a declining religious influence, the subtle Christian-God focus still prevalent at meetings, and the ever-increasing

---

34   Said by Derek Bok, former president of Harvard University.

and still ignored presence of humanist-atheism. A frequent misperception of agnostics is they are too scared to choose one way or the other. There's also the importance of the equality of women (which to some men is still a force they cannot contend with, and with some women a responsibility they refuse to embrace), the dramatic increase of young people, new sexual values, and modified categories of addiction. There's MF (militant feminism), MWGTOW (Men Who Go Their Own Way), both probably over reactions to a necessary social process. The debates rage. Recovery politics affect spiritual serenity.

And of course, there's technology (a drastic influence in itself), the addicted chaos and anger of this culture in general, and that presently at least thirty percent of the adult population are humanists or atheists/agnostics. What this means is to "demand" or suggest that the only possible avenue to recovery is limited to a 1939-style of Protestant God-forgiveness is seriously defeating to our present-day needs. Becoming spiritual is the process out of addiction, not god-believing or obedience to a 1939 Christian patriarchy.[35]

Being spiritual must now be seen to be one of two general options: (i) with some form of God as a higher power for the present sixty-five percent that are theists; or (ii), as an agnostic-atheist process of spirituality for the remaining thirty-five percent. The ratio is quickly changing, and treatment programs must respond.

None of this is meant to exclude those who choose to believe in God or choose the traditional approach. That perspective is also viable and to be supported in any recovery program. This writing is intended to increase awareness for all concerned; to open up spirituality and recovery to everyone. Dependable adult education is an essential first-step to all treatment, irrespective of beliefs.

Mr. Bok's quote cited at the start of this chapter is quite applicable to addiction. I'll amend it: If you think recovery is expensive, try ineffective treatment and relapse.

An Adult Educational Approach

(Here's the first big shift in perspective.)

Any approach to addictions recovery, whether god-believer, religious, humanist, atheist, deist, theist, or agnostic must take into account the dynamics

---

35   There is a chapter in *Alcoholics Anonymous*, To Agnostics. That chapter is not to accept agnostics, but to explain that if a person is an agnostic or belligerent to the God idea, they must eventually come to believe in a higher power (call it what you will). This is not acceptance of agnostics or atheists. The chapter is a warning, or a veiled threat, that if a person doesn't come to sincerely believe "in God" there is no hope. In the last thirty years of listening to people talk about their "faith" in God, it appears to me it's a declared conviction of many but only hopeful in strong words.

of adult education. To not do this is to promote ineffectiveness. As I learned from creating the program *Education for Abusive Men* in 1987, an educational approach was more successful than a therapeutic approach for early intervention. There are many complex issues that have proven this true, much too complex for this writing, but here is an over-view.

There is still, in the general public, a significant degree of cultural shame attached to mental illness. Thus, to categorize addictions recovery as emotional-illness therapy or as a quasi-Christian religious discipline to address moral failure, in this culture, implies it is either a mental health or religious moral issue. As regards the people in recovery, this also reinforces their almost subconscious self-perception they are deviant or morally suspect. [36]

People in school are more accepted than people in (mental) institutions or addictions treatment centers. People would sooner be told they need to learn about addiction—let's be students, rather than be subjected to a course of quasi-religious indoctrination or be a mental health case and the social suspicion associated with that. Education would alter the internally imposed shame, which is the addict's historical indoctrination into cultural disapproval. What should matter is which approach, therapy, religion, or education, offers the best chance for social acceptance, less shame, and the longer-range possibility of success. After detoxification, if that's necessary, and the stabilization of any collateral medical concerns, the best choice for initial intervention is education, not doctors for the addiction. [37]

Addictions counsellor training has often been a learning curve of a four-point program: (i) expose and explore feelings, (ii) present a God-Forgiveness indoctrination into the AA steps with some quasi-religious version of humility and prayer, (iii) encourage meetings and sponsorship; and (iv), keep proper case files on the possible success of this indoctrination for a bureaucracy. In these times, this is inadequate. Today we need counsellors and therapists to be properly trained to a high level of proficiency regarding addiction (presently quite limited), adult education (presently non-existent), psychology and relationships (very minimal), atheist spirituality (generally ignorant of such a thing), cultural influences (not taught at all), and the psychological dynamics of the AA steps underneath the religious speculation (not understood).

There has been the attendant and shallow perception that because the counsellor is sober, only they can help you. The worn-out adage that a counsellor is trustworthy because they are themselves "in recovery" carries little weight by itself in these modern times. It is inefficient in most aspects as it parallels some vague cautionary tale of a 1940 AA program—counsellors getting paid for acting

---

36   This is evident in the number of people who keep their recovery efforts secret from the general public. Social suspicion and ostracism in a perception of moral corruption are still rampant regarding addictions. This is partly related to the myth of the war on drugs (more later).

37   Many professionals of medicine and therapy would be resistant to losing their cash cow that has been so lucrative since about 1980.

like traditional sponsors. This is born out of the late-1970s recovery houses. The assumed, but mostly flawed, prerequisite for success is the sober counsellor will teach and indoctrinate the morally bad, irresponsible drug or alcohol addict into pseudo-Christian values, which is a part of the problem in the first place. This is, at best, only marginally effective for some people who already have some notable commitment to Christian values. It is marginally effective because this traditional approach leaves too many essentials unexamined.

Far too many helpers believe the game is to get the new person to adopt the AA God-forgiveness paradigm. Get sober because God wants you sober, God-is-love, pray and forgive—it's the benevolent Christian thing to do. Expose your guilt and shame, be sorry for everything, make amends for your sins, and it will eventually turn out well (review footnote 13). That makes recovery very much a religious hit-and-miss proposal which seldom works and increases repetitive inadequacy (explained later).

Today, the presentation of God-in-spirituality is more akin to Christian proselytizing than actual treatment. This is offensive to many, misunderstood by almost everyone, and a throw-back to a 1939 American culture that no longer exists. It was effective then for morbid alcohol consumption, it isn't now.

A model of adult education regarding addiction, relationships, culture, and the psychology of the steps avoids all of this and is more proximate to what needs to be achieved in recovery today. Education is easier to approach and less awkward for a shame-based clientele to participate in. It more easily undermines cultural suspicion towards addicts. The presently existing programs, with appropriate changes that would shift from subtle religion to education, would be more successful. [38]

---

38   The actual dynamics of being spiritual are never available to a new person. Being spiritual, in the arena of addiction recovery, is a verb with specific underlying values and attitudes. It is always a very slow process to acquire spiritual values and behave spiritually (the verb part). It will be available after several years of sobriety and diligent personal effort. Being spiritual is living a life that is governed by the five spiritual principles. It must be taken into account that practicing addicts and new people in recovery are living in delusion, defiance, denial, are blind to the depth of their disease, don't understand what addiction implies, are ignorant of its actual symptoms, are cynical and defensive to a noticeable degree, embody repetitive inadequacy, and are significantly dishonest and suspicious. Yes, it is that complicated. They live with no authentic sense of what has killed their spirit. Being spiritual for them is completely out of reach for a long time, as is a true sense of trust. To expect spirituality or trust in recovery earlier than five years invites more chaos—the premature imposition of non-essential demands.

Education and Trust of Process [39]

What I understood in 1987 when I was creating the *Education for Abusive Men* program for a community college outreach program, is that the briefness of a one-or-two-month program is more effectively addressed as education rather than treatment or therapy. In a purely therapeutic construct, it is too brief to be called therapy. There are many advantages to an educational approach rather than a therapeutic or religious one in early recovery.

One significant improvement is that education loses the taint of religion and its confusion, its aura of righteousness, abuses and sexism, and the need for faith. Education sidesteps all those issues and avoids the emotional confusion of God, miracles, faith, opinion, dogma, and doubt. Education and going to school also avoids the cultural suspicion and stigma of mental illness and moral failure. Trust in education is easier than trust in therapy or faith in God.

People develop stability by understanding their own addicted personality and being capable of making informed choices based in fact. This makes addiction knowledge equally important to all students. Considering that students volunteer for adult courses, like being a veterinarian or a welder, the students want to learn; they have an emotional investment in the subject. Learning about addiction has emotional investment. Learning about some questionable version of religion and prayer is not specific to the task at hand—resolving addiction. At some time in the future, after education, a student can choose a theist or atheist or agnostic approach, whichever opinion appeals. What they choose to believe in the future has no effect on what they need to learn today.

Adult education about addiction is, in many perspectives, similar to some types of therapy. In a classroom or a therapist's office people learn about their personality and then decide to change or not. People will or will not follow the insights of therapy. For theists or deists, education leaves their coveted God opinions untouched. For humanists or atheists, there is no suggestion about God or faith; for agnostics there's no pressure to believe one way or the other, therefore no conflict because all their opinions are left untouched. Education is more appealing to all concerned.

In education, the student develops a respect for their teacher and a strong interest in the subject being taught (which has emotional investment because the subject is actually themselves *vis a vis* addictions psychology). Education does not require emotional trust in anything, therapy does. The selfishness inherent in addiction consistently shows in early recovery that people are more interested in themselves than anything else and don't trust others. Education actually lowers the level of trust required which makes it more appealing to pessimistic, suspicious addicts. There's more in Chapter 3.

---

39   Regarding adult education, here I do not mean young adults that progress fairly quickly from high school to university. I mean adults that are pursuing recovery or education that is outside of the traditional structures of "school."

From one perspective, the difference is in therapy the client must develop a close bond or emotional relationship with their therapist. In education, knowledge is the strength. In therapy, the therapist is the therapy. The trust is in the integrity of the therapist and not so much in the material being discussed. When therapy is well conducted trust takes many, many months of slow progress, especially for addicts, to establish therapeutic alliance. It cannot be established in a few weeks of residential treatment. Therapy is long term; a year or longer. [40]

Initial educational programs are generally short term—weeks or months. For education to work, students must develop a basic respect for the teacher and trust that the information they are being taught is effectively relevant. Trust in education is based on the integrity and applicability of the material with some respect for the instructor. When presented properly, the information can be seen as valuable and appropriate rather quickly. Education is a mild opposite to therapy as regards trust. Value in therapy will not be appreciated for months. Value in education can be appreciated in a few hours.

Adult Education

Adult students must be approached by an educator in a way that contains and includes an underlying three-point theory of adult education. Regardless of what is being taught to adults, which could be accounting, music theory, cooking, or addictions recovery, the program must be comprised of three main aspects. It has to be appropriate to personal ability, establish germane knowledge, and be relevant and applicable. If these are accomplished with a student at the level they are capable of appreciating, it enables a meaning-focused input of information. This creates a new depth of dependable knowledge about themselves and an inner shift of perceptions regarding addictions, the symptoms, shame, fear, competence, relationships, and the steps. This is very practical and eventually results in a meaning-focused output. (More later.)

(1) Appropriate to Ability
First: Very few people, whether sponsors, counsellors, therapists, or doctors, understand how complicated this is or how to address it effectively. Certainly, they care and are interested, but there are too many simplistic assumptions about addiction, recovery, and the people who participate. Second: Seen as a "disease," that contradicts any indoctrination into a God-believing-1939 value system of prayer and forgiveness, or anything similar. That view is inappropriate

---

40 People in therapy, especially addicts, are so suspicious and defiant that authentic trust in their therapist takes upwards of a year of diligent, regular work and commitment. Addicts in early treatment are so raw that no real trust is developed in thirty or forty days of sporadic association. In treatment clients may "agree" with their counsellors and nod in appreciation but that is often as much political correctness or relief for rescue from calamity than anything else.

in recovery in this culture. It undermines the illness concept. [41] Third: Many professionals and sponsor-types over-estimate capability, or the underlying ability, in the myriad cross section of people in recovery or the complex nature of their personal addictions. There is a very limited range to what can be accomplished, taught, or understood in the first six months of transition.

Education must be appropriate to the student's level of ability and capability. It must take into account that new people in recovery are living in delusion, are defiant, notably blind to the depth of their illness, don't understand what their addiction implies, live with suspicious cynicism, have few or no authentic relationships to depend on for support (authentic is the key word here), are significantly dishonest, embody repetitive inadequacy, have trauma to resolve, and live with no credible sense of what is killing their spirit. Education must be appropriate to address all of this. Repetitive inadequacy is important; I discuss this later.

How do we teach addicts what they need to know, pertinent to their addiction, at their decidedly negative level of ability and insight, at any given point in time? [42], [43]

(2) Establish a Germane Knowledge Base

Adult education regarding addiction must establish a credible knowledge base on two fronts. First would be a firm foundation of dependable knowledge about addictions (the two major groupings), especially polyaddictions and abstinence not-available addictions, the symptoms (two major classifications), what dysfunctional relationships are, and the two rules. Second would be the psychology related to addiction that underlies twelve-step recovery; knowledge rooted in psychology that stands up to scrutiny, which then makes it reliable. From this, people develop confidence that they "know" at their own personal level what they are up against. This knowledge must be accurate and stable and dependably consistent across the range of polyaddictions, many of which are abstinence not-available and culturally approved.

When these are accomplished it fosters an inner sense of confidence, new values, and personal commitment, not a thinly veiled cooperation with opinions of morality. Education offers a reduction of anxiety and inadequacy. This establishes a germane knowledge base about addiction that is more specific than theories about God, the vagaries of faith and prayer, indecision about higher

---

41 There is an inherent contradiction between the illness concept and forgiveness. See Chapter 8.

42 The complex dynamic of the ability or inability to learn is explained in substantial detail in *The Bell Curve*, Richard Herrnstein and Charles Murray, Freepress Paperback, 1994. This is a fascinating and in-depth examination of intelligence, education, and culture. It is 872 pages and not for the faint of heart.

43 Some of the program development suggested here was based on the work of Jim Hackler, Department of Criminology, University of Alberta. *The Reduction of Violent Crime and Equality for Women, Discussion Paper 18*, 1988. This is reprinted at Appendix I.

powers, or awkwardness about atheism or future spirituality. People cannot maintain commitment when the knowledge they must depend on to make significant life choices is infused with indecision, contradiction, speculation and opinion, especially opinion that is frequently challenged.

There are thousands of different opinions about faith and God and the morality of addiction. Religious spirituality related to specific God-beliefs and atheism are opinions and frequently challenged. These should not be introduced, expected, or imposed in the first stage of recovery. This would be the imposition of non-essential demands. Decisions about faith, and where to put that, and higher powers if one wants one or not, will be made over time.

Again, one overlooked aspect to this is, each person has very unique needs *and* quite limited abilities in early recovery. People must perceive and believe this knowledge is factual and personal at their own level. It has to be seen, by them, to be relevant and dependable within the limitations of their own ability.

A reliable and trustworthy knowledge of addiction, acquired in early recovery, is what all change will be based upon. People must trust what they are taught. This allows them to commit to a new lifestyle out of their own sense of confidence; to self-diagnose and to self-evaluate. These are crucial and the foundations of wise choice. (More on wise choice later.) This does not require any discussion of spirituality or God in the first phase of treatment. (See Chapters 5 and 7.)

How do we prevent people from being overwhelmed with opinion-based, semi-religious recovery opinion they cannot understand, or they don't believe? How do they resolve the many subtle contradictions? How do we reduce their repetitive inadequacy? How do professionals offer respect so that people become interested and feel successful without discouragement, in spite of their shame and fear? Appropriate adult education presents a firm and reliable basis of addictions information that will bypass these concerns.

(3) Relevant and Applicable

Adult education must be relevant and applicable to long range, achievable goals. Recovery from addiction is expensive, in more ways than just money, and time consuming. Adults have to appreciate that any investment is worth their expense and effort. All of their addiction's education must be seen as factual and germane to personal goals, whether declared or secret. Knowledge must be molded into their personality in such a way that what they learn is seen as authentic and they can depend on it for long-term gain. [44]

---

44 For counselors: Having some knowledge of the client-centered work of Carl Rogers or Milton Erickson is of definite advantage here, as is the value of Albert Ellis' work (rational emotive therapy). The point is to have available different approaches that meet the unique needs of people that are in recovery. For everyone: Read *Taking Responsibility* by Nathaniel Brandon, 1997 and Sheldon Kopp's book *If You Meet the Buddha on the Road Kill Him*. Also, one of the very best daily reflection books I have ever read is by Sheldon Kopp — *The Blues Ain't Nothing but a Good Soul Feeling Bad*.

How do we instill in them a sense of trust that what they learn today is dependable and will benefit them in making difficult choices and the achievement of long-term goals?

If adult education does not embrace these three points—if they are not evident, then long-range commitment to a spiritually principled lifestyle in this culture cannot be maintained. We cannot expect adults to make significant life changes and embrace this difficult work based on speculation and opinion about religion and God or in ignorance of what they are up against.

What is also evident, but is unaddressed in recovery, is the defeating mindset of repetitive inadequacy which must be significantly reduced for recovery to prevail. This is a silent and deeply held counter-recovery belief that inhibits effort and commitment. Repetitive inadequacy is explained later. What all of this means at another level is that early education must be presented as an analogue base of learning and not digital or intuitive. That distinction, in itself, is an important and complex dynamic.

Analogue vs. Digital Thinking

Analogue thinking or analogue ideas are very basic and processed mentally in a logical, straight forward manner. In early childhood education children are first taught counting. Then they are taught adding, which is a simple extension of counting. *Then* they are taught subtraction (the logical opposite of adding. See 'opposites' discussed later in childhood development). Next comes multiplying. a complex form of adding, and finally dividing—multiplying backwards. This is all analogue—linear, direct, dependable, but it starts with 1, 2, 3, 4… . Children are not taught differential calculus or abstract numbers theory in the space-time continuum. These last two are digital thinking and require a solid foundation of knowledge and a certain amount of intuition and finesse.

In language, children learn the alphabet… a, b, c, d… with phonetics and pronunciation. That progresses to short words and spelling… dog, car, boy, girl. Simple sentences and short-word meaning follow, "Dick and Jane run up the hill." This is all factual and analogue. Then older children get into complex sentences and grammar (comprehension), "Why were they running? Was Jane chasing Dick? It was Tuesday and they were late for school. What does being late mean?" Later and finally, they are into intuitive and comparative meaning and complex representations of ideas in words. The first are analogue, the latter require digital comprehension—the requirements of understanding and meaning.

I repeat myself here: New people in recovery live in delusion, defiance, denial, are notably blind to the depth of their illness and probably physically ill to some extent. They don't understand what their addiction implies, live in fractured relationships, demonstrate suspicious cynicism, are significantly dishonest, embody repetitive inadequacy, and live with serious stress. They have no credible sense of what has killed their spirit or is killing them. At no fault of their own, and without insult, everything they learn must be analogue—simple, direct, dependable, and believable.

This would exclude any conversations about God, religion, morality, faith, politics, or spirituality which all require complex, digital thinking. These are beyond the comprehension of many people in recovery because they contain varying degrees of the suspension of logic and are opinion-based. It can be safely assumed they have so much cynicism and distrust it would be hard to have faith in anything not immediately, factually concrete. [45]

In a general sense of education, knowledge can only be taught in a linear sequence but that isn't the way knowledge is actually processed in our minds. When learning things, mentally there is an overlapping organized chaos. The several parts of our brain create and process emotional reactions, absorb new knowledge, develop intuition, involve perception and imagination, evaluate contradictions, assign it a value, and place it in memory storage, and all at the same time. Our minds and the process of learning are complex.

Delusion, dishonesty, fear, defensiveness, and concealed defiance are present in new clients. They carry personally- and culturally-imposed guilt as a part of the foundation of their personality when entering recovery. This, with limits on ability, repetitive inadequacy and shame, are so embedded that intuition, spirituality, faith, and complex-digital thinking are unavailable to anyone in early recovery.

The state of mind of a new person and the complexity of learning are why only a very stable and basic presentation of addiction facts has immediate impact in education. That stabilizes mental confusion and reduces shame and inadequacy by acquiring confidence in direct fact. It's the relevance of the fact that creates confidence, not the fact itself. I have confidence in the fact that Iceland is a smaller country than Canada, but that fact is not relevant to this. God or atheism are opinions. There is no confidence developed from offering opinions or presenting irrelevant facts.

If the treatment environment or intellectual presentation is too complex, chaotic, irrelevant, or expects trust in opinion; if too much depends on intuition, or too much is given too fast, the newcomer will remain confused, untrusting, and overwhelmed. There is no stability. This is an automatic set up for more repetitive inadequacya. In the chapters that follow is a brief outline for an entry-level education process to side-step all of this.

After detoxification is complete, what must be established first, is a very clear, dependable and consistent understanding of addiction. This is what allows for

---

45 It has, no doubt, been said millions of times in AA meetings, that upon attending their first meeting, "the God thing" scared people away, sometimes for years, many times forever. There is no reason to mention it as a requirement at all, until the new person decides this is what they want. Bill Wilson wrote of this in *Language of the Heart* that many AA members are too adamant about God and outspoken about their beliefs about that (my words). Being in AA is not permission to proselytize on behalf of your opinion of God.

an early commitment to recovery and long-term stability. Without this, nothing regarding transformation can be accomplished. Chapter 3 presents what would be the minimum of addictions-knowledge that should be known by people in recovery. The addict must know their enemy and who the recovery authority is—themselves. [46]

The AA steps are analogue from one to nine—direct, linear and not complex—straight-forward homework assignments designed to alter life's context. They are

---

46 Here is an important shift in concept. Consider any treatment of disease like diabetes, a flu, or cancer. Those diseases can be treated "objectively" meaning without the mental participation of the sick person. Any disease is for the most part, physically not a part of a patient's emotional character as far as immediate treatment goes. Doctors can treat a broken bone or infection in some manner independent of the patient's emotional state and personality. Next...

Any illness or disease must be studied in depth and known in great detail before it can be treated. In regular medicine the doctor understands the illness, has the knowledge, and is the authority. Their treatment of disease does not require or incorporate attendant knowledge of personality. If you are treated for a heat stroke or heart surgery the physician does not ask if you are a God believer or belligerent. They do not ask if your daddy liked your mommy. The doctor prescribes treatment and is the expert. Fair enough.

With the advent of formal/medical treatment for addictions around 1980, and the intrusion of professionals, they have assumed the role of expert and been telling addicts what they need regarding their addiction treatment. This marks the transition from addiction being an illness related to personality to a disease. This is wrong in addictions treatment.

The addict-person themselves, not the professional, must become the expert. The person learns about their very distinctive addiction-illness through education, by understanding their own unique symptoms and personality, life experience, history, values, and life circumstances. Each individual, themselves and alone, must decide on their own unique recovery protocol, never a professional. Addiction is remarkably peculiar to each person and so must be their recovery. Nothing about this is objective like a medical disease. All addiction treatment is subjective. Other than suggesting abstinence or sobriety, external protocols cannot be imposed.

Each person must become their own expert, understand their personality and addiction in depth, and decide on their own personal treatment: to believe or not believe, which god (if any), where to place faith if at all, being atheist or deist, the steps—to what degree, when and how often, what their level of commitment is to any of this, their abstinence, what their own polyaddictions are, what they decide about spirituality, how to view their family and social experience, how to cope with their personal levels of guilt and shame, how to reframe their own sense of failure, how to reframe their history, reorganize their social existence, which meetings appeal to them and how often, and which sponsor (if any). They must become the authority about themselves, assess their own illness, and initiate their own treatment. Addiction is subjective and unique, and addicts must learn to treat themselves. Being objective is the fundamental flaw of advice from professionals and peer pressure from group work. Consensus or outside opinion cannot resolve addiction. The professional, group, or sponsor can never be the authority. The addict must become the expert on themselves because the person is the illness and there's nothing objective about it.

intended to be entirely personal. They may be emotionally difficult, but they are not complex. The maintenance steps, Steps Ten, Eleven, and Twelve, are digital and complex. They are the ongoing dynamics of real-time, interconnected spiritual philosophy in daily content. The difference between context and content is necessary to understand and important in spiritual endeavor. [47]

In early recovery, effective education allows for the transformation of the client's perceptions and values about themselves and about their life and addiction, regardless of religious history or atheism. It provides a basic, dependable foundation that's essential for a commitment to effective recovery and personal change. As in footnote 46, each addict becomes the authority and the expert regarding their own addiction and recovery.

Input - Output

If the foregoing three requirements of adult education can be met—appropriate to ability, germane to addiction, and relevant to needs, this leads into what is called meaning focused *input*. That will soon be followed by meaning focused *output*. These are significant, positive consequences which eventually provide for recovery competence.

In the application of this language learning strategy to addictions treatment, it is crucial to have a meaningful input of accurate knowledge about addiction. This does not require reference to God or higher powers, which are nuanced and complex opinions within the already overwhelming demands of social conflict and early recovery. It is worthy of note that addicts and alcoholics are not suffering from a God deficiency. Nothing more than the basic truths about addiction, symptoms, consequences, the value of successful restraint, and a direct psychological approach to the first nine steps, are all that are required. Analogue. [48]

When meaning-focused *input* is established and assimilated then over time it allows for a meaning focused *output*—a properly oriented mindset based on reliable knowledge. That allows for effective participation in recovery discussions in a life of personally directed (not externally demanded) spiritual abstinence. The more meaningful the initial input of knowledge, the more meaningful the

---

47   Context is the underlying beliefs and values that a person carries in their mind—how they perceive and feel about the world. Men are nasty liars. Lawyers are generally evil. Doctors are greedy. Politicians are crooked. Women are irresponsible. "I" am an innocent victim. Whatever a person's secret views and beliefs are regarding the world is the context of how they approach life. Context is what is to be changed in the first nine steps. Content is what we do or what we are interested in in life. Parent. Skier. Gardner. Business Owner. Writer. Nurse. Musician. Painter. Chef. Teacher. Content is our day to day activities and interests, which are governed by the complexity of Steps Ten, Eleven, and Twelve.

48   This will help with the early identification of dual diagnosis, which is an under-addressed concern, more important than most people are now aware.

output will be in completing the work of the steps. Always remember there are two types of abstinence: belligerent abstinence (defiant) and spiritual abstinence (accepting). Meaning focused input—accurate education, automatically does two things. (a) It makes participation and recovery efforts more voluntary and effective. (b) It sets the stage for acceptance. Coercion into belief through descriptions of impending doom doesn't work; it never has.

Over the course of several years of continuous sobriety the transition into a spiritual lifestyle (Chapter 7) will be much more graceful. People cannot understand the nuance of Steps Ten, Eleven, or Twelve (i.e. spiritual principles) without completing the direct and detailed *input* work of the first nine steps. This is made possible by their early addiction's education.

That stable knowledge base allows a person to appreciate the reasons for the steps and that they are not meant to compensate for a God-deficiency. Adults must clearly understand why they undertake something difficult, awkward and emotionally expensive (and often-times financially expensive). Relevant adult education also lets the person know their enemy. After the enemy is known, sincerity of commitment is possible. Then later, the journey may be expanded into therapy or extended treatment where theists go one way and atheists go another. The acquisition of spiritual principles for either group becomes more graceful.

Recovery leading to spiritual transformation begins with some degree of desire to stop; to submit to treatment or a program. A person's commitment, however superficial, is demonstrated by their volunteering to attend any program. Those first lessons in addiction are critical. People in recovery must understand what they are up against. They can then become their own expert, select from recovery options, decide where they are actually going, how to get there, and why.

Repetitive Inadequacy and Shame [49]

Repetitive inadequacy is a belief connected to shame and guilt that usually begins internally during the acting out phase of addiction. It arises from the historical, repetitive failure to quit addiction while in it and is mirrored in frequent failed personal recovery efforts. It is then reinforced by ineffective interventions in treatment. "I have failed so often, in so many different ways, I now believe I am inadequate to accomplish life."

---

49   Repetitive inadequacy, as far as I can understand up until now, has never been identified and is unexamined. It became apparent to me, when working with high-recidivist clients in the 1990s, that it was a significant cause of relapse. Another of the recurring reasons for relapse is a client's commitment to atheism and no viable alternative to God being presented. Yet another is the presentation of opinion as fact. It is particularly difficult to make life commitments based on opinion. Over the intervening years I have repeatedly seen relapsing end when it is addressed through education for both caregivers and clients.

Self-perceptions of repetitive inadequacy while in active addiction are as common as bad television shows. It's a standard experience for people who are acting out. They fail at ordinary life during their addiction (see Life Damaging Consequences in Chapter 3) and fail at personal attempts to quit on their own. They fail at integrity, fail at marriages, fail at jobs, fail at intimacy, fail at anger management, fail in therapy, fail in sex, fail in parenting. These "failures" are carried into sobriety as emotional scar tissue. When people attend twelve-step programs and frequently relapse after attempts at recovery this deepens the sense of failure. Together, they reinforce a subconscious mindset of hopeless despondency. "I am a failure at life *and* at getting this recovery-thing. I've tried it seven times on my own before I went to five different twelve-step groups in three different cities and then I tried three treatment centers, two of them, twice. Obviously, I am an inadequate failure at everything."

Repeatedly experiencing failure while in active addiction, and then more failure in attempting personal recovery, and then *more* failure in formal treatment instils a deeply held belief of personal inadequacy. This becomes particularly insidious when relapsing after formal treatment. Each failure generates shame. It is one thing to make a mistake or not complete a task successfully, it is entirely another matter to feel an inadequate failure at life. The sad sarcasm is thus: A person was in therapy for a few years and made no progress. Finally, the therapist said, "Well, maybe life isn't for everybody." (I am told this was originally said by the film director Woody Allen.)

Repetitive inadequacy is a silent, major impediment to recovery. It has been unaddressed and cannot be resolved through opinions of God. Education is the only way out. [50]

Disease or Illness

There are ways that some treatment programs, sponsors, culture, and meetings contribute to repetitive inadequacy. The first is failing to deliver basic and trustworthy information about addiction as an illness. What is illness and how it is defined? What does "disease" actually mean? Which is it—disease or illness? What are the symptoms? Does anyone explain there are two categories of symptoms? How is culturally-imposed guilt instilled in a person with addiction? People get empathy and consideration for broken arms or cancer, why not me? What's the strategy for relief? What do you mean social disapproval? Why do I feel guilty for doing the right thing? Am I that inadequate? Culture and society are major contributors to this. (More in Chapter 8.)

---

50   Repetitive inadequacy sometimes has antecedents in early family of origin scripts, but that cannot be addressed when in early recovery. It may become significant in advanced recovery, much later, where it can be addressed in well-conducted therapy.

How do people learn to sense being "off" the path of recovery before it's out of control? What are the mind-games and self-talk that set up conflict and relapse? Self-talk is discussed later. How does all of this fit with anyone's history? Does disease fit into relationships and sex and personality? What's illness have to do with God, if anything?

When asked about the word disease at the National Catholic Clergy Conference in 1961, Bill Wilson answered: *"We have never called alcoholism a disease because, technically speaking, there is not a disease entity. There is no such thing as 'heart disease'. Instead there are many separate heart ailments, or combinations of them. It is something like that with alcoholism. Therefore, we did not wish to get in wrong with the medical profession. Illness or malady is a far safer term for us to use."* (And I would add, also more accurate.) In this era, we tend to use disease rather than illness. Although inaccurate, disease clearly leaves little room for discussion. "I am ill," can be vague and is certainly less dramatic. Is illness like having a mild flu? Mental illness? "I am ill..." is that slightly depressed, neurotic, or living with an ambiguous psychiatric concern? With illness there is more room for discussion and the real potential to slide into realm of mental illness. Not so with disease; it's dramatic and final.

What's more indecisive is, addiction appears to be a phenomenon. (More on this in Chapter 3.) Understanding it as a phenomenon of alienation—defective or broken relationships, eliminates much of the chaos and indecision about treatment. With this clearly understood comes a sense of confidence in focused effort and a reduction of repetitive inadequacy. This establishes a solid basis for growth and a permanent foundation of consistent information that a person can trust to self-diagnose and self-evaluate. [51] It must go far beyond the level of cliché. [52] This is essential for the confidence which is required for long-term recovery.

Another contributing factor to repetitive inadequacy and emotional belligerence is counsellors, therapists, sponsors or spiritual advisors, imposing upon new people a morality they insist the new person needs to abide by. The counsellor or sponsor imposes their personal rules regarding recovery, ethics, spirituality, responsibility, some conception of God, relationships and sexuality. They claim

---

51 The ability to self-diagnose or self-evaluate with confidence is quite important and is a side benefit of addictions education (more on this later). If a new person believes they are inadequate or incapable then being responsible, which is expected in recovery, is unavailable to them. Inadequate and incapable are carried in an addict's mind as global self-perceptions. How can anyone choose to be responsible if they believe they are incapable and inadequate?

52 Cliché: an over-used phrase: common place, trite, shallow, banal. This too shall pass. One day at a time. Turn it over. Easy does it. Have your cake and eat it too. God wants me sober. God wants me happy. Your life flashes before your eyes. Think. Think. Think. First Things First. Walk a mile in their shoes. These clichés, and dozens more, may be important in the first few months of sobriety. After that they indicate an evasion of responsibility. This is often-times related to my earlier observation about an increase in education and a corresponding decrease in literacy and comprehension. This is concealed in an abundance of cliché.

to be the authority in the client's life, and they aren't. Rather than impose doctrine, the helper should understand the unique needs of the individual, respond to that, and impose nothing. (Sponsorship in Chapter 5 speaks to this.)

Being able to self-evaluate or self-diagnose is crucial. When addiction is clearly understood that tends to neutralize any self-attack and reduce repetitive inadequacy. It contributes to the internal reduction of shame and guilt and makes for a less onerous endeavor into taking responsibility. [53]

An aside: about three-quarters of the people I work with in therapy spend the first year or eighteen months sorting out the confusion from poorly conducted interventions in early recovery and chaos about higher powers. This has been corrected by establishing a clear foundation of addictions knowledge. Without this, all ensuing recovery or spirituality tends to be chaotic and unstable because it is based on opinion. People must be properly oriented in their healing process.

It should be understood that repetitive inadequacy is a significant source of shame for the acting-out addict. Two other sources of shame are in the experiences of life damaging consequences, explained in Chapter 3, and in the second stage of childhood development, explained in Chapter 4. It must always be remembered by the counsellor and eventually by the client that, over the long term, shame must be resolved for serenity to prevail. Shame <u>always</u> arises from abusive relationships. Remember the three different sources for shame: repetitive inadequacy, life damaging consequences, and unmet developmental dependency needs. To scapegoat families for the prevalence of shame, including that addiction is somehow caused by family, is wrong. It is convenient but it is wrong. [54]

An Approach to Relationship

There are many interrelated dynamics in the appearance of addiction. One is culture; more on that in Chapter 8. Another is that it is an illness of alienation in relationship. It is not, as is claimed by so many, a family illness. Calling it a family illness may be partially accurate, but is very short-sighted and can be quite abusive, actually blaming and derogatory. Families are often scapegoated when they never should be. It is, however, an illness of relationship—*all* relationships. Bill Wilson, co-founder of Alcoholics Anonymous, wrote in Step Eight:

---

53 Culturally imposed guilt and the need for God and forgiveness for moral turpitude undermines understanding addictions as an illness. This is explored later.

54 In following the history of this, in the 1980s there was a lot of attention paid to eating disorders (rightly so). Classic eating disorders that are childhood onset are a family issue, for sure. That valid observation became therapeutically confused with the shame in alcoholism/drug addiction and the eating disorders that are adult onset which are different from the onset of childhood eating disorders. It's complicated.

"Since defective relations with other human beings have nearly always been the immediate cause of our woes, <u>including our alcoholism</u>, no field of investigation could yield more satisfying results than this one." [55] I would add to this: defective relations are the immediate cause of our relapses...

The field of investigation he refers to, here and elsewhere, is examining and resolving all relationship conflict (or at least attempting to). Mr. Wilson was quite clear that alcoholism goes far beyond the narrow limitations of family. In fact, family history or family relationships themselves as the cause of alcoholism are never mentioned in any AA literature, nor should they be. There are contributing factors to the mental set up for addictive behaviour, which are principally alienation, a never-realized sense of entitlement, shame, blame, and inadequacy in relationships. Family relationships may be a part of the cause of this dislocation, but not the cause of addiction. Family is not the cause of addiction, the addict is. Mr. Wilson clearly states that defective relations (I use the word alienation—social and personal) is the root cause of alcoholism and any conflict is the alcoholic-addict's own fault. [56] So "we" must drop the word blame from our speech and thought (Step Four chapter, *Twelve Steps and Twelve Traditions*).

There are millions of people with parents who were alcoholics and the children are not; millions of people with siblings who are addicts and they are not. What of families where the children, some or all, are alcoholics and the parents aren't? Some families are quite supportive and healthy, and the children are hard-core addicts. Some families are abusive, and the children are not addicted. How does all of that figure into our pet theories?

It is convenient for victims, the insecure/irresponsible types, or uninformed professionals, to claim it's a family disease, and provide everyone a convenient theory: Blame the Family. This "sharing of responsibility" is an easier sell to addicts than the responsibility of "It's all my fault." Addicts like sharing responsibility, which is like a 51-49 percent blame game and (of course!) the addict always makes themselves the 49 side. Yes, relationship disfunction may be rooted

---

55   *Twelve Steps and Twelve Traditions*, Alcoholics Anonymous World Services Inc. p. 80, emphasis added.

56   This is not the case with some psychological or dual-diagnosis symptoms, which may be evidence of congenital concerns or of harsh family dynamics. Care should be taken in attributing responsibility in these areas. The effort of recovery from the phenomenon of addictions is quite a unique concern. The original twelve steps did get it right in the psychology and that recovery is a personal responsibility, which responsibility is never shared. In an addict's mind If families are blamed the family shares responsibility: "If my addiction is partly their fault then my recovery is partly their responsibility." This means they leave treatment with a deeply justified sense of blame and, post-treatment, reestablish relationship alienation. Once this is established in the logic of a practicing addict, it takes months of complex therapy to reestablish responsibility.

in family but addiction is not. Addiction is not a family illness. (Review meddling with personal opinions at footnote 8.)

It is clearly stated in Step Eight in *Twelve Steps and Twelve Traditions* at page 77 that the examination of all relationships requires the alcoholic to take all responsibility for conflict and to resolve that as is best possible. People in recovery are to *"[develop] the best possible relations with every human being [they] know."* That is the principle task at hand: repair of relationships, and in the maintenance steps to prevent any conflict from arising. This eliminates relationship alienation. It's all about relationships. To reinforce this, Mr. Wilson writes in the next paragraph, *"Learning how to live in the greatest peace, partnership, and brotherhood will all men and women, of whatever description, is a moving and fascinating adventure."* The maintenance of harmony in relationships.

There is nothing unclear about this. Responsibility strikes fear into the heart of most blame-oriented addicts or counsellors. For a counsellor or a sponsor who cannot approach this level of responsibility with confidence, who themselves don't subscribe to it, leaves them in a mindset of blame. It is to be a moving and fascinating adventure (i.e. emotionally rewarding and interesting) not painful, arduous turmoil. This can only happen if there is a drastic change in views of humility. A commitment to responsibility through humility is never discussed.

The behaviour of families, parents, friends and associates are not discussed in AA literature and they should not be spoken of in meetings or recovery. This does not mean that the damage and harm caused, or the alienation in families should not be investigated. It should be and responsibility has to be taken and amends made. But family cannot be made the scapegoat for the cause of addiction. This is an illness of *all* relationships; conflict generated by the addict everywhere they go. Understanding the dynamics of relationship, from alienation to harmony, is crucial and is the basis for Chapter 4—relationships and childhood development, and the later steps. It is also important that some significant awareness be created about cultural dislocation and relationships in society (explained briefly in Chapter 8). We do have relationships in and with culture and society. This chaos promotes addiction and that should be understood.

As an aside: Nothing need be said about the necessity of God or a higher power unless that is a belief that you are already convinced of. Here, this is principally for understanding the influence of culture and the need to modify what's presented as treatment. Any indoctrination into Christian values or into being a good citizen of the commonwealth are not treatment. Gaining knowledge about your personal relationship struggles, and the conflict addicts cause in all relationships, is the start of treatment. These first chapters are, in essence, a long explanation of Step One—know the enemy and create a committed decision to remain abstinent—successful self-restraint. There's no point in going into battle with an addiction if you don't know what you're up against. Then comes step work and transformation.

This would naturally allow the new person to make an informed personally-imposed choice to remain dedicated to this long-term process with a clear but limited understanding of (a) their own addiction; and (b), the steps (explained in Chapter 5). With addictions, remember two things: understand the illness first and then the client becomes their own authority.

In the resolution of your addictions (plural intended) before you approach Step Two you must establish three preconditions: (i) rigorous honesty as a participation exercise, (ii) a determination to let go of old ideas; and (iii), some sense that you want and are committed to what the steps offer. These must come before you are introduced to Step Two. [57]

Step Two is *"Came to believe that a Power greater than ourselves could restore us to sanity."* It is quite important that people recognize the opinion-concept of a higher power. Regardless of all the rhetoric and declarations, it is an opinion, as is atheism. Regardless, a higher power isn't mentioned until after you have established sobriety, have some measure of rigorous honesty, and are committed to what AA suggests.

"Came to believe" means that it is a process over a period of time, usually longer than shorter, and "...that a Power greater than ourselves could..." Over time, we come to have a personal opinion that some version of outside help, of our own choosing and however vague, might do something on our behalf if we work for it. This is always attached to willingness, patience, and labor. This over used phrase actually means, "I desire to realize the rewards, and with determination I will diligently work for them." Religious persons believe this power is some variation of God, but there is no requirement to have this opinion and that must always be born in mind. It's a very large license to believe or not believe whatever you want regarding any version of outside help you might choose or not choose. (More on this later.)

What is implied in Step Two is that a person may come to believe a higher power of some sort is necessary; however, what that is or may be is not yet identified. A person can believe that changing their career is well and good, but until they experiment with a few alternatives they have not yet found a new career, trust what that might be, or proved it valuable. That requires time, patience, research, and investigation; that is Step Two.

Some people do believe that having a higher power would be good. Fair enough. But, at Step Two they have not yet found or identified it. Knowing that you need a new car is not the same as getting it. Believing you need some description of external help (like a higher power or a good sponsor) is not the same as getting it. Seeking that out must come during the regular participation in rigorous honesty. Rigorous honesty is not a spectator sport. Discovering what that is, and trusting your decision, is the purpose of the next seven steps. That's the investment of work and patience in order to find what you need, not what everyone else tells you you need.

---

57   These three conditions precede Step Two as implied in How It Works, p. 58 *Alcoholics Anonymous*.

The AA declaration of personal choice regarding <u>any</u> higher-power is meant to embrace acceptance of everyone's choice. There is no restriction here. There are countless stories about people who claimed a strong faith in God and relapsed. There are also stories of non-believers who have relapsed, and also non-believers and believers who stayed sober. [58] So, not believing in God, and committing to some other version of outside help can be a successful choice of getting help for some people. Three things that should be made clear are...

(1) Being spiritual does not require a belief in God or an association with religion. Whether one's personality chooses atheism, agnosticism, humanism, deism, theism, intellect, science, religion, the literature, divine presence, or old-fashioned personal commitment, will be a decision made after the three preconditions (listed above) are met. Being spiritual does not depend on divinity.

(2) Faith and belief in God, of any description, has not stopped millions of people from relapsing. Being clean and sober depends principally on an unwavering commitment to being clean and sober.

(3) Being authentically spiritual at any depth is only available after years of extended effort at Steps Ten, Eleven, and Twelve. Character defects, belligerence, being closed minded, clinging to old ideas, lack of trust, anger, dishonesty, blame, sporadic self-discipline (it has to be consistent), irresponsibility, fear, are too prevalent before this for a spiritual mindset to prevail.

A Modified Approach to Treatment

What is being presented here are possibilities for a basic adult education program and an understanding of cultural influence. [59] In the first stage of recovery, education avoids all opinions and discussions of God and faith. This accomplishes many things. Certainly, it will include all categories of new person: the atheists, the belligerent, the inadequate, the agnostics, the confused, the terrified, the humanists, the doubters, the deists, the theists and religious folks from any belief system. With education as the main initial focus, everyone will be welcomed, and opinion-conflict will be avoided.

Education must also address the dislocation of this culture, which is a serious contributing factor to the rise in addiction. The significant changes in addictions and society, in sexuality and relationship structures, and the still adamant

---

58 It is worthy of careful thought that sobriety isn't so much dependent on a higher power as it is personal determination.

59 Cultural influence is explored at some length in Chapter 8, as is a brief discussion of the use of laudanum (opiates).

presentation of an AA-God-Forgiveness approach creates several serious problems for any new person attempting recovery.

- It will be hard to get atheists or humanists involved in any god-oriented process during treatment. Any traditional AA-focused program is very critical of them.

- Religious people are up against reduced social influence and no longer enjoy a lot of cultural power. There is the denigration of organized religion, negative criticism, and drastic cultural change with attendant consequences for all concerned.

- Committed atheists or humanists will not accept a God-oriented indoctrination. Insisting they have to believe and pray or will relapse, especially when there are other options, is abusive.

- Presenting the recovery process of "the steps" as a function of finding God often provokes internal mental opinion-debates about what to believe among believers. However, focusing only on psychology includes everyone and avoids the mental uncertainty. An opinion of preference for beliefs will come clear much later.

It will be very hard for humanists or atheists to find any reliable support or mentors in the mostly God-forgiveness dominant groups. Oftentimes religious beliefs can be very subtle and righteous regarding "higher powers." It's in the nature of religion. [60]

All this chaos will ensure a higher recidivist rate and more deaths from addictions. That, in turn, creates a deeper sense of repetitive inadequacy and social dread. The social attitude now exists that treatment is ineffective and that addicts are hopeless. As I briefly detailed earlier, in these modern times, a 1939 oriented program can create a very unstable foundation for long-term recovery

---

60 See *The Language of the Heart*, Bill W.'s Grapevine Writings, AAGrapvine, Inc, beginning at p. 251, written in 1961. Taken at random: "practice the rest of the AA program with a relaxed and open mind." "faith is never a necessity for AA membership; that sobriety can be achieved with an easily acceptable minimum of it." "Perhaps three hundred thousand did recover in the last twenty-five years... maybe half a million more have come into our midst, and then went out again. ...we can't well content ourselves with the view that all these recovery failures were entirely the fault of the newcomers themselves. ...[AA carries] a sort of unconscious arrogance, God as *I* understood him *had* to be for everybody." What Mr. Wilson explains here is not that "God" must be for everybody, but the freedom of choice in how you understand "a higher power" was for everybody. Freedom of choice is for everyone. "God" isn't necessarily for everyone. The righteous hubris that everybody has to find God is still a standard mind-set in most meetings and treatment facilities. People are dying because of it.

for believers: What should I believe? I trust nothing. Or, for non-believers: I just don't buy it, never did.

God-forgiveness efforts were easy to accept, and recovery success was much higher in the 1940s because of the Christian-religious tone of that culture. Certainly, forgiveness is necessary to a Christian perspective but not to an illness perspective. [61]

The three-hundred-year long belief that drunkenness was an uncommon social nuisance c. 1500 – 1800 was replaced near 1835. Drunkenness became labelled as Christian moral depravity. Later, in 1939 and again in 1961, Mr. Wilson declared it was more of an illness (mental) than a disease (biological).

As the industrial revolution overtook everything, including massive alcohol production and the easy availability of laudanum (after 1860-ish), the established social structure deteriorated. Addiction increased both its intensity and its range of influence. Because of the Protestant-Christian Temperance Movement in the US, drunkenness became a sin of irresponsible moral corruption (which belief is still pervasive). Drunkenness wasn't commonly called alcoholism until near 1870. Now, in 2020, addiction is a cultural-dislocation illness and not a disease; an illness with a significant contribution from culture.

In a humanitarian view of this, when the addiction-illness concept is clearly understood as a phenomenon and taken out of both the religious equation and corrupt morality, forgiveness is unnecessary. In point of fact, I am aware of many people who have maintained well-conducted long-term sobriety and never forgiven anyone for anything, and they are declared atheists or agnostics. They are tolerated but not gracefully accepted in many recovery meetings. [62]

Again, none of this is meant to exclude those who choose to believe in God or take a traditional Christian approach. That perspective is viable and to be supported in any recovery program. This is intended to open up treatment and recovery to a wider spiritual awareness and make it more inclusive for non-believers. [63] Later, I discuss that one option for recovery is being spiritual in psychology. Recovery doesn't require God or a belief in God which does not detract anything

---

61   The idea of "forgiveness not required" and acceptance are explained in Chapter 8. There is more detail in *Spiritual Transformation*, cited earlier, pp. 332-352. If forgiveness is insisted upon that tends to go against the concept of illness.

62   This is not a glib observation. Acceptance requires a much deeper understanding of spirituality than forgiveness. Acceptance is much harder to achieve, and most people in recovery meetings are quietly belligerent—not accepting of acceptance or atheists. In the AA Grapevine publication *Under One Umbrella*, for atheists and agnostics, the contributors frequently make reference to the non-acceptance of atheists by the God-believers, who in the next breath, announce how accepting they are.

63   Bill Wilson, the co-founder of AA and principle author of *Alcoholics Anonymous*, spoke to this indirectly in some of his writing in the early 1960s. *Language of the Heart*, an AA publication, refers.

from theists or deists who choose to believe. If a person becomes committed to a spiritual life, there is no relapse.

Cultural Focus [64]

One of the many things that is wrong with our cultural view of addiction and treatment is our generally prejudiced and incomplete view of the illness. Bill Wilson et al presented it as a treatable illness with undertones of moral failure. The "treatable illness" part was a new and strange idea but gained favor. Then, in the early 1970s, as an outcome of the political demonizing of drug addicts, our cultural focus was grossly misdirected. Most ordinary folks were and are duped into a narrow perception of addicts as the obvious evils in society, which diminishes the illness concept. [65]

There was a myth created by politicians about a war on drugs. War is always against an "evil enemy" and any politically declared war must mobilize the population against the enemy to support that war. Drugs and drug users became a cultural-criminal enemy in 1973. Drug addicts were participating in evil and on the wrong side of "the war." Rather than being ill, they immediately became an enemy of culture, an enemy of democracy, corrupting morals, irresponsible, petty criminals, committing welfare fraud, carrying infectious diseases, doing street robberies, a burden on health care, and lazy. "Evil" drug users became the target of persecution and criminal law enforcement. [66]

In an atmosphere of war-against-criminals, the notion of illness evaporates. Criminals are always criminals first and patients second. There is prejudice and hypocrisy to be explored in how society uses the word illness regarding addiction. People who have depression or cancer are not criminals for their illness or disease. Those patients are not on the wrong side of a political war.

Since drugs became evil, drug addicts became morally dangerous (not ill), as were alcoholics morally corrupt sinners from a fundamentalist religious point of view, c. 1840. Since addicts became the enemy in a war, we now scapegoat them

---

64   This section is partly developed from the work of Prof. Jim Hackler University of Alberta, 1987. See *The Reduction of Violent Crime and Equality for Women, Discussion Paper 18*, reproduced at Appendix I.

65   Former President Richard Nixon formed the DEA in 1973. There are presently about 5,200 administrative employees and 4,950 DEA agents. The budget is approx. 3.2 billion dollars. In 1972-3 it was near 70 million dollars. (Stats available online) This does not include the thousands of drug enforcement police squads in Canadian or American city forces. In Canada there are about 60,000 serving police officers, which includes about 17,000 RCMP officers. Some notable portion are for drug enforcement. A war mentality was created against drug addicts in both countries. (More detail in Chapter 8.)

66   See *Peaceful Measures* by Bruce Alexander.

under the masquerade of politically initiated harm reduction, which is not the same as addicts helping addicts.

In the cultural focus graphs, shown next, Group B harbors well concealed moderate addiction and shame. This escalates and is exceptionally evident in Groups C and D. As an addict travels from Group B to Group D, Graph I represents that we have been taught: to focus on Group D through media, medicine, law enforcement, and politics since the early 1970s. It looks like this:

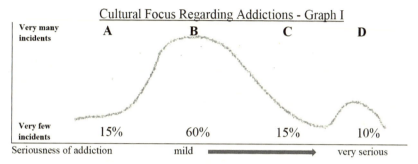

A – This group is generally non-addicted and stable in relationships; coping well with social and cultural dislocation and embraces an egalitarian lifestyle.

B – People here are addicted to socially approved addictions like religion, work, TV, sex, relationships, romance, conflict, aggressive sports, food, spending, adrenalin, exercise, body image, celebrity worship, shopping, spending, the internet, power, and shiny things. Certainly, Group B is blind to their inner conflict, unhappy, and unfulfilled in their quietly desperate lives. Group B addicts enjoy the general misperception that they are fine.

C – Addicts/alcoholics that are reasonably obvious to the general public: desperate, decidedly unhappy, frequently irresponsible and stoned or drunk, in debt, marginally employed, lost in gambling or sex, and crashing quickly. This group is in training to become the enemy in Group D.

D – The small group of hard-core alcoholics, drug addicts, street drunks, street addicts, criminals, chronic sex addicts, and outrageous gamblers. Group D has "failed" miserably in every area of life. They are the social enemy and the primary focus of the cultural drug "war" since the early 1970s.

What has been seen in research is severe addictions do not increase in population or incident frequency as they increase in severity. The more severe the addictions are, the fewer the participants and the fewer the incidents. The second hump at D is a fiction.

Society has an incorrect, two-hump perspective of addiction. Category B, the power brokers and politicians, have created this two-hump focus for their own benefit, which was one result of the myth of the war on drugs. The concern here is of two things. Category D gets probably 98 percent of the treatment focus, police attention, government funding, medical attention, criminal labels, and social disapproval, when in fact this group is at best five percent of the adult population. [67] The principle error is seeing addictions and society as a two-hump graph. [68] Our culture is actually this:

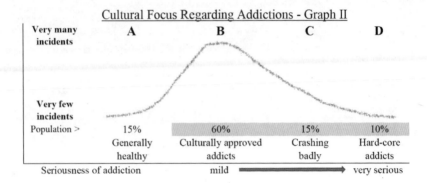

Cultural Focus Regarding Addictions - Graph II

	A	B	C	D
Very many incidents				
Very few incidents				
Population >	15%	60%	15%	10%
	Generally healthy	Culturally approved addicts	Crashing badly	Hard-core addicts

Seriousness of addiction   mild ➡ very serious

There is a small percentage, possibly 15% in group A, that are not addicted, reasonably well connected in community and not strongly dislocated. In Graph II, there are those of the population who are addicted and socially functional (Group B), the largest portion. The three factors that conceal the rampant addictions in group B are: (i) this group is perceived as socially "functional" and therefore not criticized, (ii) the addictions are mild enough to be culturally approved—whether abstinence available or abstinence not-available; and (iii), they hold social power and can keep the focus on Group D. Graph I is a political fiction. Graph II is the reality. [69]

In Graph II, the self-destruction escalates as it moves from B into C into D, the five or ten percent of hard-core addicts who are the superstars of addiction. Everyone in Groups B, C, and D, are in addictions trouble. But, the farther to the right, the worse the destruction, the fewer the addicts, and the number of incidents decreases. Media, medicine, and politicians from Group B have demonized

---

67   My percentages are only anecdotal estimates, but they are based on forty years of clinical work and research. I am probably under-estimating category B and over-estimating group D.

68   Prof. Hackler advised this dynamic of two humps vs. one hump was originally discovered in relation to alcohol and drug use as far back as 1972 by Canadian researchers. He saw a similar pattern in family violence and reported that in his discussion paper, c. 1987. In this writing I have recast it back into addictions. Prof. Hackler cites credits at Appendix I.

69   This is to say nothing of the serious complications of dual diagnosis and their increasing presence where there are bona fide mental health issues. It is apparent that the arrogance and gossip rampant in twelve-step programs promotes many ignorant and cruel opinions about dual diagnosis. There should be more compassion and simple acceptance and significantly fewer foolish opinions. Much would be gained if the uninformed would remain silent. As I have said elsewhere, and I repeat myself—it is complicated. (See footnote 96.)

Group D as the enemy. [70] There are not two humps in the population. I will refer to the A – B – C – D groups several times throughout this book. It would be helpful in your understanding of what I present if you remember them.

This culture has created a huge dislocation in community. That is a significant cause of the escalation of addiction. Later there is discussion on the two main types of addiction. Once people understand these cultural groupings, the recovery journey is easier to comprehend regardless of the addiction. Now, to change the subject…

As a long side note… One of the misunderstandings that has permeated Western civilization from about 1860 concerns Buddhism. In the 19th century, translations of Buddhist documents from Pali/Sanskrit into English were done by English speaking Protestant Christians. The main purpose of those translations was to assist in converting the Indian sub-continent to English Christianity. [71] (I'll get back to addictions in a few paragraphs.)

Those translations of Buddhist doctrine into English presented "life is suffering" as The First Noble Truth of Buddhism. This is <u>very</u> inaccurate, to the point of being wrong. The translators used the Christian-perspective English word "suffering" as a similar convenience to the Sanskrit word *dukkha*. For the translators, *dukkha* was kind-of-close to, sort-of related to Christian suffering. This is very inaccurate but was self-serving to the English-Anglican agenda of colonialism of that era—dominating the Indian sub-continent. Claiming parallels and similarities between Christianity (the British religion) and Buddhism (a belief of the conquered), made it easier to convert Indian Buddhists into English-Indian-Anglicans. Once converted, it was hoped that social obedience would be easier to maintain. (Until Mohandas Gandhi happened.)

It was long known by conquering dynasties throughout history, to enable an easier and more controlling dominance, it was important to co-opt and subsume the religious beliefs of the conquered. When politicians or missionaries try to convert people one of the things they do is they draw very vague and inaccurate similarities between religious belief systems. This is called parallelism. Christian missionaries have been abusing people all over the world in this manner for nineteen-hundred years. Near 1870 British Christians translated Buddhist *dukkha* as Christian "suffering." But *dukkha* is remarkably at odds with the Christian view of suffering.

---

70   Much of Bruce Alexander's work, presents a well-documented and examined view of cultural dislocation. He has published books to this end, especially *Peaceful Measures* which explains the creation of the war-on-drugs myth. There is also *The Globalization of Addiction – A Study in Poverty of Spirit*. For those interested, his website of the same name is worth a careful read. Prof. Alexander does not provide these percentage estimates; these are my estimates from my clinical work and teaching.

71   Three of the principle early translators were Rudolph Roth, Otto Bothlingk, and Fredrich Max Muller (all three c. 1850–1874) who did a lot of translating for Christian missionaries. Misrepresentation and manipulation through parallelism was very common in their work.

The more accurate translation would be that in Buddhist thought, *dukkha* means dislocated—life doesn't really make logical or emotional sense. Bad people win (annoying and disheartening), good people die young (unfair and sad), others work hard and finish last (exhausting), others gain privilege without merit (unjust), some others are unfairly punished (cruel), and still others work hard and get nowhere (futile and frustrating). "Life" doesn't have a normal or harmonious structure within our logical perception of it. That, and more, altogether, is *dukkha*. [72]

Suffering, pain and confusion, in a non-enlightened mind, is a recurring, experienced result of *dukkha*—apparently unresolvable pain and anguish. This is a result of dislocation, but *dukkha* is not suffering. It means dislocated—life doesn't really make logical or emotional sense. But that doesn't make for an easy comparison to Christianity, which is itself rooted in suffering and the blessings received after life is over—heaven. Very non-Hindu and non-Buddhist.

The painful reality is that life in this culture is severely dislocated. *Dukkha*. In recent decades, politicians and religious leaders say they care but there is little evidence of this (painful hypocrisy). Greed runs big business and politicians lie and deceive while they chase power (demeaning and dangerous for the disenfranchised). Cultures are destroyed by modernity (see footnote 75). Neglect, abuse, and religious terrorism are an everyday occurrence (cruelty). Politicians, business, and religious officials gather around each other to protect the criminals in their cadre from prosecution and responsibility (negligent abuse). That leaves people with a sense of hopelessness and dislocation. Our emotional and intellectual need for a sense of trust and harmony are fractured by this, and not much makes sense. This is not suffering; this is the fact of cultural *dukkha*. The British translations of Buddhist doctrine were grossly misleading and self-serving to their agenda of religious conversion.

The political power brokers (of many nations) since about 1850 have used paranoia and parallelism to create cultural enemies. Here, at home (I mean North America), politicians in our culture-of-war always need an enemy. Enemies, most of the time, are manufactured. Political enemies went from Russian Communists (cold war) to Chinese Communists (Vietnam) to drugs (an easy parallel because of returning veterans, belligerent "drug-using" hippies, and draft dodgers). Drugs and users became the internal drug-culture enemies of our society. This is not to pick on North America. All major nations had and have their own internal variation of this. Much to Mr. Nixon's surprise, his mythical war-on-drugs soon turned out to be remarkably profitable both politically and financially. [73]

In the 1970s, political enemies expanded to include drug suppliers ("nasty" foreigners from Turkey and Afghanistan to Mexico and Indo-China) and

---

72 Remember the observation of T.S. Eliot, mentioned earlier: "The hubbub of a marching band going nowhere. The drum is beaten but the procession does not advance." *The Sacred Wood*.

73 All of this, and much more, is well documented and explained in the documentaries *The Culture High*, directed by Brett Harvey (2013) and *Rat Park*, directed by Shawney Cohen (2018).

home-grown drug dealers and users who became the "destroyers our society." These enemy-groups were then quietly expanded to include other "radical" issues like homosexual rights, gender equality, and civil rights. These were all too demanding and upsetting of our "cultural stability" which really meant taking power away from the old order. That is the general underlying hindrance to social change.

All of these social radicals were portrayed, at different and various times, and to different degrees, as undermining morality, demolishing good order, evil, anti-Christian, destroying our families, an insult to God and decency, criminals, disrespectful of tradition, upsetting commerce, undermining the labour force, lazy, dangerous, corrupting minors, destabilizing democracy, a burden on "polite" society, violent, irresponsible, intentionally spreading disease, and worthy of being put down. Drug addicts became an enemy facing punitive government sanction. Each social-enemy group was seen as slightly different than, but "kind of the same" as, the others. The common denominator was being a threat to good order. "Good order" meant upsetting to white, male, heterosexual, affluent society.

This drug war was all propaganda—political parallelism in creating enemies. False or very superficial comparisons are used to lead us to believe there is a "new" enemy, which is always unexamined and easy to claim in thirty-second sound bites. Politicians and big business are more subversive and dangerous than the scapegoats they create and target. Now, back to addictions... What has all that got to do with addiction and treatment?

Creating a social enemy, addiction in Groups C and D, has had a huge impact on our views of addicts and our treatment of addiction. Politics is how drug addiction got separated from alcoholism. Politics is how Group B addicts remain "innocent." Prior to the 1960s drug addicts were a minor, usually ignored, moral-degenerate nuisance. Ordinary street junkies were mostly out of view and not given much attention. The police generally used drug enforcement on beatniks, hipsters, movie stars, gangsters, and musicians. [74]

Being a drunkard, however, was different throughout history. From about 1500 CE up to about 1830 being a drunkard, as we understand it today, was uncommon. It was viewed more of a nuisance and rare event. Around 1840, in the USA, it changed from social nuisance to a Christian sinner and moral failure.

---

74   Opium dens. Starting around 1890 and onward, smoking opium was, in a quiet way, quite popular with the financially affluent. Wilson Mizner managed the Hotel Rand in New York (West 49th Street), c. 1907. He posted signs for his hotel guests: "No opium-smoking in the elevators." That led to the 1920s Jazz-age question, "Hey, are you hip?" Smoking opium was usually done laying on your side; laying on your hip. Are you hip meant do you smoke opium? Or the street-smart introduction, "Hey, meet ____, he's hip," meaning they smoke opium. This is also where the expression 'having a pipe dream' came from, meaning an opium pipe. In the 1950s being hip or being "a hipster" meant a person was street-cool and could be trusted. Mr. Mizner is cited in *The Little, Brown Book of Anecdotes*, Little Brown & Co. (INC.) publishers, 1985.

Then, from Dr. Huss (c. 1860, Sweden), 'drunkard' became alcoholic. A medical classification of drunken behaviour came into the picture. Even though being a drunkard was now changed to alcoholic, they were still seen as a moral degenerate and an irresponsible, social failure from the US-Protestant Christian view. (More on all of this later.) However, with the successful advent of Alcoholics Anonymous (1939) followed by Narcotics Anonymous (1953), social perceptions had started to change. They went from moral-degenerate-failure to the perception of illness—for alcoholics after 1939 and for addicts after 1953 (not disease, illness).

It was a shift for a small part of the population and ideas were changing. But then came the political War on Drugs, and as a group, drug addicts, hippies, some Vietnam vets, and those "dope-smoking-draft-dodgers" became a cultural enemy. What had been a slowly growing perception of illness for drug addicts was erased in 1973. Addicts became enemies and enemies don't go to treatment they go to prison. Yes, they were called criminals but actually they were prisoners of war: loss of civil rights, unreasonable search and seizure, secrecy of enforcers, presumptions of guilt, and cruel penalties. By 1974, the myth of the War on Drugs was in full swing.

Politics were the reason for the creation of the DEA, former US President Richard Nixon's little army to fight a war against drug addicts. There was created a strong negative-perception myth of a drug addict being a threat to good social order and public safety. After about 1995 it slowly started to change from criminal-enemy back to illness... until harm reduction happened.

Cancer patients are not given tobacco. Diabetes patients are not given sugar. Whether they have contributed to their own disease or not, we spend billions of dollars to help them. Those people are worth saving. Drug addicts are given opiates. It's easier and cheaper to mistreat enemies in a war, and justify it, than rehabilitate or care for them. There is a subtle connection between the myth of the war on drugs and how we abuse addicts by giving them opiates rather than responsible treatment. It's a smoke-screen declaration of care and cheaper, too. Political indoctrination is now substituting for treatment. (See Appendix III for a very brief explanation.)

The war on drugs is a myth, and so is the myth of "helping" addicts by harm reduction. Abandoning ill people to the agony of drug addiction by giving them drugs for the fiction of public safety is never harm reduction for those abandoned. It's cruel indifference. What was obvious when "harm reduction" was initiated was the assumed decrease of crime and drug-addicted lawlessness. The original intent of political harm reduction was safer communities and less public dread. It was never harm reduction for addicts. That didn't happen, neither did the reduction of illness or crime. Harm reduction has no medical or legal credibility. It's a political agenda and has no established benefit for addicts, and for the politicians and public it's some vague placebo to reduce their guilt and anxiety.

Giving a diabetic sugar or encouraging a cancer patient to smoke is not harm reduction. Addicts are sentenced to decades of suffering at minor public expense.

They are not given treatment they are given opiates. When American politicians abandoned the illness model and created a criminal model of drug addiction onwards from 1973 addicts became disposable. They still are. Recently, it is very slowly crawling back to addiction as an illness. But, if you are a Group D drug addict, harm reduction has classified you as hopeless and not worthy of any sincere investment (except if you are famous or rich, then "they" want to make movies out of you).

This leaves culture in chaos, people living in fear and dread, with more stress, believing in lies and political rhetoric, and anxious about the future. The general public don't know they are quietly insulted by being held as stupid and treated as children who can't think. That leaves the power brokers unchallenged as regards addiction (as regards anything).

In his book *Globalization of Addiction*, Bruce Alexander explains how cultures of today are dislocated. They are severely and increasingly destroying relationships, communities, and lifestyles that used to carry spiritual and stable integrity (my words). Since the Industrial Revolution began cultural dislocation (as in *dukkha*) has gotten continuously worse. It is now global, and the destabilization is out of control. We are left in the crush for modernity with alienation and confusion as a standard mind-set (the standard pre-condition for graduation into addiction). [75]

This global alienation, destabilization, manufactured enemies, and fractured relationships are the primary background cause of the proliferation of addiction, especially to the socially approved, abstinence not-available ones. This allows society, in general, to create a sense of helpless frustration with those nasty addicts, and the subtle but abusive justifications for harm reduction. People have become empty milk cartons and broken cell phones—disposable, unless you're a celebrity.

The underlying point to be made here is social intervention must shift focus from the five or ten percent at Group D to the sixty-plus percent in Group B. The only way to reduce Groups C and D is to educate and shift those at Group B into Group A. On the graph, this will shift everyone to the left and the grossly self-destructive groups on the right will reduce. I realize this may be a somewhat utopian presentation of this, although it has born itself out in the microcosm of my private work. There is a cultural solution—the education of Group B. [76] But...

---

75   Modernity, very briefly, is the clamoring for a global market, the destruction of small communities, greed, celebrity worship, impression management, too much mobility and relocation, the clash of technology against emotional responsibility, an unstable labour force, alienation from each other, religious terrorism and political arrogance all over the world, no trust or stability in government, and a loss of personal identity. It's bigger and more complex than that, but that's the sense of it. In a generic overview, remember that we have several thousand years of traditional, small-community and family mutual support destroyed in 150 years (five generations) of industrial revolution and greed. Not good. See also, footnotes 244 and 253.

76   The Stop Smoking campaign of the 1960s through to 2000 is an excellent example of cultural

Group B embodies the power in culture and participates in socially approved addictions like greed, spending, relationships, sex, romance, sugar, mild to moderate/frequent alcohol and drug use (called functional addiction), aggressive competition, prescription drugs, smoking, the internet, beauty, pornography, sentimentality, television, religion, shiny things, wealth, and celebrity worship. Educating Group B out of this will go a lot farther and change more than the smoke screen of demonizing Group D. [77]

A major fact to realize is that the hard-core addictions of Group D do not overlap with the approved addictions of Group B. Group D, in alienation, cannot afford them and are too deep into self-destruction to be interested in shopping, chocolate cake, beauty, celebrity worship, or exercise. The poverty stricken and poor middle-class get their escape in celebrity-worship television shows. And certainly, Group B escapes scrutiny because they are a mutual admiration society—I can afford plastic surgery, two Porsches, and two vacations to the Mediterranean each year. Am I doing well, or what?

"Functional addictions" in Group B are quite harmful overall and are the enabling source of Group C transiting into Group D. Groups C and D exist because of B. But then, at a deep subconscious level, Group B wants the focus on Group D. The gang at B get to be frightened, shocked, righteous, "politically" concerned, feel superior, and point fingers at "those social failures" in Group D, they aren't us. That's how Group B gets away with it.

There are other serious health concerns that are the result of cultural stress and modernity. A short list: despondency, depression, loneliness, mental illness, suicide, stress, the globalization of addiction, the abuse of people in harm reduction, poverty, cancer, greed, religious terrorism, political abuse and indifference, sexism, racism, and delusions about political integrity. Political integrity is an oxymoron. These concerns are ably written about in other books. Some are noted in the citations (more at footnote 253). Here, within my own work and writing, I am more concerned with awareness and effective avenues to personal recovery and spiritual change.

"Every ethical system involves a psychology of conduct and depends for its development upon its idea of what (that) conduct actually is."
C. Douglass, from
The Philosophy of J.S. Mill, p. 251

---

education. It worked. In 1965 about 55 percent of Canadians smoked. In 2017 it was 15 percent (online through StatsCan). Education regarding addiction for Group B is the approach to take to reduce addictions overall. Interesting that in the 1920s over sixty percent of the population smoked and cancer was reported at one in eleven adults. After 2010 only fifteen percent of the population smokes and it is predicted that one in three people will experience cancer.

77 Celebrity worship is explained most admirably in *Empire of Illusion, The End of Literacy*... Chris Hedges (Pulitzer Prize) Vintage Canada Random House 2009. Celebrity worship: Our addicted and exaggerated fascination with the lives of famous people. What they eat, wear, and who they have sex with. This includes the ridiculous, outrageous idea that because they are famous their opinions are valid truths.

What that observation looks like transposed into addiction recovery is: Every spiritual system, like recovery, involves a psychology of conduct—the psychology and behaviour that precipitates the ability to change beliefs and values. As regards being spiritual, this might be acquiring an affinity for the governing values of equality, respect, rigorous honesty, never blaming, responsibility, seeing all annoyances and agitation as a problem initiated within one's self, letting go of old ideas, and having compassion not judgement. Adopting these ethical behaviours for new people is dependent on having a stream of responsibilities to undertake *and* witnessing excellent role-modelling and self-discipline towards that end in others.

As was suggested by Mr. Cross, a university professor back in the 1960s, if you want to know "why Vietnam?" look in your own back yard. I would modify that a little for this era. If you want to know "why addiction?" everyone look in their living room.

Chapter 3

A Basic Knowledge of Addiction — The Foundation

This chapter explains the first stage of recovery or the first step on the journey to a spiritual life (which are the same thing). The actual first step, <u>before</u> Step One, is to acquire a thorough and dependable knowledge of addiction. And again, I will remind you: This is not a general condemnation of those who use drugs or alcohol, buy lottery tickets, spend or exercise in some manner of a responsible lifestyle.

The two critical preconditions that must be established in undertaking any addiction recovery are (a) understanding exactly what an addiction is and what it's symptoms are (analogue knowledge); and then (b), with that knowledge, personal self-examination and evaluation of personal circumstances as addictive or not (insight). This cannot be done without the necessary education and it cannot be externally imposed. The old-fashioned association tests—I drank as much as you did and you say you are so therefore I am, is entirely inadequate, as is listening to horror stories from drama junkies and the life-damaging consequences from their behaviour. Both (a) and (b) must be accomplished before any of the twelve steps are attempted. Only these establish the potential for the new person to become the expert of their own recovery (footnote 46).

What I intend in this chapter is to establish a "ground zero" for addiction education. A starting place that applies to all addiction, whether abstinence available or not available, whether medium or severe, or distraction addictions like TV, or behaviour addictions like exercise, or socially approved addictions like spending, gambling, and celebrity worship. It is important everyone should at least be on the same page when we start. [78]

Modern interventions adopt the unstated belief that Group B, from the charts in Chapter 2, are just fine with their approved addictions. Even if they are addicts, their addictions aren't hard-core because they are paying their taxes and showing up at work. They are much less drastic than those nasty street junkies and dead-end alcoholics. The people in Group B are at least functional and keep the culture, consumerism, debt, and the power elite fully operational.

---

78   For the most part I will use some variation of a personal pronoun. I do not mean this to be accusatory nor do I wish to imply that all people are drug addicts or alcoholics. I would not want to include someone where they wish to be excluded. It's just easier writing.

Power brokers and politicians are often in Group B. They usually don't know, or might only suspect, that the abstinence not-available and greed-and-glitter addictions in Group B have become a necessary part of "modern" culture. [79] Education is especially required when sorting out abstinence not-available, integrated, and polyaddiction. [80] The result will be the addict can understand their situation in the polyaddictions they exhibit, and the abstinence required. The effort towards recovery will make more sense. They can identify their own specific barriers that they must hurdle, and their own chosen path to a spiritual end. A person can then decide on the spiritual position that appeals to them, why they must do what they must do, and they become the authority in their own recovery.

We must never lose sight of the fact that anyone who invests in recovery, whether private treatment or attendance at a twelve-step meeting, has some motivation for change. At the minimum there's an emotional investment to at least check it out. People, when entering recovery, are very naive about their addiction and what is or will be required. To discover what each person's motivation is, however minimal, and through education to use that to their advantage is what early recovery is about. Nothing else.

The first thing to know is addiction and its "treatment" rests on the psychology of a phenomenon. A phenomenon is an occurrence or an observable event that arises and is perceptible by the senses, which is unusual, significant, and unaccountable regarding its origin *vis-à-vis* scientific insight—addiction. A phenomenon is something that appears real to the mind and to observers, regardless of whether its underlying existence can be proved, its origin identified, or its nature understood, again like addiction.

Research offers various suggestions about genetics and abuse that are interesting. These are inconclusive and insufficient. Any proposed predictors are unreliable, as is abuse or lack of it, poverty, and family dynamics.

---

79   Spending, debt, shopping, exercise and body image, shiny things, dieting, work, sex, greed, aggression, sports violence, isolating technology, envy, are all significant and required in this culture's claims to "success." That is Group B.

80   Integrated addictions are relationships-romance-sex, as are shopping-spending. These are connected and integrated with each other in the abstinence not-available category. What is always a part of recovery from gambling addiction is understanding intermittent reinforcement—the hoped-for, unexpected big win. Intermittent reinforcement is present but overlooked in cruising bars sex addictions, adultery/betrayal behaviours, secret eating addictions, actually in all addiction when the addict scores big or "gets away with it" and believes they have escaped consequences. That's intermittent reinforcement. Abstinence not-available and poly-addictions will be addressed later.

The Relationship Between Abuse and Addiction

To make the phenomenon view easier to understand I will offer two spectra. One will represent Family Dysfunction where the left end will represent severe/ blatant family dysfunction and the right end will represent a mild/subtle variety. The second will represent Addiction, severe/blatant addictions on the left and mild/subtle addictions on the right. This is not intended to minimize or aggrandize anything or insult anyone. It's to make a general observation about dysfunction and addiction. There is a…

Spectrum of Family Dysfunction

Severe / Blatant   *Mild / Subtle*

10	9	8	7	6	5	4	3	2	1

overt sexual abuse, repetitive or severe violence, cruel, shaming atmosphere, isolation, poverty, hunger, crime, gross neglect, no support or caregiver attention

no overt abuse, minimal or no violence, minor emotional manipulation, social life, no deprivation, primarily law-abiding, support and attention

and a *Spectrum of Addiction*

Severe / Blatant   *Mild / Subtle*

10	9	8	7	6	5	4	3	2	1

crime, unemployment, sexual promiscuity, no family, homeless, chronic diseases, destitute, poverty, significant instability, chronic, visible acting out (Group D)

generally law-abiding, minimal or no sexual acting out, have family and home life, employed, have lifestyle/disposable income, reasonably stable (Group B)

To set up a comparison would leave you with a diagram similar to this:

Family Dysfunction

Severe / Blatant   *Mild / Subtle*

Severe / Blatant (D)   *Mild / Subtle (B)*

Addiction

If you are an addict, or if you know or work with addicts, consider each spectrum *separately* and estimate the overall, general state of your history in terms of (1) family dysfunction and then (2) addiction. Mark approximately where your life fits on each spectrum, and then join the points. Find several other people who are "in recovery" and ask them where they would place themselves on each spectrum. Join the dots for their choices. After several people have chosen for themselves, you will end up with a crisscrossing web of lines, something like this:

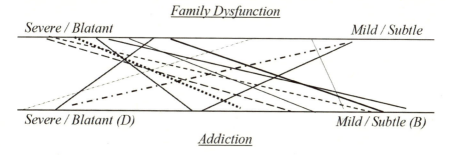

Family Dysfunction

Severe / Blatant   *Mild / Subtle*

Severe / Blatant (D)   *Mild / Subtle (B)*

Addiction

I have offered this exercise to well over 1,000 people, in various settings, in three countries, and always end with a chart like the one immediately above. Some people with mildly dysfunctional families (right end, top) ended up on the severe end of the addictions spectrum (left end, bottom) and others with severe family dysfunction ended up with "milder" addictions (or possibly none at all). You will find being severe on one spectrum *does not* guarantee you will be severe on the other.

Siblings that were exposed to similar parenting will not necessarily develop similar personality issues. The appearance or virulence of an addiction cannot be reliably predicted in relation to family issues. Yes, on a balance of possibilities, being from the severe end of "family" may tend to put you on the severe end of "addiction", but that prediction cannot be relied upon. Do not buy into the myth that because you had a horrible childhood, you must be a severe addict; or that because you had a pretty decent family, you are less entitled to be an addict or to have a virulent addiction.

There are many peculiarities in the appearance of an addiction. Its unpredictable age-onset, the widely varying degrees of its virulence, its irregular focus from television to chocolate cake to heroin, to anger and romance and righteousness, and everything in between. There is also its duration and phasic nature, its complex manifestations in substances or behaviours or both, and the inconsistent pattern of its appearance or resolution. Altogether, these imply it is unpredictable regarding its origin vis-à-vis scientific insight. No one can reliably predict if or when an addiction will start, what actually causes it to start, how bad it will be, which principle addiction it will be, what combination of polyaddictions, how it will modify over time, how fast it may or may not escalate, how long it will last, or the potential for a person to exit. It is a phenomenon which underscores the importance of footnote 46. [81]

---

81   Bill Wilson referred to the phenomenon of AA and recovery in his writing.

As regards addiction, it isn't a disease, as in cancer or narcolepsy, because there is a definite phenomenon component to addiction. It's an illness and certainly a strange one. Without an awareness of its social component of alienation in relationships and its escalation through dislocation in culture it can never be understood. This is why its history is important. The more society is unstable and punitive the more the increase in addiction.

The person must be treated and not the addiction. The solution is never available when therapists, scientists, and doctors, et al, make any addiction-phenomenon a subject of disease and DNA biology or try and impose a science of heredity. We cannot treat "addiction." The person *is* the illness. The definition of an addiction that addresses all of this when read from a spiritual mindset is...

Addiction: A *pathological relationship with a mood-altering experience that has life damaging consequences.* [82]

In simple, direct terms this is a pathological relationship or interaction (compulsive; I can't stop), with a mood-altering experience (any behaviour or use of any substance that changes my mood) that has life damaging consequences (which are harmful to me and I end up in some sort of trouble). [83]

Some differences to consider:

Illness: more emotional and mental concerns like paranoia, addiction, schizophrenia, and dual diagnosis. These are sometimes "predictable" but the prediction is never guaranteed.

Disease: more at physical concerns like cancers, the flu, infections, diabetes, gonorrhea—viruses and bacteria with cellular damage.

Injury: broken bones, burns, car accidents, falling off a ladder, cut your finger peeling potatoes.

Confusion arises when professionals treat broken bones, diabetes, poverty, unemployment, liver failure, etc., as a symptom of addiction. They are not symptoms of addiction, they are the consequences of it. Addiction exists long before the consequences become obviously destructive. It isn't a medical disease but some of the consequences of it are a medical concern. Addiction

---

82   This is from The World Health Organization pre-1987. It has since been changed as the result of pressure from the medical community and big pharmaceutical corporations. This earlier definition is the best I have found.

83   The "compulsive" aspect is addicts can't stop. This is related to Mr. Wilson's observation in Step Eight of *Twelve Steps and Twelve Traditions* and "why" sobriety is so hard to attain—dislocation in all relationships (really: all of them) is at the root of addiction. As discussed later, relationship is the very nature of our existence. Because addicts of any description are perpetually in relationship conflict we are perpetually in addiction. We cannot stop addiction when participating in sustained relationship chaos and conflict. (This culture is in perpetual conflict.)

is a phenomenon-illness that is a strange and unpredictable demonstration of dislocation or alienation in relationship and social psychology.

Life-damaging Consequences

Some life-damaging consequences, that are often not viewed as addictions related, are contained in the failure to achieve common, universal social goals like graduating from high school, holding a job for longer than a year, staying out of jail, paying taxes, or buying a car. Not to achieve any one of these is not of itself a symptom of addiction; however, if not achieving the ordinary social accomplishments is the tone of your life, there's a good chance you're addicted. The exemption-factor that addicts or alcoholics love to proclaim is they minimize any life damaging consequences and accuse others of exaggeration when confronted.

Other life-damaging consequences and destructive patterns of addictions might be:

- divorce (one or many, it doesn't matter)

- contracting or distributing sexually transmitted diseases

- patterns of medical treatment for injuries from lifestyle

- admission to psychiatric wards

- unemployment, marginal or erratic employment, excessive working hours, being fired

- being negligent or irresponsible regarding children and significant others; recurring conflict in family

- promiscuity, using pornography, neurotic or belligerent celibacy, sexual anorexia [84], adultery, infidelity, erratic or moody sexual life-style, "hunting" relationships or sex through dating clubs, bars, personal ads, internet sites, twelve-step meetings

- erratic, inconsistent, or repetitively unfulfilling friendships

- some eating patterns and food relationships (adult onset)

---

84   Sex, romance and relationship addictions are an integrated addiction pattern; one of the three will be prominent and the other two will be hovering in the background to shore-up the principle one. Addicts or alcoholics will sometimes go into a complex reaction to their relationship-sex addiction by becoming sexually or relationship anorexic. In a subconscious, emotionally aggressive reaction to perceived sexual promiscuity or relationship failure they do a hard line 180-degree change: No sex! No intimacy! This is often an emotionally destructive, angry attempt to control an addiction.

- inability to make and maintain commitments regardless of whether it's in one or many areas of your life

- violence, ongoing threats of violence, repetitive arguing and fighting, participating in violence in sports (vicariously as a spectator or as a participant), excessive competition

- gossiping and bingeing on anger and righteousness often apparent in arrogance or religious beliefs, being noticeably, frequently angry, rage binges, road rage

- having your private life noticeably different from your public life—maintaining significant secrets about private attitudes and behaviour; impression management [85]

- frequent trouble with landlords, creditors, relatives, recurring debt, financial instability

- getting drunk or stoned, having black-outs, smoking

- any drinking or drug use and driving; gambling, crime

- celebrity worship, shopping, spending [86]

- compulsive exercise, preoccupation with body image, some cosmetic surgeries

- isolation through reading, television, videos, computers, social media, internet, etc.

- obsessing and/or fantasizing. This last one is entirely concealed and difficult to evaluate. Some addicts spend most of their waking life in fantasy. Harmful consequences from that are hard to identify and understand.

If you read through the list again, many of the descriptions are very common, expected behaviours of people in Group B. This is a long list but it's necessary to create an awareness of the range of harmful consequences of addiction. To experience any one or two of these isn't necessarily indicative that you are an addict. However, if you experience a few of these to any noticeable recurring degree after childhood, you are likely an untreated addict or destructively compensating for some other serious problem. And, of course, one of the silent, long-range harmful

---

85   Impression Management: Investing energy and conscious effort into making oneself appear as one isn't—a devious self-advertising campaign designed to conceal shame, character defects, or aspects of personality that are assumed will meet with social disapproval. These are concealed by impression management. This is a significant manipulation strategy and should be carefully examined and challenged to achieve authenticity.

86   Shopping-spending are integrated addictions, as are compulsive exercise-preoccupation with image, sometimes integrated with cosmetic surgeries.

consequences of these consequences is inculcated shame, repetitive inadequacy, and a sense of failure. .

Aside from these visible consequences, addictions can be evident in a group or constellation of social behaviours; the usual visible indicators. There are five main categories, explained next. All addicts, to some degree or other, experience these. They may not admit them openly, but these five are there on close examination. There is also a series of psychological symptoms that sit underneath the social, visible symptoms. But first is to understand...

Social Symptom Constellations

In the last eighty years or so addiction has been principally focused on alcohol and/or drugs and this "condition" has been defined, classified or evaluated from a social perspective. In examining this through about forty questionnaires and intake forms from the middle 1970s to 2015, at hospitals and treatment centers, and through therapist's offices and the Twenty Questions of self-help, I am left with this view: All of the addict-alcoholic illness evaluations—from modern psychiatric assessments to lay intervention strategies, can be grouped into five categories of behaviour. There are five groups of visible, social behaviors that all alcoholics or drug addicts demonstrate. These are:

- Self-destructive or harmful behaviour to self and others, including emotional self-abuse or other-abuse. This category is directly connected to the life damaging consequences listed above. (See also Types of Abuse, Chapter 4.)

- Dishonesty, withholding, and manipulation. These may be calculated, spontaneous, deliberate, or unconscious, but dishonesty is not optional.

- Arrogance, cynically superior, living with double standards and defiant about this which conceals a deep inner insecurity. Closed-minded to conceal insecurity. Self-righteous.

- Selfish. Manipulation of others for undeserved advantage or acting charitable with various selfish agendas.

- Irresponsible and defiant, argumentative, defensive, belligerent, destructively stubborn. Blaming others.

I refer to these as the social symptoms or consequences of advanced addiction. They should be committed to memory as they are the visible indicators that an illness is present, but they are not the addiction. Fever, chills, cough, difficult breathing, chest pain are indicators of an illness, but they are not the pneumonia. Granted, these social indicators are hard to see in well-camouflaged, socially-approved addictions like anger, work, shopping, or exercise, commonly called functional addictions, but they are there.

There are also four considerations for each social symptom: (1) There are always at least two obvious addictions and one subtle addiction present. These are the primary and secondary addictions and the third unseen addiction will always be a relationship addiction. Polyaddiction is a given. (2) The personality of the individual. They will be noticeably shy, outgoing, passive, a victim, aggressive, globally angry, emotionally confused, etc. (3) The intensity and frequency of conflict and acting out; and (4), The methods of concealment or the way the behaviours are defiantly justified. These four become quite important when approaching responsibility and spiritual principles. (Chapter 7)

Each of the five social symptoms are present in every addict/alcoholic. What is unique is the presentation—how they show up. They vary in intensity, virulence, and how they are camouflaged. In one person they are dishonest at work and honest with their spouse. In another, they are mostly honest at work and dishonest on their taxes; others are dishonest everywhere. Some people hurt themselves by constant self-criticism, others by physical self-abuse, and others by aggression towards others, violence, or caustic criticism. Some addicts are focused on hurting others more than themselves, especially children and partners. Still others hurt themselves by grand sacrifice for others—martyrdom. Some people consume dangerous drugs and others participate recklessly in dangerous sports or dangerous-abusive relationships. Some are arrogant, argumentative, or very passive. People will self-destruct and hide from relationships by drinking bottles of wine in front of the TV or pornography. And, as usual, there's 1,853 variations of these.

Understand that every addict has all five social groups of symptoms and the four considerations that have to be taken into account when they participate in recovery. These social symptoms, when they are obvious, are the usual indicators used to evaluate addiction.

Misleading Evaluations

The usual symptoms considered for assessing addiction, noted above, are focused on drugs or alcohol. This is as misleading as it is narrow and superficial. Blackouts, financial trouble, drug-alcohol withdrawal, having the shakes, impaired driving, sleeping in cardboard boxes, associating with lower companions, hangovers, unemployment, unhappy home, remorse, sexual acting out, fighting, and using drugs or drinking a lot are usually seen as symptoms of addiction. These are obvious in Groups C and D in the cultural graphs. They are actually social indicators of the advanced consequences of addiction, not the addiction, itself.

I have also heard religious types claim alcoholics and addicts are "that way"... because they can't find God—if they had more faith they wouldn't be "that way." Children don't have a Ritalin deficiency. People with anxiety don't have a Valium deficiency. Addict's don't have a God deficiency.

Professionals, in general, consistently examine education, poverty, family history, abuse, employment, social defiance, social diseases, and other similar common concerns. All of this is a grossly misleading evaluation of addiction and, of course, keeps the focus on the far right, Groups C and D. This is examining consequences not addiction. We claim that behaviour modification (i.e. reduction of negative social behaviour in groups C and D) is "recovery" and never examine the complicity of Group B or society. Alienation through addict-criminalization is left out of the discussion. The psychological dislocation in culture itself or the grossly fractured self-concepts of people in this culture are not examined. (More in Chapter 8.)

People don't black out and wake up in another city in a spending or shopping addiction, and they don't have a financial crisis from nine hours of cable TV each day. But, characteristically, the end of shopping or TV binges often ends in a mental-exhaustion of clouded memory loss. Certainly, being angry and abusive or cruel—pumping oneself up with self-righteous indignation about religion isn't a mood-altering state that causes harm and abuse, it's just "fervor and passion"; not addiction. A recurring series of unnecessary injuries from extreme sports, excessive exercise or physical conflict... or four hundred dollars a month on sugar and chocolate... no addiction there.

What we have been calling addiction symptoms are more an evaluation of social behaviour, what is approved and not-approved; whether it's disruptive or not. If you are not causing trouble or being inconvenient then you are not an addict. This is misleading because they are not the addiction they are the personal-chaos results of addiction.

Psychological Symptoms

The following group of psychological conditions are present, to varying degrees, in all addicts. However, these following psychological concerns, all invisible or internal, have been left largely unexamined by clinicians, other than by Dr. Tiebout. [87] In this classification of symptoms, these mental characteris-

---

87   Harry M. Tiebout, MD/Psychiatry was an early supporter of AA. His pamphlet Conversion As A Psychological Phenomenon, New York: National Council on Alcoholism, Inc. was read before the New York Psychiatric Society on April 11, 1944. In it Dr. Tiebout made these observations about the psychology of an alcoholic: (1) Tense and depressed, (2) Aggressive, or at least quietly stubborn, (3) Oppressed with a sense of inferiority, at the same time secretly harboring feelings of superior worth, (4) Perfectionistic and rigidly idealistic, (5) Weighed down by an overpowering sense of loneliness and isolation, (6) Egocentric and all that implies in the way of a basically self-centered orientation, (7) Defiant, either consciously or unconsciously; and (8), Walled off and dwelling, to a large extent, in a world apart from others. Dr. Tiebout said nothing

tics are inherent in any addiction, to varying, subtle degrees and intensity. This psychology sits underneath the five social symptoms noted above and is what must be addressed by the steps or therapy over an extended period of sobriety. Extended sobriety does not resolve addiction. It only reduces the usual social or personal damage and makes treatment and recovery possible.

These psychological conditions are consistent with the phenomenon of addiction, and when all addictions are resolved, they often largely disappear. Bear in mind these psychological symptoms appear in the addict's personality, which then in various ways promote the social symptoms noted above. What is of additional concern is the counsellors and other professionals who usually offer guidance in recovery are not trained and/or supervised sufficiently to understand how to address these deeper, pre-existing concerns. This relegates most treatment to theories of improved social behaviour. The first one, self-neglect, is possibly the more important.

Self-neglect is a mental condition that precedes acting out. There is personal disregard and self-abuse. This is engaging in mental justifications for any behaviour that is detrimental to yourself and exemplifies a disregard for your own health and safety (like smoking, poor diet, sexual irresponsibility, reckless spending, seeking drunken blackouts, reckless driving). This is often evident in cognitive dissonance. Once self-neglect is established, which is rooted in relationship alienation, then abuse of others is guaranteed.

There are endless variations of minimizing or explaining away this mental attitude of self-destruction so addicts can maintain the delusion that they aren't self-destructive. One example is: "I'm not an addict. I know I'm unpredictable and I black out when I drink, but it's only two or three times a year." Infrequency is the self-justified exclusionary excuse. Others are, "I know I missed the kid's graduation, but they'll get over it." "Don't worry, I can find another job." "I can find another partner, there's lots out there." Because you infrequently participate in destructive behaviour; because the life-damage is subtle or it appears no one is hurt, does not exclude you from having an addiction. [88]

---

about how much his patients drank or the social consequences from that.

88 An active addict has a mind-set that believes within their own mind, all by itself and independent from the body that houses it, they are smart enough to avoid or escape any destructive physical consequences of acting out. There's an arrogant mindset that they can escape all consequences by arguing, blaming, manipulation, pleading, lying, promising, and pretending indifference to criticism. In *Spiritual Transformation* there is a detailed discussion of this at Appendix IV. Treatment for some people means a manipulative holding pattern to prepare for more acting out. The tighter they are wrapped in arrogance and delusion the farther down the scale of destruction they go. An addict "hitting their bottom" is a common phrase. What this means is an internal mental realization has happened: The addict becomes aware they can no longer and are unable to create lies or manipulation strategies to avoid reality. This is the reason they generally stay away from insightful therapists or assertive partners, because their manipulations are not tolerated, they are identified and exposed. (See the Preface). Hitting bottom means they have

Neurosis isn't usually talked about as a part of an addiction. Neurosis is a mental-emotional disorder, characterized by strong inner conflict, which does not have an organic cause. The symptoms of neurosis are insecurity, anxiety, irrational fears, or depression but not to the degree that a person would be incapacitated. The anxiety and inner conflict must be significantly disproportionate to the external conditions, but the person can still function in community. Many neuroses disappear in the normal course of getting recovered and going through proper twelve-step work, but the more serious ones don't. Addicts are neurotic to some degree. [89],[90]

Denial is an unconscious, automatic ego defense that's characterized by an inability to recall or acknowledge painful truths, realities, thoughts, or feelings. Denial is a mind-survival technique of "not remembering." All addicts have denial to some degree. To all addicts: Congratulate each other that you're in denial, it helped you survive your self-imposed crises so you could enter recovery.

Repression is common among addicts and is different from denial in that it begins with a more conscious, willful effort. It's not automatic. When reality is repeatedly painful, memories and emotions from conflict are consciously thrust aside (like willful forgetting). Over years of repetitive willful forgetting, the incident is repressed out of memory.

When trauma is frequent or continuous, or when addicts continuously act out and regenerate crises and trauma (which trauma is greatly escalated by drama), the denial and repression become almost permanent. Developing denial and repression, and to some extent being neurotic, are ways addicts compensate and survive. These prevent them from being proportionately aware of the realities and pain in the circumstances of their life. They can be greatly reduced by sincere recovery work and well-conducted therapy.

Assumptions. Addicts often base their values and beliefs on assumptions. These are rooted in ignorance, supposition, and prejudice. Assumptions keep people trapped in destructive, limiting thought patterns. This leaves prejudices, judgements, and stereotypes unchallenged.

---

exhausted their own delusions. If early recovery is presented with opinions (about God, being a trouble-maker, prayer, and moral corruption) the addict will create stronger secret opinions about their ability to act out and their delusional ideas about escaping consequences. After all, thinks the addict, my opinions about me are more valid to me than yours are. This is one reason for education being essential—no opinions. Reaching bottom is convincing themselves they are out of delusional options and have no more escape strategies. It has little to do with the degree of degradation.

89   From *The Language of the Heart*, Bill W.'s Grapevine Writings, "[the alcoholic] cannot avoid becoming a neurotic—to some degree or other." p. 266. Carl Jung advised that neurosis was a way to avoid legitimate suffering.

90   Bill Wilson refers to this in the AA pamphlet *Three Talks to Medical Societies*, an Alcoholics Anonymous publication.

Shame is arguably the most powerful emotion and the greatest block to human development. Other emotions are certainly influential, but none carry the power to contaminate personal awareness or defeat personal accomplishment to the degree that shame does. In short: It is the emotion that separates us from ourselves—internal alienation. Shame demands that we be "human doings" rather than human beings. [91] (More on this in Chapter 4.)

Some addicts are shamed in childhood significantly less than others, and yet are not shamed to the degree that would correlate to the vicious addictions they demonstrate. Not all, and sometimes very little, of an addict's shame came from their family of origin or caregivers, and it is irresponsible and abusive to insist otherwise. (This was discussed regarding repetitive inadequacy and harmful consequences.)

Isolation. Addicts are psychologically isolated from themselves (by denial, shame, and repression) and have no dependable sense of self. This alienation is often referred to as a shame-based identity and (with repetitive inadequacy) is one of the most important things to address long-term. [92] They are also emotionally isolated from everyone in their lives; lonely and secretly afraid of people, believing they are misunderstood or persecuted which is sadly often the case. (More in Chapter 8 on persecution.) There is a definite avoidance of connection with others.

Fear. Addicts and alcoholics live with a disproportionate, usually overwhelming sense of fear. This can be an unfocused fear from early childhood development. Certainly, they are afraid of people and afraid of being found out. They usually conceal this well. Recall the observations of R.D. Laing in the section Who is this book for? above footnote 5.

Guilt is an externally applied (learned) emotional state. Some guilt is imposed by the addict on themselves because they misunderstand the illness. There is also culturally imposed guilt which addicts tend to agree with. Society and families harbor beliefs that addiction (alcohol, drugs, pornography, etc.) is a moral corruption, which defeats the declaration of illness or disease. There's more on guilt and moral culpability in Chapters 4 and 8.

Selfishness is an aspect of being irresponsible and intrinsic to addiction. It shows up in four ways: (1) The manipulation of people and circumstances, or the disregard for the rights and dignity of others, to avoid exposure of your own shame, frailties, fears, and mistakes. (2) Any behaviour that avoids personal responsibility or accountability and unjustly (irresponsibly) externalizes responsibility onto someone or something else. (3) Avoiding exposure of your limitations, defects, errors, or resentments at the expense of others—making others guilty, bad, wrong, or responsible for your own faults and misdemeanors.

---

91   The phrase "human doing" carries an edge of satire from over-use. Nonetheless, it is appropriate here.

92   "No dependable sense of self" is explained in more detail in Chapter 4.

(4) Expecting or demanding in any situation a larger share of privilege or entitle-ment—making thirty percent of the effort and insisting on seventy percent of the rewards and credit.

Irresponsibility permeates all aspects of an addict's life. Here's a short list of behaviours that are irresponsible in a spiritual life: accusing, admonishing, arguing, attacking, avoiding, blaming, censuring, cheating, complaining, con-demning, deceiving, defending, defying, demeaning, disregarding, embellishing, evading, exaggerating, finding fault, gossiping, hiding, invading, lying, mini-mizing, moralizing, petulance, pouting, rebuking, reprimanding, undermining, whining and withholding. Addicts are masters at irresponsibility.

Cynicism, among other things, embodies a belief within the cynic that they are superior to whatever they are cynical about. It's often rooted in assumptions about the shortcomings, failings, or hypocrisy of others. It implies the cynic's self-held conviction about their own superior character attributes and/or superior insight and wisdom.

Arrogance is the demonstration (or secret existence) of a belief in some per-sonally held superior quality, accompanied by a patronizing or dismissive attitude towards others. One common understanding of arrogance is that it's the opposite of humility. With arrogance, there is isolation.

Within a recovery program, there are three obvious paradigms of arrogance and these are very often silent. (1) Believing you are the smartest or most per-ceptive or most experienced person around and because of that you don't need help. (2) Believing you are (or someone else is) the sickest or the most depraved person around, so nobody can help. (3) Believing you (or someone else) is the most worthless or useless person in the room, and nobody should waste time giving help. These are arrogant and you're isolated, afraid and lonely, even if you aren't aware of it. [93]

Fantasizing and **obsessing** are serious components of addiction. However, since having some fantasy is a healthy part of being creative *and* it might also be obsessive fantasy within some other emotional health issue, I mention them here with reservation. For addicts, fantasy and obsessing are instant ways of mood altering, which makes them a secret, significant factor in perpetuating any addictive cycle. In the cycle of addiction (shown later in this chapter) these contribute to Distorted Thinking at position 2. Self-talk plays a significant role in this. Fantasizing and obsessing are also significant in the generation of drama and the inability to resolve pain. [94]

---

93 If "we" had been born before 1900 many of us would have been long-ago dead from heart attacks, strokes, violence, cancers, etc. Being born after 1950 makes longer life a function of medicine. It is certainly arrogant and righteous to claim God-miracles where none exist. Medi-cal effectiveness? Yes. Miracles? No.

94 Resolving emotional pain is incredibly complex and too intricate for extensive discussion here. There is pain from trauma and abuse. There is pain from unmet needs. There is pain from shame and from excessive guilt. There is also an exaggerated sense of pain from drama. The pain from

Cognitive Dissonance is a very complex concern in many people in this culture and of serious concern to people with addiction. [95]

In a too-brief explanation, it is the conflicted mental chaos of rapidly switching between two opposing beliefs, one of which is harmful. I *know* smoking is bad for me; I am buying cigarettes. I *know* drinking or gambling are bad for me and my family; I'm going to the bar and casino this afternoon. I have known for two years my marriage is done; abuse, distrust, arguing, betrayal, lying, we've tried three romantic reunions and I *know* I have to leave... we're planning a romantic getaway next month. I *know* I have to use a condom but.... And on it goes, cognitive dissonance.

Cognitive dissonance is especially evident in recovery groups and their relationships. Many people in recovery declare all manner of convictions and beliefs about faith, God, love of their fellow members, and commitment to the steps and program; it's all so wonderful and I am so committed. They certainly sound sincere in meetings. Yet, they so quickly behave in transparent contradiction to their convincing speeches about acceptance, spirituality, recovery, commitment, honesty, and health. They gossip, criticize others, argue, and are obviously not spiritual in so many ways. They believe the speech and act otherwise.

In the reduction of cognitive dissonance, for insight in recovery, there are three elements that should be addressed. (i) Education to understand that cognitive dissonance exists underneath anxiety and is a primary factor in repetitive inadequacy. When acting out in any addiction dissonance disappears and a false sense of peace exists. This is the root-source for addicts reporting that they felt calm when acting out—no more dissonance. (ii) Examination of the mind-set addicts have they are smart enough to manipulate others and escape any consequences of participating in destructive behavior. They think they can plead, beg, argue, promise, intimidate, or talk their way out of trouble. This is the belief that allows them to not contemplate any possible consequences that might arise in the future. (iii) The belief of innocence: This isn't my fault it's someone else's fault and "they" have to fix it (rationalization of blame). In subtle terms, "my dissonance is someone else's fault."

Altogether, the principle strategy to reduce cognitive dissonance is to acquire new information (education in facts, not opinion) that will counteract the dissonant conflict. Information is presented, particular to each individual, that

---

drama is experienced as very real, but it is from the exaggeration and fiction in the drama, not from any authentically existing incident that sits under the drama. The resolution strategies are different. This is examined in some detail in *Spiritual Transformation*.

95   Leon Festinger, A *Theory of Cognitive Dissonance*, 1957. People strive for a mental consistency, a psychological harmony, so they can function mentally in the real world. People who have mental contradictions ("I know this is good, but I do the opposite bad thing") have a severe but subtle dissonance between believed values and behaviour as opposed to consonance (harmony). There is mental distress and justification for the dissonance, which is especially true in addiction.

increases an awareness of the benefits of consonance (agreement and compatibility) and how each person can eliminate the contradictions between negative behaviour—drinking, shopping, chocolate cake, too much salt, and a positive belief that successful self-restraint and recovery are beneficial and necessary.

Religion always contains dissonance in their beliefs, and often so does belief in a deity (not always). Adherence to spiritual principles doesn't. Kathryn Schultz's book *Being Wrong*, cited elsewhere, has relevant discussion of cognitive dissonance.

Do not use psychiatric words like denial, repression, neuroses, depersonalization, ego, abandonment issues, dissociation, or cognitive dissonance unless you're well informed and know exactly what you're talking about. Even then, there must be a compassionate reason for saying them at all. All of this is put here to make people aware of the very complex inner symptom concerns that are associated with addiction.

Misuse of complicated psychological words hurts people and is very often motivated by bias and prejudice. Millions of people, for thousands of years, have been spiritual without psychiatric words that dissect and analyze anyone's character. Unless you are truly compassionate, and very well informed, don't use them. [96] Practice successful self-restraint with abstinence not-available addictions (actually all addictions). Practice self-restraint with unspiritual thoughts. Practice this with harsh judgments and anger. Work patiently at completing the step assignments in the order presented and most of this will disappear.

A final note: The five constellations of social symptoms and the psychological attributes may seem overwhelming. They are moderately resolved to some noticeable degree by sobriety, step completion, and a general participation in an array of meetings over a few years. Substantial resolution and authentic spiritual peace require a very deep commitment to the spiritual nature of the steps (very rarely seen) and some long-term guidance with a quite inciteful therapist or mentor. Ordinary sponsorship is insufficient for significant spiritual awareness.

And so finally, we are left with two categories of symptoms—social and psychological. Regardless of how obvious or subtle, these will be **chronic** and

---

96   There's a lot of unexamined power mongering and mean-spirited labeling of character in our society. Certainly, many psychiatrists, other doctors, therapists, religious officials, and poorly informed addicts are guilty of this abuse. Very often it's elitist, self-righteous, and unnecessary. This relates to uninformed comments about dual diagnosis at footnote 69. And finally, these psychological symptoms of addiction, regardless of how obvious or subtle, will be chronic and entrenched. They will be so pervasive that the addict will be unaware of their all-encompassing nature. The ever-thickening manual of mental disorders (the DSM), and the addictive, common-place lifestyle of legal prescription drugs are to me disheartening. We live in a culture of irresponsible hypochondria orchestrated by big business. This is an aspect of people being disposable which I discuss in Chapter 8. *The Myth of Mental Illness* by Thomas Szasz, M.D. 1961, is worth close examination, as is M. Foucault's *History of Madness*. These are challenging reads and not for the faint of heart.

entrenched. The social symptoms are often mislabeled as social defiance and rebelliousness which gives rise to the perception of addiction as some form of defiant moral corruption.

Addiction is a unique from of mental malady where the cause is hidden in the secrets of self-destructive alienation. This is to be seen and discovered by the addict, no one else. Then recovery will prevail.

Blindness to the Illness

Both categories, together, will be so pervasive that the addict will be unaware of their all-encompassing nature. With either group of symptoms there is always a blindness to all of this. For the most part, addicts or alcoholics, in the early stages of becoming one, are most often unaware that they are crossing some invisible line and descending into addiction. There are several reasons for this, here I will describe the only most important ones.

Having an addiction is living trapped in those psychological symptoms but they exist in a very complex and interconnected social pattern—like a three-dimensional spider's web. Each one of the five social symptoms are contributing to the other four. Each of the psychological symptoms are also connected to the five social symptoms. It is a three-dimensional spiders web of symptoms and issues. It's complicated.

A person gets addictions-sick everywhere and throughout their entire personality all at the same time in very shallow increments. It's usually a slow, creeping atmosphere which is impossible to notice. If you get a headache or break your arm those are localized and noticeable and stand out from the rest of you that isn't affected. When someone gets some illness or disease other than addiction, it affects certain aspects of their life but not every aspect of it. Other illnesses have a defined boundary of influence. They're noticeable because the condition is experienced in a specific area. Not so with addiction.

Addiction is a global personality-attitude-belief malady that is prevalent everywhere in a person's life. It is not noticed because of its gradual appearance everywhere. Addiction affects everything about an addict's life: how they brush their teeth, how they make love, how they drive, how they talk, what they eat, what art and music they like, how they think, how they work, how they celebrate holidays, how they earn a living, how they sleep, how they dress, how they comb their hair... literally everything is affected by addiction. Addiction is an all-encompassing state of existence.

Because it is a slow, creeping fog that takes a long time to become apparent, and it affects every area of personality, the people in Culture Group B don't know they are in it. They are blind to it. Groups C and D are usually aware because of the socially blatant consequences. [Being spiritual will eventually be an all-encompassing state of existence; the opposite of addiction, but more on that later.]

Addicts have a broken relationship within themselves. A psychological and spiritual truth is that whatever is happening inside a person's mind, if they are abusing themselves or neglecting themselves disrespectfully, lying to themselves in their thoughts, that will be reflected in how they behave in all their external relationships. All addicts are relationship-addicted.

The relationship between an addict or alcoholic's internal, secret mindset of self-abuse and their external destructive behaviour is seen in two ways. One is a broken, harmful relationship with substances or behaviours or distractions. The other is a broken or dysfunctional relationship with people, all of them. The underlying psychological crisis is externalized into every relationship an addict has. Some form of relationship manipulation and dishonesty, which are outgrowths of shame and fear, make all relationships power struggles that generate abuse and damaging consequences.

Addicts and alcoholics never develop relationships with insightful, honest people. They develop relationships with people who will suffer their dishonesty, neglect or abuse which fits with the other person's unconscious need to be treated that way. [97] This is relationship addiction, a more accurate description than codependence. Then both people get what they want, one to be a form of irresponsible abuser and the other to be a victimized martyr. Both will act out in their resentment, dysfunction, martyrdom, and harm themselves. There is nothing heroic in this ongoing persecutor vs. martyr-like self-abuse in relationships. Relationship addiction co-exists with, and underlies, all other addictions, hence, polyaddictions. This is a constant condition.

There is a presenting, primary or visible addiction, very often thought to be alcohol, drugs, sex, pornography or gambling. Underneath that is always relationship addiction and sitting beside that is at least one other addiction, like smoking, anger, television, exercise, shopping, etc. Polyaddictions are a given situation that must be examined.

The Addiction Cycle

Addiction operates in a cycle which gradually increases in severity and complexity and the addict creates various addiction substitution scams. There are many theories on the origin of this cycle but discussing the origin is not the main purpose of this book. Here, we are more interested in interrupting or stopping the cycle. The discussion usually begins at (1) and progresses clockwise. [98]

---

97   This is explained later in the section Ego Formation.
98   This cycle was introduced to me through the work of John Bradshaw (1933 – 2016) who was significant in bringing an awareness of the need for recovery and therapy to the public. Two books of his that are important are *Healing the Shame that Binds You* and *Bradshaw on The Family*.

Richard W. Clark

The Cycle of Shame

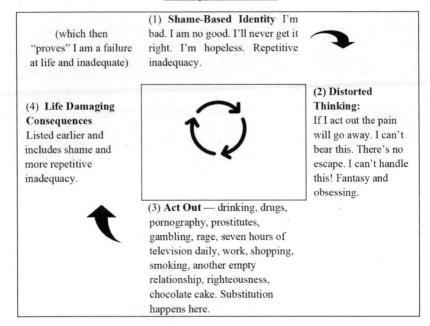

(1) **Shame-Based Identity** I'm bad. I am no good. I'll never get it right. I'm hopeless. Repetitive inadequacy.

(which then "proves" I am a failure at life and inadequate)

(2) **Distorted Thinking:** If I act out the pain will go away. I can't bear this. There's no escape. I can't handle this! Fantasy and obsessing.

(4) **Life Damaging Consequences** Listed earlier and includes shame and more repetitive inadequacy.

(3) **Act Out** — drinking, drugs, pornography, prostitutes, gambling, rage, seven hours of television daily, work, shopping, smoking, another empty relationship, righteousness, chocolate cake. Substitution happens here.

The opinions on the origin of a shame-based identity at (1) are wide-ranging. What must be understood is that a great portion of this shame arises from repetitive inadequacy and from life damaging consequences. The period for intervention to stop the cycle is at positions (1) and (2). When an addict is in acting out (at 3) or in the immediate experience of life damaging consequences (at 4), interventions are rarely successful. [99]

Abstinence Available or Abstinence Not-Available

Although it may sound tedious, this next section is of significant importance. This presents the two main categories of addiction which will be either Abstinence Available or Abstinence Not-Available. This is crucial information when people are trying to establish successful self-restraint or stability in sobriety

---

99   There are various sources for a shame-based identity. This cycle itself, regardless of its antecedent causes, generates shame, guilt, and repetitive inadequacy. A shame-based identity could be from social-historical consequences of addiction, from repetitive inadequacy, or influenced by some early childhood/social circumstance. Not all families are guilty of inducing shame; some yes, all – no. If there is actual clinical evidence of childhood-origin shame, there should be no (or very minimal) attempt to resolve this in early recovery.

and challenge any addiction-substitution scams. And, as I noted earlier, some addictions are integrated, like relationships-sex-romance and all addicts live with polyaddictions. Failure to understand these concerns is of significant influence in the high relapse rate. What must be remembered is these two categories require different approaches to abstinence and early recovery.

Abstinence Available Sobriety or Successful Self-Restraint	Abstinence Not-Available or Successful Self-Restraint
These are addictions to alcohol, tobacco, drugs, and gambling (which often includes the socially encouraged forms of lottery and bingo). Here, the addict can clearly establish complete abstinence; hence, an abstinence available addiction. [100] NOTE: *From the Cultural Focus Graphs, abstinence-available are usually Groups C and D addictions, and commands virtually all government and treatment attention, funding, policing, research, and press coverage. Yet, these are the least common of the addictions and underneath them, they always harbor abstinence not-available addictions.* *Sex, pornography, relationships, work, television, religion, spending, shopping, chocolate cake, movies, computers, celebrity worship, internet, and violence (usually Group B) are much more prevalent and destructive to the human condition and the environment.*	These are addictions to anger, adrenaline, work, relationships-sex-romance, food, computers, power, money, competition, shopping-spending, body image, celebrity worship, etc., where complete abstinence is never available, and culture often encourages them. [101] Addicts desiring recovery must *first* establish an ethical and credible standard of "healthy" normal behaviour at Step One before any other twelve-step work begins. This means they establish and maintain a standard of behaviour that, if it were not met, would be considered a relapse. The difficulty is the standard is subjective. Complete abstinence is not available for these addictions. Successful restraint is required and has to be negotiated between personal perceptions, instinct, environment, and pre-existing psychological issues, all of which cause all manner of confusion. It easily lends itself to irresponsibility, repeated failures, smoke-screen sobriety, and constant relapse, which are guaranteed to set up more repetitive inadequacy.

Within these two categories there are hundreds of secret struggles addicts contend with. "How do I buy prostitutes or cruise singles bars spending thousands

---

100 Here I refer to gambling as deliberate wagers and various games of chance. Yes, it's a "gamble" to cross the street, but the generic risks of life are not what we're discussing here.

101 Relationship addiction is the more accurate representation of what was formerly referred to as codependence.

of dollars and not hurt myself?" "How do I watch two hours of porn a day and find fulfilment in my relationship?" "How do I get drunk or shoot dope five nights a week and be healthy, too?" "How do I spend $350 a week on things I don't need and feel good?" "How do I lie to everyone and have trusting relationships?" "I want to commit adultery and have a fulfilling marriage." "I love to gossip about everyone but never feel trusted by others." "How do I watch TV for seventy hours a week and have a life?" "How do I refill six prescriptions a month for uppers and downers and mood-altering drugs, or buy $235.00 of mood-altering retail counter drugs and still have emotional insight?" "How do I eat fifty-three chocolate bars, two bags of M&Ms, and one cake every week and feel good?"

The logic of successful self-restraint is: "If I stop myself right now from ___*insert destructive behaviour*___ then I will... keep my family, not declare bankruptcy, not get a divorce, avoid psychiatric wards, not get arrested, not lose my job, not get stiches or have to take antibiotics." The logic of successful restraint (which is problem prevention) is lost in an addict's delusional thinking about escaping consequences. This was explained to some degree at footnote 88.

Over years of acting out, as the life damaging consequences become more apparent and destructive, an addict creates subtle and very complex justifications and thought patterns to rationalize their self-destruction. By tweaking their memories, they find ways to fill in the memory gaps or explain and defend their blatantly self-destructive behaviour. [102] At the minimum this includes:

(1) creating enemies or pseudo-allies where none exist,

(2) minimizing their own culpability,

(3) exaggerating self-blame; and,

(4) exaggerating, blaming, or minimizing, the influence of others.

Relationships

All of this is about conflict in relationships. As explained in Chapter 4, we cannot *not* be in relationships. First: Steps One to Seven are to heal the inner conflict within the addict. They must get themselves honestly sorted out before anything else. Second: Steps Eight and Nine are designed, with humility as the governing principle, to repair harms and correct historical, external conflict in all relationships. This is always second. The consequence of these efforts is the sincere realization of the promises. Finally, third, are Steps Ten, Eleven, and Twelve. These are to prevent conflict, maintain healthy relationships, and create a deeper sense of spiritual behaviour.

---

102 Sometimes this extends itself into confabulation, which is explained in *Spiritual Transformation, Third Edition*, a footnote at page 177.

For practicing addicts or alcoholics, and many in recovery, relationships are power struggles to:

- to prevent others from finding out the truth (about anything)

- to maintain control (of every situation) [103]

- to be taken care of and looked after by others

- to be rescued from responsibility

- to justify or continue acting out.

As was discussed earlier, this is not a family illness, it is a relationship illness. All relationships in a practicing addict or alcoholic's life are fractured or dislocated power struggles. There is no emotional intimacy anywhere. The phenomenon of addiction exposes itself to the world as a disease of broken relationships...

- destructive relationship within themselves in the addict's mind; how they treat themselves (with negligence and disrespect).

- destructive relationship with acting out (behaviour, distractions, or substances) and reckless disregard for themselves, their health, social guidelines, and the environment.

- broken/twisted, dishonest relationships with *everyone*.

It is a social and religious misperception of addiction that it's a deliberate, defiant and intentional exercise by the addict to be mean and irresponsible—moral corruption. This view is a religious-cultural prejudice. Moral corruption that requires forgiveness, like kidnapping, isn't the truth of the matter for addiction. It is illness. No one seeks forgiveness for illness. Addicts and alcoholics are often more perplexed by the whole self-destruction thing than anyone else. But, with the prejudices that are rampant in the views of addiction, they can't talk about their own puzzlement without being scolded.

Groups C and D addictions are always a downward spiral into chaos, illness, shame, loneliness, financial poverty, isolation, possibly jail, and (probably) a too

---

103 Maintaining control isn't always to be the boss. Some people, who assume a position of helpless victim, maintain control by getting others to continuously look after them. People can "think" themselves into being helpless or ill. Both genders play into this irresponsibility. This is the reverse of aggressive dominating: be completely helpless to remain in control (passive aggressive). The power is in irresponsible helplessness. Resentment becomes intrinsic to either party whether the role chosen is helpless or dominate. But this must be balanced with some compassion because there are critical diseases and illnesses that are ongoing, and some people do require frequent attention and care.

early death. Group B is a long-term holding pattern of addiction and isolation. Hence, the two rules. Learn them.

Two rules:

1) People die from addictions.

2) I cannot change the first rule _and_ it applies to me.

To eventually achieve some semblance of spiritual serenity, and to stabilize the path to get there, the information that is outlined in this chapter should be understood and committed to awareness. This is the required education. By understanding this a great skill is developed—the ability to self-evaluate and to self-diagnose. [104]

Within our personality, addiction shows up everywhere, in multiple disguises, always as polyaddiction, and in everything we say, do, think, believe, and feel. I mentioned the addictions substitution scam. I.e. drinking three days a week, four days of television, one day of shopping. (or) Four days of food bingeing, one day of sex, television every night. (or) Get sober from alcohol and smoke more and use porn. (or) Quit drinking and smoking, start shopping and exercising until you're exhausted and broke. Addiction substitution scams switch things up day-to-day. To escape addiction and achieve a true spiritual harmony is a great accomplishment. We must always know where we stand in relation to addiction, its symptoms, and recovery. Education allows for this.

After the first four or five years of diligent sobriety and step-effort, entering a responsible, spiritual lifestyle will be possible. (Chapter 7) By learning what's outlined in this book you can soon self-monitor and self-evaluate. In this way, you will be able to recognize when and where you are deviating off course, when you are substituting addictions, or in some change-up scam. You can then self-correct before your relapse is flagrant.

What clients or newcomers should come to understand in their initial phase of recovery—what they should achieve in the first year or so—is being quite aware of and committed to these following principles or behaviours. The first four are essential and entry level to the world of recovery.

- (1) Sobriety - don't act out. Practice successful restraint. Compare your behaviour to the five main social symptoms listed earlier and self-search

---

104 We are taught to self-diagnose regarding common-place illnesses: colds, flu, headaches, sprains, bruises. This is a part of being an adult, and so it should be with addiction. Knowing when you are demonstrating symptoms at the level of self-neglect, dishonesty, withholding, manipulating, selfishness, arrogance, and defiance is essential. This is experiencing symptoms but not being drunk or stoned. Addicts must be able to self-diagnose and self-evaluate to prevent relapse from progressing unchallenged. This relates to the addict becoming the expert as described in footnote 46.

your attitudes and emotions regarding the psychological symptoms. If you don't you will live in Rule #1, dangerous at best.

- (2) Rigorous honesty all the time about yourself (from How It Works [105]). You are your own Honesty Police and honesty is not a spectator sport. This is how, over the long term, you challenge substitution scams.

- (3) Abandon your old ideas (from How It Works) which old ideas are usually related to the five social symptoms of addiction. Old ideas must be replaced with ideas or goals of being spiritual. The result was nil until we let go absolutely. [106]

- (4) Learn what addiction actually is; what it means. Understand the symptoms deeper than clichés and acting out.

- There are two ways to relapse. (i) In early recovery it is to start acting out again—you "suddenly" relapse out of sobriety into using again. (ii) In later recovery, after Step Nine, relapse is to abandon or ignore spiritual principles—to relapse out of spiritual behaviour into addictive behaviour. You are again acting like an addict: lying, manipulating, arrogant, frequently angry or defiant, blaming others, selfish... but still sober. This is relapse.

- There is never any spiritual or psychological reason to blame anyone for your addictions or the problems that arose from them. Drop the word blame from your speech and thought. (From *Twelve Steps and Twelve Traditions*, p. 47.)

- Attempt to maintain a healthy, no-conflict relationship with everyone. The other person may want conflict, but you do not have to engage in it.

- There is nothing to prove to anyone; nothing to convince anyone of, there is only you to convince yourself. Never argue about opinions and avoid an endless or meaningless argument. It is a sign of true spiritual endeavor when a person chooses loneliness over conflict.

- Whenever you are disturbed or upset there is something missing in your spiritual program or an ignored problem in some relationship. To be upset is only human—everyone should expect to be upset sometimes—just quietly "nudge" yourself back into spiritual principles and get on with the business of your life.

---

105 *How It Works* refers to the two-and-one half pages beginning at page 58 in *Alcoholics Anonymous*. It is read at the beginning of most AA meetings. There are important reasons for this. See Step Two in *Spiritual Transformation*.

106 There are hundreds of old ideas to be abandoned. Here are a few: One lie won't matter. I won't get caught. They won't find out. I can handle it. No one can be trusted. I can do this on my own. I'm smart enough. I don't need help. It's partly your fault. I have to do it my way. It's not that bad. No one can help me.

As regards therapists, counsellors, sponsors, groups and treatment, there is this: *"Because we live in such a degenerate age, we rarely meet a teacher endowed with all the necessary qualifications. In this age of conflict spiritual masters will exhibit both faults and virtues. No one is absolutely irreproachable. Therefore, examine well those [who claim] to excel in virtue before beginning to study with them."*

Reported to be said by Pundarika, 1100 CE.

This has not changed in the intervening 1000 years. In one Buddhist treatise it recommends taking upwards of five years to choose your teacher. Granted, this may be a little extreme, but choosing quickly is worth a note of caution. Choose mentors or spiritual advisors carefully for they can only guide you short of where they have gone. Irresponsibility in them will show up in you. But from another perspective, anyone who is sober a few years is a strange human being to those in the first few weeks of recovery. Always bear in mind that for the most part, sponsors, groups, counsellors, and spiritual advisors are temporary. It may be advisable to move ahead in spiritual discipline by changing your advisors.

"If you are trapped in a cage of illness, turmoil, and fear, the door always opens from the inside." [107]

---

107   This is taken from the instruction manual *Body Energy Healing*, by Richard W. Clark, copyright 2004, p. 19. Available from the author. This is expected to be published in book form late in 2020 as *Four Corners of Almost Perfection: Maintaining Health.*

Chapter 4

Relationships and Childhood Development

How important are relationships? Relationship is our very existence and if a person intends to make progress into a spiritual lifestyle, this next section is worthy of careful consideration.

We are created by relationship (our parents). We initiate our existence and are born through relationship (with our mother). We exist and survive in and by relationship (parents, caregivers, extended social circle, relatives, and environment). There's relationship with food, sex, emotions, love, romance, and a few other things. We can never be out of relationship. Everything about our life and existence is embedded in relationship. "I am relationship." There is no escaping this. [108]

Governing Energy

As adults all we can do is define our relationships by how we each assign a governing energy. Each of us creates every relationship with some type of energy attached to it. This energy can be loving, joyful, safe, affectionate, honest, sensuous, sexual, romantic, resentful, shameful, defensive, dangerous, angry, fearful, suspicious, intimate, secretive, or deceitful. There's some type of governing energy or governing attitude which is assigned by you that defines the relationship. Again, we must be involved in relationships in some manner and we assign a governing energy and attitude to each one.

We often change the governing energy. We change the relationship energy from love to resentment, from pleasure to suspicion, from suspicion to affection, from affection to romance, from friendly to sexual, or romance to anger. In a spiritual life we are supposed to make a sincere attempt to change all relationship energy to some version of positive through the psychology and work of the steps. It's not always possible but the attempt must be made. That's all well and good, but each of us must be aware that relationship is our existence and there is a governing energy to each one. [109]

---

108 Certainly, there are many levels and aspects of health or dysfunction in relationships, to varying degrees, but regardless of this, existence is relationship.

109 Changing the governing energy is part of the important dynamic of Steps Eight, Nine, and Ten

Like sex and water and food, relationship is fundamental to the core of our existence. A person cannot choose to *not* be in relationship. We can leave or absent ourselves from people or things but that's often a relationship governed by resentment, fear, anger... avoiding. All we can do is define our attitudes and participation by the governing energy we assign to each situation. After achieving successful abstinence, and eventually approaching Step Eight, the first thing at Step Eight is to accept that as an adult you are responsible for conflict. In the past you chose the governing energy and have perpetuated it by guilt, resentment, or blame, all by yourself; no exceptions.

There is a sequence to the resolution of any life of crises. First you heal your inner judgements and dislocations; resolve inner emotional conflict. Then reduce your judgements and cynicism, stop blaming, take responsibility for your participation and attitudes. You change your inner world view (context). Then you take responsibility for the conflict you generated with everyone. This is done honestly, without blame or complaint, and then finally, you heal any external conflict as best you can. You change the governing energy and live a spiritually principled life. This doesn't mean you have to socialize with them or marry them, it means you set everyone free of your judgements with compassion. [110]

If you are honest and committed to healing the resentment and fear (chaos) within yourself first, there will eventually be resolution to the chaos in external relationships. What happens in concert with this is old ideas are abandoned and then it is possible to take complete responsibility for conflict at a social level. Steps Eight and Nine are conflict resolution and Ten and Eleven are conflict prevention. This perspective is rare in recovery discussions and is quite foreign to most people in this dislocated culture.

Dislocation and Trauma – It's Complicated

Dislocation and trauma aren't the same thing. **Trauma** from an incident is anything from being battered or assaulted, falling off a ladder, or to being yelled at. There is developmental trauma—emotional wounds and neglect from

---

and the meditation portion of Step Eleven.

110 This paragraph. "There is a sequence..." is the shortest version of the psychological steps that form the path to being recovered. These are accomplished, for believers, with the help of their chosen higher power. For agnostics or atheists, they are accomplished by desire, seeing their value, and persistent determination. This is no different than someone who had a tough life with disadvantages who desires sincere success being a teacher or an architect. They sense and see the long-range value of being that. They follow the instructions of education, therapy—whatever, and work hard. They are personally determined, don't complain, don't blame, and eventually realize their goal. Determination and hard work get the credit for them becoming a good teacher, not God. Addiction recovery is no different. Out of a tough life (various addictions) people see value in recovery, work hard, are persistent, and succeed. Some people strongly believe a higher power is necessary for this, others don't. This is an opinion of choice, don't argue about it.

childhood, and full-system trauma from acting out, severe electric shock, near drowning, and major illness. These types of trauma have both common and unique requirements for their resolution. As mentioned earlier, the resolution of pain and trauma is quite complicated.

Whatever event initiated the trauma, that circumstance itself generates different emotional reactions and psychological concerns depending on any number of variables. To make it even more complicated, there are influences in memory and perception and the creation of drama. This is discussed in some detail in *Spiritual Transformation*.

Dislocation (Buddhist *dukkha*) was discussed earlier as regards parallelism. It's that sense that life doesn't operate how we expect it to or how we demand it should. As was discussed, good people die young, mean people win, bad things happen to good people, we try hard and don't get anywhere, and many people work hard and finish last; rather unfair, isn't it? For many people, it's confusing that life doesn't work out fairly or smoothly. Life's capricious unfolding dismantles our sense of fairness and creates dislocation. The often-times deliberate cruelty of religion and politics makes this worse.

Life and our view of it (for many people) categorizes life as unfair and dislocated. That makes being alive a source for resentment and bitterness. What is common is that a profound spiritual dislocation exists within culture and within addicts. The psychological mindset of not fitting in, repetitive inadequacy (whether real or imagined), dislocation, self-neglect, or self-annihilation sits at the core of all acting out.

Addiction is a phenomenon that manifests as defiant, self-negligent behaviour as a way of compensation for all of this. It is seen as constant conflict: relationship conflict, conflict between the addict and the world (unstated and seldom understood), conflict with everyone in their life (often silent), and conflict within the addict's mind, their values, perceptions, behaviour, and self-worth; alienation. These are core issues of spiritual dislocation. [111]

Conflict

Conflict: a state of opposition. The opposition of incompatible wishes or desires within a person and the internal and external distress that results from this; indecision and fear regarding personal circumstances and choice—the inability to stabilize the mental chaos. Cognitive dissonance. This internal struggle and chaos generates social conflict, and this is usually externalized by blame and anger onto an outside agency (a spouse, a boss, a family member, the neighbor's dog). There is also significant conflict in aspects of identity. [112]

---

111 Too many people approach life as a problem to be solved (dislocation) rather than a situation to be appreciated—spiritual acceptance.

112 Identity Conflict: A very complex disparity between how people act publicly, how they act

The sincere resolution of internal conflict is actually rare. What is usually achieved is some self-assigned level of being good enough and usually ends with collusion to maintain social acceptance. That mediocre level of recovery is obscured by socially approved addictions, emotional concealment, impression management, or in some cases bragging about struggles and accomplishments. Attempts at conflict resolution often regress to aggression and brow-beating to establish dominance or compliance. Whoever has the best memory for misdemeanors wins because they can overwhelm the other person into submission.

Oftentimes conflict will be generated as a mental exercise to avoid responsibility (blaming). However, the real source of conflict is internal and often subconscious. The AA literature advises rigorous honesty is essential, addiction is a self-imposed crisis (it is our own fault), "we" must work towards letting go of old ideas, and never blame. Without resolving identity conflict to some notable degree; without accepting responsibility (never blaming), and without substantial emotional truth, these suggestions from the AA literature are impossible.

Developmental Dependency Needs.

This section outlines the dynamic of shaping your identity as an infant during the first four stages of childhood and personality development.

1st **Stage** — 0 - 1 ½ years: Basic Trust vs. Mistrust (pre-verbal)
Children and infants (almost everyone, actually) have no means to self-regulate their responses to their environment. Negatively, this is called trauma. Children and infants are *always* influenced by what they encounter. How caregivers respond to an infant's physical needs, and what attitudes are displayed to the infant,

---

privately, and their internal mental chaos/conflict about who they are and how they see or want to see themselves. They don't have clear insight about "how and why" their decisions have taken them to wherever they are at and can't appreciate what they want to be or how to get somewhere else. There's no stability about their identity (*Who am I, really?*, the title of a book by Sheldon Kopp). They sense being trapped in a social presentation scheme that they didn't choose, cannot escape, and is not authentic. The mental conflict is a series of emotional shadows and very subtle: "This is not me. I am not *this* person, but I don't know how I got here, who I am, and I want to be something else, but I don't know how I to get to where I don't know that I want to go." It is much more common than we realize. They sense all of this, knowing neither how to escape the public presentation scheme nor how to decide who they want to be, and cannot achieve some authentic stability about themselves. This is greatly increased by cultural instability and especially true for alcoholic-addicts. It can be somewhat resolved if sufficient spiritual work is completed and rigorous honesty and responsibility are embraced. It is usually long and arduous to escape. For the more serious spiritual student well-conducted therapy is required.

establishes in their developing nervous system that the world is or is not friendly (safe or unsafe). If bodily needs are met as they arise and are not neglected, and they are exposed to affection and compassion, the world is interpreted as trustworthy. If bodily needs aren't met, or they are subjected to poor handling and negative emotion, infants become unconsciously mistrustful about the safety of their existence. This is a pre-intellect, pre-verbal limbic brain construct of energy that alters their nervous system. Severe ongoing abuse in this stage results in psychopathic-type personalities and/or multiple aspect personality disorders.

2nd Stage — 1 ½ - 3 years: Autonomy vs. Shame and Doubt (pre-verbal)

Autonomy, a kind of emotional and physical independence, is the realization of separation. The infant is becoming "itself" in an unconscious physical way. Infants will acquire awareness to eventually challenge their world by achieving physical *self*-definition. Separation into autonomy, "I am me, not us," is the infant's primary task at this stage.

Personal muscle control and rules around toilet training are confusing: Rewarded for holding on in the car. Scolded for holding on on the toilet. Rewarded for letting go on the toilet. Scolded for letting go in the car. Patience without criticism is crucial here.

Criticism and disapproval at this second stage of development are never understood by the infant. If punishment or scolding happens—stern face, angry voice, neglect, impatience, rough handling, it generates shame and an ingrained fear of moving from attachment to autonomy. The world then becomes unsafe and the infant learns to hide their needs and emotions because of anxiety and shame. The child will avoid autonomy (separation) for fear of receiving more shame (displeasure) from any authority figure. Unless resolved, this is carried for life.

Shame and doubt at this stage result from an implied allegation of failure from a caregiver. [113] This disapproval (implied "failure") is sensed in the criticism of receiving impatience, a stern face, scowls, an angry voice, other scolding, or non-gentle handling. The child will experience doubt and fear and will be emotionally or nervously confused. Under four years old a child cannot understand rules. They cannot understand what motivates criticism and displeasure, which results in internalized shame.

With their inability to understand, and the unnamed fear of reprimand, they develop shame and anxiety—an internal boundary of hiding and self-concealment. This is the result of sensed criticism or outright abuse. Autonomy is

---

113 This "alleged failure" is never an actual failure. The infant is receiving disapproval from some caregiver rooted in the irresponsibility or anger of the adult. This is the internalized shame of the adult being transferred to the child—the inner-personal transfer of shame. Impatience with the infant is included in this dynamic. In the case of children this is always an indictment of the caregiver or parent, never the child.

abandoned. They become "not themselves" and become an approved extension of the authority figures that shamed them.

As a young child they always conceal their autonomy because of early shame and anxiety. Years later, when progressing into being a teenager and an adult, the person won't know their capabilities. They now live just on the edge of success and unconsciously doubt themselves. Rarely will they try anything new or adventurous unless it is an angry reaction to emotional confinement.

In their future, the person will see themselves as not being valued and having no potential. Being an individual becomes dangerous because of the real possibility of criticism, rejection and disapproval from some person that is supposed to provide safety or is seen as an authority figure. Ongoing abuse or neglect in this second stage is visible later in adults as a personality bound by shame, and disorders or issues of strong neurosis, accepting or dispensing abuse, personality disorders, and anxiety. When investigating this remember for addicts or alcoholics there are two other sources for shame. [114]

3rd Stage — 3 - 5 years: Initiative vs. Guilt (post verbal)

This stage can only be negotiated safely with an ability to understand abstract rules and concepts which are a function of language. Language and intellectual development must be available at a very basic level to achieve a healthy and realistic sense of guilt.

Taking initiative, which is built upon autonomy from the second stage, is a *self*-declaration of preference. This allows a child the possibility of independent choice and success. But while acting on the impulse to do something, i.e. taking initiative, a child has to negotiate rules. Rules are words. Appropriate guilt is related to understanding rules and taking initiative but acting on impulse (taking initiative) creates the possibility of scolding and displeasure from authority figures. If a reprimand happens it will be misunderstood and reprimands that are not understood always prevent a person from taking initiative on their own behalf because of anxiety, shame and guilt. It is very delicate. [115]

Two intellectual developments that signal a child is near the end of this stage, and can understand very <u>simple</u> rules, are "opposites" become understood and

---

114 Stern faces of displeasure, frowns, impatience, and angry tones, and also happy faces, pleasant sounds, and gentleness have all been recognized by infants as young as one or two months. By three months old infants easily sense their environment and are tuned in to love or displeasure. Some experts say by one month old they sense well. I believe it's more like from conception.

115 A child is almost three years old. Taking initiative: Impulse to action. They think, "I want an apple." What rules apply? Wash it first. Don't eat before dinner. Don't waste it. Taking initiative: Impulse to action. They think, "I want to go over there." What rules apply? Ask permission first. Don't cross the street alone. Watch for cars. Wait for Mom or Dad. Don't go outside alone. These are rules that a three-year-old cannot understand. At three years they will act on impulse to do what they want (initiative and autonomy) but are unaware of the rules that govern their behaviour or any consequences. They won't understand any reprimand or scolding.

simple logic questions, like "Where'd the bread go?" are asked and simple explanations are accepted. [116]

Guilt means you broke a rule. Most rules are the abstract and arbitrary whim
of the authority figures in a family. Guilt is about breaking rules and rules are
abstract and particular. Each rule must be understood and examined in relation
to the guilt that accrues from infraction, again arbitrary. [117]

<u>Good Rules (left) Bad Rules (right) and the elimination of Guilt.</u>

The experience of appropriate guilt, change the behaviour.	The experience of inappropriate guilt, change the rule.
Wearing seat belts is good and reasonable rule. You get a ticket for not wearing a seat belt. You feel guilty. You should. If you change your behavior, and wear seat belts, the guilt goes away.	Assume "Keep family secrets" is a historical family rule. As an adult, you go to therapy and are honest. You feel guilty breaking the family rule and telling family secrets. This sets up a dilemma: honesty in therapy is good, but you have to break the family rule of secrets and that's bad. You can't heal without feeling guilty for breaking the family rule of keeping secrets. Here: change the rule and guilt goes away.

Language and meaning must be clear so that rules are understood. The intensity and appropriateness of guilt is dependent on the comprehension of language
and understanding the concepts of rules and contracts. This makes guilt a post-
verbal experience. [As a side note for religious believers, guilt is not necessarily
evidence of sin.] [118]

---

116 Opposites cannot be understood until well into this third stage of development. Hot vs. Cold,
   Left vs. Right, Up vs. Down, are opposites. They may know hot and cold, but "opposite" is an
   intellectual relationship. When that is understood then *very simple* universal rules like please
   and thank you can be comprehended, not before and not more complicated than that. "Where'd
   the bread go?" is from a *Calvin and Hobbes* comic strip by Bill Watterson. Calvin puts bread in a
   toaster. He waits. The toast pops up and he asks Hobbes, "Where'd the bread go?" In the mind
   of a four-year-old that's a complicated before-and-after logic.

117 Relationships between people, in all but two situations, are contracts. Contracts have rules. Relationships with infants/children, with those who are mentally challenged, and higher powers
   if you have one, are covenants. Contracts and covenants are remarkably different. (see *Spiritual
   Transformation, Third Edition* for a full explanation.)

118 Should children be raised with no rules at all, doing whatever they want without restriction,
   they may become adults with an inordinate belief in entitlement and privilege. Too many rules
   can be as harmful as none.

However, with fear and shame present from the first two stages, appropriate guilt is never available. What happens is the child becomes an unconscious extension of the approval and punishment dynamics of the authority figures that govern their life. This results in three concerns: (i) an inordinate sense of loneliness, (ii) an unhealthy ego posture of self-blame; and (iii), to avoid the possibility of censure, they never take initiative for their own benefit.

Shame – I am wrong and bad. I am a mistake. (A total, universal self-condemnation.)

Dysfunctional Guilt — I can't do anything without getting punished or criticized. I am always wrong, so I won't do anything. (This means that repetitive inadequacy has been established.)

When shame is fused with dysfunctional guilt life becomes a singular experience of always failing at "something." If you defeat recovery efforts by adhering to old, abusive or unhealthy rules you'll get depressed or angry at yourself. That's a setup for relapse. If you don't examine old rules and let go of old ideas, which are often related to the five social symptoms discussed earlier, recovery is always unstable. This is especially true when there's misunderstandings about claiming addiction is an illness and seeking forgiveness for being sick. This truth, that addiction is an illness, cannot harbor any sense of moral turpitude.

Appropriate Guilt — I made a mistake, or I did a thing wrong; a single incident of error. This only applies with prior awareness and understanding of the rule that was transgressed. In a healthy situation, people must only feel as guilty as they agreed to within that relationship and must have prior knowledge of whatever rules are in play.

The Denied Person Construct – A Metaphor for Shame

This begins the discussion of a shame-based identity. When a deep-seated anxiety that life is unsafe, from Stage 1 is coupled with shame from Stage 2, all relationships are contaminated. While reading this, remember there are three sources of shame for the addict-alcoholic: family of origin, life damaging consequences, and repetitive inadequacy.

The left figure (with solid circle around the heart) is a shame-based personality. The person is "separated" from themselves. The figure on the right (dotted circle) would be generally healed or integrated.

A Symbol for Shame (left) and Self-Acceptance (right)

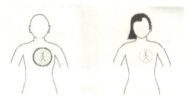

Shame-based Identity (Left)	Integrated "Healed" Identity (Right)

The left figure is an unconscious impression management scheme. An authentic personality is bound by shame and concealed inside the tight inner circle. It is terrifying to confront this shame-based existence where the person has no awareness of an authentic self. The person is separated from themselves. They don't know who they are.
 	
    In this, there is no dependable sense of self. They are unsure and cannot depend on themselves for wisdom or direction. Shame or addiction decides everything.
 	
    This harbors unfulfilling lifestyles, neuroses, serious insecurities, anxieties, and controlling fears. Shame causes relationship addiction, and <u>that</u> is the basis for all other addictions; never knowing who you are—always impression management. Others don't really love "you" they love the role you are playing. This is an existence of internal turmoil locked inside by shame—the solid line barrier.
 	
    The unacceptable parts (like sexuality, intelligence, interests, assertiveness, passions) are an experience of shame and hidden. There is a significant lack of self-awareness and insight from denial, repression, shame, etc. It is self-denying, self-destructive and unconscious. It is not fully resolvable via self-help.
	I am Me—authentic, integrated, and fulfilled. I have a freely chosen internal value system, emotional clarity, effective insight and self-awareness that is appropriately expressed. Assertiveness is available in relationships (especially in intimate, romance, sexual ones) with an absence of self-destructive behavior.
	
	    The right figure shows the concealment line broken and the person has assertive access to their real character. These people display a clear sense of fulfillment and purpose in life and relationships, always acting on self-determined values and trusting themselves.
	
	    They have awareness of an authentic self where they are integrated between character, emotion, values, passion, interests, and behaviour. They are not controlled by denial, shame, exaggerated fears, or hopeless, abusive, stagnant relationships. They are not hiding anything; an internal locus of control.

Shame-based personalities (figure left) are blind to their true character. Some of this may have come from family of origin, but certainly much of it came from the consequences of addiction and repetitive inadequacy. And, of course, the purpose of well-conducted therapy or spiritual transformation is to travel from left to right.

4th Stage — 5 - 8 years: Industry vs. Inferiority (social independence)

Children are expected to attend school which means there is some element of absence from their parents. Here, they navigate simple social independence. School requires participation with peers (negotiation), participating in a new social experience (an expansion of normalcy), and interacting with new authority figures like teachers or school bus drivers. They must understand new, simple rules. This requires tones of both assertiveness and cooperation. This is industry; making a social effort to accomplish with the risk of not succeeding. This is impossible for the child to realize when excessive fear exists from the first stage, shame exists from the second developmental stage, or significant guilt from the third stage. This is inferiority.

Loneliness [119]

The more subtle issue beyond shame is loneliness, which relates to a very elusive sense of dislocation and isolation—a symptomatic, quiet side-issue to addictive acting out and often present in sobriety or successful self-restraint. Loneliness in addiction recovery is rarely spoken of and has a similar emotional character to the loneliness and isolation many people experience in relationships. As with many things in addiction, this is complicated.

The Action and Cycles of Loneliness

In the diagram below, begin at the top left shaded box, Start Here (1). That will take you directly to the shaded box in the middle of the diagram, Quiet Loneliness. From Quiet Loneliness there are one of two cycles that people, especially addicts, go through. Either cycle begins at Quiet Loneliness and a choice is made.

119　In the late 1980s there was a survey conducted amongst counsellors/therapists in Canada. They were asked what they thought the #1 mental health concern would be for Canadians after the year 2000. The response, by over seventy-five percent of the respondents, was loneliness. Loneliness resulting from the disintegration of traditional values of community, the absence of long-term stable employment in later years, forced retirement, the isolation from illness, anxiety about retirement and poverty, and loss of family and friends. Loneliness is not feeling sincerely connected in a relationship of value. One considered issue is the disparity in life expectancy, for men 8 – 10 years younger, and what that would mean in their later years. There's more on loneliness in Chapter 8.

The cycle indicated by numbers 2 to 6 (upper right cycle) is healthy. The unhealthy cycle indicated by letters A to E (lower left side) is a set up for relapse and being unhealthy. [120]

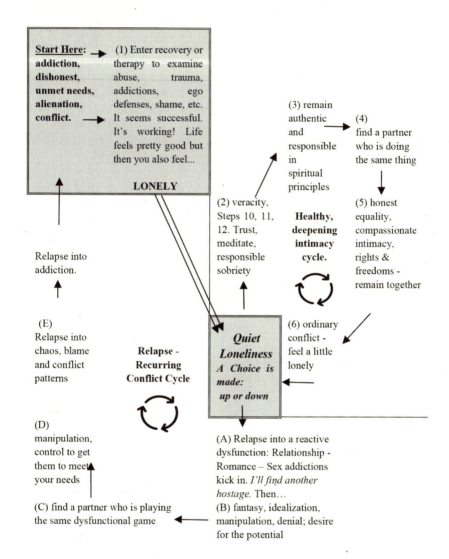

---

120   For people who claim happiness or a fulfilling life, loneliness is often too embarrassing to admit. It would undermine their declared faith in the power of God or their happiness "in program" to admit this depth of loneliness.

Ego Formation [121]

As we all know our mind, which is an emergent and invisible property of our brain, does all manner of things. Organizing memory. Processing information. Evaluating situations. Making decisions. Passing judgments. Deciding behaviour. Manufactures emotions. Our mind takes in external information, balances it against some instinctual, internal concern we may not be aware of, makes an assessment of it, matches it up with what's already in storage, and assigns it a value of risk and immediacy. Then our mind advises our body to do something with that mental risk assessment: say something, keep silent, leave, stay, talk, punish, argue, be angry, hit something, run away, lie, hide, cry, pout, blame, laugh, smile, be embarrassed or not. All of these behaviours, and there are many others, are what we refer to as your "personality." Your inner, silent mind evaluations and balancing motivate the external behaviour you present to the world. That is you.

Within our mind is a component of the mind, like a governing software program, that coordinates and organizes all of this. That silent thing in your mind that balances information from all sources and coordinates it to motivate your behaviour is your ego. Anyone's ego is actually their own mind coordinating and balancing of all the information of their life against what's in their mental storage units.

Yes, there are many differing opinions of ego, some quite complicated. However, in the arena of addition recovery, having an understanding of motivation and behaviour will significantly contribute to spiritual recovery. It will make it easier to understand why we have to make difficult recovery demands of ourselves and commit to this spiritual course of action.

An ego is the organized conscious mediator of whatever you experience. The ego's job is to set up a complex balancing act between our inner instinctual needs (the matrix of the soul) and the life circumstances we are exposed to (the corporeal universe).

Situation: You live in Calgary. It's March. As you walk to the bus stop to go to work a person is standing quietly, waiting for the bus, wearing beach sandals, a bathing suit, sunglasses, and a straw hat. A beach towel hangs around their neck. They quietly sip their coffee while they wait for the bus. Your mind evaluates this, places it in memory, and passes judgment. You react in some manner that your ego has decided you should act.

Situation: You are having lunch with a friend. A person walks in for lunch and sits at another table. Your friend quietly raves on about how desirable they are; really sexy! Your friend will behave in some manner close to what their mind has decided they should. That is their personality. You think the stranger is okay but nothing to sell the farm over. Your egos have each assessed the information about the stranger differently and made a judgement. Depending on hundreds

---

121   There is extensive discussion of Ego in _Spiritual Transformation, Third Edition_, at Appendix IV.

of variables, the stranger is assessed and personal behaviour is displayed. Your behaviour will be different from your friend's. That is one presentation of ego. Then between you and your friend, your relative egos have evaluated the other's view of the stranger, assessed it and made judgements accordingly. Your personality (your ego's assessment) requires you to act in some way that supports your ego's assessment of your friend.

Situation: You are in a recovery meeting and someone is strongly declaring "We all have to find God, thank you Jesus. Salvation is at hand!" Your ego evaluates this, files it away with whatever is already in your mind, and you make judgements and act according to your ego's assessment of the situation. Confront them publicly? Don't? Present an argumentative point of view? Say nothing or quietly say something later? Your decision is your personality demonstrating your egos' assessment of that situation.

Situation: You are standing in a store parking lot and you witness an adult scolding a child. The child is crying. Your ego will notice this, evaluate it, place it someplace in your mind, and you behave in some manner. That behaviour is your personality which is the visible result of what your ego has evaluated.

In each of these situations, in every situation, you will behave in some way peculiar to you. Your own unique, internal, instinctual drives and needs will be matched against whatever else is in storage from your history and balanced in accordance with the world you are exposed to. Your personality is the visible result of how your ego balances things out in the world you inhabit.

An Ego Balances and Coordinates

Matrix of the Soul	EGO is my personality	Corporeal Universe
fear, sexuality, hunger, social association, awareness of the mystery of life (by what-ever name or definition) CORE INSTINCTS AND NEEDS	⚖ My Personality is the visible result of the invisible mind-agency that negotiates, mediates, and balances these opposing realities	Everything in reality including your own physical being and IMPOSED SOCIAL DYNAMICS YOU ARE EXPOSED TO

In addiction this ego-balancing act is always balanced selfishly or self-destructively. My needs first and second, your needs a distant third. That is the personality of an addict: selfish and self-destructive. Life is automatically balanced so that whenever something happens they don't like or can't control, they decide they want something, or maybe-possibly have to be honest about, there is no consideration for others: quit, leave, get drunk, or pick a fight. Balanced selfishly. Martyrs balance oppositely; I'm last behind everyone else. I'll suffer on your behalf. Yes, I will absorb the indignation because you are so much more important than me. This is a non-spiritual, negative balance of others first. Addicts are me first. That's why many codependent relationship addicts (martyrs) choose addicts (tyrants)—they both get what they want.

In order to become recovered (spiritual) it is important to know what we are asking of ourselves in recovery. In this process we are demanding things of ourselves. At meetings they discuss rigorous honesty. You demand this of yourself. They talk about meeting attendance. You insist you attend meetings. They describe tolerance or meditation and you demand these things of yourself. They explain getting involved in group responsibilities, so you "force" this on yourself. Each addict should be able to answer these questions: What am I doing to me and why? In my effort to recover, what am I really demanding of me? To what advantage for me? [I know it sounds too esoteric but that is what is happening in your mind.]

In a shallow, ineffective manner of opinion, usually what is presented is that we are to demand of ourselves a belief in God. With no evidence, and ten-thousand contradictory opinions, couched in all manner of righteousness, we "insist" and demand that we have to believe in God. In actual fact, that is the least important of all the demands that you must impose upon yourself in early recovery.

Whoever demands God beliefs of you is demonstrating how their ego has balanced their emotional anxiety against the world they have been exposed to. What's wrong here isn't their demand for themselves of their own perceived need for God. Fair enough. What's wrong is their ego has also decided they have to impose this and demand belief from everyone else. Ineffective and punitive at best. There is no stable recovery in demanding of ourselves or others the adoption of God beliefs. Eventually deciding that you, yourself, have to believe may be a valid option of your opinion for you.

If a person in recovery has to demand of themselves change in some major way, what is the change that's required? When we understand what we are actually "doing" to ourselves in this game of recovery—why, what for, and how do I do this to me?—leaves recovery people in a very favorable position. They can, with reasonable certainty, understand the value of their effort in future events.

This is quite important to understand. Being shown this (taught it), that by completing the steps and demanding this effort of ourselves, we will eventually adjust our personality so our ego balances everything differently. We adjust the way we process life (context). We don't change life but change our ego's balancing from selfish or self-destructive to being balanced by spiritual principle. That's the "why" of all our effort. Everything is now balanced differently.

Your ego will be just a "big" as it ever was, but the governing energy will be spiritual principle and not selfish destruction. This guarantees that any situation that you encounter in the future will have a value added by you—your participation with compassion and equality. Recovery people demand these drastic changes of themselves, by their own effort of self-discipline. That's the only point, here. Always be aware that it is a dead-end street to attempt to reduce your ego. An ego cannot be eliminated or reduced, but it can be refocused.

Aside from all of that, probably all that's required here, is to understand the four general (ego) personality structures for addicts/alcoholics and of course for many other people, too. The balancing act of unfulfilling relationships are built around:

ATTACHMENT: The caregiver the child depended on for safety is also the source of danger it needed to protect itself from. If you can't win, learn to love losing. Learn to adapt to the caregiver's mishandling, abuse and neglect as if it were an acceptable expression of attention and caring. As an adult: My partner or counsellor or doctor criticizes me and lectures me therefore they care.

ISOLATION: If you can't run away, withdraw and hide. Learning to conceal and deny your own needs for the erratic security afforded by satisfying a selfish authority figures' wishes. As an adult: Hiding your own needs, having secrets, and isolating are an escape from a painful, helpless situation. Having a "secret fantasy life" of wishes and preferences and being disdainfully distant often conceals isolation (and then subtle guilt may materialize because you feel like a fraud).

MERGER: If living your own life is too scary, be lost in a crowd. Be obedient to whatever is expected by the authority figure or the group; become a robot-extension of the parent or group and submit to the party line. As an adult there's no separate self of their own and people suffer an inner, lonely solitude living under the shallow, dangerous mantle of compliance. Family, church, cults, some fellowships, secret society, military, dominate partners and therapists, and the like, all require merger and suppression of any creative individuation.

DEFIANCE: Emotional isolation and a strong character belligerence towards doing anything that anyone suggests they should be doing. This defiance is to conceal fear and insecurity. As an adult they show strong opinions of judgement. They are always right, no one will ever understand them, and everyone else is wrong. Let's argue about everything and live with simmering resentment and disapproval.

These ego structures are created, or the stage is set, in the early stages of childhood development. One of these will be a dominate feature in adult relationships and of course people can overlap or alternate between them.

Because of how we are, usually our partners "love" our impression management schemes and not our authentic selves. We desire the possibilities and illusions of a perfect relationship future more than accepting it as it really is. The secret thought is, "It will be just wonderful when... ." Addicts often project a fantasy relationship into the future. Relationship addicts are a little bit in love with the person (who has their own impression management scheme operating) but mostly in love with some version of a perfect future which they will struggle to orchestrate.

How many times have you said or heard: "I didn't sign up for this!" "I thought I knew you…" "Who are you, really?" "I can't believe that you actually did that." "I wish I'd known that before I…" These, and 257 other similar expressions, indicate that the relationship is now experiencing a breakdown of the impression management schemes. Reality is creeping in.

In well conducted (group or private) therapy and spiritual transformation we need to learn: (a) that we defend, (b) how we defend—attachment, isolation, merger, defiance, blame, judgement, impression management; and (3), what we defend against—our fears, anxieties, shame, and discovering any truth about ourselves. [122]

Here are a few points to be mindful of:

- Fulfillment is based on an inner choice regarding personally developed values, interest and desire—an internally focused locus of control. Locus of control means who's in charge or who's values govern behaviour. Are these my values I live by (internal) or someone else's values? Do I allow myself to be controlled by values and beliefs that are imposed upon me? (external)

- Self-realization means your values and their expression are firmly rooted in the confidence of your choices and, in personal relationships, you are generally indifferent to the external demands of other's values. Agreement is offered out of an independent, informed choice, which means there are no grounds for complaint if the plan doesn't work out.

- Realize that to create external conflict is always some inside turmoil reflected outside.

- The resolution of relationship conflict is usually a "power and dominance" model of compromise and negotiation, which is always temporary.

- Internal healing must always be first, then followed by adoption of spiritual principles as the keys to not creating conflict—problem prevention.

- Dilemmas and indecision are always rooted in inner turmoil and resolved from the inside.

- Acceptance of self—understanding addiction as an illness not a disease or moral corruption, taking responsibility and never blaming are the first keys to serenity.

> *If external rules demand externally imposed conscientious behavior and infraction promotes punishment, then goodness is only political. People despotically governed will lose their moral sense.*
>
> Kung Fao Tzu, 500 BCE

---

122   This is developed from the work of Thomas Szasz, Carl Whittaker, and Sheldon Kopp.

Fifty Percent Wisdom

There are two beliefs and two possible truths which are a set up for a life which has a fifty percent chance of bad decisions or a fifty percent chance of wise decisions. These are:

Beliefs:	(1) I believe I am in danger.	(2) I believe I am not in danger.
Truths:	(3) I am in danger.	(4) I am not in danger.

If you believe you are in danger (at 1) and you actually are in danger (at 3) you can make wise choices.

If you believe you are in danger (at 1) and you actually are not in danger (at 4) you cannot make wise choices.

If you believe you are not in danger (at 2) but you actually are in danger (at 3) you cannot make wise choices.

If you believe you are not in danger (at 2) and you actually are not in danger (at 4) you can make wise choices.

There is only a fifty percent chance of a wise decision depending on what you believe and the truth of the circumstances. Aside from all of that there is the...

The Probability of Ineffectiveness

There is a cultural mindset in beliefs of "good vs. bad," "right vs. wrong," "acceptable vs. unacceptable." In religion there is sinner vs. saint; in conduct there is moral vs, immoral. These are a value system of duality and this culture carries a system of approval-disapproval in its perception of goals and process. This is a typically western way of assessing behaviour. Duality creates an adversarial position rooted in personal perception.

A sixty-one-year-old person has sex with a twenty-two-year-old person (consensual both ways); homosexual or heterosexual – doesn't matter. Good? Bad? How Bad? And for which one, the older person or the younger person? Someone betrays their marriage vows. Good? Bad? How bad? Drug addiction: Good? Bad? How Bad? Bankruptcy: Good? Bad? How bad? Duality requires that you have to pick a position. Gambling addiction; pornography addiction—Good? Bad? How bad? Fundamental religious beliefs vs. militant atheism: Good? Bad? How bad? Duality demands you take a position of approval or criticism.

Duality creates the possibility of a seventy-five percent chance of moral "failure" when in transformation (anomie in a social construct). This means in any "transformation" process there is a seventy-five percent chance of it being spiritually ineffective. There are...

positive goals	in a positive process
negative goals	in a negative process

Here is an example as regards recovery from addiction:

Goal (+ or -)		Process (+ or -)
Positive Goal: I want to be in a loving, fulfilling relationship and be spiritual (positive)	by	acting with integrity, being honest, responsible, and respectful. A positive process.
I want to be in a loving, fulfilling relationship and be seen as spiritual in recovery (positive)	by	lying, misrepresenting, acting a role, creating false impressions of me. A negative process.
I want to be in a relationship so my partner will look after me and make me happy and pay all my bills. I need a parent. A negative goal.	by	being somewhat responsible, somewhat honest, showing some integrity and respect. A reasonably positive process.
I want to be in a relationship so my partner will look after me and make me happy and pay all my bills. I need a parent. A negative goal.	by	lying, misrepresenting, acting a role, enticing, creating a false impression of me. A negative process.
	OR	
I want to be a spiritual person and help others recover. (+)	by	working hard at self-discipline and sincerely living by spiritual principles. (+)
I want to be a spiritual person and help others recover (+)	by	memorizing a bunch of passages and speeches and jokes so I can impress people. (-)
I want to look like a spiritual person so I can impress people and get a lot of compliments (-)	by	working reasonably hard at self-discipline and mostly abiding by spiritual principles. (+)
I want to look like a spiritual person so I can impress people and get a lot of compliments (-)	by	memorizing a bunch of passages and speeches and jokes so I can impress people. (-)

This can be substituted for just about any enterprise. In spiritual addiction recovery, if any part is negative it is all negative. A culture of duality has set this up where three of the four available situations in either example are unspiritual. The path of recovery that is laid down in the twelve steps, whether spiritual or psychological, avoids both the Fifty Percent Wisdom trap and The Probability of Ineffectiveness.

Relationship— Sex— Romance Addictions

These three addictions are integrated; they exist in concert with each other and they are emotionally bound together. Relationship addiction shows up as two things—a significant inner disharmony people are blind to and conflict with others. That inner disharmony and external conflict shows up socially as self-abuse, self-neglect, irresponsibility, dishonesty, or various types of harm in relationship behaviour like abuse, betrayal, manipulation, attachment, isolation, merger, dishonesty, or defiance. There's a certain martyrdom and aggrandized suffering in many relationships which are subversive aspects of addiction. And, many relationship addictions are attached to a latent (waiting in the background) romance or sex addiction.

We often hypnotize ourselves into a romance fantasy that is a delusion of possibility. The fantasy always contains perfect love, perfect sex, or perfect harmony. Whether delusional or illusional, it's a manufactured fantasy because perfect partnerships are never available. What this looks like in our minds is we are often in love with the potential; in love with what it will be like "when... it gets perfect." People become infatuated and in love with the fantasy. Then they create a relationship that is partly a relationship with the fantasy (obsession of sorts) and partly with the person. Both people are presenting an impression management scheme. Of course, neither person is ever as perfect as the fantasy so everyone's soon disappointed and in turmoil. That takes them into conflict and judgement or another relationship.

Initially there are traits that attract you to a person: He's so outgoing. She's so assertive. He's so neat and tidy. She's so financially organized. Those qualities will eventually be recast by you to be a source of complaint. He's so outgoing becomes he's a flirt. She's so assertive becomes she's stubborn. He's so tidy becomes he's a compulsive neat freak. She's so financially responsible becomes she's cheap. This is the testing phase of a relationship in order to trust its stability around the loss of illusion; loss of fantasy.

Aside from that, there is the projected improvement scheme—it will be just perfect if I can get them to stop wearing those torn sweats or stop smoking. It will be perfect if I can just get her to wear less makeup or him to stop with all the sports watching. It will be perfect when I can get the other one to lose twenty pounds—to "improve" in some way which I will struggle to orchestrate.

Rather than love someone as they are, we romance ourselves into desiring the possibilities. We love the fantasy possibilities, searching for true love in the future. This means, "Yes, I do (mostly) love this person now, with all their flaws (ho-hum), but I will love them more and truly when I get them fixed up," which never materializes or never lasts. "It would have been perfect if they had just changed in the way I had suggested (insisted) they should." A relationship addict's version of "true love" is a euphemism for a relationship dominated by their rules.

These embody emotional hiding and generate constant power struggles. The subsequent, usually silent control tactics and complex manipulation schemes demand constant attention. Relationship addiction is present in all relationships in an addict's life, not just their intimate one. A significant side note is this can be a complicating factor in your relationship with your sponsor, therapist, or higher power if you have one.

If you are acting out in relationship addiction you cannot heal or develop spiritually. You can only develop more subtle control tactics or a more complex impression management scheme.

Styles of Relationship:

1. Absolute Strangers
2. Temporary Social Contact (airplane passengers, theater patrons)
3. Infrequent Acquaintance
4. Frequent Acquaintance
5. Recreation - sporadic or regular
6. Work / Career, regular contact
7. Friendly, casual
8. Friend, regular
9. Best Friend
10. Therapist, Mentor, Counsellor
11. Sexual – not committed
12. Intimate – committed [123]
13. Family [124]

"Sexual" can happen anywhere. Sex addiction, adultery, or pornography use are often rooted in a conflict-isolation dynamic where emotions related to shame and anger are severely suppressed. In pornography addiction there is the fantasy of control and perfection with no emotional involvement. These create the illusion of safety and damages any intimate relationship. They are always harmful.

The amount of shame, denial, fear, guilt, or anger you live with; repetitive inadequacy; your internal self-concept; your values and feelings about sex, all of

---

123 Bill Wilson wrote for a Grapevine article (p. 57 *The Best Of Bill*) regarding sponsorship, "*And if the sponsor's next following case turns out in later time to be their best friend (or romance) then the sponsor is most joyful. But they well know... happiness is a by-product...*" Edited for pronouns.

124 Do not include any detail of incest or sexual abuse in Step Five. Note those separately. They are for the ear of a well-trained professional.

these unseen concerns govern whom you pick for a partner. We always get what our subconscious wants.

Dating is actually that process of going "people shopping" for a complimentary personality structure. When you find the one that matches what your unconscious beliefs require, that's the one you'll choose. If you've asked five consecutive, different people out on a *second* date and they all say 'No,' you are deliberately (subconsciously) orchestrating that situation because your relationship context is rooted in rejection. Whatever you get in relationships is what you want, regardless of your declarations to the contrary.

Remember that everything we have created in this culture is about sex, except sex, that's about power. That's where this culture and rampant addictions have taken us. Two shame-based people create a relationship of compensation and hiding. Their unconscious decides. There are serious contractual rules in play here. [125] Two reasonably "healthy" people create a relationship of informed choice (this is equality). The more the issues have been resolved, the greater the integrity in personal choice.

The five rules of relationship, which appear to be universal, are:

1) You cannot be "out" of relationship. Not being in relationship is a fool's delusion. All that's available is to define how you participate *in* relationships (the governing energy). Your life is the active dynamic of relationships and the governing energy you assign to each one.

2) Whatever dynamics are present in one relationship are present to some degree in all your relationships. Every relationship is a mirror of, or a reaction to, all your other relationships. We are subtly consistent.

3) We choose long-term, intimate partners that will align with our deepest needs and secret values. People are mostly unaware of what these are. Before their exposure, these are hidden under impression management schemes. Over the long-term, however, the chosen partner will demand we expose these insecurities. Or, if you are in repetitive, short term relationships and "can't commit" that's also an exposure of your deeper insecurities related to context and values. [126]

4) Our intimate partners will reflect our deeply cherished self-judgments. This is subconscious and usually a subtle and complex reflection of the

---

125 All relationships between consenting adults are contracts. Explained in detail in *Spiritual Transformation, Third Edition*, cited earlier.

126 Context vs. Content: In culinary arts a chef prepares food (that's context) but what do they prepare? French cuisine, vegan, Asian food, soups and sauces, or fast food, is the content. Architects design buildings (that's context), but that may be houses, shopping malls, hospitals, or really big doghouses (content). Context: life is unfair, women or men are nasty creatures, all people are notoriously dishonest. Content: guitar player, teacher, counsellor, or plumber. Steps One to Nine alter context. Steps Ten, Eleven, and Twelve govern behaviour in content.

relationship with the parent you have the most unresolved conflict with. Gender is irrelevant. Addicts cannot escape this truth.

5) In any on-going close relationship of intimacy or friendship, each person is equally capable of bringing love and harmony or conflict and fear into the relationship. This is the unalterable fact: Neither person is emotionally healthier than the other, regardless of how obviously it appears otherwise.

You are the boss of only you and self-discipline is the key to everything. Never create excuses to avoid self-discipline. Push through being uncomfortable, which can be from the compassionate observations of a wise mentor or therapist. Observations (not instructions) when offered with kindness and compassion and aligned with spiritual principles are actually priceless. Unless you are rigorously and sincerely honest, and discipline yourself accordingly, any recovery will be political impression management. You must be willing to challenge your old ideas; challenge them enough to make yourself seriously uncomfortable, *and* with serenity, persevere through the discomfort you or others generate. [127]

Misunderstanding of Choice

It begins with unconscious self-delusion about ourselves. Addicts make pretty speeches and create a lifestyle acting-role for themselves: tough person, victim, vamp, sensuous, cruel, shy, home-body, smart person, sympathetic, helpless one, indifferent, caregiver, warrior, comedian, needy one, princess, etc. Then they create a lifestyle accessory list their true love will have. "I want a specific type of lover with these specific attributes... insert height, weight, appearance, age, hair colour, vehicle, preferred music, hobbies, wardrobe, career, income, shoe size." This is a casting call for a role in your movie. "Today I'll wear the red scarf, it goes nicely with that coat." We make a shopping list for a suitable partner, which is usually only your partner being a comfortable accessory for your desired lifestyle (as on dating websites).

This creates a romanticized fantasy story like *Harlequin Romance* novels, or the desired romantic relationship in a film. Happy-ending, fictional romances. [128] These create unreal expectations in relationships. In our making decisions

---

127 Persevering through discomfort is explained in Negative Capability, Chapter 8. Being serene when moving past discomfort is explained in a different way in Nearing the End, at the end of Chapter 7.

128 Books in the romance novel genre place their primary focus on heterosexual relationships and romantic love. The story must be between socially admirable people: attractive, clean, tidy, with some mild value-conflict to overcome, and lead to an emotionally satisfying/happy, optimistic ending with the inference of sexual satisfaction in the last seven pages that fits with

about relationships, our unconscious needs or unexamined issues actually make the choice:

- my anger chooses
- my need to punish chooses
- my insecurity chooses
- my need to please chooses
- my need to be seen as successful chooses
- my horniness chooses
- my needing a caretaker chooses
- my need to have status chooses
- my need to complain chooses

- my need to show off chooses
- my need to be a hero chooses
- my need to dominate chooses
- my need to be abused chooses
- my need to be obedient chooses
- my need to be defiant chooses
- my addiction chooses
- my envy chooses
- my loneliness chooses
- my need to act out chooses

Four Principle Power Struggles

(In 10,000 Variations)

<u>Double Standard</u>: I can't, you have to. I'm allowed, you aren't. I can do this, you can't. If you defy my double standard, I'll get mad, shout, pout, get sick, or betray the relationship.

<u>The Follower</u>: I won't decide anything. You tell me what to do and I'll do it. Secretly, as soon as you tell me to do something I don't like or is hard, I'll do it, but I'll resent and punish you. You tell me what to do anyway.

<u>The Morality Police</u>: I absolutely demand that other people behave in the way I insist (imposed righteousness). If they don't, I'll resent and hate everyone and abuse them or myself.

<u>The Dictator</u>: I'll impose my standards and values and perceptions on my partner, and they had better act in a way that I approve of. If they don't cooper-ate, I'll punish them. If they don't let me punish them, I'll leave.

---

cultural approval. They became popular after the first world war. There are presently 200 million regular readers of this fiction. It generates about 1.1 billion dollars in sales each year, and these are the most purchased book in North America. The readers are women between 18 and 45. Statistics are also very high for romantic movies, especially on low-cost internet sites like *Netflix* (large selection for small financial investment). Some information indicates two or three ro-mantic movies each evening. I have interviewed people who have admitted watching the same movie (men—action, women—romance) fifty or sixty times in succession. Often this represents addiction and a fantasy compensation for loneliness, fear, and shame.

Richard W. Clark

Types of Abuse

I created this list as a part of an education program I developed and taught in communications and gender issues at a college. I include it here for two reasons. First, it deepens the awareness of abuse and provides some behavioral boundaries. This is important in addicted relationships because addicts so seldom understand what a non-abusive relationship is. This list makes the power struggles open for examination and reasonable to discuss as a part of relationship, respect, and emotional health.

The second reason is, in the long term, it will help to reduce relationship conflict and abuse. People in general, and certainly addicts, quarrel over definitions and specifics of abuse. All of the types of abuse listed will fit into more than one category. [129]

PSYCHOLOGICAL AND EMOTIONAL ABUSE

- exerting power or control (dominance)
- intimidation; being demanding
- threats of violence to anyone, including threats of suicide
- excessive or furious jealousy
- disrupting routines
- ignoring, suppressing, withholding, editing, or disagreeing with feelings
- insult or ridicule religion, race, traditions, friends, family, significant things
- prohibit or restrict employment
- threats to children, pets, property; acting inconsistent or erratic to keep confused
- prohibit, interfere with, or defeat emotional growth or health
- deny access to support or family
- lie or be evasive; withhold information
- threats to use information from past
- unequal access to recreation, hobbies, health, leisure, education
- threats to abandon
- punishing children unfairly or unequally
- destroy / damage personal property
- manipulate, lie, deceive, keep secrets
- breach of confidence, gossip
- public or private ridicule
- forcing dieting or eating
- withholding feelings or support
- tell sexist or racist jokes
- demand dress codes; forcing or demanding changes in cosmetics, hair styles, wardrobe, jewelry
- subjected to reckless or unsafe driving
- dishonest about birth control
- brag about or describe past affairs

FINANCIAL ABUSE

- forcing excessive financial responsibility or unequal responsibility
- withhold money, unequal access to funds
- unequal pay
- hiding money or financial secrets
- not supporting or denying employment

---

129 This list was compiled by men and women. All were abusers to some degree and had volunteered to take an education course on family violence. The actual list was longer. It has been edited to cover the main points.

109

SEXUAL and PHYSICAL ABUSE (they overlap)	
• use as sex object • ridicule or minimize sexual or intimate feelings • criticize partner and others sexually • constant arguing about other's preferences and wishes, accusing, blaming • undermining, trivializing • comparing partner to others • making sexual accusations • not respecting sexual boundaries • withholding sex or affection • forced to have sex with objects or others • dangerous or embarrassing sex • forcing to use pornography	• pushing, grabbing, shoving, shaking, kicking, choking, slapping, biting, and threats of this • kept from leaving or locked out • ignoring needs or withholding health care • refuse or withdraw help during sickness or poor health • hit with things, throwing objects at • having affairs/adultery • abandoned while in danger • murdered, stabbed, shot, kidnapped, raped • withholding STD information • forcing sex, exercise, travel, work • touching or fondling against will

This list is directly related to the first social symptom of addiction, self-harm and harm to others, which can easily be called abuse. When defining what abuse is men and women (generally) have a different perspective.

Men tend to describe abuse as being dominated by others through fear, coercion, and threats. Being punished for non-compliance or disobedience. Men see it as the "putting on" or the imposing of values or behaviors. Women tend to describe abuse as actions, words, or behaviors, or the exercise of power that takes something away from another person. It's a loss of rights, demeaning of self-worth, loss of safety; having less personal influence or viewed as a lesser person in value, dignity, and respect. Women usually describe abuse as a denial and disentitlement to equality—not being treated as an equal.

Being defensive and using political double-talk, benevolent dictatorships, resorting to patriarchal religious rules, claiming "the other person abuses me too," or whining "I'll stop when they do," are never a defense for abuse. Also, those who proclaim victim-status must accept responsibility for placing themselves in a victim-position. Because assertive equality is difficult or even formidable, that is not automatically a defense to being a victim. Seeking guidance is wise.

Sexual Conflict [130]

All of this applies equally to heterosexual and homosexual relationships—no exceptions. Sex, for humans, has a unique characteristic where our expressions of sex will draw into it problems that belong elsewhere. Expressions of sex/sexuality are wide-ranging: How we make eye contact, how we dress, words we choose, tone of voice, how we behave socially and sexually, how we do or don't flirt. Remember that everything in this society we have created is about sex, except sex, that's about power. Any religion's view of sex is also about power. That's where this culture and its religious prejudices and rampant addictions have taken us. In intimate relationships, sex is very often the arena of struggle for non-sex problems. There are four reasons for this.

1) Sex is INSTINCTUAL and therefore dependable – we all have it, and we all know we all have it. *And*, we all know we can take advantage of having this instinct.

2) Sex is EXPENDABLE, not like hunger or thirst. We can offer or withhold intimacy without risk to life. The energy of sexual cooperation is easily made into a reward-punishment battle ground. If you don't behave the way I want you to behave in my life outside of sex... then you're not getting what you want in sex.

3) Sex is INTERPERSONAL. Even in masturbation, there's someone else involved. The fact that there's other people involved, even in fantasy, sets up conflict that intrudes from other areas of life.

4) Sexual desire is VULNERABLE. The subtle ease with which we can control and manipulate our own or another person's arousal is used to advantage. We can very easily change moods and influence others regarding desire and desirability. Being desired or desiring are complications in the competition and power dynamics of sex.

These four aspects invite conflict from other areas of life into sexual expression. Conflict in finances, parenting, jealousy, housekeeping, driving, diet, unmet needs from childhood, broken promises, suspicious behaviour, failed commitments, perceived neglect, are dragged into a couple's sexual life.

Next to that, there is the cultural shame around sex and the imposed cruelty of religious morality. *In Defense of Atheism* by Michel Onfray examines this in some detail. There are often unstated or subtle roles in sexual expression.

---

130 This discussion is intended for the realm of sexual expression for generally ordinary people and recovering addicts/alcoholics in their everyday lives. It is not to be applied to the twilight-zone pathology of psychiatric sexual issues.

There are many variations of these subtle dynamics and rules that happen in sexual relationships:

- Dominance – Submission
- Parenting – Dependency
- Caretaking – Cared For
- Capable – Incapable
- Initiator — Responder

- Persecutor – Victim
- Aggressive – Passive
- Demanding – Compliant
- Angry – Tender

These may be very subtle and when one person changes the rules, without agreement, conflict results. Sex is not where most conflict originates but it is where most conflict ends up. The general rule of monogamy in this culture is your partner is supposed to be the only source of sex. For addicts who have poor problem-solving skills, who are ashamed of themselves and of sex, or live with religious persecution, it will guarantee that general conflict be transferred into the arena of sex.

The inability to understand this and to resolve conflict is, of course, a primary set up for adultery, betrayal, and use of pornography (which are particularly harmful). And, if a person quits this relationship and moves on, they eventually end up in a similar situation. [131] For addicts/alcoholics, and of course for many others, relationships are very conflicted. It is advised in Step Eight that we are to develop the best possible relations with all others and that conflict in relationship is the cause of our alcoholism.

Recovery is made more complicated by the drastic cultural and sexual changes that have arisen since AA was organized eighty years ago. The struggles related to gender equality, civil rights, dignity and equality for minorities, more open sexual expression, and many other social concerns like the internet, immigration, easily accessible pornography, dating sites, and cultural destabilization, makes relationships and sex a gluey morass of complex issues. There is an important requirement in Step Four regarding sex. This is described in Chapter 5 and at footnote 152.

This is especially true in the area of gender equality and the changing roles in sex, committed relationships, raising children, finances, and marriage. Some people cannot handle equality because of the required sharing of influence. Others cannot embrace the responsibility inherent in an equality mindset. Abandoning power or money is harder than most people realize, as is taking responsibility after a life of compliance. Judgements around this are often quite fierce. All of this makes understanding abuse imperative. These are usually the more complex

---

131 One reason (there are others), one reason adultery or weekend affairs appear to be more fulfilling sexually is they don't have the complex, historical, unresolved emotional baggage that longer-term relationships have.

issues for long-term, later recovery. Just be aware that these "issues" exist, and know you are affected by them.

Maintain abstinence or successful restraint at all costs and sneak up on being spiritual as best you can. Be patient with yourself when completing the steps. You have undertaken a journey that requires great courage. Treat others with respect and be rigorously honest with a well-informed, trusted spiritual advisor or therapist. You will find your place. [132]

Change Your Perceptions

A quick glance will show you either an older woman with a head scarf and a large nose or a younger woman looking to her right (large nose becomes jaw line).

---

132 One problem with honesty in relationships is most addicts in recovery are living with quite poor insight regarding themselves. They are completely unaware of their concealment strategies or manipulating behaviour and can only be honest at a superficial level. And, of course, the anxiety about the consequences of honesty are terrifying. The ease of its expression and depth of honesty will change over time.

Chapter 5

The Twelve Steps
(and a few related topics)

Regardless of whether you are in formal treatment or a twelve-step self-help group you should be mindful that:

1)   An addiction is a pathological relationship with a mood-altering experi-ence that has life damaging consequences.

2)   All addicts live with polyaddictions—more than one addiction operat-ing at the same time. One of these polyaddictions is always relation-ship addiction.

3)   There are the five social symptom constellations of addictive behaviour. These are important and I will refer to them several times. If at all pos-sible, write these out until they are memory-accessible.

> (i)   Self-destructive or harmful behaviour to self and others, including emotional self-abuse and other-abuse.
>
> (ii)   Dishonesty, withholding, manipulation.
>
> (iii) Arrogance, cynically superior, living with double standards. Closed-minded and defiant about these to conceal internal doubt, shame and insecurity.
>
> (iv)   Generally selfish. The manipulation of others for undeserved advantage or recognition; acting generous with concealed selfish agendas (impression management).
>
> (v)   Generally irresponsible and defiant, belligerent, openly or silently stubborn, argumentative. [133]

---

133   Arguing is a strange endeavor. If it's an argument over a fact, don't argue. Search online or go to the library. If it's an argument over an opinion, don't argue, it's just an opinion. Always remember, God's existence or non-existence is an opinion. John Bridges advises in *How to Be A Gentleman*, Rutledge Hall Press, 1998, that a gentleman never argues over anything, except that which may save a life. My position on addiction and recovery may sound argumentative and unyielding, but these are issues that will save lives.

114

4) Addict-alcoholics have no sense of their own or another's rights and responsibility. These were outlined in the Introduction. Review them now.

5) For addict-alcoholics, relationships are conflicted to some degree. As per Step Eight, that conflict must eventually be resolved (or at the minimum a sincere attempt must be made). The phenomenon of addiction always manifests socially as self-destructive relationship conflict, both internal and external. For the practicing addict-alcoholic all relationships are power struggles...
   - to prevent others from finding out the truth (about themselves)
   - to maintain control (of every situation) [134]
   - to be taken care of and looked after by others, or at least not challenged
   - to be rescued from responsibility
   - to justify and continue acting out
   - to maintain impression management

6) There are abstinence available addictions and abstinence not-available addictions. These have important distinctions described earlier which must be considered at and after Step One.

7) Addiction in Groups C and D are always a downward spiral into chaos, illness, hospitals, jail, and (probably) a too early death; hence the two rules.

The Two Rules

1) People die from addictions.

2) I cannot change the first rule *and* it applies to me.

Remember them. Once you understand these rules, recovery begins with a commitment to abstinence or sobriety at any cost. Up to this point, this has been a long, drawn-out description of understanding addiction and Step One. Next comes a realization of the need for a major shift in the context of life. That begins at Step Two. It is appropriate here to outline spiritual principles. These are:

---

134 Maintaining control isn't always to be openly dominant. People who adopt a position of helpless victim or have a perpetual relapse pattern can maintain control by getting others to continuously look after them. Both genders play into this irresponsibility. The power is in any irresponsible, feigned helplessness to find a rescuer. This must be carefully balanced with some wisdom because there are illnesses and dual diagnosis concerns that are ongoing, and some people do require frequent help and compassionate attention.

Spiritual Principles

#1: Respect for the Physical Body

Respectful physical self-care—respect for the body, as demonstrated by healthy caring for our physical being—for others as much as ourselves. Not damaging myself or anyone else through squalid living, toxic diets, violence, addictions (including smoking), greed, irresponsibility, selfishness, or physical or emotional abuse is crucial. [135] If you're damaging or neglecting the care of the body, your own or another's physical or emotional health, you cannot be spiritual. [136]

#2: Veracity

This is a style of being honest and describing your perception of truth or reality that incorporates gentle trustworthiness. Honest communication that is angry or blunt without respect and consideration for others will be received as abusive. The listener will view the speaker as selfish or inconsiderate. Any truth or wisdom will be held suspect because of the manner in which it's delivered. Veracity is honesty with kindness and compassion. [137]

#3: Humility

Most often misunderstood, especially by people seeking spiritual transformation, humility is rare and elusive. There are two aspects of humility that must be incorporated in both behaviour and attitude in order for it to have integrity.

---

135 Harmful, destructive behaviour is a classic part of addictions. And, if you are an active addict/ alcoholic, including smoking of any description, you are at the minimum, emotionally dishonest and manipulative. You are also harming yourself, others in your immediate circle, and a long-term subtle burden on the community.

136 A commitment to general health should not be interpreted as any kind of fanaticism or compulsive behaviour to exercise or diet. A reasonable or sincere approach to health is all that is required. Yes, I included smoking as harmful disrespect. Making a successful effort to quit smoking, regardless of how difficult in the beginning, is an important part of a spiritual life. No exceptions. If you smoke during your recovery efforts you might soon become a nicer person, but you cannot be authentically spiritual.

137 See *The Language of the Heart*, Bill W.'s Grapevine Writings, beginning at p. 259, "This Matter of Honesty." Taken at random: "The problem of honesty touches nearly every aspect of our lives." "Self-deception... reckless truth telling, which are so often lacking in prudence and love." "...nothing less than utter honesty will do." "Half-truths or inexcusable denials; an exaggerated belief in [our] own honesty." "Deception of others is nearly always rooted in deception of ourselves." "...unconscious deception. The prideful righteousness of 'good people.'" And, I'll end with this one: "Is any action or criticism on our part really necessary?" If it affects you directly, yes.

The **first,** generally ignored but essential requirement for humility is adhering to a sincerely egalitarian philosophy as the foundation of all relationships. Being egalitarian must be universal and operate generously and willingly, without criticism or blame regarding gender, age, health, ability, talent, culture, religious preference or not, entitlement, height, weight, politics, disability, tattoos, afflu- ence—egalitarian about *every* category that people use to classify each other. Respect and equality are especially required of theists and atheists for each other, of any religion for any of the other religions, or from any culture to any other culture. To interact with anything other than equality is evidence of racism, elitism, sexism, assuming privilege, double standards, justified abuse, etc., and fails to honor the universal truth of apparent unity that underlies all categoriza- tions of life. In the pursuit of humility equality is always primary. This is relation- ship humility.

The **second** requirement for humility, and secondary to the first, is for theists and deists. "Humble in the sight of God." This is the religious and common focus of any discussion about humility, which deftly avoids egalitarianism. This requirement is participating in the sincere honoring of your view of your "higher power" (a *very* broad definition). Your interpretation is entirely a personal choice of opinion, as is everyone else's. However conventional or unconventional, you decide on yours, and you honor it. For any believer in God to criticize, attack, or demean any other belief on the basis of religious superiority is arrogant hubris; nothing humble there.

For addiction recovery, the primary principle of humility isn't with God, it's being honorably committed to egalitarian compassion—social humility. Being "humble in the sight of God" and an arrogant abuser with people is a horror story of recovery. Social humility takes you into relationship harmony, which is the point of Step Ten. Relationships must involve more than your own selfishness and being secretly devoted to that. Being committed to something like verac- ity, responsibility and equality that would have spiritual integrity is the desired goal. [138]

#4: Charity

Charity, common in the jargon of many people, is generally understood to be a theological virtue of religion. It is always some variation of "giving things away"—giving away your time, giving away money, volunteering to drive others around, donating old clothes, working at the soup kitchen. These social endeav- ours are important and their social necessity is not under examination here. What qualifies or disqualifies charity as having spiritual integrity is the invisible agenda underneath the "charitable" behaviour.

Charity may be socially admirable but unspiritual when offered because the giver feels guilty, sorrow or pity for the recipient, or tries to impress anyone (most often and especially themselves). The motives for charity may be wanting a tax

---

138   This was explained in Victor Frankl's book *Man's Search for Meaning.*

break, rescuing the recipient out of some responsibility that is the recipient's to meet, trying to collect salvation points with God, offering it with judgements of who's worthy and who isn't, offering charity to live up to other people's expectations (especially shadow-expectations from the past), or wanting social admiration. The unrecognized, *un*spiritual mental setups that motivate charity are insidious. [139]

Charity is important. Generosity of compassion with humility, without hint of reward, are intrinsic to the spiritual value of charity.

#5: Responsibility & Obedience

Certainly, these are easily viewed as separate qualities, but as regards being spiritual, they are so closely related and interdependent that I present them together. These two attributes, which comprise the final spiritual principle, are usually abhorrent to addicts in general, to angry people, and to victims. This principle doesn't harbor well in our culture of victim-hood, disposable consumerism and greed.

If people value an idea like honesty and observe that value, then they would be honest. They would be responsible for, and obedient to, "being honest." If someone is responsible, then they would be willing to be held accountable for not being honest when they weren't. Or, if people hold kindness as important then they should self-discipline themselves to behaviours and words of kindness. They would voluntarily be kind. i.e. responsible to themselves to offer kindness in trying or awkward circumstances. They would hold themselves fully accountable if they weren't kind. If they were kind or honest only when it was convenient, or only to certain people, or only when people were watching, or were unwilling to be taken to task when they weren't kind or honest, then these would be conveniences used for impression management. It is the same for anything that a person declares as valuable or important.

Be responsible and obedient to the first four spiritual principles; that becomes your recovery job.

These spiritual principles are applicable to every aspect of every situation and relationship in life. Haphazard adherence to them is not evidence of spirituality; it's evidence of convenience and impression management. For people who are recovered and living within the maintenance steps, these are not negotiable or optional. If you embrace shallowness and hypocrisy in short order your abstinence will be at risk.

A person cannot ignore any part of any of these principles and claim spiritual integrity. All are equally important, and they are acquired (generally speaking) in the order they are presented. #1 leads to #2, leads to #3, etc. All five principles are contained within each of the three maintenance steps, Ten, Eleven, and Twelve.

---

139   Joshua Loth Liebman, in his book *Peace of Mind*, Simon and Schuster, 1946, speaks to this.

What makes these spiritual principles (the right column in the following chart) essential to recovery is that they directly counteract the five social symptom constellations of addiction (the left column). Remember, the phenomenon of addictions always shows up as conflict and corruption in relationships at three levels: dissonance and conflict, shame, guilt etc., in the addict's mind; in their relationship with substances or behaviours; and in their relationships with people. [140]

Social symptoms of addictions are the left column, and each major symptom of addicted behaviour is the direct opposite of a spiritual principle. Study this chart. Notice that all of them, left or right column, is a direct function of the governing energy of relationships. [141]

Addicted Social Behaviour transformed by the first nine steps to Spiritual Principles ➡ 10 – 11 – 12	
1) Self-destructive or harmful behaviour to self and others, including emotional disregard, disrespect, and gossip. (Governing energy: shame, envy, anger, bitterness)	1) Thoughtful and considered self-care and respect for others which would exclude all gossip. (Governing energy: respect, affection)
2) Dishonesty and manipulation. (Governing energy: fear, shame, anger, guilt)	2) Veracity, regardless of the situation. (Governing energy: trust, respect)
3) Arrogance, cynically superior, living with double standards; isolated. Argumentative or belligerent. (Governing energy: fear, shame, resentment, envy)	3) Humility: egalitarianism and possibly a considered respect for a higher power of your understanding. (Governing energy: acceptance, patience, compassion)
4) Generally selfish, manipulation for undeserved advantage, or acting charitable with various secret agendas. (Governing energy: shame, fear, desire to control)	4) Charity of spirit, which would include compassion. (Governing energy: respect, interest, caring, humility)

---

140 See *The Language of the Heart*, Bill W.'s Grapevine Writings, AA Grapevine, Inc, p. 238. *"If we examine every disturbance we have, great or small, we will find at the root of it some unhealthy dependency and its consequent unhealthy demands* [on others]."

141 Notice that recovering from a traditional medical condition like diabetes, high blood pressure, or healing from a broken bone, doesn't have anything *directly* to do with relationships. A body can get sick and get better without altering all the relationships in that life. Not so with addictions.

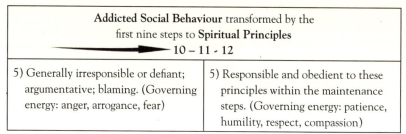

Addicted Social Behaviour transformed by the first nine steps to Spiritual Principles ——▶ 10 – 11 - 12	
5) Generally irresponsible or defiant; argumentative; blaming. (Governing energy: anger, arrogance, fear)	5) Responsible and obedient to these principles within the maintenance steps. (Governing energy: patience, humility, respect, compassion)

The only way to transit from addicted to spiritual is to embrace the psychology in the first nine steps. And, as I have said, that can be with or without God, prayer, or religion; as an atheist, a deist, an agnostic, or a humanist. Those nine steps get you from left to right. The purpose of the maintenance steps, Ten, Eleven, and Twelve, are to keep you living in the right column and enhance your serenity in healthy relationships. They keep you away from the two rules. This is what it means to be recovered from a seemingly hopeless state of mind and body. Spiritual principles are problem prevention.

Misalliance of Commitment

Problems arise when people undertake these steps with a wrong focus. Generally, these are: Beginning Step Two too soon before really understanding the importance of having a solid base of successful restraint (sobriety) at Step One. They must also understand addiction and its symptoms as an illness, not a moral deficit or disease. Very, very few people understand this. Accomplishing Step One is more subtle and complicated than most people believe. Ask: Are you committed to resolving an illness or seeking forgiveness for being morally corrupt? (Chapter 8 explains this.)

If you are a deist or involved in a religion, in addition to recovery, the steps are designed to recreate or enhance a relationship with a higher power that you may or may not call God. You must establish a relationship with that. For God-believers, be advised that addictions recovery requires more faith than any traditionally understood religious faith.

In these modern times, we must accommodate being an atheist or humanist and trust in the psychology of the steps. A different kind of courage and commitment to the human spirit is needed and is sufficient to complete the steps and be recovered. After you have achieved some measure of abstinence, sobriety, or successful restraint (whatever you call it), decide if you are aligned with the group "God-Deist" or the group "Agnostic-Atheist." Pick your team according to your preference. Remember, you can change your mind later. But be advised, that to evasively waffle back-and-forth is a set up for an on-going misalliance of commitment.

Each of the twelve steps has two benefits. (1) Each step embodies spiritual principles and develops a spiritual lifestyle. (2) Each step also promotes psychological truths that contribute to psychological integration and peace of mind. One benefit is attached to the other.

If you are a religious type or a deist, that is fine and excellent for you. Your alliance would be with a lifestyle of beliefs around a program that is supervised in absentia by your version of God. "I believe in God" is an entirely subjective-opinion point of view. It applies to no one else. Always work towards acceptance of other points of view. If you are a humanist, atheist, or agnostic, also subjective, align yourself with a commitment to compassion, rigorous honesty, and the first aspect of humility: equality in a life governed by spiritual principles. For everyone: Don't harbor subtle criticism or nasty opinions about other points of view. When you get to footnote 148 reflect carefully on how to mind your own business.

Error in Perception

Many people view the steps as tools to get through onerous and trying times— an acquired group of skills that are used to fix problems. [142] This misperception of a toolbox-of-steps arises when spiritual principles, or the tasks of the first nine steps, are recast from context (what they are) into content (what they are not). Footnote 126 has more information.

For addicts in recovery, the context changes from being selfish and dishonest; argumentative and judgmental everywhere (addiction context) to being kind, honest, accepting, and compassionate everywhere (spiritual context). Whether you are a guitar player, a business owner, or a school-teacher, you will approach life differently. You changed the context in the first nine steps: a new attitude everywhere you go and in everything you do. The content of your life: parent, taxi driver, house painter, factory worker, may or may not change, but whatever you do will be governed by spiritual principles (context) rather than manipulating selfishness.

These first nine steps are assignments to teach you how to truly change your personality and your views of life; changing the way you participate in "life"— not what you do but how you do it. These first nine steps are definitely not tools to fix a problem, they are complex psychological exercises designed to change your personality. This new context will offer a later benefit of how to prevent problems from arising. There is a huge difference between fixing problems and knowing how to not create them. As a brief aside: If a person has been sober for some considered time, the fact that they are "in" a problem means they are responsible for it *and* they weren't spiritual in the first place when they created it.

---

142 Please remember that all problems are some type of relationship conflict.

The "maintenance end" of the program is not designed so you can constantly fix problems that you repeatedly create, it's ultimately designed for serenity and problem prevention. That is acceptance and compassion in social humility.

What follows is based on the many references in *Alcoholics Anonymous* and *Twelve Steps and Twelve Traditions* that clearly indicate that the solution to addiction, and the achievement of serenity, is a life governed by the maintenance steps and spiritual principles. [143] The first nine steps, through self-discipline, will address problems that your addiction (a self-destructive, unspiritual attitude) created in your past. That is the specific dual-purpose of those nine steps: changing the context of your life views and repairing harms you caused in past relationships. If you don't change your life's context you cannot amend the harms you caused. These are hand-in-glove related.

None of the steps were originally designed to allow you to resolve any psychological deficits, although that does happen. Neither are they designed to maintain sobriety. Abstinence is simply being determined, in whatever manner, to not drink or use or act out, one day at a time. Successful restraint is determination. The steps, such as they are, are principally for the creation of a spiritual life and to alter the psychology that is essential to that. [144] Steps One to Nine will greatly modify your mental attitudes and secular life. When completed with committed self-discipline they actually change your personality. [145]

It's far too easy to be mediocre in your being spiritual. There is the culturally incorrect association of spirituality with religion. There's the increasing disparagement of religion and the significant increase in atheism. Along with other influences, there is a definite collusion between people in recovery to applaud mediocrity and social compliance. With all of that, it's easy to settle for "good enough" because this is such hard work. Being spiritual and the underlying

---

143 The AA literature refers to spiritual principles but those are not articulated, they are vaguely implied. Mr. Wilson was only four years sober when *Alcoholics Anonymous* was published. As many of us have experienced, four years of sobriety only allows for very limited personal awareness, which would also apply to Mr. Wilson. His observations in later writings, c. 1960, demonstrate a much deeper insight and complex wisdom from a Christian perspective.

144 AA jargon, in recent decades, is perpetually focused on surrendering to God, talking about feelings, and subtle complaining life isn't going according to plan; if not that, then subtle "missionary work" to convince others to believe in God. Rarely (if ever?) has anyone spoken to the valid and necessary psychological benefits of the steps when done sincerely and in sequence. The psychology is worthy of much more attention than it gets and should never be subservient to the God-thing. Regardless of anything else, you are always charged with self-discipline. As only one example for people quitting alcohol: Is it God's job to keep you out of the bar or your job not to go in? That is hard for many addicts but is an essential component to this.

145 This is the point made earlier about changing context in the first nine steps. In the psychology of well-conducted therapy, which can be quite valuable, a person can go far beyond what is achieved in these steps. However, the steps, within meetings, do offer enough dependable support and psychology to create a spiritual life.

psychology are very closely related to each other. Religion or God isn't required for either one. It is optional but not required. As a person completes the steps, there's both spiritual and psychological improvement, which are strongly inter-connected. [146]

The disastrous result of doing the steps with a belief they are a toolbox for conflict resolution is a misunderstanding of purpose. You are unspiritual when you create any conflict. If the steps are simply "tools" then you can continue to be unspiritual, act out in character defects as it suits you, and whenever you create conflict use your "toolbox" to escape a problem you never should have created in the first place. The steps, over the long term, are designed to prevent conflict, not to fix it. If you have done the steps and are still generating notice-able conflict in your life, then you missed the point. Only Step Ten is to resolve wrongs or harms done while living a spiritual life. You "should" progress from occasional conflict that requires amends, to seldom and then to hardly ever. A life that is not completely governed by the maintenance steps cannot maintain recovery from addiction.

.Let's back up to a point before sobriety, before abstinence and the steps, within active addiction. Addicts, for the most part when acting out, live with the illusion of unity and competence. Whether chocolate cake, sex, shopping or alcohol, while they were acting out, the sense of isolation and shame disappears. Anyone in a program longer than five years has heard a thousand times: "I never knew who I was." "I don't know who I am." That is a statement about estrange-ment from self. That separation was hidden by acting out.

Acting out creates a false sense of unity that hides a broken personality. That broken personality (shame, cognitive dissonance, loneliness, conflict, fear, etc.) disappears when acting out but that always ends in a destructive way. While acting out, feeling "complete" is a delusion and the actual result is self-anni-hilation. Bear in mind, too, there is the other equally devastating illusion that spirituality or serenity are present when conflict is absent. [147]

For what it is worth, at this point, memorize the five social symptoms of addic-tion and their opposite, the five spiritual principles (noted in the chart above). Doing this will make everything that follows easier to understand and generate a deeper trust in these steps.

The purpose of *Alcoholics Anonymous* noted on page 45 of that book is to help you find a power greater than yourself which will solve your problem. That may be God and it may be trust that all you need is a commitment to the psychology within the steps. Support through meetings is crucial for either belief. [148]

---

146   There are some valid psychological indicators that being spiritual is more readily available out-side of a religious organization than within one. That is better left to another writing.

147   Many people think that serenity is the absence of conflict. No, that's just an absence of conflict. Serenity is much more than no conflict. (See Chapter 7.)

148   Your recovery may be governed by God or by psychology. For theists or deists, with the help of their chosen higher power. For agnostics or atheists, the process is accomplished by wanting

For all of the adult conflict in your life, it is your fault and the resolution of conflict is your responsibility. Never lose sight of the fact that "you" are the problem, not alcohol, not your family, not the police or the government, not other people, not sex or chocolate cake. You may not have instigated the conflict, but you may be choosing to perpetuate it to try and win some useless argument out of a meaningless power struggle. This is why it is more important to learn problem prevention rather than problem solving.

Trust the maintenance steps and spiritual principles. They will carry you through difficult times and go a long way to prevent problems. This means there is some combined psychological harmony and social serenity when psychology and life are governed by spiritual principles. This can be seen and appreciated in a sincere life of serenity. Long-term life is graceful.

Recall Mr. Wilson's observation cited earlier that conflicted relationships are the cause of our alcoholism. (Step Eight, *Twelve Steps and Twelve Traditions*) Each step has three general purposes: (1) to shift your inner dislocation and conflict into harmony, (2) to create an internal, spiritual mindset *and* lifestyle; and (3), to bring serenity to your social existence. (1) and (2) *always* come first.

What follows is an examination of the steps. The psychological detail is necessary because of need for that insight, which provides a valid alternative for atheists and agnostics. Finding God or some variation of being religious (or something like that) is important to some people, but always secondary to spiritual harmony and the creation of a psychologically integrated personality. Here is an examination relative to spiritual principles and the psychology within each step.

Spiritual Principles (A Reminder)

1) Respect for the body; yours and others'.

2) Veracity.

3) Humility (in two parts).

---

recovery, seeing the value of recovery, and persistent determination to follow the instructions (the steps, honesty, responsibility, etc.). This is no different than someone who had a tough life of poverty and neglect and sincerely wants success. They discipline themselves to be in therapy or school or a long apprenticeship and work diligently to that end for a long time. They see and appreciate the long-range value of the path of self-improvement they have chosen. They follow wise suggestions, work hard, are personally determined, don't complain, don't blame, and eventually realize their goal. People applaud their determination through difficulty. Addiction recovery is no different: Out of a tough life (addiction) people see the value of recovery, decide they want it, work hard, are properly supported and guided by others, are persistent, follow the psychological/social instructions, and succeed. (This relates to what was described in footnote 46.) In all fairness, where lies the credit for either one?

4) Charity of Spirit.

5) Responsibility and obedience to the first four principles.

If you attend to the maintenance steps or spiritual principles with diligence you will realize each one has a direct connection to all relationships. Your attitude and behaviour in relationships has to be drastically adjusted. Here are the steps from the larger perspective of their general purpose, their spiritual intent, and their psychological benefits. [149]

The Steps

Step One – I am ill, not a moral degenerate.

"We admitted we were powerless over alcohol—that our lives had become unmanageable."

. Comments: Step One is to create a new awareness about your history. It is to shift self-perceptions away from morally degenerate failure to addiction-illness (not disease). What must be learned first is how to live with some measure of peace with sobriety and abstinence. This is self-discipline. Step One is in the past tense. Once sober and committed to that, alcohol or drugs or other acting out are in the past. Sharing about "the past" in detail has sinister implications for healthy spirituality and is not a part of the recovery equation.

The dash is used to set off an appositive phrase meaning what follows the dash is an explanation or definition of what preceded it. "—that our lives had become unmanageable." is an explanation of the first part, "We admitted we were powerless over alcohol—". They are the same thing in different words, and both are past tense. There is not the first half or the second half of Step One. Believing that Step One is in two parts sets up a series of complex and unnecessary problems. (See *Spiritual Transformation*)

It is unnecessary and harmful to impose insight questions regarding family systems or expect any awareness of relationship dynamics from new people. It sets up the possibility of disingenuous responses, resurgence of overwhelming shame, and repetitive inadequacy. Many counsellors, themselves, are quite naive about family dynamics. Ask of new people only what is relevant to what is to be accomplished. At Step One are they to resolve the complex dynamics of family systems theory or to establish sobriety? Complex analysis here is largely premature and a detriment to getting established in successful self-restraint.

Purpose: To reframe your perceptions of your past; to shift the view of your acting out from morally corrupt to illness. This is much harder than it seems. It is to admit and eventually accept truths about your self-initiated, self-destruction

---

149   All of the steps are quotes from *Alcoholics Anonymous* or from *Twelve Steps and Twelve Traditions*, published by AA World Services, Inc. Reprinted with permission.

and the consequences of your addiction. It will begin to begin to establish the first, second, and fifth spiritual principles and lay the foundation for the third principle.

Spiritual Result: To understand the hopelessness of continued acting out (the elimination of blatant self-destruction). This is the tentative entry into the world of recovery and seeking a solution.

Psychological Result: Through early abstinence, the obvious and immediate reduction of mental chaos, self-destruction, and conflict; the awareness and eventual understanding of illness, *and* to begin to abandon guilt and moral degenerate thinking. (Again, this is harder and much more complicated than it would seem.)

Step Two – Understanding the need for guidance.

"Came to believe that a power greater than ourselves could restore us to sanity." For atheists this can be understanding the need for guidance and trust-worthy outside help. The reducing of alienation and isolation. It would be similar to initiating a proper effort to not blame, commitment to rigorous honesty, establishing successful restraint, and self-discipline, with disclosure to a trusted and insightful mentor are required. "Reaching out" to God or anyone that can help achieve these goals is essential.

Comments: According to its position in "How It Works," Step Two comes after successful abstinence is well established and rigorous honesty has become a participation exercise. It takes time and commitment to reach Step Two. A person is not ready for Step Two until they understand four things: (i) The over-riding importance of rigorous honesty and regularly engaging in that. It is not a spectator sport. (ii) They know what letting go of old ideas means and demonstrate that in some tangible way. (iii) They know what addiction is (from education) and what recovery means that's deeper than a sense of humor and sober dances. (iv) They are willing to go to *any* lengths (meaning stay sober at all costs). Only then are they ready for Step Two. This necessary, long delay between Steps One and Two is because of the impatience and shallowness of modern recovery, i.e. get sober, do the steps right away, and live happily ever after in chaotic relationships. In this era, there are the significant complicating factors of polyaddiction, abstinence not-available addiction, social dislocation, and socially approved addictions that require this delay.

Restore means exactly that. At some point in the distant past you were generally okay. You became ill and are now restoring yourself to health. [150] There are four different kinds of spiritual newcomer described in *Twelve Steps and Twelve Traditions* and one more new type described in *Spiritual Transformation*. Entering

---

150 From the AA pamphlet A *Member's Eye View of Alcoholics Anonymous*, "To believe that the alcoholic who approaches AA is an unprincipled, untaught barbarian, suddenly transformed by the previously unavailable spiritual illumination of the Twelve Steps, is, to me, utter foolishness."

into a spiritually disciplined life, whether theist or atheist, requires self-examination and a specific effort to undermine your pre-existing belligerence and doubt to achieve a life of responsible and compassionate honesty. Belligerence towards all of this exists and needs to be challenged.

It's never a matter of forcing yourself to believe in anything. Desperation is a poor basis for motivation into a spiritual life. Desperation for abstinence, possibly, but not for spirituality. That is why, in How It Works, the word then is inserted where it is… *"then you are ready to take certain steps."*

Purpose: To begin to reorganize and lay the foundation for ongoing changes to your perceptions regarding the illness, responsibility, spiritual corruption and its resolution. This will eventually establish a new context for life, the commitment to spiritual integrity. This is the only common starting point that everyone shares in twelve-step recovery, supposedly a commitment to spiritual behaviour. The actual reading of How It Works at most meetings is to establish Step Two, the common starting point for everyone there. How It Works is an actual explanation of Step Two (see *Spiritual Transformation*). [151] This also lays the groundwork for the third, fourth, and fifth spiritual principles.

Spiritual Result: The recognition for theists that willpower directed towards an increased interest in finding a higher power, or for atheists a sense of authentic commitment to responsible healing, is required. Pursuing a spiritual life is the commitment necessary and the eventual solution. There's clear direction the steps are the path for spiritual transformation.

Psychological Result: Experiencing legitimate pride through continued successful abstinence, social stability via meetings, the reduction of social alienation, and over time coming to believe that a commitment to the steps will provide a spiritual solution (not a God solution). This is called the rewards for effort. Step Two is probably the most important step. It establishes a realization of the need for significant changes in beliefs and a commitment to a new context for life. A sincere effort at self-discipline is essential to accomplish this.

Step Three — I've decided I'm Committed.

"Made a decision to turn our will and lives over to the care of God as we understood Him." The atheist version would be making a sincere decision to commit to rigorous honesty, responsibility, and the maintenance steps to achieve a spiritual lifestyle. For atheists, eventually at Step Eleven, your commitment would be to mediation not to prayer.

Comments: Making this decision does not mean you can turn your will and life over or that you can live by those principles. You have only decided to do this. Deciding you want to become a veterinarian, or a pastry chef, does not mean you can do it. It's only a decision. A decision is not an accomplishment; work and focused effort must follow. The recovery rhetoric about turning it over

---

151 A commitment to God may bring comfort but resolves nothing about your addictions. A commitment to spiritual principles does.

and taking it back, the Step Three chaos, is evidence of ignorance of what a decision actually is and what that requires. Making a decision is only that and nothing else. The steps following Step Three teach you how to achieve your goal—spiritual abstinence.

Purpose: To commit oneself to, and to marshal and focus personal willpower towards, an all-encompassing spiritually oriented lifestyle, in terms of both will and life. "God" by any name, may or may not, fit into this. Again, for atheists and humanists, it is the decision to eventually achieve a spiritual lifestyle. (See Chapter 7.) The development of the second, third, and fifth spiritual principles happens here.

Spiritual Result: Understanding more of what will be required in the future as regards your decision. The direct relationship between honesty, responsibility, eventual serenity, and the steps should be a drawn conclusion.

Psychological Result: The experiences of life are organized around a twelve-step social structure (friendship and meetings), and a basic trust that (most) program people aren't lying. There are a few people who sincerely care and (might) know what they are doing. Those are significant social changes for an addict. And, since having achieved sobriety and completed these first three steps, all of that combined has allowed for a corresponding mental change: the substantial reduction of mental chaos and doubt. That mental change allows you to contemplate actions and decisions with more clarity of thought and certainty. This creates a tentative, but regular and stable social interaction that parallels the beginning of trust in the program itself and stability in relationships.

However, problems do sometimes arise when people parade around meetings and groups thinking they are dating clubs, "insisting" on contact information, pretending they know more than they do, or stare at others trying to collect masturbation fantasies. This might include unwanted hugging or holding hands during a prayer. If people sense personal discomfort, they must be supported in firmly saying "No" to any unwanted attention or intrusive behaviour.

Isolation abates and life becomes gradually less chaotic. The relationship between serenity, responsibility, and honesty is a considered realization. Based on their inner experience, it is a safely drawn conclusion that the steps are the path to this success.

Step Four — This is me.

"Made a searching and fearless moral inventory of ourselves."

Comments: This is not an inventory of sins, lies, or misdemeanors. It's a list of emotions (jealousy, insecurity, fear, anger, selfishness, etc.) in relationships, which motivated your irresponsible, destructive behaviour of controlling and blaming others. There are only three columns. The word blame must be dropped from speech and thought, including blaming alcohol or drugs, others, or even yourself. Take note that Step Four asks nine questions about your sexual behaviour, two questions about your resentments, and only one question about your fears. There is something significant about that ratio: nine vs. two vs. one. [152]

Purpose: To create an awareness and belief that misaligned and out-of-control instincts (especially sex) are made worse and never resolved by blame, dishonesty, resentment, or attempting to control others. We must understand that all conflict and the addiction that arises from that are all self-imposed. The ever-deepening awareness of the first and third spiritual principles will lay additional groundwork for the fourth and fifth spiritual principles.

Spiritual Result: An increasing desire to experience spiritual calmness and acceptance (which avoids problems by not creating them).

Psychological Result: This new "self-insight and awareness" about blame and resentment creates a determination to focus willpower on spiritual development, meaning responsibility. This recognition of value-for-effort encourages addicts to strive to reduce their own character defects through a determined effort to not blame. It increases a commitment to recovery. This is a subtle set up for humility at Step Seven. [153]

Step Five — Someone else knows.
"Admitted to God, to ourselves, and to another human being the exact nature of our wrongs." For atheists, omit the God part. The rest is as-is.

Comments: This admission is limited to what was specifically identified in Step Four. Childhood issues are to be left out of this conversation. There are three reasons for this. (1) Step Five listeners are usually not qualified to respond to sensitive information about family of origin or the dynamics of abuse or neglect. This is a very complex psychology. Them saying or suggesting the wrong thing is much worse than offering patience and compassion to delay until sobriety and other supports are well established. (2) In treatment, there is insufficient time or trust to make any progress in resolution of childhood concerns. Even if the listener is qualified, they shouldn't be attempting resolution of childhood or family dynamics in this limited, short-term context. (3) At this early stage of awareness, the client-new person has neither the insight nor trust to present the necessary information. They have not developed the basic internal emotional

---

152 Talking about sex in meetings is frowned upon and notoriously avoided and is almost always misunderstood. Yet, it is a very significant part of recovery as is seen in Step Four. Again, notice that Step Four asks one question about fear, two questions about each resentment, and nine questions about each sexual partner. That says much more than can be written here.

153 In Step Four, the problem *appears* to be that you resent others and don't get along with people and are sexually selfish, but that isn't your problem. The addiction underneath the conflict is the problem, but that isn't really the problem, either. It's spiritual corruption and alienation through the absence of spiritual principles—that's the problem, which sits underneath abstinence and sobriety and conflict. It is always an inside job. The external is an expression of the internal.

structure required for that disclosure. Resolving childhood "issues" is extremely time consuming and complex. The stage must be set for success to prevail. [154]

Always end your Step Five with a polite thank you. Saying a prayer for grati-tude, maybe, if that is *your* choice, not the suggestion of the person hearing you. No Step Six or other suggestions. Stay focused on rigorous honesty in disclosure, no blaming, and take responsibility for the conflict generated by your own acting out. Other than thank you, nothing else is required and nothing else should be suggested when you are done.

Purpose: To take complete responsibility during accurate self-disclosure for your self-imposed crisis and defects of character. This will establish a style of self-disclosure that exonerates others from blame and responsibility. You assume personal responsibility with one person at a very limited public level. There's practice of the second, third, fourth, and fifth spiritual principles. This sets the stage for understanding Steps Nine and Ten.

Spiritual Result: A new awareness of social humility. A very subtle aside for deists or theists is the proper context for prayer is established within this step.

Psychological Result: Acceptance at a social level, through the interaction with the person chosen, will create an experience of less shame and guilt. This is often described as "feeling stronger and more determined" (a sense of psychologi-cal integration). With the admissions of responsible truth, repetitive inadequacy is reduced.

After Step Five, review all your earlier step work to make sure all is in order and nothing was overlooked before moving to Step Six.

Step Six – The Most Difficult Awareness

"Were entirely ready to have God remove all these defects of character." For humanists and atheists: I became entirely ready to understand the overall impor-tance of social humility.

The original Step Six is a poor representation in words of the requirements of this most difficult step. It requires a lot of careful thought, awareness of its importance, and a determined "thinking" effort (as in Step Eleven meditation).

To understand what is required, a more accurate wording would be: I became entirely ready and willing to increase my humility so I could remove my defects of character from all my relationships. This links it directly to very important sentences in Steps Seven and Eight, *Twelve Steps and Twelve Traditions*. (Step Seven may be the next most difficult step. More later.)

---

154 There are some *rare* exceptions, usually in treatment. Approach the disclosure of childhood abuse or any sexual acting out with very sensitive compassion. Sobriety must be well established, much longer than a few weeks, and several criteria of therapy must be established before any long-term resolution can be attempted. The necessary foundation cannot be established in a few weeks of sporadic interaction. Any mishandling of disclosure by the counsellor will eventually have to be paid for by the client. And, it should never be attempted with a counsellor that lacks proper training. If they are trained but have little experience they should be supervised.

Comments: The point usually missed here is Step Six is the preparation for active humility. No more talking about it; prepare to do it. This is very difficult at Step Six and significant in all the remaining steps. It demands an increase in trust that a spiritual lifestyle is what you must accomplish. With or without God, you are becoming willing to live by spiritual principles. Step Six is where we commit to abandoning our addiction survival skills (manipulation, disrespect, belligerence, selfishness, anger, arrogance, dishonesty, withholding, irresponsibility, and blame) and prepare to commit to social humility: compassion, honesty, respect and equality. This commitment is the larger difficulty. The in-your-face acquisition of active humility is why it separates the shallow from the sincere. [155]

Purpose: To create an internal spiritual mindset of personal willingness and determination to remove character defects. This really means to completely abandon old survival skills. Your defects of character, which allowed you to survive your addiction, have been blocking the pursuit of humility. Character defects are the detours away from enlightenment. There's a deeper entrenchment of spiritual principles two, three, and five. Additional groundwork is laid for the fourth spiritual principle. From this point forward the key to everything is social humility.

Spiritual Result: An actual shift in the perception of a higher power and its personal purpose. For everyone, that may only be a more-clear understanding of the overriding importance of humility. Again: From Step Seven forward the key to everything is social humility.

Psychological Result: There's a reduction of socially imposed guilt and a clearer understanding of character defects. These are particularly important and associated with a successful Step Five and earned insights from contemplation at Step Six. This enhances an emotional commitment to a spiritual life and generates a sustained effort at recovery. Life conditions are noticeably improving which reduces repetitive inadequacy. This entrenches the idea that recovery is a personal reward process—value-for-effort invested, and that humility will improve relationships and serenity. It sets the stage for more trust in relationships, consistent honesty, and a stable lifestyle. (Sometimes new-comers will notice their life is getting boring.)

Step Seven – The Key to Reducing Character Defects
"Humbly asked him to remove our shortcomings." For non-believers, it is necessary to become committed to humility in all areas of life, especially in relationships.

Comments: Steps Two, Six, and Seven, are the least-discussed steps. They are arguably the most important but also the least dramatic. [Step Twelve is the

---

155 "This is the step that separates the men from the boys" is the first sentence in Step Six, *Twelve Steps and Twelve Traditions.* I am not enamored of the sexism the phrase implies, but it was intended to point out the significant difficulty involved here. The necessary commitment and determination are often more than most people can muster. Be compassionate.

most ignored.] Creating action-adventure stories about acting out, terrors in early recovery, anguish at Step Four, the horrors of making amends, or the heroic efforts of carrying the message, are unnecessary drama. No one ever describes their monumental struggles over being humble. Who wants to talk about boring humility? And as an aside, if a person actually did understand humility as a voluntary commitment there could be no grandstanding, complaining, or self-proclaimed suffering.

And yet, the quietly subtle implication in Step Seven is humility is the key to everything that follows and essential to the reduction of defects of character. Many people avoid these three steps (two, six, seven) because of the effort required to understand them and to actually contemplate what they mean. They are absent of drama and quite intimidating and are therefore avoided.

The vague ideas and significant misconceptions about humility, God, religion, and addiction, make this step awkward to approach. To embark on understanding Step Seven demands a significant change in personal awareness. It requires a definite effort offer humility in all areas of life. Side Note: Very often addicts are reluctant to embrace humility because they think it means that the bad guys will get away with being bad or people who hurt them will escape punishment. This is tricky business.

Humility, as a principle of recovery, is discussed in this book in Chapters 5 and 7. It is presented for both theists and atheists. For theists and believers, humility requires both aspects. For humanists and atheists, it only requires the first aspect; equality. For humility to be authentic it must, for everyone, have acceptance and compassion as the governing energy in all relationships.

Political recovery, smokescreen sobriety, impression management, and social approval become insufficient. [156] I suspect that because this is sensed, and those important changes are feared, Step Seven, and likewise Steps Two and Six, are slyly avoided. People perpetuate cliché conversations to sound sincere and avoid showing how little they know. Empty words keeps them confused. It's very easy to evade responsibility in cliché speech, hence the need for education more than praying.

Purpose: At a deep level to understand that humility is the only successful way to reduce character defects. A person can focus on, review and debate anger and selfishness until the world is free of dirt. To offer humility makes for correct focus. Humility is actually the key to everything past Step Seven. A

---

156 Smokescreen sobriety is related to polyaddictions. I'm sober, I don't drink (but secretly I smoke dope). I am clean and sober (but eat handfuls of pills with codeine and a bottle of *Nyquil* every night). I don't do pills, street drugs or alcohol (but it's only a small chocolate cake and four doughnuts a day). I don't do drugs and have a good diet (but there's compulsive masturbation and two hours of internet porn a day). I quit gambling (but smoke more and buy prostitutes). There are a thousand variations of smokescreen sobriety—the addiction substitution rackets. These are usually addressed in sequence, the biggest first then the rest are challenged as recovery progresses.

commitment develops to embrace a realignment of personal priorities, which will enhance devotion to a spiritual lifestyle through a willing demonstration of the five principles.

After rigorous honesty, humility has the highest value in serenity and the personal discipline to achieve them is most difficult. It requires significant effort at Step Eleven meditation (when you get there) and commitment to living a principled life (maintenance). More groundwork is laid for the third and fourth spiritual principles. This is crucial because humility is the only thing that leads directly to the reduction of character defects. [157]

Spiritual Result: Sensing the steps as the most reliable path for the courage to transform. Courage here, comes from trust that continued success along the route can be depended upon. This expands the principle of humility to embrace all human relationships and is the fundamental requirement for Steps Eight, Nine and Ten, and for spiritual heliotropism (explained later). Being humble in *all* relationships with *all* people for spiritual success cannot be overstated. There should be a general absence of annoyance and selfishness with everyone. This is intrinsic to the third and fifth spiritual principles.

Psychological Result: The realization of non-religious humility, equality, and rigorous honesty in relationships are far more important to recovery than a relationship with a higher power. The governing effort in all relationships becomes a desire for compassion and the spiritual attitude of humility in approaching all life circumstances. Relationship harmony is much more visible with everyone because there's a direct perception that serenity in all relationships is possible through acceptance, honesty, and equality.

By this time, addicts have become more selective about their associations so as to excuse themselves from conflict. Consequently, they exhibit fewer defects. This, in part, leads to being accepting and more respectful of others. Part of active humility is not introducing stress into, or meddling in, the lives of others. Meddling includes gossip and slander which is a secret form of meddling in other's lives. Avoiding conflict through self-discipline at Steps Ten, Eleven (Meditation), and Twelve is the beginning of a basic spiritual wisdom, as is choosing loneliness over conflict. [158]

---

157 It must be born in mind, for any number of reasons, that many people in recovery cannot approach this level of commitment. Religious heritage, long-forgotten childhood issues, dual diagnosis concerns, prejudice, education, ability, unexamined belligerence, and age are influences. Being abstinent and not making things worse are where this starts and is good enough for some people. This is to be respected.

158 *"We needn't be always bludgeoned and beaten into humility… a great turning point in our lives came when we sought humility as something we really wanted, rather than something we must have,"* and, *"The whole emphasis of Step Seven is on humility. … we now ought to be willing to try humility in seeking the removal of our other shortcomings…"* Twelve Steps and Twelve Traditions, pp 75, 76. Humility is the only character-defect reduction strategy that actually works.

Step Eight – Preparing for Social Reentry

"Made a list of all persons we had harmed and became willing to make amends to them all."

Comments: You must be determined through a commitment to spiritual responsibility and equality to care for the welfare of others, especially those you have harmed. You must be willing to go to any lengths to realize the importance of humility at Step Seven as the only thing that allows the identifying harms caused to be thorough. This was explored and understood at Step Seven. Don't join Step Eight to Step Nine or be reluctant to be specific because of your anxiety about an impending Step Nine. Just make a thorough list of harms.

Purpose: To list and identify harms caused by your character defects to all others (and the probable amends required) *and* to take complete responsibility for these harms. This is a clear demonstration of spiritual generosity and devotion to the impending social responsibility at Step Nine. There's much more acceptance of the spiritual principles, especially the second, fourth, and fifth.

Spiritual Result: A deeper intuition around the spiritual benefits and freedom inherent in taking complete responsibility, regardless of the personal cost. Your history of conflict must be resolved by you, or at least a sincere attempt made to do so. Relationship conflict and dishonesty are the principle results of addiction and the major cause of all relapse.

Psychological Result: The confident anticipation of less social and inner-personal tension and less guilt because of social responsibility that will be achieved at Step Nine. Unaddressed relationship conflict is one principle cause of unresolved adult-onset shame, living a life of avoidance, and relapse. To identify this conflict at Step Eight allows some emotional relief of anxiety and fear that had been present for years. There is always some relief when there is an end-in-sight to burdensome complex problems. Step Eight is often accompanied by a subtle intuition that "if it works," Step Nine will offer emotional freedom and less social restriction. The proposed resolution of inner turmoil, when at Step Nine, is made easier if you are very clear on the concepts of illness and humility rather than moral guilt and atonement (which most people aren't).

Step Nine – Repairing the Past — I have to go back from whence I came.

"Made direct amends to such people wherever possible, except when to do so would injure them or others."

Comments: The exception "when to do so would injure them or others" is a very limited exemption. Pointing out or reminding others of your own former selfishness or meanness and disreputable conduct, and them becoming uncomfortable about that, is not harming them. Do not rescue yourself out of responsibility with this feeble excuse. [159]

---

159 From *Alcoholics Anonymous*, p. 79: *"…we have decided to go to any lengths to find a spiritual experience… no matter what the personal consequences may be… we must not shrink at anything."* Yes, we each find our own personal standard of responsibility here. You will experience serenity com-

What has become popular is the phrase "living amends"—staying sober and being a responsible, nice person now. Yes, there is some long-range valid trust established in staying sober, but that does not excuse a person from the awkwardness of truth and responsibility. Living amends are after sobriety but what about before? What shame or fear causes you to avoid confronting your abuses and hide in living amends? [160] A sincere demonstration of regret, and a willingness to be examined, whether or not any actual amends can be made, goes a lot farther than staying sober. The people harmed are at the very least entitled to a conversation to hear your sincerity. It demonstrates responsibility for past behaviour.

Purpose: To repair the harms done and damage caused, and to sincerely facilitate peace in the lives of other people. Sorry doesn't count. This requires you to demonstrate humility through social responsibility.

Spiritual Result: A deep and direct experience of the five spiritual principles often happens. There's a substantially different sense of freedom, in such a way that the promised promises are now appreciated as the direct result of spiritual self-discipline and commitment. [161]

Psychological Result: A clear sense of getting along better with other people; feeling more peaceful in personal and social situations, with an awareness of self-confidence from your own effort. This establishes longer-term healthier relationships. [All of this effort—*all of it*— is to first reduce mental dissonance and then to create a sense of belonging in conflict free relationships. In its most basic elements that is what this is all about.]

During Step Nine there is a definite sense of social freedom and it generates a valid self-respect through responsibility and the increase of confidence. Shame, guilt, social fear, and repetitive inadequacy are diminished. The promised promises become a real and tangible presence. [162]

Whether it's a God-oriented or a humanist-psychological process there must be this awareness: External conflict, in too many successive doses, meaning several bad things happening close together, whether caused from emotionally

---

mensurate with your commitment and effort. Strength and direction can come from commitment and trust in the written program probably more than from some version of a higher power, which is an individual preference of opinion.

160　In some situations, with the aged or infirm or mentally challenged, living amends may be the best a person can do. Don't hide accountability behind living amends.

161　The promises are listed in *Alcoholics Anonymous*, page 84. For atheists, the statement "We realize God is doing for us what we cannot do for ourselves" does not apply. Atheists do it for themselves and the people in their lives. From another, deeper perspective, everyone does this for themselves, and if you don't do this for yourself, you can't do it for anyone else.

162　*Spiritual Transformation*, *Third Edition*, has several pages of detailed analysis of The Promises being the result of a determined social and psychological effort. The promises are not accidental, they don't arrive until Step Nine is almost done, and they are not a gift from a higher power. They are the direct result of your own hard work. Nothing is free, especially the promises.

bad decisions or not, can be turned into a calamity of magnificent proportion. Drama must be avoided in making amends to prevent calamity.

A misunderstanding is evident when people say things like: "I'm mad or scared about _(insert circumstance)_ so I'll do another Step Four." (or) "I'm fighting with _(insert name)_ so I'll do another Step Eight-and-Nine." The fact that they are being said means the conflict was caused by unspiritual behaviour in the first place. These, and similar statements, show a misunderstanding of what the steps and spiritual principles are to accomplish, which is problem prevention, not conflict resolution. To say those things, indicates the steps are used as situational problem-solving techniques. (We are back to the tool-box metaphor here.) That is not what they are intended or designed for.

The steps are not a social-conflict resolution game. They are is to create and maintain a spiritual personality. If you can accomplish this then you will stop generating conflict. There is no perfection only commitment to progress—not progress in solving conflict quickly, but progress in not creating conflict at all. Problem prevention. Yes, there will be conflict in the world but you creating it or participating in it will be optional.

It is also an error in perception, when working through the steps, to believe of yourself that you were completely defective from the moment you were born. It is dramatic self-abuse to believe that you must repair everything about yourself. This is ignoring the meaning of the word restore in Step Two.

As a parallel example: You're driving your vehicle and get a flat tire. You don't abandon your car, go back to university, get an engineering degree, and redesign the construction of tires and the vehicle wheel assembly. Fixing the problem is changing the tire. Fix what's wrong and get on with the trip. In addictions recovery, getting recovered means you fix what's wrong with yourself, appreciate what isn't, and get on with the trip. There are three perspectives to "wrong" here. What you think is wrong with you; what others think is wrong with you (which are both probably inaccurate), and what is actually in need of adjustment.[163]

The steps, up to Step Nine, are the context of transformation, which isn't direct "problem solving." They're to redesign your personality and to change your view of life so you (a) stay 'sober,' (b) can become more spiritual; and (c), fix the problems from your past which you have been ignoring. Addicts must change their attitudes, beliefs, and values which they used to justify their acting out (self- and other-abuse). Their blaming and complaining must eventually stop, after all it is a self-imposed crisis which demands a self-imposed solution. Abandoning old ideas, taught by completing the first nine steps, is essential to recovery and a spiritual life.

Altogether, the spiritual principles learned by completing the first nine steps create a spiritual foundation for a new life. That new life will be generally

---

163 Remember: From the AA pamphlet *A Member's Eye View of Alcoholics Anonymous*, *"To believe that the alcoholic who approaches AA is an unprincipled, untaught barbarian, suddenly transformed by the previously unavailable spiritual illumination of the Twelve Steps, is, to me, utter foolishness."*

absent of conflict for you, the individual, and include a distinct awareness of the promises.

Steps Ten, Eleven, and Twelve — The long haul.

10. *"Continued to take personal inventory and when we were wrong promptly admitted it."*

11. *"Sought through prayer and meditation to improve our conscious contact with God as we understood Him, praying only for knowledge of His will for us and the power to carry that out."*

12. *"Having had a spiritual awakening as the result of these steps, we tried to carry this message to alcoholics, and to practice these principles in all our affairs."*

Comments: The maintenance steps are quite different from the first nine. Maintenance steps, these active spiritual behaviours (being spiritual is not a spectator sport), are intended for the prevention of problems. They're interdependent themes of a spiritual lifestyle—coping with life spiritually. When, on the rare occasion, conflict does arise, then they enable spiritual problem solving. But, never lose sight of the fact that this is primarily problem prevention. [164]

Steps Ten, Eleven, and Twelve are not separate tasks that are completed independently of each other. They all happen together. They reflect the intricate, ongoing participation in a spiritual life—problem prevention first, problem solving second. Because of this intricate relationship they are here examined together. [Recall digital, complex thinking in Chapter 2. This is it.]

At this point, at this entry level of being spiritual, and having regard for a consistent level of commitment, you are recovered. Each of these maintenance steps have all five spiritual principles acting within them. This requires that the definition of relapse change after Step Nine. Relapse is now related to spiritual principles. When you abandon spiritual principles, are dishonest, sarcastic, angry, punitive, arrogant, abusive, disrespectful, irresponsible (whatever), you are in relapse—you may be sober but not living spiritually. You are again living in the symptoms of addiction. After Step Nine, that's relapse.

Purpose: To maintain being recovered; to prevent problems from arising but when they do, to solve problems spiritually and to enhance and deepen a sincerely spiritual lifestyle. Remember it is a spiritual awakening, which means a personality change, not a realization of God. All five principles operate in all three steps.

Spiritual Result: A continuing, deeper awareness of spiritual harmony (aligning yourself with the energy of compassion and acceptance). Life is less chaotic. There's fewer problems, less conflict, and it's more stable.

Psychological Result: Recovered addicts get along quite well with people. They can offer compassion and acceptance in all relationships and approach life with humility. They establish a network of conflict-absent, healthy relationships. Life

---

164 Albert Einstein was reported to have said: "A clever person solves a problem. A wise person avoids it." From *If Ignorance is Bliss*, John Lloyd & John Mitchinson, Bloomsbury House Pub, p. 55.

is not chaotic and is stable. There's a deep sense of confidence that, with a proper attitude, problems can be largely prevented. Problem solving becomes secondary to problem prevention.

Spiritual living—approaching life with humility, equality, a gentle rigorous honesty, being responsible, never blaming—as a general lifestyle, becomes standard conduct. When life becomes chaotic, recovered addicts avoid blame and accept responsibility. They establish a lifestyle that challenges their character defects and intrusive behaviour rather than challenging the people around them. They amend various subtle harms and disrespect to others. [165] Whether viewed as spiritual or psychological, the maintenance steps result in:

(a) more consistent and dependable serenity, regardless of what events occur,

(b) life having less of a personal, selfish agenda, and taking on more of a spiritual agenda (the difference is important),

(c) a greater devotion to acceptance, honesty, compassion (which means never blaming) and problem prevention; and,

(d) noticeably less meddling in the affairs of others, which includes no gossip. There's a certain benign indifference to what's going on around them; gracefully minding their own business, which is a definite aspect of humility.

Step Twelve does not have, within it, a secretly-coded permission to do missionary work. The adage of attraction rather than promotion will have a definable presence. This enhances personal integrity and requires exerting your will, which means making an effort, to demonstrate your commitment to this process. It means you demand of yourself a life which embraces the five spiritual principles.

As with the other steps, psychological benefits are realized within Steps Ten, Eleven, and Twelve. However, traditional psychology (the style of therapy from the 1950s onward), cannot include spirituality in its mandate. Those therapies were designed and developed to accomplish social compliance and reintegration, not spiritual integrity. And, any religion, in any of their social presentations, are

---

165 With the overwhelming presence of recovery houses, treatment centers, and doctors "treating" addiction (all paid twelve-step work), and in recent decades the notable absence of any discussion or recognition of the maintenance steps, the recidivist-recovery mindset is both insidious and dominant. This developed partly from intrusive cultural dislocation, discussed elsewhere. I cannot find in either of the two original AA texts any hint or reference to "perpetual recovery" or repetitive step completion. I cannot find any discussion in them of a general expectation of relapse behaviour. I can find several references to becoming recovered. As mentioned elsewhere, doctors are invaluable in treating the consequences of addiction but should be very cautious advising on the treatment of addiction itself. Doctors and treatment centers are not spiritual advisors.

inadequate to enable a personally designed spiritual life. Whether good or bad, religions are intrusive in that they strongly advise what is required.

A thing can only accomplish what it is designed for. People don't go to a grocery store to renew their driver's license. Grocery stores aren't designed for that. We don't go to restaurants to buy winter tires. We don't go to the SPCA to buy televisions or toothpaste; wrong place. If you want to cook an egg don't buy a dust mop. Any organized religion is not designed for psychology and are themselves spiritually suspect. Classic psychology isn't designed for spiritual transformation, it is also spiritually short-sighted. Any effort at transcendental meditation is a misalignment of purpose with recovery. TM isn't a suitable substitution at Step Eleven. This is explained later in this chapter as regards the three types of meditation and what they are supposed to accomplish.

However, both traditional therapy and religion are more visible in this culture and socially easier to access. Neither are designed for addiction recovery. There is no disgrace attached to going to "church" and congratulations from many quarters for attending therapy. It is easy to get social compliments for attending religious functions or going to therapy and being a "good" taxpayer/consumer. These don't oppose culture and are seen as "good" which really means not threatening to society.

Fear and dread within society, when faced with Group C and D addicts, are a consequence of abusive politics. There's a strong presence of ignorance about addiction and a sense of helplessness to deal with that. Ignorance, fear, and dread; welcome to the modern era of 2020. Socially approved addiction in Group B is never addressed, nor is the overall related dislocation of modernity. Inefficiency and failure in recovery and treatment are from invalid perspectives of addiction and treatment and participation in thinly veiled religious propaganda. Yes, a spiritual life for everyone... but religion, some psychology, medicine, and God are easily counter-productive. As the philosopher Terrence McKenna said: *"The cost of sanity, in this society, is a certain level of alienation."* As so it is with being spiritual, it generates social alienation and cultural disapproval, as does addiction. Interesting that the illness and the solution (addicted and spiritual) are both outside of acceptable social norms. This cannot be ignored.

It's easier to get social approval if you accept the cultural imposition of addicts being "bad." It's easier to get social support if you seek forgiveness for being mean and apologize for being an addict. Degrade yourself; it works. Participate in some quasi-religious group (moderate or otherwise) and be indoctrinated into Group B addictions. However dangerous, this is only ersatz comfort in social compliance. Without a sincere spiritual mindset, which opposes traditional religion, resists classic psychology, and will alienate you in modern culture, there is no safe recovery from addiction. [166]

---

166 Obedience to the five spiritual principles, which usually invites social suspicion, is hard to justify in our culture. People will wonder why you work so diligently to live by spiritual principles. The rewards of a truly spiritual lifestyle: compassion, humility, acceptance, are held in low regard in

The risk for addicts, in not choosing the more difficult spiritual orientation to life, leaves abstinence at risk and their integrity dependent on the cooperation of fate. This is often seen in continuing moodiness, complaining, bragging, self-ishness, isolation, gossiping, anger, general discontent, expressing disapproval, disregard for the emotional rights of others, being belligerent or demanding, recurring impulses to act out, ongoing deceit, frequent brief relapses, and the ongoing presence of socially approved addiction.

Prayer and Meditation

For addicts of a theist or deist view, prayer can be a tricky business. Sometimes an over-dependence on prayer or TM-meditation are chosen by the emotionally lazy. They do pray a lot but avoid a more self-demanding commitment to the steps. They experience an automatic belligerence towards humility and certainly a laziness towards Step Eleven meditation. In later recovery this reluctance to meditate as per Step Eleven—that indolence, is vicious enough to prevent them from meditating at all, and they relapse and die because of their refusal to pursue a spiritual lifestyle. Reading it is not the same as meditating on its instructions. In any event, any half-effort ensures they will remain in turmoil and conflict.

Many people stay just on the very edge of recovery, only dipping their toes in the waters of spirituality. This reluctance to pray properly for theists, or to undertake correct meditation for everyone, or to make only an intermittent effort at self-discipline (doing only what's convenient) is evident in all manner of mediocre recovery and collusion in socially approved addiction.

Prayer

Prayer is: *1. a. A reverent petition made to God or another object of worship. b. The act of making a reverent petition to God or another object of worship. 2. An act of communion with God or another object of worship, such as in devotion, confession, praise, or thanksgiving. 3. A specially worded form used to address God or another*

---

this society, especially in view of the effort that's required. Nothing is free, especially spiritual integrity which is essential for a life free of addiction. It is surprising to me how many people claim to pray a lot, secretly hoping for a lazy person's version of spiritual serenity. "Please God, give me what I haven't earned." "Please God, change this reality I have created to something I like." They don't trust the actual work of the steps or meditation (as per Step Eleven), and don't take responsibility to embrace the effort required. They can't mind their own business in a compassionate manner. So, they pray and complain a lot, hoping for unearned rewards in recovery. However, I do acknowledge that resolving addiction is much harder than most people anticipate. The initial ten years of diligent effort can be mentally exhausting.

object of worship.[167] In order to explore prayer, it is important that theists all start from a common place; a grounded orientation. I've divided prayer into three broad classifications to provide a basic sense of awareness. This is just a place to start.

Prayers of Petition

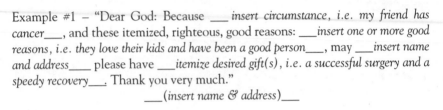

Example #1 – "Dear God: Because ___ *insert circumstance, i.e. my friend has cancer*___, and these itemized, righteous, good reasons: ___*insert one or more good reasons, i.e. they love their kids and have been a good person*___, may ___*insert name and address*___ please have ___*itemize desired gift(s), i.e. a successful surgery and a speedy recovery*___. Thank you very much."

___*(insert name & address)*___

Example #2 — "Dear God: Because ___*insert circumstance, i.e. I am in pain and going crazy and my boss wants to fire me*___, and these itemized, righteous, good reasons: ___*insert one or more good reasons, i.e. I am in recovery and I don't want to relapse, and I'm trying real hard, and I have two kids, I'm trying to be a good person*___, may I please have ___*itemize desired gift(s) i.e. some sobriety for another day and some peace of mind in recovery, and maybe a better job*___. Thank you very much."

___*(insert name & address)*___

This is nothing more than the person asking their God for a present. Whether stated or not, there's always a justification and "good reasons" for petitionary prayer. The person praying has decided they have somehow earned the right to be noticed by (their) God. They are sincere and well-behaved, or desperate, and so God should listen to them. "Hey, God, pay attention to me, please. I'm sincere." Or, they're tired of anxiety and suffering and if they get their requested present from God then for sure they'll really behave. It's a one-sided conversation with requests. Asking God for gifts is the essence of the serenity prayer: *God grant me the serenity to accept the things I cannot change, courage to change the things I can, and wisdom to know the difference.* [168]

"*Our immediate temptation will be to ask for specific solutions to specific problems, and for the ability to help other people as we have already thought they should be helped.*" [169] The person is telling their God what they want. Even with devotion

---

167   *The American Heritage® Dictionary of the English Language, Third Edition,* © 1996, Houghton Mifflin Company. Electronic version.

168   There are reasons for prayer, and reasons why sometimes it seems to work, but that's for another book. Petitionary prayers are always justified in the mind of the person praying. It cannot be justified to pray for the death of someone in a fiery car crash because they were late for lunch or didn't come to your party. Be very cautious about justifications for petitionary prayer.

169   *Twelve Steps and Twelve Traditions,* p. 102.

to a higher power, and reasonable integrity based on the five spiritual principles, all petitionary prayer runs the risk of complications of selfishness. There's no way around this.[170]

There are drawbacks to petitionary prayer. If you coincidentally get what you want, it tends to lead you to be self-righteous and self-congratulatory. "Hey, look what God did for me!" If you pray and don't get what you want, it tends to lead into feeling forsaken; that you're doing something wrong. Is God ignoring me? Does God like others more than me?

This can undermine commitment and may lead to abandoning a life of prayer. "I'm not praying any more, God never listens." You may increase your effort to the point of being obsessive: "When I get this prayer-thing perfect, then God will hear me, and I'll get what I want." "When I finally get rid of all my character defects then God will listen to me." Any time you superimpose Santa Claus on God you set yourself up to justify your selfishness or demean your own character. There is no escape from either possibility.

The novice at prayer often misperceives prayer-time with (their) God as similar to an audience with royalty, or a job interview with the head of the corporation: shoes shined, don't swear, fingernails clean, hair combed, and be on top of the agenda. Don't waste time, God's busy running the universe. This creates needless anxiety and all manner of corruption in spiritual principles for theists.[171]

Prayers of Contemplation

This style of prayer is sometimes called Prayer of Quiet, where suppliants become still within their heart and peaceful in reverence. They communicate to their higher power without doing or expecting. In using some wisdom from Taoism, it might be described as *Wu Wei* in prayer—accomplishing without action; acting deliberately but with deliberate non-purpose. This unique, prayerful meditation takes you to rest with your personal perception of your personal God.[172] This is an opinion very unique to each individual.

---

170 It is interesting that in many groups the serenity prayer is no longer a prayer—a quiet supplication to your personal God, it's more a glee-club chant where people all hold hands in a big circle and pump up solidarity. That's not a prayer.

171 For Christian liberals and moderates a well written and thought out approach can be found in John Shelby Spong's book *Rescuing the Bible from Fundamentalism - A Bishop Rethinks the Meaning of Scripture*. For the philosopher, there is Mortimer Adler's book *How to Think About God: A Guide for the 20th Century Pagan*.

172 *Contemplative Prayer*, by Thomas Merton, Image Books, Doubleday, 1996, although sometimes esoteric, is a valuable guide to contemplative prayer, which makes it a fine volume for learning about prayer for those so inclined.

Prayers of Gratitude

These are a communication to God offering gratitude and praise, asking for nothing in return. In those religious perspectives that superimpose Santa Clause on God, when something "nice" happens, like your drunken relative is well behaved at the wedding reception, or someone survives their surgery, or you find a parking spot... well, you've received "a present" from God and polite people say thank you. As regards this particular type of prayer, you're essentially telling your higher power you're pleased and grateful for getting your own way. There is no humility in these prayers.

For recovered addicts with a much deeper spiritual perspective, prayers of gratitude mean two things: (i) gratitude they are no longer causing harm in the lives of others and can contribute to another's peace by offering a considered wisdom and by gracefully not interfering; and (ii), gratitude for everything, including hardship. Gratitude to be able to demonstrate commitment. Besides that, calling anything hardship is only an arbitrary, self-serving interpretation of some circumstance. It usually means that something has happened that you don't like, or you expected yourself to be exempt from calamity. This is related to the observation of Boethius cited in Chapter 7.

Prayers of gratitude are not to be offered because the bus was on time or somebody found their lost puppy dog. Gratitude must go far beyond social convenience. As advised by the spiritual masters, for believers it is an active recognition of the perpetually available state of love and grace. Gratitude is an appreciation for the implacable grandeur of the experience of our humanness through spirituality, regardless of any circumstance. This, with equality, embodies humility. (See the quote of Albert Camus at the end of Chapter 8.) [173]

Meditation

There is far too much misdirection and outright foolishness as regards meditation in addiction recovery. I've divided meditation into three categories. These general categories are to clarify the issues of meditation as it applies to the instructions for recovery. The three types are quite different practices, they require a different approaching mind-set, and have different intended results. The distinctions are important and will enable you to more clearly appreciate what the original twelve-step program advises.

1) Meditation *of* Transcendence (Two Subtypes: Intellectual and Physical)

The discipline of Transcendental Meditation (TM) originates out of the ancient Eastern religious philosophies of Hinduism. There is reasonable probability that meditation, as a certain style of very ancient yoga, could go back 4,500 years to the Mohenjo-daro and Harappa cultures of India. From there,

---

173   Sometimes, more than we realize, compassion is as simple as quietly minding our own business.

overlooking its long and complex history, we jump ahead to 1955. Generally, Transcendental Meditation, after 1955, is referred to as TM by its North American participants.

Here, the interpretation of TM is, it is intended to take you above, and at the same time temporarily disable, the distractions of mind-commotion, energy blockages, and sentient chaos. Or, in other disciplines, to release healing energy as in Kundalini. When done effectively, TM takes you beyond the dislocation of your mind to achieve a state of "blissful absence"—a peaceful mind through transcending. In one way, is intended to create an ersatz harmony that resides "above" the broken images of perceived truth, hence the use of the word transcend. [174] There are two basic approaches to TM.

TM — Intellectual: This would be meditations that require no movement and demand focused intellectual concentration: sitting quietly, generally immobile, concentrating on breathing, and/or concentrating on OM or other sound mantras in a meditative posture. This is to temporarily abandon and rise above mind-commotion and sentient chaos.

TM — Physical: In this group are Tai Chi, Qi Gong, and some yoga; those that incorporate movement and balance with mindful concentration. This physical discipline isn't specifically intended to transcend the spontaneous mind-chaos. It is to create harmony and connection between your physical and mental dislocation.

In either discipline, when done well, TM helps you to rise above the chaos and broken images of ordinary consciousness, to enter a state of mental calmness and physical, situational harmony. This is valuable, but for addicts in recovery this is not what is required by Step Eleven. There is evidence that to only do TM, and to avoid Step Eleven meditation, will create a spiritual stagnation with no changing of old ideas and no access to humility.

2) Meditation *of* Safety (Guided Meditation and Therapy)

---

174 "*...broken images of perceived truth.*" It is proposed in Hindu philosophy, beginning (probably) 4,500 years ago, in what is now Pakistan, and more recently from about 475 BCE in Buddhism, and from about 1100 CE in Zen Buddhism, that what we see and think about what we see about ourselves and others is false but believed to be a real truth. See yourself in a mirror—there you are—it's you! In those three practices of Eastern insight: Mohenjo-daro, early Theravada Buddhism, and 12th century Zen the belief is you don't see you. It's a very broken image of perception; a mirage of you. It's like a badly cracked mirror with many pieces missing, you see only partly you. Our mind is only a mirror and always reflects broken images of ourselves and others; of everything. Our mind's images of truth and life are broken misperceptions—illusions or delusions. TM is designed to transcend this not to fix it; to absent ourselves from these incomplete, fractured and chaotic images, sensations, and mind-commotion for a short while. In TM we sit temporarily in empty mental peacefulness. For addiction recovery this is not to be substituted for Step Eleven meditation.

Meditations of Safety are a therapy construct and sometimes referred to as Guided Meditation. These became popular in the mid-1970s with the growth of the self-help movement and the cultural impact of therapy and counseling. The student/client is guided through a mental focusing exercise designed by a therapist. "Picture a safe place..." "Imagine you are a child again..." "Picture a place from your past when..." This to create new insights or a sense of peace or harmony and safety. Meditation of Safety can be important in some situations but does not apply to Step Eleven.

Be very cautious about guided meditation. It can cause more difficult recovery, as in smokescreen recovery, and conceal unexamined irresponsibility. There must be a very specific psychological agenda and the guide must be very well trained in several disciplines. [175]

3) Meditation on Wisdom (Step Eleven)

Addicts have to transform their personalities, not transcend them. They must dismantle the dislocation and chaos, not avoid them. What needs to be clarified is the meditation suggested within Step Eleven is not TM and not a meditation of safety. Step Eleven recommends a unique meditation on the wisdom of someone else. This is a crucial practice that challenges the recovered addict's self-limiting beliefs, old ideas, and prejudices. It is intended as a way to access someone else's wisdom and achieve an active humility—being humble rather than sitting around talking about being humble.

If addicts are to reduce their defects of character, and enhance their spirituality so they can allow spiritual principles to more influence their lives, they must consciously let go of their old ideas through humility. As was said at Step Seven, (social) humility has become the key to everything spiritual. This is accomplished by people forcing themselves to appreciate the wisdom of others through thoughtful reflection—hence, meditation *on* wisdom. You study carefully the wise thoughts of someone else.

Rather than transcending the human condition, i.e. having empty-mind, with no conscious contact with anything, which is the specific goal of TM, or hiding from your chaos in guided meditation, Step Eleven advises us to "improve our conscious contact...". That means to deliberately develop a disciplined awareness that promotes insight and humility. Step Eleven meditation is to improve conscious awareness not to avoid it. It is how addicts abandon self-limiting ideas, dismantle old defense mechanisms, and alter their beliefs and perceptions. Step Eleven meditation is a focused, deliberate, and self-initiated exercise of responsible self-discipline. This is crucial: Meditation on the wisdom of others is active humility, which creates insight.

---

175 Many, certainly not all, gurus and therapists can be duplicitous in presenting themselves as meditation masters. Use caution when seeking guidance here and have some idea of a long-range goal that can be explained and understood and is relevant.

The original twelve-step literature provides one example for a meditation on wisdom and offers instruction at the same time. There isn't a Step Eleven prayer. They chose a popular Christian prayer of that era to use as an example of how to meditate as regards recovery. [176]

The Instructions for Meditations on Wisdom: *"Well, we might start like this. First let's look at a really good prayer. We won't have far to seek...."* And, *"The world's libraries and places of worship are a treasure trove for all seekers."* [177] The Christian prayer they chose was a teaching example. Here are the basic instructions. First, find <u>any</u> spiritual writing that appeals to you. Then,

> *"...reread* [the material] *several times very slowly savoring every word"*
> *"...try to take in the deep meaning of each phrase and idea"*
> *"...drop all resistance..."* and *"...debate has no place."*
> *"...rest quietly with the thoughts of someone who knows"*
> *"...ponder what its mystery is"*, and
> *"...seek all those wonders still unseen"*

The goal is to *"...experience and learn* [and to]*... be strengthened and lifted up.,"* [178] Step Eleven, as regards practice and intent, has nothing in common with transcendental meditation or guided meditations of safety. It has everything to do with re-education, being open-minded, and letting go of old ideas. Pick any spiritual writing that appeals to you, any psychology that you might be influenced by, and study it. Figure out what the author is trying to teach you. Use this discipline

---

176 Step Eleven meditation is the only effective avenue to humility. It is both essential and time consuming but accomplishing any measure of humility is always difficult. Mr. Wilson presented Step Eleven to us at least twenty-five years <u>before</u> this culture had any awareness of the Eastern practice of TM, and decades before "therapy" had any formal social standing. His insight regarding Step Eleven meditation is of outstanding value for later stages of humility and long-term serenity. The muddle we are now in regarding meditation has a parallel similarity to what happened in Buddhism. The Buddhist rituals most people participate in today are religious. There is some agreement that religious Buddhism, that is now attached to transcendental meditation, is not how it started. What we are generally exposed to in modern representations of meditation (after about 600 CE), are variations of TM, not what Buddha Siddhartha practiced. Siddhartha meditated and thought about complex problems regarding personality, cultural turmoil, dislocation, and religious conflict evident in his era (c. 500 BCE) as did Da Mo at Shaolin in China near 500 CE. They were trying to identify problems, offer solutions, and understand, not to transcend. And, from *Secrets of the Blue Cliff Record*, writings from 12th century Zen Buddhism, trans. by Thomas Cleary, p. 211: *"Buddha-knowledge is the knowledge derived from contemplation of existing things."* Step Eleven meditation is devoted to insight; to read and study carefully the wisdom of others regarding existing things. It is meditation to aid in changing our selfish personalities, not to transcend or avoid them. Step Eleven meditation is essential to humility. Guided meditation and TM, although important, do not qualify as a part of Step Eleven. As regards Buddhism, I intend another book that will speak to this in some detail.

177 *Twelve Steps and Twelve Traditions*, pp. 98, 99.

178 Ibid., pp. 99-100.

of meditation to reflect on how your defects limit you. Open your mind to other possibilities. This is essential if you wish to achieve a deeper humility, which at Step Seven was presented as the key to all future change.

Keep It Simple

This is one of the clichés that is frequently declared in recovery: Keep It Simple. There are problems with this. Addiction and recovery are not simple. The illness is very complex, as is evident from this book. There are two categories of symptoms, social and psychological. There are two categories of addiction, abstinence available and abstinence not-available, and they each have different requirements for successful restraint and abstinence. Addiction symptoms are elusive, they easily modify themselves. There is blindness to the subtle nature of addiction, polyaddiction, smokescreen recovery, and integrated addictions.

There is the cultural demonizing of some addicts, persecution of other addicts, and cultural approval of some addictions. There is often-times inappropriate medical and religious interference in a spiritual process. The transformation exercises—the homework assignments—that have to be completed, called the steps, can be confusing, especially when combined with outdated, punitive religious views and opinions of morality. Significant difficulty and failure frequently arise because of the notable dysfunction in the people who would offer help in recovery. And finally, understanding all of this complexity, helping others to understand this, and accomplishing any meaningful spiritual recovery, is exhausting. It requires significant effort, time, attention and support, compassionate guidance, patience, and personal self-discipline. It is definitely not simple.

For some people, being obedient to religious doctrine like forgiveness and prayer, living with an imposed morality, or seeing addiction as a moral deficit, can be a detriment to progress. It adds a complexity that can be quite difficult to sort out. It's difficult to find some emotional balance in the midst of all of this—being bombarded by all manner of challenging and subtle contradictory opinions. That only demonstrates how complicated addictions are and how peculiar they are to each person. This requires we must depend on fact as much as possible. (This takes us back to the importance of education in early recovery.) Becoming recovered cannot be made simple.

It is still suggested that those in recovery keep it simple. From reading the literature, what is meant by "keep it simple" is to keep your approach to all of this simple. Offer yourself patience. Find some small piece of willingness or commitment within yourself. Undertake the steps one at a time, in a simple and direct manner, in sequence. Patience and a wise mentor are required.

The steps are numbered for a reason. Don't bounce around. No going back over them again and again. Don't wander in circles through the first nine steps.

That makes it significantly more complicated and creates repetitive inadequacy. Keep it simple by developing trust in the instructions in sequence. Do what these steps tell you to do and try not to anticipate problems. Planning a spiritual future is always a long-shot-guess and easily sets up disappointment before anything happens. Life is regularly uncooperative.

Be cautious about seeking guidance from people who are chaotic, sarcastic, trapped in cliché speeches, entertainers, or poorly informed. There are a lot of them. When people circle back through the steps month after year, or attempt to address Step Three very day, do a step series every year, that makes it impossible to progress beyond repetitive inadequacy. It is evidence they don't really trust the steps to accomplish what they are supposed to, or don't trust their own efforts. They have evaluated their own level of commitment or success as inadequate. [179]

When the steps are completed as instructed, patiently, in detail, without any altering or substitutions, the benefits are quite noticeable in all areas of your life. Always remember, in addiction recovery half measures avail you nothing. Ignoring the maintenance steps and crashing around the first nine over and over again sounds like a half-measure to me.

When these were written Mr. Wilson was unaware of the overall impact these steps would have on the world. His writing from the 1960s expressed his hopes that it would have a significant impact, and it has. He managed to capture and explain an exact process that is reflected in depth psychology and parallels a few of the better spiritual disciplines around the world. It is a soft reflection of the early forms of Theravada Buddhism, through some elements of Taoism and Benedict and The Rule in the 1500s, to some of the compassionate suggestions of humanists in the twenty-first century. Mr. Wilson (indirectly) captured the essence of psychological transformation for alcoholics that exists underneath its first religious presentation. What is left for us to sift out and notice the relevant and necessary psychology (psychosocial requirements) of spiritual recovery and the related insight psychology that sits underneath the quasi-religious rhetoric of the 1930s. We now, also, have to push back from the presently-existing subtle view that permeates treatment that recovery is for socially deviant behaviour and to achieve social compliance is never the goal. (See Appendix III.)

---

179 This is repetitive inadequacy, discussed earlier, and it is more insidious than most people imagine. Education based on the facts of addiction is the only resolution strategy. There is also this: When you passed from Grade 4 into Grade 5 you managed three Cs, three Bs, and one A. You passed. Now, as you approach your third year of university there is no need to redo Grade 4 to get perfect marks. It was good enough then and it is still good enough. Sincere devotion, patience, good guidance (the literature) and a painstaking effort are good enough for completing the steps. There are safeguards for oversight in maintenance. You may say you believe and trust the program but if you repeat it once a year, do you really? I understand completing Steps One to Nine two or three times because it is a learning process, but more than three or four times is evidence of doubt. (Repetitive Inadequacy)

In some quarters of recovery programs, these steps have been substantially altered in their assigned requirements. As was written earlier, one major problem in recovery is unnecessary demands and intrusive questions too soon. The original steps, as laid out, are exceptional in that they ask for no more than is exactly required and expect no more than an addict is capable of, at any particular place in the steps, which are both crucial to successful recovery. To ask for more than is actually required or more than they are capable of, from a fear-ridden, distrusting, shame-muddled person, creates self-doubt (inadequacy), confusion, and more shame. For many subtle reasons like insecurity, arrogance, fear, repetitive inadequacy, and impatience on the part of helpers, they ask for more than is required. That is itself a set up for imposing anxiety, guilt, self-blame, anger, and (more) repetitive inadequacy on those they help.

Recovery and spiritual transformation are an exact science. There are no mysteries to this discipline. The exercises must be voluntarily self-imposed exactly as written. As Manly Hall wrote in 1928, *"The unfolding of [a person's] spiritual nature is as much an exact science as astronomy, or medicine…"*. [180] It should always be remembered there are essential psychological insights within the steps that are gained as you complete them. Whatever you are supposed to learn from any step cannot be appreciated or learned until you have thoroughly understood and absorbed all the preceding work.

It is best to follow the psychological instructions exactly. Your beliefs regarding a higher power, or not, is a choice of personal opinion that will solidify well after you are involved in step work. I will point out three things.

- If there is a struggle between God-praying vs. Spiritual Principles/ Psychology, spiritual principles and psychology always take the more important position.

- Being spiritual does not require any belief in God, nor does it require any religious doctrine. It is very feasible to be spiritual and be an atheist or a humanist (more on this later).

- In the cultural trilogy of God-Spirituality-Psychology, spirituality and healthy psychology are closer to each other than religion is to either of them.

Spiritual Heliotropism

Heliotropism is when a plant, like some tropical flowers and sunflowers, throughout each day, rotate to follow the path of the sun. It is the directional growth of some plants to follow the path of sunlight. Heliotropism is a growth

---

180   *The Secret Teaching of All Ages*, Manly Hall, p. 120. He referred to our spiritual nature not beliefs in God. You may have a belief in God, which is fine, but for recovery it is not necessary.

strategy. My experience in spiritual endeavor, especially in the sequence of the steps, is identical—it is a growth strategy. When completing any step of the first nine in the manner and sequence prescribed, and regularly participating in medi-tation on those steps as advised, I was (I am) left with three things.

The first is a fulfilled sense of meaning to the step just completed. The step itself makes sense in the independent manner it is laid down. There is an under-standing of what it means without any connection to any other step. Its psycho-logical purpose is made clear. Second, is knowing the step's importance as one piece of the larger Getting Recovered Program (the first nine steps). In perfect sequence, altogether, they take me out of addiction. Any of the first nine are only one of nine building blocks that are actually an intricate connected resolu-tion strategy to exit addiction. The third level of awareness is once recovered (in maintenance steps and spiritual principles), each of the first nine steps have a unique contribution to long-term maintenance. Each one has an intent and purpose slightly different in relation to the last three steps. Getting recovered is uniquely different from maintaining it.

It's like trusting the importance of learning the alphabet in grade two. I trust that what I learned back then about letters (analogue) was valid forever. Now the alphabet, which I never question, appears in all of my life, from reading product labels, to reading subtitles in a film, road signs, texting, negotiating complex con-tracts, understanding philosophy, to writing my books (all digital). There is never any reason for me to doubt the alphabet or relearn it. I don't have to go back and review vowels and consonants on a yearly basis.

Once the steps (one to nine) are learned and assimilated into your values and lifestyle, you end up in maintenance; deepening your spiritual perspectives to life. There is never any reason to doubt the first nine or return to any of them. They are permanent underpinnings to being recovered. They are like the alphabet is to writing words; they become understood as having been the training ground for maintenance and the foundation of everything in a spiritual life.

There are built-in safeguards when Steps Ten, Eleven, and Twelve become an internal self-discipline. When approached in that manner, there is never any reason to wander through those nine steps again and again. That repetition is, itself, an indication of lack of trust or doubt, often brought on by repetitive inad-equacy or faulty counsel from others. [181]

When the steps are completed and trusted, people will become naturally curious about what comes next—a spiritual heliotropism to explore the next step and go there. There never needs to be any external or internal demand put upon ourselves to push ahead. We never have to force ourselves into "prog-ress." (Actually, forcing yourself into spiritual progress isn't spiritual or progress.) However, within the maintenance steps there is no pushing ahead, there's

---

181 I do understand that repeating the first nine two or three times may be necessary, after all it is a strong learning curve. Still, repeating them after ten of fifteen attempts indicates something, but it isn't trust or faith in the program or confidence in yourself.

nowhere else to go. What happens in "maintenance" is becoming curious about the intricate relationship between those three steps and the depth of serenity that is possible. Rest quietly with their efficiency in problem prevention. Spiritual heliotropism—there is a spiritual curiosity that draws you on with confidence.

Sharing at Meetings

The suggested guidelines for sharing at meetings, according to the AA literature, are:

(i) We share in a general way what we used to be like, what happened, and what we are like now—1/3 for each (not what *it* was like and not what other people did). That would exclude long, boring stories of our chaotic autobiography.

(ii) We must drop the word blame from our speech and thought.

(iii) We explain our own spiritual awakening—how we have changed as the result of these steps and the value of commitment to the step instructions. [182]

Yes, it's boring.

Don't complain or report on how you are being treated by anyone. No gossip about others; no inventory-taking of anyone else. No direct details of how you are so let down and misunderstood by others. Practice silence about any member of your family, spousal units, in-laws, out-laws, workmates, people on the bus, other programs, therapy, diets, sex, dating, citizens of the commonwealth, ex-spouses (or their lawyers), the police, or sponsors who act like the police. Practice compassion and acceptance about other addicts and their addictions, about other groups or program members, authors of books, or anyone's obnoxious behaviour. Practice silence about religious commitments, atheists, or outside organizations and events. Take what you like and leave the rest. [183]

You should very rarely talk about your drinking or acting out at the meeting/public level. It's boring. We've heard it all before, and you're being a martyr, looking for sympathy, or trying to impress someone with your heroic struggles.

---

182 These are my words for the guidelines found in *Alcoholics Anonymous* (p. 58/59), and in *Twelve Steps and Twelve Traditions*, in that book's chapters on Steps Four and Twelve. The guidelines of Step Twelve may be the most ignored suggestion in all of recovery. Sharing is examined in more detail in *Spiritual Transformation*.

183 This is intended for guidelines and values in spiritual recovery. We all have opinions and passions run high. Be careful in discussions about any emotionally charged subjects or how recovery works and how society should manage itself.

Public degradation or showing off about how "bad" you were or the calamities you have survived (with details!) are not recovery.

Your intimate history, which is important, is to be a private conversation with a trusted advisor who should be advising you to avoid this at a public level. Yes, details in proper therapy, but there is no progress in long-winded survival stories. If you are a sponsor, never talk about who you sponsor. Again, in confidential, private conversation with your own mentor about how you sponsor, but never publicly and never in any detail about who you help. If you do, that's a betrayal of trust and anonymity.

Refer only to yourself and your relationship to the steps and your personal effort and struggles about rigorous honesty, letting go of old ideas, and how you take responsibility for your life. Sponsors role-model spiritual behaviour and explain the benefits of the steps. That is Step Twelve.

Anything other than that is gossip, bragging, complaining about suffering, righteousness, seeking some degree of sympathy, trying to impress someone, or making yourself a martyr. This is the hubris of making ourselves the hero of our recovery story. "Let me tell you, in glorious detail, my opinions about how I have suffered and faced daily calamity. Gather around one-and-all and hear my tale of woe. I have overcome all odds...!" This should not be at a meeting or public level. Support and direct explanations of your interpretation of the steps? Yes. Advice and complaining? No.

It is not okay to talk in a general way about "them"—anyone them. Complaining and gossip about others like workmates, bad drivers, encounters with drinkers, irresponsible pet owners, ex- or present spouses, bad traffic, other addicts, or family, is rampant in meetings and goes unchallenged. Those "others" are never there to defend themselves and it's only your biased opinion.

The general meeting rule, which is reasonably well observed within twelve-step groups, is no cross-talk or commentary about other people's sharing. Interesting that no cross-talk or commentary is one of the more respected rules which then enables the insidious, irresponsible gossip that pervades meetings. None of the wiser members can say anything about improper sharing. To point out the damaging and unspiritual nature of this complaining gossip in a meeting would break the rule of no cross-talk. How convenient to enforce a rule that defeats spirituality and allows unspiritual behaviour in a program that is supposed to be spiritual. Acting like alcoholics and pretending to be in recovery; how convenient. This is evidence of how meetings have become very dysfunctional therapy groups.

To share about chaos and personal struggles, in any great detail, is necessary but only for the trusted ear of a professional or your sponsor/spiritual advisor, and only then if they can keep a confidence. Recovery meetings are not therapy groups and people are not to discuss other people or brag about their heroic suffering and struggles. Briefly, yes, but always include information on a step or spiritual principle used to stop that personal hubris.

"*Having had a spiritual awakening as the result of these steps, we tried to carry this message to alcoholics and to practice these principles...*" (Step Twelve). That is a very straight forward guideline and probably the most ignored instruction in all the literature. Here it is backwards: We tried to explain to alcoholic people, who wanted an explanation, that we had a personality change and stayed sober and "relatively serene" because we did these steps. We remain committed to being honest and responsible in our lives. (Sounds boring.) That has nothing to do with itemizing the shortcomings of stubborn drunk relatives, rude bosses, unruly kids, barking dogs, sleeping with strangers, or bad drivers.

There are many honest, emotionally moving, ordinary stories of success through commitment. They are, by implication, demeaned by the grand tales of debauchery, violence, abuse, failure, trainloads of alcohol, degradation, escapades of crime, and vainglorious suffering and relapses. When recast as humor or presented as the drama of recovery these are seriously damaging. When you hear them, don't laugh. Flamboyance defeats spirituality and creates isolation. The tellers are expressing deep insecurity and shame. They need compassion and guidance in a confidential manner, not applause at a public level. Humorous stories of your embarrassment in recovery bring a quiet laugh of identification and that is wise.

Never say "we" in carrying the message. That means, by definition, you aren't sharing, you're imposing your interpretations and beliefs on others. In a convoluted way you may also be soliciting sympathy. Your experience of recovery is yours and should not include others in your beliefs and opinions. Let others choose to identify with your story by its personal presentation. When you say "we" some will think "me too," others won't. Do not imply that you are smart enough for everyone because your general opinion about "we" is assumed to be accurate. That is the imposition of your opinion on everyone else's truth. The intensity and difficulty of recovery, beliefs, perceptions, and misdemeanors of anyone else will be different from yours and your opinions should not be suggested as any kind of universal truth.

Fellowship is not the solution. Meetings are not a collective social agreement. Holding hands in a circle for the serenity prayer makes it a glee-club chant, not a prayer. I suppose as much as we all "want" to be like everyone else, fit in, and have a friendly peer group, all participants are very unique and whatever is said about "everyone" is sure to be wrong for someone. The underlying fact for people in recovery is if you are gossiping, complaining, imposing your opinions, or including everyone by declaring "we are all this or that," you are in irresponsible judgement. This ignores the guideline that you are not to take anyone's inventory and are not being responsible, accepting, or spiritual. Step Twelve is so restricted in its focus that sharing has to stay quietly personal about your changing personality to avoid a community collective voice, which is fatal to a spiritual lifestyle. Quietly tell only your story in the first person (grammar) and let others decide if they want to share your ideas.

The fact that you slept in a ditch with or without a gun, sold your body, got in 987 fights or no fights, gambled away all your money, drank in the closet, were divorced, liked wine not scotch, abandoned your kids or had no kids—any or all of this should be mentioned in no great detail and only in brief passing. Never share anything at a meeting you wouldn't want on the six o'clock twelve-step news. Expecting confidentiality or respect from a group of unknown strangers, in a casual social setting, in a gossip-laden community, with a proven background of dishonesty, resentment and blame, is unwise bordering on foolish. Again, it is wise to discuss this in detail for personal insight but that is only for the trusted ear of a well-informed mentor, spiritual advisor, or therapist.

In three parts: Share mediocre, brief, general stories about your past personality: dishonest, mean, angry, lonely, depressed, selfish, arrogant, etc. That's what you were like. Mention briefly "drunk stories," your hard-core junkie stories, your sex escapades, jail time, perpetual job loss, spending sprees, or crime, and never in glorious detail. Talk very little about this at a public level. These are for the ear of a trustworthy mentor, spiritual advisor, or a therapist. Public bragging or complaining has no merit in pursuing a spiritual lifestyle. Talk also in some detail about what happened to get you commit to this lifestyle. What happened to make you change your mind? And finally, talk in more detail about doing each of the steps and how that is the key to everything: "Having had a spiritual awakening as the result of these steps..." . [184]

People are in recovery to understand their emotional turmoil, relationship conflict, the path of the steps, and to take responsibility for conflict in a spiritual manner, not to aggrandize their debauchery, martyrdom, or suffering. There are three reasons for this. (1) There can be no humility in bragging or making yourself out a hero, and especially no humility or spirituality in being an entertainer. (2) Our memories are often flawed, exaggerated or minimized. Keeping stories to a minimum helps to avoid inaccuracies. (3) During our drinking or acting out we did enough degrading or embarrassing things. There is no need to continue that by debasing ourselves in our stories. There is a lot of gossip in and around meetings. Gossip is inaccurate and unkind. Protect your dignity.

Serenity is determined by your work on the steps, not your ability to tell stories or make jokes. Stay focused on personal commitment to the steps. Share about what happened in the transition from being drunk or stoned; from general acting out to "I'm now in a program." Remember that as soon as you introduce yourself as an addict or alcoholic you have qualified yourself. You don't have to

---

184 Many of us are so damaged it will take many years to accomplish recovery. Be patient. Abstinence and successful restraint at all costs. If you do relapse get back into meetings/recovery as soon as possible. That is very important, but it's more important to not relapse in the first place. Don't leave and come back, just stay. For new people, sharing gory detail and bad behaviour may be all they have to talk about—the damage and corruption. Keep that part very brief at the public level and talk about gratitude for the program, the opportunity you have taken advantage of, and your successes at whatever changes you have made.

prove it by example. Explain how you achieved successful abstinence. You'll get more out of it, so will they.

Telling acting out stories isn't the solution it's living in the past. Living in the past and gossiping about others isn't carrying the message, it demonstrates an addiction mindset. These defeat the ability to live in the solution, which are the steps and spiritual principles. Talking about the steps and your work on them has no flamboyance in it. Rigorous honesty, never blaming, letting go of old ideas, etc., is carrying the message and it's rather boring.

Talk about what you did to affect your spiritual transformation: reading literature, calling sponsors or being one, socializing with program friends, devotion to abstinence, service work, studying the literature and other meditation. Share your "silly stories" about recovery which goes a lot farther than detailing debauchery. Tell about your studying the approved literature and how hard it is to do what you're told according to the steps. Especially talk about your struggles with rigorous honesty and acceptance. Never share anything about anyone else.

Share what you are like now: more honest, less mean, not as angry, less lonely and depressed, not so selfish, maybe less arrogant, more accepting, etc. Not so scared, not as suicidal, more friendly, more insightful, more responsible, more caring and generous... that's what you are like now. And it's from praying (if you do that), meditation (for everyone in the style of Step Eleven), being honest, responsible, participating, being committed, and completing the steps as instructed. Page 107 of *Twelve Steps and Twelve Traditions* refers; notice the line that begins: *"He has been set on a path..."*.

Hugging at meetings is optional. If you are uncomfortable with it or suspect some ulterior motive, say no to it. That is your right. Here are three reminders about sharing at meetings:

(1) **Never** talk about "they" or "them" or anyone other than yourself unless it's a brief reference to someone who was kind and supportive. We must drop the word blame from our speech and thought. Don't gossip. Don't refer to "we" in your personal story. Using "we" assumes you know everything about other people and are including them, not knowing if they want to be included. Maybe your "we" doesn't apply to them. Let others decide where they belong without you taking their inventory.

(2) **Never** relate details of anyone else's story, including people that you encounter outside of meetings socially or social incidents that, in telling, may demean or be embarrassing to them. Don't discuss another's character or that you hear Step Fours (called Step Five). Don't ever attempt humor at some else's expense.

(3) **Never** say anything publicly you don't want on the six o'clock AA news.

Sponsorship

"*So cooperate; never criticize,*" which is a pretty tall order for alcoholics and addicts, even sponsors, whom, I understand, are to share only their experience, strength, and hope (which does not include making up recovery rules and imposing their opinions). It's amazing how, in the midst of a conversation that is called "fellowship" or sponsorship, or sharing, so many people conveniently forget the injunction to never criticize.

A sponsor is a person who is supposed to do special and important work, called sponsorship, with a charitable spirit and without fanfare. Without fanfare includes not dropping hints about how hard you work or how many you sponsor or how many hours you spend on the phone, or how many you saved with your prescient insight. Most of that is a variation of bragging. Sponsors shouldn't speak at meetings about sponsoring people. There's no valid reason to. [185]

Sponsorship or mentorship is working with others. Fair enough. As a mentor: Never force yourself or your opinions upon anyone. Don't moralize and lecture or dwell on the hopeless feature of the malady. Discuss this as an illness with explanations of how you got well. Use everyday language, not religious language. Share how you straightened out your past, not what a bad person you were. Remember your way is not going to be their way. Never talk down to anyone or impose your values. Encourage others to develop their own spiritual conscience. It is a waste of time to keep chasing someone; they want what you have, or they don't. Do not participate or take sides in any quarrels in their life. Especially do not give advice that you are not competent to give or should not give at all. Don't make up suggestions that are not in the literature. [186]

It would appear logical that sponsors would willingly adhere to the tenets of the twelve steps and encourage but never demand similar behaviour from those they help. "*You can help when no one else can.*" "*You can secure their confidence when others fail.*" "*...you can be uniquely useful to other alcoholics.*" Side Note: That is not confidence in you but confidence in the program. I suppose in a perfect world, new people could be made to understand that it is trust of the sponsor and confidence in the program's guidelines. [187]

---

185 Gossiping at meetings is usually safe. There's "no crosstalk" so you won't be challenged about this unspiritual behaviour, and because those people you're analyzing, or criticizing, aren't there to defend themselves. Interesting how many of us like to pretend we're generally innocent and have good intentions when we trash someone's character. Sponsor: a person taking responsibility or who pledges support for another or an organization. Mentor: an experienced and trusted advisor who counsels others. Sponsorship was appropriate in the early decades of AA; introduction into a hard-to-find, closed group. It is not appropriate now. Mentorship is somewhat more suitable.

186 *Alcoholics Anonymous*, pp. 90-97, and *Twelve Steps and Twelve Traditions*, p. 111.

187 *Alcoholics Anonymous*, pp. 89.

A mentor has an important and significant obligation to strive for genuine integrity. When a sponsor, or a therapist or mentor lives with conflicted values and spiritual negligence, are themselves unethical, or participate in any culturally approved addiction, those they help will not be able to get recovered. It's difficult enough to face alcohol or other abstinence, or successful restraint in abstinence not-available addictions, the steps, and spirituality without having to negotiate through hypocrisy in people who hold themselves out as helpers. In circumstances where the sponsor has questionable integrity, to hold the newcomer responsible for all their difficulty is reprehensible and ignores the program injunction to never blame. [188]

Share your experience (through the steps), strength (belief in the program), and hope (for more serenity in the future). Do not share your opinions. If you do offer an opinion be very clear that's what it is and any cooperation with it is optional. Disagreement with your opinion cannot carry censure. Rather than dispensing advice, demonstrate your own obedience to spiritual principles. Never demand compliance from anyone. When you offer advice or create and impose rules you go from sponsor to parent or personality consultant. Sponsors and mentors in recovery are not personality consultants or relationship advisors. [189]

When a sponsor shares their experience, strength, and hope they remain a sponsor. Sponsors can't really go wrong if they gently guide all discussions and efforts back to spiritual principles—some relevant passage from the AA reference texts. It's not up to the sponsor to solve the other person's problems. A sponsor doesn't have to be precocious, prescient, wise, powerful, entertaining, or amazing, they have to be compassionate and willing to follow the instructions.

The mentor's "job" is to (a) teach problem prevention via spiritual principles, (b) demonstrate spiritually-focused problem solving when necessary; and (c), to point out to those they help how to identify any relevant literature guidelines when completing the steps. Eventually, new people should not depend on the sponsor or meetings. Sponsors show other people how to depend on the original literature and the truths embodied in that. Spiritual transformation and that lifestyle is an inside job, dependent on adherence to the maintenance steps and

---

188 *Twelve Steps and Twelve Traditions*, p. 47. *"Where other people were concerned, we had to drop the word "blame" from our speech and thought."* Complaining is indirect blaming.

189 A mentor's job (or therapist, for that matter) is to make themselves and the other person a little uncomfortable by always reaching for higher and better spiritual possibilities. The decision to participate or not, and to what degree, always rests with the individual. In fact, anyone in recovery or those recovered, either wants what the program offers, or they don't. The potential for very deep spiritual serenity is there. There is nothing to argue and no pressure or cajoling required. The usual mentor/sponsor is not your friend and shouldn't behave as if they are. If they are your friend they can't do their job because of the political investment in a friendship. But at the same time, as they gently push you "forward" out of your comfort zone, they are also to make you feel safe and respected during your awkward transition. Fun eh?

self-discipline. It is not dependent on anything external. Opinions about higher powers (or not) are never subjects for debate.

There's no place for arguing when carrying the message. None. The mentor demonstrates sincere spiritual behaviour (acceptance, responsibility, compassion, honesty). They share their experience (re: getting sober and becoming committed), strength (in trusting the instructions), and hope (to have more serenity and to help others). The other person either wants what they have, or they don't. What's to argue?

Bill Wilson, *et al*, discovered the process and wrote *Alcoholics Anonymous* and *Twelve Steps and Twelve Traditions*. Underneath the 1939, historical Christian focus, and with the inclusion of relevant cultural developments and psychology over the intervening generations, it has proven itself time and time again.

Be patient. Understand clearly this is an illness not a disease or moral deficit. Find and trust a sincere spiritual mentor. Follow the instructions without proclaiming any rhetoric about God. Whatever you believe Do thoroughly what is suggested. Whether or not people adhere to the instructions is for them to decide. Their ideas about higher powers are always opinions and their level of commitment is for them to decide. *"Rarely have we seen a person fail who has thoroughly followed our path."* (From *Alcoholics* Anonymous, p. 58). Following the path is most successful when that choice to follow it is freely made without coercion, doom-and-gloom rhetoric, and without opinion. After quite a bit of hard work, all will be well.

> *"If one cannot state a matter clearly enough so that even an intelligent twelve-year-old can understand it, one should remain within the cloistered walls of the university until one gets a better grasp of one's subject matter."*
>
> Margaret Mead [190]

---

190 As quoted in *If Ignorance Is Bliss, Why Aren't there More Happy People?* Ed.: John Lloyd & John Mitchinson, Advanced Banter Press, 2008, p. 98.

Chapter 6

Emotion & Communication

Applied Problem Solving in Personal Relationships

As is pointed out in Step Eight, and discussed elsewhere, broken relationships and dislocation are a principle antecedent cause of addiction and relapse. This is at all levels from family relationships, through intimate relationships, to friends and business relationships. From this, addicts are afraid of people, especially afraid of intimacy, terrified of honesty (offering or receiving it), and generally incapable of responsibility or trust. There are many aspects to this nasty relationship chaos that society is in. In addiction there's conflict in all relationships and, as outlined earlier, everything is relationship.

One part of inept communication comes from the inability of people to listen. Many people don't actually listen, they wait for the next opportunity to talk, to criticize, or defend themselves. There's impatience from significant others, which is often silent: I'm busy; I only have a few minutes. I'd rather be doing something else. Here we go again I've heard this before. Say something intelligent for a change. This isn't interesting. Don't bother me with this. People sense this and are hurt by other's impatience and patronizing, subtle insincerity but cannot challenge it or protect themselves from it. Received criticism or the imposition of guilt, or any presentation of superiority, generates arguing and defensiveness. [It's painful to wander through life always defending yourself before you are attacked.] That's the game of this culture.

Impatience, exasperation, criticism, and the imposing of guilt (blaming) are often sensed and are evidence of disrespect and disinterest—not caring. These contain a built-in attitude that (my) time is being wasted (by you) by your repetitious and irresponsible behaviour. Addicts cannot protect themselves from this in early recovery. Remember, what you love is what you give your time to and recovery requires time and compassion.

Other chaos in communication is from the inability of addicts to talk openly with congruence. Their interior life is a bewildering muddle of contradiction, fear, shame, guilt, and cognitive dissonance. They are incapable of being clear on what they think, feel, believe, or value—they just don't know. Addicts are unsure and they ramble on, change their mind, and resort to cliché recovery conversation.

In quiet reflection, picture an over-view of how complicated addiction is—what you have read thus far: The punitive rejection of some addicts by society because they are "morally deviant." Socially imposed shame and guilt. Rampant power mongering and greed in politics and big business. The psychological symptoms, especially cognitive dissonance. The types of addiction, with cultural encouragement of some and condemnation of others. There's identity conflict (explained at footnote 112), the fusion of fear, shame, and internally imposed guilt, repetitive inadequacy, the abuse and chaos in religion, an inability of addicts to think clearly, the terror of honesty, and the inability to create boundaries or self-protect. In the middle of all of that, try and stay sober.

All of this is <u>very</u> overwhelming, which is why people resort to cliché communication—they dance around this disordered complexity with a bare modicum of honesty. They try to say, without sounding stupid, "I am not this addict person; I am but not really. I don't know what happened, who I am, how I got here, or what to do about it. I do want to be someone else, but I don't know how I get to where I don't know that I want to go." I have heard ten-thousand times, "Do you understand what I'm trying to say?", and ten-thousand other times, "I am sorry I am not clear about this." Clichés are a safer, even if inefficient, way to try and make sense of this.

This society is terrified of honesty, of being known, and quite afraid of being held accountable for our abuses. Part of this evasiveness is related to repetitive inadequacy—even if everyone was honest, most of us would resort to defensive blame and wouldn't know what to do with the honesty, anyway.

There's the built-in scheme for addicts and other fear-shame-based or righteous people, that not communicating is a safety measure. Silence is self-protection. They can't be challenged or disagreed with if they say nothing. Being evasive, saying little, speaking in vague clichés, are always a guarantee that any conflict will be resolved in your favor in your own mind. Mentally, everything ends to your satisfaction. If you create an honest, open dialogue you will be held accountable and might not get your own way. So, say nothing and win all the debates.

In a short-form view of this: People hide and destroy themselves in addiction because of their general inability to create healthy, honest, respectful relationships and maintain them. All of the concerns that have been discussed to this point: sexuality, religion, atheism, culture, addiction, developmental dependency needs, cognitive dissonance, honesty, "the steps," sponsors, therapists, fear, guilt, shame, inadequacy, <u>all</u> of these are issues of relationship. Poor communication is a major contributing factor to failed relationships and failed relationships are the major contributing factor to failed recovery.

Oftentimes people are at a loss and seriously distressed because they have looked for answers and found none that were relevant. Their efforts were met with opinions, disapproval, and social ostracism when endeavoring to make serious changes to themselves or their lifestyle. Good communication, which is actually applied problem solving in relationships in real time, can be risky, but it is a major contributing factor to the resolution of many existing problems. Good communication goes a long way to problem prevention. The better people can listen on a deeply non-judgmental level the better addicts will communicate and then the dynamic of healing will be present. Please do not underestimate the importance of what's in this chapter as regards healthy relationship.

Part 1 – Emotion
We Cannot Not Have Feelings

It's important to know and remember that we can't not have feelings. People can't choose not to experience emotion. Certainly, if a person spends years and years hiding their feelings it will seem like they don't have any emotions at all, but they do. With some people it may seem like all they ever have is one emotion—angry all the time, nothing else—just angry. Someone else seems depressed all the time. Yes, we can choose to hide, translate, or minimize feelings but we can't not have them.

Experiencing emotion is the result of chemical changes in our bodies and, depending on what the emotion is, it signals us to do something. Symbolically and literally, having feelings means to be disturbed and to be moved to do something. Emotions prepare your body for some type of action. They are energy demanding attention within yourself. We are supposed to "move" with our feelings.

The word emotion comes from the French word *esmovoir*, which itself comes from the Latin word *exmovere*.

EX - MOVERE — *ex...* (to disturb); *movere...* (to move away)
Fear is the emotion that moves you to **run away**.
Anger is the emotion that moves you to **protect** yourself.
Nervous is the emotion that moves you to **caution**.
Joy is the emotion that moves you to **celebrate** life.
Happiness is the emotion that moves you to **play**.
Sadness is the emotion that moves you to **cry**.

Responding appropriately to your emotions is what animates your body and indicates you are alive. Not responding to emotion is being frozen. Having a very limited range of emotional expression is being "emotionally shackled." Be aware of the distinctions between having feelings (we all have feelings—no choice) and acting on feelings (a choice of how we act) and responding appropriately to feelings (respect and personal self-care).

Anger has been getting a lot of press in the last fifty years. Anger is one of our emotions that cannot exist independent of other emotions. When anyone feels angry, they will also be experiencing another emotion hidden by the anger.

The anger will often make the other emotion invisible. This second feeling is always some derivative of fear, shame, impatience, a sense of entitlement, overwhelmed, etc.

When you feel angry search within yourself to identify what other emotion motivates it. Address the other emotion, not the anger. Stop blaming. In this way, reacting with anger will eventually become optional.

Myths About Anger

From ancient times, various cultures and philosophers had perceived anger as unhealthy—a loss of face, dangerous to express, a thing that will complicate issues, cause trouble, and cloud the mind from reason. This changed with some of the observations of Charles Darwin (c. 1850) and the subsequent research into sociology. [191]

There are two kinds of anger. There is instinctual/survival anger and cultural anger. This is about cultural anger, which is a product of our self-esteem, attitudes, values, and cultural education. It's especially how strongly we believe we are supposed to get our own way and blame and condemn others when we don't—an exaggerated sense of entitlement, which is overwhelmingly common. These myths are about cultural anger and need to be examined.

Myth #1 - Anger is an essential emotion that we must live with.
Anger is different in different cultures. Some people are quite successful having very little or no anger. Reacting with anger and expressing it is a choice. We are taught that having power and getting our own way is good. Cultural anger is an effort to dominate some situation you disagree with. It is often emotional abuse and we can learn to live without it. Anger is a method to get your own way—to intimidate someone into giving you what you want. This is culturally learned behavior, which means it can be unlearned. Anger is not an emotion that we must be controlled by.

Myth #2 - If a little anger doesn't work, then a lot will.
Believing "more is better" is a fundamental gimmick of our culture. It doesn't work in the case of anger. When you become angrier (pushing yourself from annoyed to furious) you are simply trying to intimidate or control the situation and attempting to get your own way. Anger that is used to dominate people and situations is damaging to everyone concerned. Stop punishing people and

---

191 If you are serious about eliminating anger, I encourage you to find and study *Anger the Misunderstood Emotion*, Carol Tavris, Simon & Schuster, Inc. 1989, and *Taking Responsibility*, Nathaniel Brandon, cited earlier. Albert Ellis' book *Anger, how to live with and without it* is also a valuable read.

pouting when you don't get your own way. This should not be confused with anger when protecting yourself from physical harm.

Myth #3 - People learn from experience.

If this were true people wouldn't get into destructive relationships time after time. Without new problem-solving skills and insight, which for the most part are learned by careful self-examination and taking responsibility, personal experience usually only allows people to go around in circles. Regarding emotions, talking about them and gathering new information (outside of your experience) is what you need to break the cycle. Experience isn't necessarily the best teacher.

Myth #4 - Old habits and attitudes require a long time to change.

This myth arose in various contexts, one of which is early psychoanalysis. Theories were being developed, a lot was experimental, and yes, therapy can take a long time. This isn't about therapy, it's about anger. The slow progress that some people make in reducing anger is a reflection of their willingness and how effective anger has been to help them get their own way.

Cultural anger always comes back to personal responsibility. The fact is, once you acquire new information about anger, you will change as fast as you want to. Often people will exaggerate their difficulty as an excuse to avoid change. You will either do it or you won't. There's a cycle here. The more you tell yourself it's difficult, the more reluctant and fearful you are. It's the same thing with abstinence or quitting smoking, or leaving an abusive relationship, you can scare yourself out of it.

Myth #5 - You cannot remain competent in a stressful situation.

That depends on what you believe about your feelings and your responses to them. If other people are responsible for your feelings (living with an external locus of control, i.e. being subservient to others) that will dictate whether or not you "lose it." When you are in charge of your emotions, an internal locus of control, you can influence your responses to circumstances. Remaining competent in a stressful situation often depends on your belief about who's in charge of you.

Myth #6 - Everyone has a breaking point.

Yes, maybe as a prisoner and subjected to psychological or physical torture, and yes, if you repress the emotions underneath anger or exaggerate everything by drama and blame. No matter how much you wish you weren't, you are always in charge of you. Personality is a matter of moment-to-moment choices that are made in the routine situations of everyday life. Who you are today is from the decisions you made yesterday. If you decide you can't handle it, or ignore difficult choices, you won't. If you believe you can handle it and promptly use the skills, you will.

Myth #7 - Anger cannot be eliminated.

An infant spills a glass of water and you smile and wipe it up. A teenager spills a glass of water and you're angry. Think of the many times you wanted to be angry but weren't because you knew it wouldn't work. Dealing with various authority figures often requires anger self-management. Withholding anger in one situation and then later spewing it all over someone else is abuse. People don't like to admit that their anger is always a selective process that they use to their advantage. Choosing to be angry allows choosing to be not angry.

Myth # 8 - An eye for an eye is best—fight anger with anger.

The majority of the time when you get angry with someone, they become angry or are secretly resentful. Manipulation and revenge are frequently the long-range cost. Using anger to fight anger always entrenches the conflict. Cultural anger is always wounding. Using anger to fight anger escalates the conflict and complicates the issues.

Myth #9 - The real reasons for anger are from your childhood.

This is externalizing responsibility for your anger and selfish attitudes and blaming your childhood or parents. This may be a good reason for therapy but it's a poor excuse for an unfulfilled life. It's never an excuse for abuse which ends up in a blaming/guilt cycle. Yes, it can be important to discuss the past for clarity and understanding and to achieve some emotional healing. That's a complex issue of therapy. You can still reduce anger without blaming your past.

Myth #10 - Angry people are mentally ill.

Yes, a few angry people are mentally ill. If you believe cultural anger is valid (i.e. angry because you didn't get your parking spot) that's a belief that supports entitlement. It justifies anger in people who advocate for privilege, power, and aggression. Anger is not an issue of insanity. Angry people are playing at a dominance game.

Don't approve of anger, your own or others', and don't routinely accept it in your life. If you do approve of anger it will be used against you and your life will be reduced to a struggle for control and retaliation. People who live a life generally governed by sarcasm, resentment, abusive humor, or anger can never embrace compassion and cannot live a spiritual life. The uncomfortable fact is, it is easier to justify anger than to take responsibility for it.

Good collaboration skills, accepting responsibility, believing in equal entitlement, and teaching ourselves it is fine to not get our own way, will go farther to eliminating anger than mental hospitals and medication. Decide to give up your anger—just stop expressing anger and look for the emotion associated with the anger. [192] Here it is…

#1 - Take complete responsibility for yourself, your anger and rage, aggression, judgements, inappropriate behaviour, sarcasm, and menacing threats to frighten people. These are your choice to abuse others and are all completely your responsibility. Your expressions of passive rage and manipulation and your sense of entitlement are all your responsibility. [193] #2 - Learn about the range of your emotions and develop an inner sensitiveness to what they are. Know your feelings and be aware of what they are telling you to do. #3 - Learn to use feedback as a communication skill rather than using anger as a control tactic (explained later).

In the following volcano metaphor, I offer a theory about escalating emotions and feedback. It is a metaphor that helps you focus away from anger onto the associated emotion. There is a sequence shown in the image.

There are the basic emotions, at the bottom, like fear, shame, jealousy, loneliness, etc. and the immediate opportunity to discuss these by offering feedback. This often prevents escalation into arguing and abuse. Without feedback, or intervention at this lowest level of internal turmoil, the original emotion is then escalated into anger and that anger becomes the dominate feeling. This will quickly lead to the denial of personal rights and abuse as listed in Chapter 4.

In the middle of the escalation there are control issues—a psychological point of view, within someone, that requires them to manipulate a given situation so that they are in charge of what happens. There is self-talk meaning the silent dialogue that goes on in someone's mind—what they think to themselves. And, there are the influences of socialization and culture meaning how people are molded by the values, rules, and imposed expectations of our society and culture. For any number of reasons this leads to acting out. This sequence can happen in two minutes or three months.

---

192 This is in the arena of ordinary relationships, not in the shadowy area of psychopathology.

193 A quiet surliness or lack of interest in the welfare of others is often the expression of being emotionally frozen. There is unaddressed anger and punishment expressed in this selfishness.

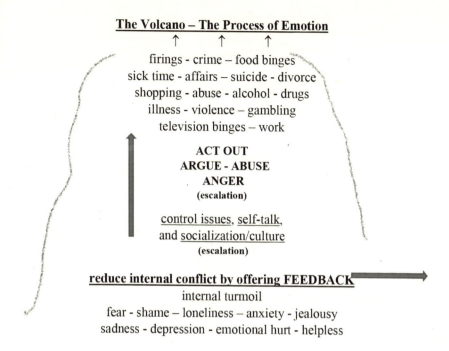

The Volcano – The Process of Emotion

↑   ↑   ↑

firings - crime – food binges
sick time - affairs – suicide - divorce
shopping - abuse - alcohol - drugs
illness - violence – gambling
television binges – work

ACT OUT
ARGUE - ABUSE
ANGER
(escalation)

control issues, self-talk,
and socialization/culture
(escalation)

reduce internal conflict by offering FEEDBACK

internal turmoil
fear - shame – loneliness – anxiety - jealousy
sadness - depression - emotional hurt - helpless

Knowing that you are not a victim of addiction as a personal punishment, and taking responsibility for yourself, is a matter of believing that whatever state your life is in is your fault. That is the first rule of being spiritual. If you are in an abusive relationship, you put yourself in it, get yourself out. If you complain your partner is a liar, you are dating the liar, move away from that. If you are married to an adulterer, you married them, get yourself out of it. If you're complaining your spouse is repeatedly financially irresponsible, you married them, deal with your irresponsibility for being there, not theirs. Get yourself out of it. If your lover or "closest" friend is angry, abusive, disrespectful, you volunteered to be there, volunteer yourself out of it.

Outside of random calamity (like earthquakes and plane crashes) your life is your fault. The joys and successes are also yours to appreciate. Even after random calamity, you are responsible to clean up the mess. (Fun, eh?) Pat yourself on the back for your life—you did it all by yourself.

Feelings

This exercise will require effort and discipline. You should know how your emotions show up, what they are, and what they want you to do. Remember an emotion moves you to do something. This should be natural, but the majority

166

of us have been well trained to translate our emotions like sadness, loneliness, anxiety, fear, or shame, into an aggression emotion like rage, disapproval, racism, jealousy, judgement, sexism, anger and criticism. Or we suppress or deny them as in some types of depression. Here's a few common emotions:

Fear	Nervous	Calm	Joyful
Anger	Peaceful	Anxious	Happy
Irate	Safe	Serene	Grief
Ashamed	Irritated	Pleasure	Despair
Embarrassed	Shy	Lonely	Worried
Sad	Content	Self-conscious	Jealous

There are variations of these, but this is a good start. Look these up in a dictionary. Learn what they mean. Imagine yourself feeling that feeling. What does that emotion move you to do? Imagine a situation where you would feel that emotion. Look for it in movies and watch actors act it. When it's anger, identify and examine what the associated emotion is. Monitor yourself frequently. Learn about the range of emotions that you feel throughout the day and notice what provoked them.

Emotional Deafness and Emotional First Aid

People suffer from unaddressed emotional wounds. We have all experienced an emotional wound at some time in our lives. When people are emotionally hurt **emotional deafness** happens. They can't hear things that are said to them—the emotional pain overrides thinking and hearing.

In order to begin helping someone who is in a lot of emotional pain you first have to help reduce the emotional deafness. Telling them to forget their pain, to ignore it, to demand they stop, or it's the wrong feeling, never works. In fact, giving instructions will make it worse. A person has an "emotional injury" that must be attended to. In order to help them you have to give emotional first aid.

Emotional first aid is a way of helping someone heal from an emotional wound. It's similar to regular first aid, except you are dealing with an emotional rather than a physical wound. Sincerely demonstrating the skill of Emotional First Aid will help. What you do is:

1) Acknowledge and recognize the other person's emotional pain. It's real to them. It doesn't matter that you can't understand it or might disagree with it. It's important that you let them have their feelings—recognize their feeling and accept the person. You don't have to agree with either them or the feeling, just offer respect. Clarification or discussion can come well after the fact.

2) Make an effort to understand the emotion and the situation from their point of view. Their perceptions are true for them. Work at seeing it their way and let them be aware that you are respecting their point of view.

3) Communicate to them, in a supportive way, your acknowledgment of what they are experiencing. Communicate this without guile. Be calm, don't speak too much. Keep your own judgments out of it.

Everyone is entitled to their own feelings. That may make you uncomfortable but that's the way it is. One of the ways to cause trouble in a relationship is to control someone by suggesting, demanding or hinting that they change their feelings. Telling a person what to feel, what not to feel, or how much to feel; advising them to cheer up or settle down; suggesting it's about time they "let it go", or disagreeing with their feelings, will get you into trouble. (There may be a very few situations in carefully conducted therapy where planned instruction may be necessary.) Do not control, manipulate, limit, suppress, minimize, or exaggerate another person's feelings.

Perceptions [194]

Our perceptions are related to how we think, our attitudes, prejudices, beliefs and social learning; what's in our mind. We experience life at #1. Everything is then assessed and evaluated at #2, and the cycle begins.

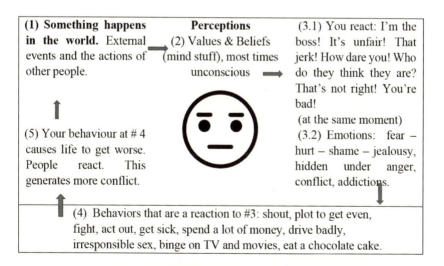

(1) Something happens in the world. External events and the actions of other people.

Perceptions
(2) Values & Beliefs (mind stuff), most times unconscious

(3.1) You react: I'm the boss! It's unfair! That jerk! How dare you! Who do they think they are? That's not right! You're bad!
(at the same moment)
(3.2) Emotions: fear – hurt – shame – jealousy, hidden under anger, conflict, addictions.

(5) Your behaviour at # 4 causes life to get worse. People react. This generates more conflict.

(4) Behaviors that are a reaction to #3: shout, plot to get even, fight, act out, get sick, spend a lot of money, drive badly, irresponsible sex, binge on TV and movies, eat a chocolate cake.

---

194 This section on the influence of values is adapted from Dr. David Burn's work, *The Feeling Good Handbook*.

Realize that you really are powerless over other people, their behavior, and external events (at #1 and #5). In many situations you are powerless over what you feel. Emotions are influenced by chemicals which your body produces as a result of your perceptions, selective memory, trauma history, and a collection of other things. You do have control over your thoughts and behaviors (at #2, #3 and #4). You can change your values and your perceptions. When you challenge yourself and accept responsibility for your behaviors, you will be less irritable, struggle to control other people less, and enjoy life more.

Conflict – Self Talk

Self-Talk Sets Up Conflict

What we say to ourselves often makes issues and emotions bigger and more complicated. There are five ways that we think, called self-talk, which make conflict, anger, and emotional chaos difficult to eliminate. This is related to #2 and #3.1 in the diagram above. It originates from what we were taught, the way we perceive and think, the life we are exposed to, and what our expectations, values, and assumptions are. Self-talk is how people distort things. [195]

1) Perfectionism

Conflict escalates when it's associated with perfectionism. This means using a lot of 'you should' or 'you shouldn't' in speech and thought. You (or they) should have or shouldn't have done… *whatever*. There's a long list of self-recrimination and criticism of others. [196] Aside from the fact you mistakenly believe you are entitled to expect perfection from yourself or others (which is a way to escalate shame) a part of the human condition is making mistakes—being wrong is sometimes important. [197] You maintain arrogance by criticizing. Here are some situations where perfectionism is found.

One is in situations where you think you should lecture others or chastise yourself. Perfectionism allows you to criticize and justify anger and disappointment with others who are less efficient in those areas that we excel at. I.e. "You shouldn't ever be late for work! I am never, never late!" "You should be neater; dress better!" You justify your anger and criticism because another person isn't

---

195 There is positive self-talk that is a form of guided meditation that is used to calm down or reduce mental tension and conflict. What is presented here is more understanding the escalation of conflict through negative self-talk.

196 Self-recrimination is very often related to not understanding the phenomenon of addiction as an illness (which is a strange dynamic in itself). People instead report it as a disease or subtly agree with society that it's somehow deliberate—a moral deficiency of sorts. This fits neatly with an addict's built-in self-disparagement. It is neither a disease nor a moral corruption.

197 It is outside of the direct purview of this book, but worthy of study is *Being Wrong, Adventures in the Margin of Error*, by Kathryn Schulz, Harper Collins Pub. 2010.

as talented or compulsive as you. In supervisor-subordinate or parent-child relationships a person in authority harps on performance and demands perfection to maintain control or power through the inner personal transfer of shame. There are a thousand variations and combinations of these in relationships. In any of these situations people become angry and damage a relationship because someone acts just like a human being.

2) Stereotyping and Globalization

When you think that someone is a jerk, a bum, or a liar, whether or not you say it out loud, you are seeing that person in a completely negative way. You have ignored any part of them that is good. That is globalizing or stereotyping.

Conflict cannot be resolved if you think stereotyped thoughts. When you stereotype someone everything about them is flawed. The person has no good qualities. You objectify them which justifies them as a target for your judgements. This allows you to feel superior. You will have to continue to label and stereotype others in order to feel good.

People sense this and will be hurt, insulted and probably angry. They will tend to be self-righteous about your stereotyping them. The battle is about defending against false accusations. Anyone who is stereotyped is wrongly accused.

Stereotyping, Defenses, and Innocence

Start here:

#1 "You're lazy!"

 A globalization or stereotype which is 20% true and 80% false. *The person who hears this will defend against 80% that isn't true.*

#2 "You're a liar!"

A defensive reaction to the 80% false accusation in #1. This reactive accusation is also itself 20% true and 80% false. *The person who hears this will want to defend against the 80% that is false.*

#3 "You're a complete jerk!"

 Again, a defensive response to the 80% false portion from stereotype in #2, which is also 20% true and 80% false. *The person who hears this will defend against the part that is false.*

From there it escalates back and forth to the point of chaos, abuse, or violence, everyone trying to defend themselves.

In order to keep your dignity, you must defend against the part that is false and the conflict will then escalate in the effort to defend yourself. So, what can you do?

In reality, the other person isn't a totally worthless jerk, or a complete idiot, regardless of how much you insist they are. Nobody's completely perfect or completely terrible. Instead of trying to prove they're a total anything, which can't be done, exit the cycle. Be honest and very accurate about your concerns. If you stop stereotyping by being accurate and specific as in feedback (explained later) the other person will have to stop since there's nothing for them to defend against.

3) Jumping to Conclusions

This type of self-talk is about being able to predict the future and claiming to know the unknown.

a) **Mind Reading** is when you believe you know what someone else is thinking in any given situation. It really means you believe that others are thinking the same things you would think in the same situation. Should someone have done something you think is "bad," you get angry at them because you would be bad if you did that. Your faulty belief is that others believe the same way that you believe.

b) **Fortune Telling** happens when you claim to know exactly what another person will do in a situation in the future. You can predict events and you "know" how someone is going to act or how events will turn out. You're a fortune teller, which often generates defensiveness and anger in you before anything happens.

c) **Assumptions** are a self-talk problem related to stereotyping and based on inadequate or inaccurate information—you're filling in your own blank-spots with what you think the information should be. You believe communists are bad, but you've never met one. You "know" that all women are greedy or that all men are mean. When you act on assumptions you will generate anger or defensiveness before you know what you're talking about.

So, in the **Jumping to Conclusions** category of self-talk you generate conflict in your mind.

Mind Reading: You get angry because you would get angry.

Fortune Telling: You get angry because nothing has happened yet.

Assumptions: You get angry because you don't know what you're talking about.

4) Exaggerating or Minimizing

First there is an event—a car accident, losing a job, a divorce, getting drunk… and an inner-personal evaluation of it. A fiction is created in relation to the event so that everything is out of proportion. Problems cannot be solved with drama attached to them. Whichever you do, minimize or exaggerate the event or the responsibility, is dependent on where you try to place blame or how willing you are to accept your share of the responsibility.

If you're trying to avoid responsibility, you might sound like this: "It's not that bad. I mean, come on now! Relax! It's not a big deal." You minimize your responsibility and minimize their evaluation. In other situations, you exaggerate the other person's share of responsibility: "Oh ya? Look what you did! You did this and that and the other thing, too! And, I only did this little tiny thing!"

The other person knows you're minimizing or exaggerating. They'll defend themselves and challenge you because of that. Everyone becomes angry at your manipulation of minimizing or exaggerating their behaviour or your own.

5) Justice and Fair Play

This type of self-talk is based on a person's philosophy of life and what they believe. Angry people and victims often justify their anger or bad attitude by believing that life isn't fair.

Fair is an abstract concept people have created. We like to believe life is supposed to be orderly and ethical and can't understand the "unfairness" of it. This is based in the philosophy of duality, a version of good-vs-bad, that was explained earlier; now it's fair-unfair. There is no line between them. Many people insist that life be fair, and if it can't be "fair" at least it should be reasonable. When life isn't fair or reasonable, people often get angry, pout, get depressed, eat a cake or two, isolate, watch porn or get drunk (stoned too). It's quite common to binge on television or film where the good guys triumph against all odds (or the bad guys finally win). Emotional reaction to "unfairness" is personal and quite insidious.

Calamity, illness, and "bad luck" are generally random and invite the perception of unfairness into our thinking. The circumstances you were born into are random. Often, we are irresponsible and don't want to admit it. We made poor choices knowing full well they were not the better choice but wanted to play with fire. When we get burnt we pout and complain and reorganize our reasoning, so we don't look quite so foolish or irresponsible.

Some people seem to escape great calamity, which is an indication of its randomness not their special exemption. When calamity doesn't happen to people we think are "nasty" then life is unfair. When calamity visits those that we believe to be good it's very unfair.

Life just *is*. The biggest gang decides what's fair. That's one of the dangers of democracy—tyranny of the majority. Democracy is the best of what choices we have but that doesn't mean it's fair, it just means that sometimes the majority of people want something you don't. When you think something is unfair or unjust and get angry, it usually means one of two things:

- You don't understand that life is capricious; there's no logic. Life isn't reasonable or unreasonable. Everyone gets sick sometimes and everyone dies once. It seems that fate is against you, which is quite frightening; or,

• Your ideas about the rules-of-life are different and other people are not playing by your rules. It's not necessarily who's is more-right, it's just your rules are different. [198]

When another person acts in a way you think is unfair, often you will try to manipulate them by argument into your value system. You want them to change their mind. If you lose it's dangerous, you label them a jerk for being stubborn or foolish for not listening to your (excellent!) reasons. Expecting justice and fair play from life are emotional invitations into conflict and disappointment.

These five thinking patterns: Perfectionism, Stereotyping and Globalization, Jumping to Conclusions, Exaggerating or Minimizing, and Justice and Fair Play, are relationship nightmares. The actual problem cannot be solved because self-talk hides the actual problem. What we speak in our minds is very subtle and causes issues and emotions to become more complicated.

It has become apparent that people must (by self-discipline) form the habit of silence to some degree; to think about what they need to say and what they intend to accomplish by speaking words before they say anything. Impatience to brag, complain, or blame motivated by self-talk, are high on the list of what needs to be examined in the more advanced spiritual life. This restraint of tongue and pen will, over time, take you closer a quiet mindset; a reflective and thoughtful votary of truth in silence.

Part 2 – Communication

We Can Not Not Communicate

We communicate clearly or not clearly, but we cannot choose to *not* communicate. If a person slams a door, they communicate contempt, or anger, or fear, but they are not *not* communicating. Ask someone how they are, and they ignore you—what are they communicating? We cannot *not* communicate. The styles of communicating are varied and complex.

Setting the ground rules for communicating will sound tedious. It is each person's responsibility to communicate clearly and difficult at first to examine *everything* you say and how you say it. To be honest, direct and vulnerable can be difficult. At first, communicating clearly is time-consuming, hard work, and can

---

198 This does not endorse the obvious wrongs like violence, racism, or inequality. I am reminded of a cartoon in the *Calvin and Hobbes* comic strip, by Bill Watterson. Hobbes looks on sympathetically as Calvin complains about life. Calvin pouts petulantly that life is very unfair, and he demands that life needs to be unfair in his favor.

be embarrassing; however, it is essential to defeat your self-destructive patterns and avoid unnecessary relationship conflict. (Here, we are back to the source of relapse and addiction: conflict in all its forms in relationships.) It is important to select words and construct sentences that fit with what you are talking about. Here are two examples to consider.

"I feel like going to a meeting." As it stands, that is emotionally unclear. Are they saying they feel lonely and want to go to a meeting to see friends, or they feel happy and want to go to a meeting to share joy? "I feel like going to bed." This is also unclear. Are they saying they feel horny and bed is a euphemism for sex, they feel ill and want to recuperate, or they feel tired and want to go to sleep? (Yes, I know it sounds tedious.)

As written, neither sentence is emotionally clear. The sentences sound like they are about feelings, but only indirectly and assumptions or interpretation is necessary. They are actually about behaviors. Using the word "feel" in these sentences, if they are to be accurate, requires more information. "I feel _emotion_ and I want to go to bed."

Addicts in any addiction are irresponsible. They have little insight of themselves and often communicate by inference and camouflage. And, of course, when someone misinterprets the inference addicts get to argue and blame. Any attempt at clarity and accuracy is worth the effort. Being clear is one of the three guarantees to achieve healthy relationship. The other two are rigorous honesty and compassion.

With all the complaining that some of us do about communication and its importance to the human condition, we have to take more personal responsibility. Know what you feel, say what you mean, and do as you say, especially in the sphere of addiction, treatment, and recovery. Know what you feel (insight), say what you mean (accurate honesty) and do as you say (trustworthy and dependable).

There is a dynamic called the emotional rackets. Emotions can be translated: fear to anger, anxiety to terror, loneliness to depression. Regarding anger, this is always associated with another emotion. It's a racket of emotional translation. Fear, jealousy, insecurity etc., can be translated into anger. Anger can be translated into depression or sadness.

Remember that emotions move you to do something. Anger moves you to protect yourself. Since anger is the emotion of protection it tends to put people on the defensive—you protect yourself by anger and they want to protect themselves from your anger. Discussing anger and trying to resolve conflict at the level of anger is rarely successful. The feelings associated with the anger—fear, anxiety, shame, loneliness, jealousy, whatever, is the topic that will bring resolution to conflict.

Our responsibility is to be clear and honest, without blame, in how we communicate. Know what we feel, say what we mean, and do as we say. It is our responsibility to be accurate and articulate. Communicating to understand conflict or to resolve it is most effective when you style your emotional information as in...

Feedback

Feedback is efficient, doesn't manipulate, and is empowering to all concerned, but there is risk. The risk is that if you offer feedback as recommended here, you will be left with clear information that often leads to resolution of conflict. But... the resolution of conflict requires making difficult choices.

PART I — What Feedback is.

feed•back (fêd'bak') n. 1) a reaction or response to a particular process or activity: to get feedback from a speech. 2) information derived from such a reaction or response: to use the feedback from an audience survey. [199]

In communication, feedback is people providing you information about how something you do or say is received by them. Giving feedback can also be called emotional self-care—not repressing or translating emotions, which allows you to describe your own truths, without imposing those truths on others. It is disclosing, without abuse or manipulation, what your emotional responses are to someone's behaviour. [200] It is also setting boundaries, which are emotionally- or behaviorally-defined limits of interaction.

Feedback announces your interpersonal boundaries and is the least threatening way to tell others how their behaviour affects you. It's the most effective way to disclose information about your emotions regarding the behavior of another person. It contributes to significant changes within yourself and how others view you. [201]

None of this implies that feedback must cause some change in external circumstance. The receiver of your feedback isn't required to respond in any particular way to the feedback. It's apparent from the thousands of conversations I've had about this that people associate feedback with something negative. There's an awkward anxiety about giving feedback and a defensive posture about receiving it. It appears people are reluctant to use feedback because it is so pointedly accurate, and they are left with no space to argue. This severely limits our willingness to impart information in ways other than ordering and demanding.

---

199   Random House Webster's Dictionary © 1992 (edited).

200   Review where feedback is placed in the metaphor of The Volcano.

201   This is shifting the locus of control of your life from external to internal.

Millions of words have been written about the games in communicating. "Games" is a euphemism for power struggles and manipulation that create degrees of tension or conflict in a dysfunctional relationship. [202]

Our willingness to offer feedback correctly; to communicate honestly and accurately, is always directly related to how devoted we are to the other person and how willing we are to be emotionally honest. For anyone not dedicated to emotional health and honesty, feedback (as presented here) is risky business. You'll quickly find out who cares about you and who doesn't. Should you receive feedback, you will be put to the test of actually demonstrating how much you care.

PART II — How to Do It.

There are two parts to feedback. There's a description of emotion (yours) and a description of an external circumstance (someone's behavior). Here's the specific formula of what you say when you provide feedback—nothing more, nothing less:

"**I feel**   *specific feeling word*   **when you**   *specific behavior*   ."
An accurate emotion

Be accurate in describing your feelings and accurate regarding the specific behavior of the other person. It's an in-the-present communication skill of facts. Here are three examples:

"I feel **afraid** when you **yell at me**."
"I feel **ashamed** when you **tease me**."
"I feel **hurt** when you **ignore my feelings**."

If the speaker of these examples is being honest these represent accurate facts—there's no opinions, no judgments, no labeling, no threats, no demands. Emotions are facts, no different than a fact in chemistry or physics. Embrace an attitude that the facts are friendly. [203] It's the fact that these are facts that makes feedback so effective and significant.

Giving feedback prevents emotions from being suppressed or translated. It is active emotional self-care and gives clarity to your interaction with others. Expressing your emotions in this way keeps you in charge of yourself without manipulating or threatening others.

---

202 All relationships (except two, those with children and with mentally challenged people) are contracts of one form or another. *Spiritual Transformation* goes into this in some detail.

203 The psychotherapist Carl Rogers believed that the facts, whatever they are, are friendly. I agree, and that brings us back to accurate education. Facts. When people get facts they can trust, without opinions or demeaning observations about morality, they often do the right thing.

Anger in its various forms is the emotion that maintains isolation. If emotion is always expressed in terms of anger, then intimacy is unavailable. This is worthy of repetition: Anger moves you to protect yourself and blame. Since anger is the emotion of protection it tends to put people on the defensive—you protect yourself by being angry and they want to protect themselves from your anger. When angry, identify the other emotion and focus on that in the feedback.

There are only two reasons for talking about your emotions in a non-blaming way. One is that you look after yourself—in several aspects that's the primary reason. The other is that you provide factual information to someone about you and their behavior in a way that isn't demanding. By doing it as I have described, you provide information without judgement. Absence of judgment or blame is important here. Feedback is:

> **"I feel** _specific feeling word_ **when you** _specific behavior_ **."**
> *An accurate emotion*

PART III — Guidelines for Effective Feedback

(1) Focus feedback on describing specific behaviors. If you call someone a liar, they will receive it as an attack. However, if you point out that you feel hurt or confused because they are contradicting themselves—said this and then later said something else; obviously one is inaccurate or a lie—they can begin to act responsibly for that specific behavior in <u>that</u> situation. For you to accurately describe a person's behavior is being fair.

(2) Articulate your emotions in terms other than anger. When people are angry they always experience at least one other emotion. Anger is isolating, designed to protect and keep others away or to intimidate them into doing what you want. Make an effort to focus on the other emotions. Figure out what you are afraid of or embarrassed about and discuss that. Anger may be expedient but is very ineffective in interpersonal problem solving. [204]

(3) Focus feedback in the present. It's very difficult to respond to and resolve conflict that happened "a while ago." Feedback is discussing feelings and behaviors as they happen, or, within reason, as soon as is possible. As you practice you will become more spontaneous in this; however, if the best you can do for now is to give feedback after the incident then start there. The goal is to make feedback an in-the-present skill.

---

204 To further complicate things, some people have a hard time expressing anger. If this is you, then when you offer feedback make an effort to include <u>both</u> the anger and the other emotion at the same time. "I feel angry and hurt when you tease me." The other emotion must be included, because it's at that level where the problem will be solved.

(4) <u>Do not generalize or make stereotype statements</u>. If a person makes general statements ("You *always*..." or, "You *never*...") the statement is not accurate. Because of this, the person who receives the information will become defensive.

(5) <u>Do not give advice or make needs statements.</u> Giving feedback without advice or demands allows the other person to be responsible and participate as a free agent. Any demand for change invites defensiveness. People can behave as they will and are free to choose their response to feedback, whatever that may be. There should be no request for change or any needs statement.

(6) <u>Feedback keeps the rights of the other person in mind</u>. People need to maintain their dignity and are entitled to participate in the solution to the problems that affect their lives. People are defensive or hostile when they receive feedback that's given loudly, shames them in front of others, removes their right to choose, or when it's sarcastic. It's important to respect the other person's right to participate with dignity.

People will frequently complain: "I talked about my feelings and the other person didn't change," or, "I gave someone feedback and they didn't stop doing it." The person who gave feedback was more concerned with controlling the other person and expedient problem solving. They're complaining that using feedback didn't get them their own way. Feedback is not a trick to force the other person to change their behavior.

When you give feedback that is ignored or ridiculed there are now two issues. (1) The emotion and behaviour in the original feedback; and (2), feeling hurt or scared they don't respect you and ignored your feelings. This is new information about lack of respect in that relationship that will help you make an informed decision.

Keep talking about your feelings and be specific about their behavior. Do not deviate from this formula and, if possible, do it without anger. Only in this manner can you gather accurate information.

Avoid analyzing why a person behaves a certain way. Avoid psychiatric terms. That gets off topic and people get defensive when you analyze them, and besides that, it's only your self-centered interpretation of their behavior. When you're giving feedback, if the other person cares, they will support what you are doing. Giving and receiving feedback in this manner will provide accurate information about your relationships. It allows for informed choice.

How someone responds to your feedback is their business. Don't end up in a power struggle about them not responding the way you want. As uncomfortable as it sounds, others are entitled to be rude and ignore your feelings. How they respond will provide information about their attitude towards you and the relationship.

PART IV — Setting Boundaries

Giving feedback is setting boundaries. Setting boundaries is telling people that their behavior is, to you, comfortable or uncomfortable.

In a situation where you give this style of feedback, it will allow the receiver of your feedback to respect your feelings without themselves being defensive. They may be defensive but there is no real need for that because it's facts not opinions or stereotyping. They can demonstrate how important you are by the respect they show. Should they not respect your feelings (demean or ignore you) this would be factual evidence they really don't care about you and they're not willing to improve the relationship. Decisions will have to be made.

PART V — How to Receive Feedback

Someone gives you this feedback: "I feel **hurt** when you **tease me**." If you want to enhance the relationship it is your responsibility to honor the other person's feelings. Respect what they are saying. Do not accuse the person of being too sensitive, or that they deserved it, or it was just in fun (teasing that hurts never is). Don't tease them more, disagree with them, argue, or claim they misunderstood. Offer Emotional First Aid.

They are giving you feedback. Offering feedback is a very caring thing to bring clarity to a situation. Do not cover up your own embarrassment or guilt at having hurt someone. Any response other than acceptance is just trying to take the heat off yourself.

When someone gives you feedback properly, it's just factual information. It isn't necessarily good or bad, it's how you respond that counts. The person who gave you feedback has the right to feel what they feel and say it. Yes, it's often uncomfortable when someone gives you feedback, but you still have choices.

PART VI – Needs Statements and Control

Addicts are generally focused on control and accumulating power and influence (the more the better). This protects their secrets and keeps others at emotional distance. None of these are healthy for committed, loving relationships. It is extremely difficult to opt out of wanting to control. This is an example of unhealthy feedback:

"I feel **hurt** when you **lie to me**... and I **need** you to **stop lying** to me."
   (emotion)   (behaviour)   (needs statement)

Adding that needs statement, "I need you to stop lying to me" is a demand for behavior change and exactly what this is not about. Needs statements demonstrate a cultural value system of dominance, severely dislocated and abusive, that is inappropriate in recovery, love and intimacy.

There's often a misunderstanding about what caring is. Have you had someone say to you, "If you really loved me you would..."? Doing what somebody else wants is not always evidence of caring. Our culture is entrenched in the notion that altruism and obedience are the higher good and are thought to be morally excellent. This is rooted in 18ᵗʰ century European parenting and religious indoctrination. [205]

The authority which demands sacrifice may be parents (If you love your Mommy then you will...), or it may be love (If you really love me then you would...), or politicians (If you love your country then...). The higher good of sacrifice may be loyalty to a myth (blood's thicker than water), or it may be God (If you really love The Church or love God then you will...). These claim that self-sacrifice to a "higher good," whatever that might be, is better than emancipation from emotional slavery. The demands are always serving the needs of the person or group making the demands and not you. You will then betray yourself in an existence of sacrifice. [206]

Freely chosen values are not possible in addiction. Your complicity in the altruism-and-obedience game will leave you forever lonely and unfulfilled. Caring for others is good. Altruism and charity can be good but approach these with caution. The emotional conspiracies and schemes of people who expect obedience or demand sacrificial altruism, and your offering either of them at the expense of yourself, are always harmful.

> "I feel hurt and scared when you yell at me... (feedback)
> and I **need** you to stop **yelling**." (needs statement)

Feedback with a needs statement attached to it, as above, should be heard like this: "If you were a nice person you would do what you're told. Stop yelling. If you don't do what I tell you, you're bad." It's actually a control tactic—a demand in a polite, political package.

This needs statement (a demand for behaviour change) shifts the focus from facts—feeling hurt and yelling (both are facts) into a political power struggle about obedience, to stop or continue yelling. "If you love me you will do what you're told."

This promotes bargaining and compromise as the standard of behavior in the relationship. "You bossed me around today and I did what I was told. I'll boss you around tomorrow." This eventually leads to: "I sacrificed and gave up more than you did." Conflict resolution will then be reduced to the vicious game of who

---

205   This is admirably explained in Alice Miller's books, especially *For Your Own Good: Hidden Cruelty in Child-Rearing and the Roots of Violence.*

206   See Nathaniel Brandon's book *Taking Responsibility* for an enlightening point of view on altruism.

has the better memory and exaggerating obedient self-sacrifice to instill guilt and compliance.

Making political demands or needs statements means there is little regard for the other person's right to behave as they want and their right to participate in problem solving. It is important to remember that all of us can behave as we choose, with the ensuing consequences. Should the receiver dismiss the feedback, it may be because they are being defensive about being told what to do. That won't allow for intimacy or trust.

Our culture can negotiate contracts but can't negotiate emotion. We are very uncomfortable with process-and-emotion and have little patience for things that cannot be reduced to a four-minute conversation (as long as a set of TV commercials).

There may be doubt that the other person is dedicated to you or the relationship. If feedback delivery and response are respectful, feedback will promote interest, trust, and caring in your relationship. Unless a person knows how to respond to the feeling content (Emotional First Aid) they're left with the traditional cultural position of negotiating for power. Be aware that:

1) Feedback doesn't disempower anyone. Dignity can be maintained. Both people can demonstrate caring when feelings are respected.

2) If no one is criticized, neither person has to sidetrack into being defensive. There are only two facts on stage: the emotion and the behaviour.

3) There's no implied demand; there's no threat; there's no defensiveness required. There are no power struggles. Respect is established and further exploration is encouraged.

4) Feedback with a needs statement is a relationship of demands. Feedback without a needs statement is a relationship of respect.

5) If the response is considerate and respectful that provides positive relationship information. If the response to the feedback is ridicule, argument, or justification; if the response is inconsiderate or uncaring, this non-supportive behavior provides new information. (It usually just verifies old suspicions.)

Feedback: "I feel *specific feeling word* when you *specific behavior.*" Then, wait to see what happens.

The Attending Behaviours

There are some misconceptions about what it means to listen. It's more than just "hearing words." Most people don't listen, they wait for the next opportunity to talk. Some people get discouraged when they realize how much effort goes into listening properly or the self-discipline required to be considerate. There are six behaviors that show that we are really listening (or attending) to another person.

1) Verbal and Non-verbal Following — Verbal Following is making sounds, or saying short phrases, that show you are listening. Examples might be "Wow!" "Uh-huh." "Humm." "I see." [I know it sounds pedantic.] The speaker knows you are hearing what they are communicating. These should not be said too frequently as this would be taken as interrupting. Non-Verbal Following is attentive body movements that indicate your awareness of what is being said, (hand movements, head movements, mild gestures, shrugs, nodding, facial expressions).

2) I – Thou — There should be an equal relationship between the speaker and the listener. Martin Buber developed the concept of I-Thou and I-it in communications. [207] In I-it, one person is seen as lesser and having minimal or no influence in the interaction. I-Thou communication is both people having equality and influence when they communicate. Here are the three possibilities:

> I - thou. When the speaker puts themselves in the dominant position, or they take more authority than they are entitled to.
> i - THOU. When the speaker puts the listener in the dominant position and gives away their own influence.
> I - Thou. When both persons have equal responsibility and input into the conversation, with respect for emotions and rights. Both maintain their dignity.

3) Body Posture — Your general posture will convey your interest. When possible, shift your body a little so that you are facing, the speaker.

4) Eye Contact — Making eye contact involves looking directly, but not staring, at the speaker. Usually the speaker will glance away while they formulate another thought. Generally, it's the listener's job to make the effort to maintain eye contact in a sincere and relaxed way.

5) Relaxation — Let the communication flow as naturally as possible. If there are any hidden agendas (secret goals of the interaction which one person conceals from the other) there is no relaxation.

6) Paraphrasing — If you briefly rephrase, or state in your own way, what you believe the speaker said, you can determine whether or not you heard what was intended. It reflects back to the speaker two important things: you understood the nuance of their message, and you are interested and

---

207 See *I-Thou*, by Martin Buber

care about what they say. [208] As the listener, it may be appropriate that you ask questions that clarify points of confusion.

If people are invited to talk freely and you listen well, without impatience or judgement, eventually everything said makes sense. When people are interested, they do most of these attending behaviors already. [209] It's a matter of fine-tuning the ones you are weak on. It's your responsibility to communicate clearly. Attending to the other person requires patience and compassion, which shows you are interested.

Opening Lines

What's often overlooked is knowing how to begin a sensitive and painful discussion. Usually someone is going to be shocked and emotionally hurt. Our lives may change drastically. Someone will be angry, and this often deteriorates into an argument.

Undisclosed emotions, fears, and anxieties will contaminate problems. Self-talk escalates issues. Suppressing feelings is costly. Here are some ways you can begin any sensitive conversation:

"I have something difficult to talk about. I'm anxious and I don't know what to say."

"I'm feeling ashamed (or sad...) about something and I need to talk about it—but I'm afraid to start. I'm nervous."

"I'm worried (or scared, or frightened) about telling you something. I don't know how to start because I'm afraid I won't say it properly."

Each of these examples introduces the topic in the least threatening way (variations of feedback). It presents a non-threatening notice that the conversation is important. It identifies the significance of what's going to happen, and it gives the receiving person some warning to prepare for the conversation.

Time Out

People need to learn how to stop disagreements before they become abusive. A Time Out is a way of facilitating this—intervening before they get out of hand. Taking a Time Out means <u>you</u> disengage from the argument temporarily to figure out your own part of the conflict. One of the people will want to fight to the

---

208   For interesting perspectives on conversation and receiving attention, read *The Pursuit of Attention*, Charles Derber, Oxford University Press, 2000

209   If you are involved in a long conversation that you aren't interested in, but are acting interested, what isn't being said? Is your fake interest a manipulation?

bitter end—to force the other person to agree, to win, to teach them a lesson (punishment), which is often why you ended up in an argument in the first place.

When you realize you are in an argument consider taking a Time Out. Get off the "argument" subject. Work to prevent it escalating. Avoid blaming statements that start with, "But you..."

A Time Out is one person temporarily excusing themselves from the conflict. When you take a Time Out, say, "I'm feeling angry. I'm taking a time out so I can calm down. I'll be back in about a half an hour," or "I'm really confused and angry. I'm taking a Time Out so I can figure out what I'm doing wrong. I'm going for a walk. I'll be back in about twenty minutes."

Talk only about yourself. The other person isn't involved in your Time Out. That keeps you in charge of you, the only person you are really in charge of. A Time Out is a direct communication about yourself, there's nothing unclear about it. You introduce that you are taking one and then you leave for a short while.

Here's the harder part... when you are on a Time Out, concentrate on your own emotions associated with the conflict. (The Volcano.) Don't analyze or blame the other person. (Self-Talk) Take personal responsibility. Don't drink or use drugs. Don't justify your behaviour. These make it worse. If you're angry enough to need a Time Out, you shouldn't be driving. Don't sit and brood—walk or jog slowly. Quiet motion will help you think clearly about your behaviour. Decide what your hidden agendas are. Resist the impulse to win the argument.

A Time Out is a contract so return when you say you will. That demonstrates you are being dependable. When you return discuss what you realized about yourself. Use "I" statements and don't blame. A Time Out is about self-examination not manipulating to win. The other person is entitled to do this too. You are choosing a behavior that demonstrates caring and willingness to resolve the issues. This is one part of positive conflict resolution which takes time and effort. It isn't easy.

Arguing Fairly

An argument is usually about something underneath the verbal disagreement. First, identify emotions that are associated with anger. What were you feeling or thinking hours or days before the argument? What disapproval or resentment did you conceal before it started? What long-standing tension has been exposed? Discovering this will help you to identify what the conflict is really about. It takes courage to be honest and to trust the other person is also being honest. If there are hidden agendas this won't work.

Admit your emotions about the issues you have discovered. Avoid escalating the anger and talk about the related emotions. Anger keeps everyone on the defensive. Be responsible and don't blame or manipulate (that'll be the hardest part—addicts love to blame and win).

Invite the other person to describe their feelings and listen to what they say. Their feelings are as true as yours. Acknowledge what they are telling you. Try to understand it from their point of view. [Yes, I know it's tedious.]

Arguments are about who's going to be the boss or trying to prove the other person is the bad one. A necessary component to resolution is to decide what you did to contribute to the argument. If there's respect and caring neither person needs to settle for being obedient. If you insist on being right this will end up in a resentful, blaming/guilt cycle.

> The difficult part is honesty without blame.
> The complicated part is sorting out the emotions.
> The humble part is admitting your own fault.
> The fear part is admitting being wrong.
> The embarrassing part is disclosing the history that's been avoided.
> The self-conscious part is giving up your need to win.
> The risky part is sharing your secrets.
> The end result is discovering what the conflict is really about.

For people in addiction recovery read the list again. It outlines the common struggles in recovery and sobriety: honesty without blame, sorting out the emotions, admitting fault and being wrong, disclosing the history that has been avoided, giving up a need to win, and discovering what the addiction is really about.

Dishonesty always generates more confusion and conflict. When people in conflict honestly share their hidden agendas, the real problem will be identified. Now they can solve it with regard for the feelings and rights of everyone involved. During the resolution of conflict be mindful of your common and complimentary interests: We both want _this_. We both want to arrive _here_. We both agree _this_ is good. Identifying complimentary interests builds empathy, trust, and a sense of team-work. Then collaborate on opposing interests.

Interpersonal conflict that is addressed by power and dominance always leaves resentments that reappear again and again. Emotions are denied, dignity is lost, and getting even becomes the type of existence that you live. The relationship degenerates into a series of "making deals."

This chapter is about communicating and (hopefully) resolving conflict. It might be implied from how this is written all relationships should be saved, or all conflict can be resolved. It's not my intent to present some Pollyanna-type of relationship heaven. Some couples should separate. Some relationships or friendships come to an end (some quickly, some slowly). Break-ups and endings are a part of life. Some conflicts cannot be resolved, they've been going on too long, are too repetitive, someone's too stubborn, too much interference from others, too much fear, too much bitterness and resentment. At least this process allows you to be more graceful in agreeing to disagree.

"To escape looking at the wrongs we have done another, we resent-fully focus on the wrong [they have] done us." Step Eight. And, *"It is a spiritual axiom that every time we are disturbed, no matter what the cause, there is something wrong <u>with us</u>."* (Emphasis in the original.) Step Ten. [210]

Small Group Needs

Everyone is a member of a small group—our families, our work, a small circle of close friends, a couple. There are three needs that you have a right to advocate for on your own behalf. You should recognize that these apply to all members of the group.

Inclusion: This means being a part of something, and not just a hanger-on. Everyone is included and has a sense of belonging.

Affection: This is having a sense of safety and consideration, having your personal involvement respected. You can give and receive support and give and receive caring.

Influence: There must be a shared sense of power—having influence is important but having more than someone else easily leads to abuse. You need to be able to exercise a fair degree of influence.

If you are experiencing problems in a small group reflect carefully about yourself and the others in the group. Offer this information for discussion.

> Which of these three do you have or not have?
> Who appears to be giving these up?
> Is anyone denying these needs to other group members?
> Who appears to be demanding a larger share of these?
> How does the group lose when these do not exist for everyone?
> Be sensitive to maintaining these in your relationships with others.

Summary

All of this is difficult and tedious—the first several times you try it. Making a relationship strong and safe takes a lot of effort and hard work, more than most

---

210 Both are from *Twelve Steps and Twelve Traditions*, the Alcoholics Anonymous publication, pp. 78 and 90. These two statements may be the second and third most ignored guidelines in all of the AA literature. The first is at Step Twelve, carrying the message and talking about the steps as the method of recovery.

people are prepared for. In order to be in a safe, healthy relationship, everyone concerned must contribute to the resolution of the problems that concern their lives. You must take responsibility for yourself.

This chapter covers what you need to know in order to communicate and negotiate yourself into healthy relationships. Usually people hope there's a simple magic trick I'll provide that makes it easier. There isn't any secret information that has been left out.

The key is committing yourself to the hard work of demanding only of yourself rigorous honesty. Be responsible and accountable for being evasive or vague or for your history of being an outright liar. This is always a demonstration of affection and respect. There are no shortcuts to clarity; no less risky way to disclose your emotions; no more expedient way to make a relationship safe. This is how simple (or difficult) it is.

As I said at the beginning of this chapter, addicts are afraid of people, especially afraid of intimacy, afraid of being known, and incapable of responsibility when acting out. In addiction there's conflict in all relationships and, as outlined in Chapter 4, everything is relationship.

Communication, here I call it applied problem solving in personal relationships, is crucial to addiction recovery. The better people can listen on a deeply non-judgmental level the better others will communicate and then the dynamic of healing will be present. Please do not underestimate the importance of what's in this chapter.

Chapter 7

Spirituality and a Principled Life

There are a few ideas that have to be understood when people talk about "spirituality" or "principles." These are vague words and their meaning changes from group to group and person to person. This first section is to offer information that will establish some common ground for understanding.

There is "I am spiritual." That's like saying I am tall, as an adjective. Then there is "I am spiritual," which is like saying I am running, as a verb. Other people talk about spirituality like it's process of relocating or moving—I am going to a spiritual life (I am going to Calgary). There are people in twelve-step programs and religions who bandy the word spiritual about like they are talking about the weather—everyone talks about it, but there's a hopeless futility that nothing can be accomplished. And, for many people, there is the implication (in error) that being spiritual must contain some form of God belief. Altogether, this brings us back to the quote from T.S. Eliot in the Preface: *"The hubbub of a marching band going nowhere. The drum is beaten but the procession does not advance."*

Some questions are: What is a spiritual principle, anyway? What is a principle as opposed to a rule? Are the steps principles or are they just homework assignments? Within twelve-step programs the steps are often viewed as principles. Are they? The steps may be called principles by uninformed common consent, but the steps really aren't principles. Principles are not rules. Rules are arbitrary. The steps are not principles, they're homework. Principles are what decides the context for life. The differences are important.

Another confusing misperception is that spirituality must be contained within religious beliefs. Religious people can't agree on God, so how can they agree on something as vague as spiritual principles? But being "spiritual," the word itself, is emotionally loaded with God and religious innuendo. Almost no one as far as I can understand, can see a spiritual life available to atheists. This is a common but false perception. [211]

---

211 As advised in *Alcoholics Anonymous*, those people who struggle with the idea of God, or are belligerent about that, can choose their own conception of God—call it what you will or view that how you want. We are advised in AA that any interpretation of "God" is acceptable. Fair enough. The AA Christian-oriented belief of 1939 is there is a god, but within the meetings of the first three decades, members got to call "God" whatever they wanted. This is fine, for believers. For atheists, changing the name of the opinion from God to 'the energy of the universe' is

A principle is an all-encompassing code of conduct, like rigorous honesty or compassion, that governs all behaviour; the context for life. Rules are arbitrary, socially convenient, and change frequently: the meeting starts at 8:00 pm, the speed limit is 50, take your shoes off at the door, say please and thank you. These rules govern the content of life and are arbitrary. The steps are neither rules nor principles, they are actually homework assignments. Within each assignment (each step), is how you learn spiritual principles. A person looks at a map to see how to drive to a certain address. The map isn't a principle, it's a guide. Complete the steps to travel into a spiritual life; the steps are the training-guide to arrive at a principled life. A person learns about these principles through the steps, but whether they adhere to them or not is another thing.

So, whether acting in concert with spiritual principles or not, whatever your principles are, are the governing agency of personality (context). Rules are arbitrary (content). The steps are homework assignments to learn how to exit addiction. This was presented in Chapter 5 and will be reviewed later. In attempting to bring clarity to the chaos of spirituality, there is no small task ahead of us.

One of the hardest things for insecure people to do, especially self-righteous people, is to mind their own business and leave others alone with their rules and beliefs. This seems to be particularly true about religious people who are strong believers. Their insecurity around others with different beliefs and atheists is often quite apparent, which is a block to addiction recovery. Insecurity is evident in proselytizing movements that encourage missionary work or religious conversion programs. Certainly, this is cruel and egregious when they create excuses for violence and harsh judgements, which judgements are nothing more than fanatical opinions.

Contrary to many opinions, I do not believe humans are at heart spiritual beings. History has demonstrated, for all of history, that we are violent, our cruelty knows no bounds, we torture and abuse everything, and ignore or abuse people we claim to love. We can rationalize anything. People are dangerous when crossed, sneaky, and vengeful. That sits at the instinctual core of who we are as animals. Sharks imbued with selfishness and long memories for revenge.

Then, we add to our animal nature the dislocation and abuse inherent in modern culture. There is racism, sexism, violence, political abuse, global poverty, gross consumption, lunacy holding places of power, stress, celebrity worship,

---

still believing. That is parallelism in religious beliefs (see Chapter 2). If you are an atheist and believe there is no god, which is fine, then there is no god. It's all opinion anyway, and by definition, atheists don't believe. In dealing with atheists, suggesting they change the name from God to some other euphemism for God is still God, just by a different name. "That which we call a rose by any other name is still a rose." Wm. Shakespeare, *Romeo and Juliet*, Act II, Scene II. Changing the name doesn't mitigate or absolve it of its meaning. Atheists or agnostics can become spiritual by being committed to achieving spiritual principles. Each step has a purpose related to psychology, listed in Chapter 5, that is quite sufficient. The issue is commitment, not belief. See footnote 25 regarding agnostics and footnote 110 regarding being determined.

greed, environmental destruction, and irresponsibility. This culture breeds and approves of some addictions, ostracizes and demonizes some addicts, and sends most addicts to outdated treatment (indoctrination, see Appendix III) so they can return to an addicted, unspiritual culture. At the risk of criticism for repetition, as I said earlier, we rescue addicts from a fire and send them to live in a burning building.[212]

The majority of people are socially-approved Group B addicts. (Cultural Focus Graph II). It's sometimes surprising to me that anyone ever accomplishes anything spiritual. When we examine the effort of those few who created a truly spiritual life in some observable way, what was required of them makes most people cringe and avoid the effort required.[213] To actually be spiritual is difficult. It goes against our deep seated, instinctual animal nature and against this culture. It's a potential we all carry—to be spiritual, but so is the easier potential to be cruel and righteous. Selfishness and greed are more accessible and partly why we fail at being spiritual so often *and* why so few people actually accomplish it. Becoming spiritual (as a verb) that is a visible quality of life is not easy to accomplish.

In this chapter I will explain the qualities of a principal. Then I will present what the spiritual principles are and apply those principles to addiction and the social symptom constellations (from Chapter 3). Later, I will point out how deists, theists, agnostics, atheists, and humanists can all be spiritual. Finally, there will be a short exposition on how the twelve steps of *Alcoholics Anonymous* are a path to successfully live a spiritually principled life for everyone.

Fundamental Qualities of a Principle

"Principles, unlike values are objective and external. They operate in obedience to natural laws, regardless of conditions." [214]

Principles, unlike rules or values, are universal and objective. They would govern behaviour in all situations. A spiritual principle would represent an authentic truth and hold within the principle itself a universal theme that went beyond personality, rules, culture, or religious beliefs. A principle would be the foundation out of which attitudes and behaviours could emerge that enable a person to rise above (be spiritual) or descend below (be soulful), the ego-constructions of self-serving convenience in any culture.

Spiritual principles must take us beyond the limited vision of personal opinion and rules. They should also be above the pettiness of politics, the abuse in power

---

212 In this, I speak of North America. I have travelled many places and see other countries trying hard to catch up to our madness.

213 Aldous Huxley wrote of this in *Huxley and God: Essays.*

214 *Principle-Centered Leadership*, Stephen R. Covey, A Fireside Book, Simon & Schuster, 1992, p. 19.

mongering, the corruption inherent in religion, and the addiction in culture. A bona fide spiritual principle would embrace all of the generally recognized virtues, regardless of the cultural tradition through which they are perceived. In this instance they would also include whatever qualities recovering addicts would have that demonstrate being recovered.

The general chaos and confusion about spirituality occurs most often when people take something as universal as "spirituality" and distort it with personal interpretations and opinions that cater to their coveted prejudices, defend their religious opinions, and conceal their insecurities. They claim, with judgement and criticism, that their interpretation is superior to others' interpretations. Sometimes they are so arrogant about their superiority (so insecure) they'll kill you for being different.

Principles must be broad and flexible enough to be available to everyone at a deeply personal level. To allow something to qualify as a spiritual principle (as opposed to a rule, which is arbitrary and situational) is no mean feat. Each of the five I suggest is a principle because it satisfies the following twelve qualities. These are listed in random order. A spiritual principle must be:

- Universal enough to accommodate all endeavor, whether atheist or theist, beyond the narrow limits of culture,

- Respectful of any personal symbolism of deity or humanist-atheist belief system,

- Broad enough to encompass the generally recognized virtues,

- Restricted enough to exclude the more universal vices,

- Tested enough to be trusted,

- Simple enough to understand,

- Complex enough to require reflection,

- Demanding enough to require an effort to accomplish it,

- Idealistic enough to be always worthy of respect and just out of reach—to keep people humble in their pursuit of it,

- Specific enough that it can be approached with confidence,

- Achievable to a degree that people can realize personal progress; and,

- Profound enough to be above pettiness.

<u>Five Spiritual Principles</u> [215]

The abuse and chaos of religions: rigid opinions, contradictions in prayer and faith, condemnation of outsiders, religious violence, prejudice, racism, sexism, superlative God-opinions, claimed miracles, deceit, arbitrary rules, social irresponsibility, and assumed superiority, make being spiritual within a religion almost impossible. Being spiritual is challenging because people have complicated this with religious dogma, and as noted immediately above, make various outrageous proclamations that are foolish to many, including preposterous claims of superlative religious beliefs. There's all manner of perpetual righteous abuse that goes unchallenged. These deny humility absolutely.

Spirituality, through secular principle (honesty, kindness, etc.) may be difficult to attain, but very practical when achieved. It side-steps all religious hypocrisy. Each of the five principles I recommend for a spiritual lifestyle satisfy all twelve qualifications. Additionally, there are only five of them so people can comprehend how they interrelate. These principles can be internalized and become the governing values of truly spiritual people.

Recall the earlier discussion of how we assign a governing energy to relationships. Spiritual principles allow you to assign a compassionate, accepting energy to all you do. What may be more important is these five allow the adherents of different faiths to peacefully interact while maintaining different beliefs. For addicts, they counteract the five social symptoms of addiction.

Regardless of the circumstances people find themselves in, recovered addicts would demand only of themselves adherence to these principles. They would be the governing energy of all behaviour. To the uninitiated they are probably overwhelming and thought to be untenable and viewed with disbelief. However, with willingness, patience, and labour (i.e. desire, devotion, and diligence), right association, and completing the homework assignments (the steps), they are within reach of anyone who is desirous of a truly spiritual way of life. With long perseverance and wise council, they can take a person well beyond the conventionally enlightened. [216]

I refer to a Manly Hall quote: *"The unfolding of a man's spiritual nature is as much as exact science as mathematics..."* [217] The assumed and varied debates and

---

215 This section is a reframed version of Appendix II taken from *Spiritual Transformation, Third Edition*, cited earlier.

216 Marshall Frady, in his book *Martin Luther King, Jr.*, Viking/Penguin Books, 2002, p. 186, offered this observation about Dr. King: *"King was indeed passing now into that far country of all true prophets ultimately: that lonely region beyond the conventionally enlightened...."* People don't have to be prophets; however, the investigation at Step Two and the decision at Step Three to become spiritual have no limits attached to them. It is voluntary and so the standard to aspire to is that set by the principles and not by collusion in mediocre social convention (meaning religions, politics, and socially acceptable levels of addiction).

217 *Secret Teachings of All Ages*, Manly P. Hall, Tarcher/Penguin Books, 2003, p. 120.

opinions about God, religion, and atheism may be esoteric, controversial, and unending, but all anyone can do is express their opinion. The everyday application of spirituality is none of these.

These five principles appear to me to govern ethical, spiritual endeavor. These will, when willingly complied with and taken altogether, create spiritual integrity. "Willingly complied with." means to be voluntarily obedient to them (desire, devotion, and diligence).

Principle #1: Respect for the Physical Body and Respectful Self-Care

It is long believed in the perennial philosophies that the Atman-Brahmin (God for the Western ideas of religion), resides within us and access to this is through ourselves. [218] Our soul should that exist, from one perspective, is the access point to, and the residence place of, the dark void out of which we arise. Our soul appears to be independent of any opinion about God. From there, we can access an integrity of living in two seemingly opposite directions. People can be drawn into an appreciation of the dark, sublime mysteries of primal life and love (soulful) or can rise above to the call of light and spirit (spiritual).

Being soulful is very different from being spiritual. Soulfulness is sincerely honoring and cultivating the strength, frailty, mystery, and power at the core of our being alive in a way that doesn't harm or impinge on the corporeal universe. Soulfulness is directly attached to our sexuality. The counterpart to soulfulness is spirituality. That might be described as manifesting the action of our individual personalities "out" towards the world. That might be a form of love that is contained in compassion for others, in a way that cooperates with spiritual principles. Harmonizing soulfulness and spirituality may be the intended journey of life.

This ultimately begins and ends within each of us. It is our bodies, our emotions, our sexuality, and our thoughts and values through which this is experienced and expressed. Spirituality is accomplished by challenging ourselves. Our bodies are the place where the essence of soul and spirit meet, and it all begins within our own physical being. Your body is literally the home of your soul and spirit, as is everyone else's the home of their own. You must have an internally negotiated contract with yourself about decent self-care. [219]

---

218 According to *Alcoholics Anonymous*, in the final analysis, it is deep within us that the Great Reality is found (p. 55). The "Great Reality" is usually interpreted to be some metaphor for God. That is one point of view of opinion. But it may also be that the great reality is a realization of the over-riding importance of successful restraint, veracity, humility, letting go of old ideas, and never blaming. These are also a great reality that doesn't include any higher power. Either one is yet another opinion.

219 For those of a theist focus there are two similar opinions of God residing within us, found in *Mysticism In Religion*, by Rev. W.R. Inge, University of Chicago Press, 1948, Chapter 3: Attributed to St. Paul: "*...the spirit dwelling in us, or of our bodies... 'the body' as the 'tabernacle'*

Respect for the body, as demonstrated by healthy caring for our physical being—for others as much as ourselves—is essential. Not damaging ourselves or anyone else through squalid living, toxic diets, smoking, shame, violence, addictions, greed, irresponsibility, selfishness, or physical or emotional abuse is crucial. If you're damaging or neglecting the emotional or physical health of your body or another person's you cannot be spiritual. Nurturing the residence of the spirit or the soul is the starting place for all transformation.

It was written over a thousand years ago:

"The pledge of the vajra body [human body] *is to never disrespect the body of any being, male or female… because each possesses the nature of the body of enlightenment. The pledge is to… not cause distress to oneself or another by instigating feelings of guilt, etc., because all sentient beings possess the nature of enlightened mind. The pledge… is to never speak harsh words but always gentle ones that please and do not upset others because all beings have the nature of enlightened speech."*

> Indestructible Nucleus' Ornament Tantra
> The Treasury of Knowledge
> Jamgon Kongtrul (trans. Kalu Rinpoche)
> Book Five (of ten volumes), p. 270

Principle #2: Veracity

This is a certain style of being honest and describing your perception of truth or reality that must incorporate compassion. Presenting your truths without consideration is cruel and not a part of veracity. Realize that honest communication that is angry or without respect for others may be honest but will be received as abusive. The listener will view the speaker as selfish or rude, and the truth or any wisdom in the truth, will be held suspect because of the angry manner in which it's delivered. People who are angry and honest are seen as more self-righteous and mean than honest.

Spiritual people are consistently and gently honest about themselves with all people, in all situations, at all times, regardless of the cost to themselves. This disables impression management, which must be absent for any sincere spiritual endeavor. If you are honest with kindness and compassion, other people's reaction to your honesty is their concern, not yours.

In microscopic truth telling, spiritual people always offer respect, courtesy, and dignity to others, regardless of the nature of what needs to be told. [220] You

---

of the soul while we live here [on earth]*."* And, from Rev Inge: *"The body must be reverenced and preserved from defilement… it is the temple of the Holy Spirit."* I do not intend Christian hegemony in this. *The Kabalah* teaches similarly, that what we consume or use (good or not good), so it is that we become. Many other religious traditions, and particularly the original Buddhism and the compassionate middle road, promote respectful self-care with equal style and grace.

220 Microscopic truth telling is a descriptive phrase that I find particularly applicable. It is from *Conscious Loving*, Gay Hendricks, Ph.D., & Kathlyn Hendricks, Ph.D., Bantam Books, 1990,

cannot be spiritual if you are mean while being honest or political as a justification for being dishonest. Either way, you are closer to relapse. Being spiritual always requires gentleness, trustworthiness, and courtesy in microscopic truth telling; no exceptions. That is veracity. [221] (Recall the comments on being a silent votary of truth at the end of the section on Self Talk.)

Principle #3: Humility

Humility is largely (mostly? almost always?) misunderstood, especially by religious people or those seeking spiritual transformation. Humility is rare and elusive. It is becoming more so with the increase of culturally approved addiction and the depth of collusion in recovery that mediocre is good enough. (See Appendix III.) There are two aspects of humility that must be considered in both behaviour and attitude in order for it to have integrity.

The first (ignored) requirement for humility involves adhering to a sincerely egalitarian philosophy as the foundation of all thoughts and behaviour. Demonstrating equality, in attitude and outlook, must be universal, and operate generously and willingly regarding gender, age, health, ability, talent, culture, skin tone, education, religious beliefs or not, politics, height, tattoos, language, and affluence—equality about *every* category that people use to classify each other. As soon as we get superior, righteous, judgmental, sexist, irresponsible, xenophobic, or patronizing about anything (including the divorce lawyer for the other side) there can be no equality and thus, no humility.

People have intellect and the ability to choose values and behaviour. Unlike crows, iguanas, or sharks, which operate on instinct, people have choice which imposes responsibility for behaviour. We are charged with the stewardship of our own conduct. Spiritual humility can only be found in egalitarianism. This must be self-imposed and extend out to other living things and the earth as a matter of respect and consideration.

Humility requires a fundamental prerequisite to all interaction be a sincere belief in equality; a compassionate respect for everyone. To interact with anything other than this, regardless of the situation, is evidence of racism, elitism, arrogance, sexism, condemnation, entitlement, assumed privilege, etc., and fails to honor the universal truth of harmony that apparently underlies all categorizations of life. A personally chosen, sincere, egalitarian philosophy for all of life is

---

Chapter 4. Here, see footnotes 132 and 137 regarding honesty.

221 In T.S. Eliot's book *The Sacred Wood*, Dodo Press, 1920, Mr. Eliot wrote an article on William Blake (1757-1827). In that article Mr. Eliot observes of Mr. Blake's honesty: *"It is merely a peculiar honesty, which, in a world too frightened to be honest, is peculiarly terrifying. It is an honesty against which the whole world conspires, because it is unpleasant."* Jumping ahead to 2020, I don't know that it has changed at all in the intervening 199 years.

the over-riding element of humility and the mandatory spiritual requirement at hand. [222]

This relates back to Step Seven in that social humility is the principle antecedent condition to the reduction of character defects. Approach all relationships with compassion and equality, that we are all equally entitled and valued, so it is then impossible to abuse, deceive, or take advantage. This is problem prevention and we abandon all character defects in the dynamic of humility.

The second requirement for humility is for people with religious or deist beliefs. This second condition, always subservient to the first, is participating in the sincere honoring of your version of your form of higher power. Sadly, this is the historical focus of discussions about humility—a person's relationship with (their opinion of) God, which leaves available racism or prejudice and entitlement. That excuses believers from any adherence to equality.

A person decides and honors their own higher power in some worshipful, self-effacing manner; humility in service to God. Since this is entirely personal, and without intrusion from others, it is easy to become self-righteous about God and humility. Equality is easily lost when God is telling you yours is the only and best way to believe. This second aspect of humility, subservience in relation to an opinion of God, is the habitual view taken. For some people God might be "love," or a universal, governing energy in the universe, or the general director of everything. Your chosen place on this spectrum is a valid choice for only you and no one else.

Atheists must focus only on the first requirement, equality. Theists focus on both requirements. It must be remembered, whether religious or not, you cannot embrace humility without the first requirement of equality. "I am humble but don't let them live in my neighborhood." "I am humble, but I am entitled to more than you." "I am humble but this gender-equality thing is wrong; men (or women) really are the bad guys." "I am humble, but this homosexual-rights thing is not how we do things around here." And in addiction recovery, if you cannot embrace humility you cannot recover.

Principles that embody equality and acceptance, with no righteous dogma, will foster humility and serenity. Egalitarianism requires you to participate in relationships with compassion and acceptance, thus willingly incorporate a commitment to spiritual principles. This is quite enough to achieve long term sobriety and for many, if pursued with diligence, will carry you beyond the conventionally enlightened.

A "higher power" is the socially safer phrase now in vogue and is left to the interpretation of the individual. Your idea may be clear or not; you may believe or not. Regardless, be committed to something—honesty, respect, not blaming... emotional integrity. Commit to equality and shared entitlement and honor those. Should you consistently insist on these behaviours for yourself it will be enough to affect recovery.

---

222 Equality, as described here, was spoken of in the earliest forms of Buddhism.

Humility is the primary prerequisite for thoughtful participation in all relationships and immediately beside that are acceptance, rigorous honesty, and
compassion. As has been said, according to Step Seven, humility is the principle
factor in the reduction of character defects. It requires a deeply willing participation in an egalitarian lifestyle *and* the regular and sincere commitment to something more than a selfishly-oriented belief system.

Principle #4: Charity

Charity, common in the vernacular of religious people, is generally understood to be some variation of "giving things away"—giving away time, giving
away money, volunteering, donating old clothes, working in the soup kitchen.
What qualifies or disqualifies charity as having spiritual integrity is the personal
agenda underneath the behaviour. That agenda is often invisible to the individual in introspection.

When charity is offered with any underlying agenda: social advancement or
salvation, getting a tax break, for good publicity at meetings or church, to allevi-
ate guilt, then the charity lacks spiritual integrity. Yes, it's admirable and certainly
necessary, but for the addict in recovery it's spiritually suspect. In other words,
charity is socially necessary but may be unspiritual because the giver feels guilty
or pity for the recipient, tries to impress anyone (especially themselves), wants a
tax break, rescues the recipient out of some responsibility, or tries to collect salvation points with God. If there are distinctions of who's worthy of charity and who
isn't, if it's offered to live up to other people's expectations (especially shadow
expectations from the past), or to generate social admiration, it isn't spiritual.
Charity may be socially necessary but oftentimes is spiritually questionable. The
unspiritual unrecognized machinations that motivate "charity" are deceptive. [223]

"*St. John of the Cross put the whole matter [of charity] in a single question and
answer. Those who rush headlong into good works without having acquired through contemplation the power to act well—what do they accomplish? Little more than nothing, and
sometimes nothing whatever, and sometimes even harm.*" [224] Charity is always necessary, but for the recovering addict, it will often be harmful to both the giver and the
receiver without appropriate self-love, respect, compassion, and humility, as sincere
prerequisites to the charity. It will be impression management and manipulation.

---

223 Joshua Loth Liebman, *Peace of Mind*, Simon and Schuster, 1946. "*There is too much undissolved
wrath and punishment in most religions… Conscience, abetted by this kind of punitive religion, doth
indeed make cowards of us all.*" (p. 37) And, on charity that's used to atone for guilt or sin (charity
with unspiritual motives) Rabbi Liebman wrote in a letter: "*Dear Madam: Nothing could prevent
you from visiting [your shortcomings] on the victims of your humility. I advise that you love yourself
properly before you squander any love on others.*" (p. 39).

224 *Huxley and God: Essays*, Aldous Huxley, p. 175. With careful consideration this applies in carrying the message. Offering support does not include rescuing with demands or arguing.

Being generous (charitable) with your experience, wisdom, time, kindness, or spiritual courage through role modeling will be advantageous in the long run for people undecided about spiritual transformation. There's no tax deduction for compassion or respect, but these offer dignity and create a healing environment.

Principle #5: Responsibility & Obedience

These two attributes, which comprise the final spiritual principle, are usually abhorrent to addicts, angry people, and victims. Responsibility and obedience don't harbor well in our culture of victim-hood, disposable consumerism, and addiction. Certainly, these two attributes are easily viewed as separate qualities, but in regard to spirituality they are so closely related and interdependent that I present them together. (It always sounds pedantic to analyze common sense, but here it is necessary.)

If people value an idea and are respectful of it, then they would be responsible in relation to it. And, if one idea they value is being responsible, they would be willing to be held accountable for not being responsible to the value of responsibility they claim they have, which would be responsible to adhere to it and irresponsible to not adhere to it. (Yes, it's circular—dizzy yet?)

For example, if people hold kindness as an important value then they "should" be kind. They would be responsible (to themselves) to offer kindness during trying or awkward circumstances. More importantly, they would hold themselves fully accountable if they weren't kind. If they were kind only when it was convenient, or only to certain people, or only when people were watching, then kindness wouldn't be a value, it would be a convenience for impression management. Boethius' statement applies here: "*A wise [person] ought no more to take it ill when [they] clash with fortune than a brave [person] ought to be upset by the sound of battle. This is why virtue gets its name, because it is firm in strength and unconquered by adversity.*" [225]

A person who willingly pursues a relationship with a higher power or tries to live in harmony with life in a spiritually principled existence, ought not to take it ill or complain when their stated values crash up against their own human nature, frailty, and defects. Someone who volunteered to recover from addiction,

---

225 *The Consolation of Philosophy*, Boethius, Penguin Books, 1969, p. 144. In practical application, if a person values veracity they would be pleased and gracious when their own honesty was difficult to express. Being honest with kindness when this is difficult is the spiritual opportunity to prove it is of value. Being honest when it's easy proves nothing. Be thankful when faced with difficult spiritual choice; you volunteered. In intimate relationships, in recovery, difficulty is the opportunity to prove your commitment. What gives virtue and a spiritually principled life value is consistency in trying times. Virtue: Faith, hope, and charity, are the three Christian theological virtues. The Christian list of secular/social virtues are prudence, justice, fortitude, and temperance. Courage and honesty are not considered to be virtues.

regardless of the addiction or its intensity, would view all internal, personal struggles with their unspiritual impulses and temptations as an opportunity to prove they are dedicated to what they claim they value—a spiritual life of compassion and responsibility. At the minimum that would be successful restraint, veracity, responsibility, and the other spiritual principles in the maintenance steps. There is pride and success in being firm in commitment during difficult times.

If you accept a gift that you declare you value highly, you are and would be responsible to take care of it. You are responsible for things that belong to you. Your life was given to *You*, no one else. As a person in recovery, your "recovery life" was an opportunity to choose and you made the choice. Abstinence and the opportunity to be spiritual were choices you made; no one else chose this for you. Your life and health, your transformation, your cherished mementos and shiny things, your lover, your sobriety, all "belong" to you. Only you are responsible to take care of them without complaint.

Responsibility: In recovery you didn't volunteer for an easy job, you volunteered for a very difficult one. Maybe we should tell people that, which is the point of education. Truly spiritual people are willingly and completely responsible for themselves, their conduct, their thoughts, and their feelings—for their life and everything in it—*without complaint*. Without complaint is the hard part. Granted, at times you are not responsible for what is done to you, but you are responsible for cleaning up after it, again, without complaint. Hold yourself responsible for the entire state of affairs in your life. Never surrender this responsibility. Anything else requires blame and defeats being spiritual. That denies you serenity.

More importantly, since addiction is a self-imposed crisis and you volunteered for the job of becoming spiritual, all the responsibilities and hard work of recovery are self-imposed. A self-imposed crisis requires a self-imposed solution. This includes letting go of old ideas throughout your recovery. You are either running away from your past (the popular point of view) or you are walking towards spirituality (the rarest point of view). The focus of walking towards being spiritual is more effective than running away.

Obedience: If you aspire to or claim to be spiritual then you must make a sincere effort to follow these five principles, which are embodied within the maintenance steps. Steps Ten and Twelve are moment-to-moment participation exercises that you must do to maintain mental and social harmony: problem prevention. Recovery, like honesty, is not a spectator sport. Step Eleven meditation is for regular guidance towards humility. However, it seems there are very few credible <u>spiritual</u> mentors within recovery or religion. Each of us must be guided to finding our own spiritual conscience. This is why reading and meditating on credible literature is better than relying on the disorganized opinions of "fellowship."

Spiritual principles (and compliance with them) govern the way you manage all your endeavours. It's only compliance that proves you hold them of value and are responsible. Principles are only principles if you adhere to them through difficult times. Be completely responsible for yourself and obedient to the principles of spirituality, otherwise you're not obedient, responsible, or spiritual. [226]

These five spiritual principles are applicable to every aspect of every situation and relationship in your life. Haphazard cooperation with them is not evidence of spirituality, it's evidence of convenience and impression management. For people getting recovered, they are not negotiable and only available if you're willing to avoid shallowness and hypocrisy. The avoidance of shallowness and hypocrisy require self-discipline. Self-discipline to adhere to the maintenance steps is the correct use of the will. Participant, not spectator.

As operating principles of life, these are not available unless you have completed the first nine steps (or some very close identical process) with a painstaking effort of thoroughness and patience. For addiction recovery, spiritual transformation is an exact discipline in the manner outlined.

The psychological insights realized through the steps, with or without a higher power, are sequenced in the only process I have ever found that has lasting positive effect. Heal internally and take complete responsibility (Steps One to Eight). Make a sincere and determined effort to repair and heal *all* past relationships (Steps Eight and Nine). Maintain and enhance all of this on a continuing basis (Steps Ten to Twelve). A person cannot disregard any part of any one of these steps, or the spiritual principles that underlie them, and claim spiritual integrity. In detail and sequence, every aspect is equally required to become recovered. And, of course, abandoning commitment to them always has dire consequences for the addict. [227]

A parallel truth is whenever a recovered addict's life is unsatisfying, conflicted, or lonely they're not living within these principles. They're being ignored in favor of socially approved addictions, collusion in mediocre recovery, petulance, sex, blaming, revenge, dishonesty, or desire for control. That's the paradigm of the human condition in the illness of addiction. [228]

---

226 Being spiritual is the most difficult journey that anyone can undertake. And, as explained by Aldous Huxley in *Huxley and God: The Essays,* that's why there are so few saints.

227 The only alternative is to choose atheism; to choose instead a strong and consistent commitment to integrity, honesty, abandoning old ideas, etc., explained at footnote 148.

228 Always bear in mind that there are some mental health concerns that can defeat recovery and, even with excellent mentors and personal effort, the steps will prove insufficient. Medical intervention can be most valuable for depression or dual diagnosis. Yes, many people are still opinionated and suspicious about "psychiatry," but it does (often) work. People and their psychiatrists are to be viewed with compassion not suspicion. One of the more unique and exasperating aspects of ongoing emotional turmoil or recurring relapse is blaming the new person when they are provided inadequate care or inaccurate education. It may also be that people in frequent relapse are refusing to make difficult life choices about bad situations (relationships, employment, family, friendships, residence, etc.) and repeatedly put themselves back into chaos and abuse. They have been "almost rescued" from a fire and go back to live in a burning building. It's very complicated. In order to be spiritual, people are required to make definite, difficult choices based

Always bear in mind that being spiritual or humble is not restricted to only those people who believe in God. Although, I'm sure there are adamant religious folks who would disagree. Being spiritual is a certain way that we interact with each other and how we care for the earth.

If you are a religious fanatic of sorts and are critical of other religious disciplines that are different from yours, you cannot be spiritual. If you are wandering around society trying to convince everyone your religious opinions are best (missionary work) you cannot be spiritual. If there is no equality, there's no acceptance, no respect for others, and no humility. You can be righteous and religious but cannot be righteous and spiritual. This applies to twelve-step members who are quietly adamant that everyone has to believe in God.

There is no humility in righteousness, calling recovery or sobriety a miracle, or claiming privilege (nothing in these are egalitarian). There is no charity of spirit. There can be no compassion in religious or personal righteousness.

To explain this as simply as possible I have divided the general population into three categories. (1) Religious folks/theists who believe there is some form of God and are religious to some degree. (2) Deists who believe there is a higher spirit that is involved in their life but are not religious. (3) Humanists, atheists and agnostics who don't believe there is a God (or are undecided) and are not religious. All three groups have the opportunity to be spiritual according to these five principles and there is no reason for conflict.

For religious people, if you are not righteous about your religion and regardless of the religion you belong to, that organization will advise you on how you are to perceive God. Each religion has different perspectives of this opinion and is valid only for itself. These should be honored in your discipline of Step Eleven prayer and humility, especially egalitarianism, in the third spiritual principle. Along with that you would respect and never criticize other views and abide by the other spiritual principles. [229]

For deists who believe there is some sort of spirit or higher power at work and are not religious, abide by spiritual principles. Regarding humility, including egalitarianism, you would honor and respect your concept of a higher spirit that appeals to you, personally and accept all other positions as valid for them. If you were of a mind to pray to this spiritual power that would be included in your daily recognition of Step Eleven and in the third spiritual principle. This need not be arduous or complicated. All other views would be viewed with acceptance.

For atheists, agnostics, or humanists who are conducting their lives with integrity and do not believe in any higher power, the first part of humility that

---

on factual information not opinion. It is very important that self-appointed twelve-step "gurus" never misrepresent themselves and never impose opinions, especially when attached to mental health concerns. Compassion is always better than dogma.

229 There is some movement within Christianity, as observed by Michel Onfray, cited earlier, and shown in the Ontario survey (See Chapter 2) to declare being an atheist-Christian who adheres to traditional Christian values but does not believe in God.

embraces egalitarianism is the foundation of your life. Equality without criticism or judgement. That would require an absence of anger and blaming *and* include the other principles. You would not harbor sarcasm or righteousness towards believers. Living in this manner of acceptance would allow for an atheist or agnostic spiritual life.

Being spiritual, beyond any limited social perceptions, seems monumentally difficult. Social participation in modernity (discussed later) or maintaining a Group B addiction is easier but not spiritually healthier. That it's easier is an illusion only because moderate addiction is more popular, and we're trained from birth to live that way. It's the transformation into a spiritual life that seems insurmountable. Once you are well on the way to achieving it, being spiritual is much easier and more graceful than corruption or addiction or righteousness.

When children are allowed to be spontaneous, they eat when they're hungry, stop doing something when it hurts, and sleep when they're tired. The impulse to self-care and self-respect is innate. Honesty is natural and makes sense—it takes no effort. Truth is graceful and the facts are friendly. [230]

Children are taught how and when to deceive. I've often heard an adult counselling a child to be dishonest and the child asks with some confusion: "But why can't I tell?" [Years later, parents wonder why teenagers lie to them.] It's also very natural to be egalitarian. People are taught racism and prejudice, especially religious prejudice. They're taught arrogance about culture and God: "You're wrong and my way is better." This righteous arrogance can be quite subtle and careful thought is required to eliminate it.

The List, which follows, is a point form of realization. The top part is cultural in origin and people minimize their own accountability. Being spiritual, as in the bottom part of the list, must be self-imposed and pursued because it is counter to the top part of the list. The transformation isn't easy. Likewise, some people are suspicious of the mysterious energy of metaphysics (quantum physics) that appears to underlie everything.

The List

Anger is the ocean we swim in.
Blame is irresponsible.
Arrogance is taught.
Greed is culture.
Violence is cruel.
Competition is shaming.
Selfishness is society.
Fear is learned.
Honesty is natural.

---

230 "The facts are friendly" is an expression attributed to the psychotherapist Carl Rogers.

Love is spontaneous.
Affection is contagious.
Patience is peaceful.
Humility is graceful.
Collaboration is respectful.
Kindness is safer.
Responsibility is easy.
Compassion holds them all. [231]

Being spiritual often generates insecurity in others, especially regarding veracity. Rather than examine their own fear of truth they justify their insecurity and attack someone who is more honest. Be wary of the unregenerate person whose propensity to blame, criticize and disrespect others creates a dark labyrinth that keeps them off of the path of spiritual transformation, even though it appears (to them) they're on it.

A spiritual lifestyle is an all-encompassing state of existence. You will miss the mark, which is the nature of being human. When in error you only have to make amends where required and quietly refocus your energy and intellect back onto these principles. According to *Alcoholics Anonymous* this is the proper exercise of willpower. [232]

From wherever you are right now, at this immediate point in your own transformation, you are a newcomer to whatever lies ahead. The future, and how to deal with (a) our imaginings about the future; and (b), what it capriciously, eventually ends up as actually being, comprise the inherent uncertainty in life. In the face of this uncertainty, in order to appreciate the implacable grandeur of life exactly as you have been given it, consistently and voluntarily demonstrate the five principles: respect for the physical body, veracity, humility, charity, and responsibility and obedience. The serenity achieved is the confidence to attend to whatever we are dealt in a timely and respectful manner.

Where do I learn the principles?

Completing the first nine steps with a thoughtful and painstaking effort teaches the spiritual principles that are contained within that homework. But then, following your completing each step, comes the much harder part—you have to self-discipline yourself to continue to follow the instructions. Once you learn what is required you are required to follow the teaching.

---

231 Over the years a few people have asked to reproduce this list large size, framed, to hang up. That is okay provided you have included Richard W. Clark and this book title as the source. It cannot be for resale, only for limited personal use (maximum two or three copies).

232 *Alcoholics Anonymous*, p. 85 – "this is the proper use of the will."

The first nine steps are preparation for the maintenance steps and being recovered.

Learning Spiritual Principles

Each step teaches underlying spiritual principles.		You are now prepared for:
One teaches	principles 1, 2, 5, and a foundation for 3	Daily Sobriety
Two teaches	principles 3, 4, 5	11 & 12
Three teaches	principles 2, 3, 5	11 & 12
Four teaches	principles 1, 3, with preparation for 4, 5	10 & 12
Five teaches	principles 2, 3, 4, 5	10 & 12
Six teaches	principles 2, 3, 5, with preparation for 4	11 & 12
Seven teaches	principles 3, 4	11 & 12
Eight teaches	principles 2, 4, 5	10 & 12
Nine teaches	principles 1, 2, 3, 4, 5	10 & 12
Ten, Eleven, and Twelve have all five spiritual principles within each of the maintenance steps…		**Live Recovered**

What this means is if, and it is a big if, you approach the first nine steps with integrity, and learn to trust them, you are fully prepared for the maintenance steps. When you live consistently in the maintenance steps there is never any need to repeat the first nine steps, ever.

As I reflect on how these five principles coalesced in my mind, I'm very aware of my gratitude to the monks, imams, priests, ministers, and rabbis I have the pleasure of knowing, especially the Buddhist monks—Theravada and Zen practice. Also, gratitude to the therapists and spiritual advisors that helped me; my clients, friends, and students who were very generous with their trust of me. And finally, I offer respect to the authors of the many fine books I've studied, for their courage to put their views in writing for all to see. [233]

Nearing the End

I hope I have managed to convey a general sense of how complicated addictions and recovery from them are. Now that we are nearing the end of the path

---

233 Worthy of special note are: William James for *The Varieties of Religious Experience*, Modern Library Classics, 2002; Huston Smith for *The World's Religions*, HarperSanFrancisco, 1991; Aldous Huxley for *The Perennial Philosophy*, recently by Harper Collins, 1994, and *Huxley and God: Essays*, Jacqueline Hazard Bridgeman editor, HarperSanFrancisco, 1992; Gerald May for *Will and Spirit*, Harper Collins, 1982; Sheldon Kopp for several of his books; Nathaniel Branden for *Taking Responsibility*; and Bill Wilson for *Alcoholics Anonymous*. Footnote 27 has a list of other authors.

of knowledge and conscious understanding, and if you have managed to read all of this with a thoughtful mind, there is one thing left to offer. It is subtle but I believe we must now answer:

- How is a long-term commitment to this difficult path of advanced spiritual recovery, in this culture of chaos, gracefully accomplished without struggle or self-persecution? (or) How is it accomplished without selfishness and righteousness?

- The nuances are delicate in progressively deeper spiritual perceptions. How do you arrive at some mind-place where you are never chastising yourself into cooperation? (or) How do you manage compassion and acceptance for yourself when addicts are so critical and judgmental?

- After all is said-and-done, with or without deities, it is always an inside-to-outside game of responsible self-discipline. How do you offer acceptance and compassion when you are constantly affected by your own shortcomings and the outside misdemeanors of life?

The way is in the knowledge of "affinity and concordant paths." It is to attain understanding of how to create and maintain a mind that aspires to awaken affinity with a concordant path to a truly spiritual life. Yes, it may sound complex but with a little careful thought, this ancient Buddhist idea is understandable, and you don't have to be a Buddhist to get it. First...

Affinity is a spontaneous or natural liking or sympathy for someone or something; an affection and respect towards someone or something. **Concordant** is being in agreement or in harmony with someone or something. I.e. Their high regard for honesty is concordant with—consistent with, their behaviour with people.

For those of us who have developed affection and fondness for some interest, we have created a unique place of calmness in a world of turmoil. This is concordant affinity. The only place I have ever heard it spoken of has been in my discussions with Buddhist monks and what has been written in *The Treasury of Knowledge – Buddhist Ethics* (Book Five) by Jamgon Kongtrul, translated by Kalu Rinpoche. The brief summary for Buddhism is found in the translator's introduction at p. 23. Here, I apply it to spiritual recovery.

Examples: For some it may be gardening. You find pleasure in it. Your flowers are attractive and calming. Your vegetables are tasty. Gardening is important to you and you affectionately think about gardening when you are not doing it. That is an affinity for gardening. *And,* you abide by a proven set of guidelines for what is best for growing things. You have an inner affection for gardening, and you understand and follow—you gracefully cooperate with the best gardening rules. That would be a concordant affinity for gardening and will result in success.

For others it may be playing or creating music. It brings joy and harmony to you and your life. You have affection for your instruments, you cherish them and care for them. You have consulted with experts and follow the "best rules" for excellent playing. This is concordant affinity for music. Or, it may be meditation in some manner of Step Eleven—a calm peaceful affection for this pastime. You are cooperative with the best rules for this meditation. Or, it may be walking in the woods, cooking, or an affection for time in conversation with a lover or close friend governed by respect and honesty. Concordant affinity. In spiritual pursuits this would naturally exclude activities of aggression, manipulation, or competition.

Affinity and being concordant are essential for commitment and gracefulness in the long-term way that being spiritual is accomplished. For those of us here, a long-term commitment to spiritual principles through maintenance steps is maintained by developing an affinity for this and the concordant path that nurtures such affinity…. maintenance steps and principles. The connecting thread between one's ordinary condition and the states of acceptance and compassion is the affinity for awakening.

Early in recovery from addiction, say the first ten years, the chaotic past is easily available for recall. Bad memories are still clear, and motivation is often based on the desire to not recreate that chaos. Early participation is motivated by not wanting to reexperience nasty circumstances. Fair enough.

Later, in this effort at recovery, at Step Seven, there "should" be a transition in motivation from running-away-from-the-past to pursuing social humility. That shift to humility becoming attractive (discussed earlier at Step Seven) when it happens, is the birth of affinity. You see and understand the value of social humility and have affection for offering it in all relationships. Hopefully, at Step Seven, affinity for humility becomes the motivator for deeper spirituality with a developing respect for the concordant path of the maintenance steps as they embrace spiritual principles.

In spiritual-recovery terms: After the memories of alienation and degradation have faded, to remain gracefully motivated to long-term cooperation within a spiritual life is built upon (a) the conscious attraction and affection (affinity) to live spiritually; and (b), knowing the bona fide guidelines in the maintenance steps will promote and nurture a long-term involvement with spiritual principles. That is the key to ever-deepening spirituality.

This effort must be on behalf of both one's own and another's welfare because you cannot transmit what you do not have. Without benefit to yourself there can be no benefit to others. That connecting thread between having an affinity for a spiritual lifestyle *and* the achievement of this through spiritual principles and maintenance steps—between our ordinary life and the almost-realized truly spiritual life, is the affinity and concordance for long term commitment after painful memories have faded.

What this means is: (1) Before a long-term, spiritual life can be accomplished gracefully to any degree, there must be some mental-personal attraction to wanting this. Remember, affinity is a spontaneous wanting and liking for something, a person, or a value. There must be a natural attraction, an affinity, for principled living. And (2), That affinity must be concordant (in harmony and consistent agreement) with "being" spiritual as outlined in the maintenance steps and spiritual principles.

During each day, the white noise in the background of your ordinary life would be being attracted to living by spiritual principles and embracing a quiet cooperation to act concordant with the outlined guidelines. The maintenance steps are the concordant path that nurtures this deeper affinity for a spiritually principled life. Side Note: Having a concordant affinity for AA meetings is rather different than concordant affinity for spiritual principles.

Without concordant affinity, the only way to achieve long-term recovery is to persecute yourself with faded bad memories and criticism to push yourself into staying, which is always unfulfilling and tenuous at best. We are usually imperfect, or at best sometimes we can be close-to-perfect for a few moments when concentrating. When off the path, all that is required is noticing our affinity for this life, a smile of acceptance, refocusing our effort, making an amend where necessary, and a gentle mind-nudge to reclaim principled living. Affinity makes this graceful when concordant with spiritual principles and a life governed by them.

I'll close this chapter with the words of the actor and author Peter Coyote. He once said in an interview: "Consistently reach for the most enlightened possibilities in any given situation."

Chapter 8

It is not by locking up one's neighbor that one convinces oneself of one's own good sense.

F. Dostoevsky [234]

Addiction and Society
The War on Drugs
Cultural Dislocation and Stress
Is Forgiveness a Contradiction?
Negative Capability

Addiction and Society

In writings earlier than 1500 CE, alcoholic drunkenness is rarely mentioned. The perception of drunkenness from near 1500 CE up to about 1800 was that drunks were a not-too-common general nuisance. Regular, daily consumption of wine and ale were common, but excessive or morbid drunkenness was rarely mentioned. Shakespeare made it of particular note in *Othello*, near 1603. The quote from *Othello* is noted near the beginning of this book. Later, excessive drunkenness was worthy of attention in the records of the Hudson's Bay Corporation, in their isolated outposts in the Canadian wilderness in the 17th and 18th centuries. Prior to 1800, however, society's response to drunkenness was not persecution or accusations of sin. There were no medical or professional investigations into "heavy drinking" as there had been for various other social concerns like diseases, prosthesis, war wounds, or surgery. Most of what follows will principally be about alcoholism and addiction in the United States where Alcoholics Anonymous began.

There was a big shift around 1835 in the United States. From then, drinking began to carry Protestant-religious condemnation. Drinking was described by them as religious-social degeneracy and moral failure (sinning). So... with the formal organization of The Temperance Movement in 1840 in the US, any person who consumed alcohol, of whatever amount, was seen as a sinner, or a

---

234 From *A Writer's Diary*, Fyodor Dostoevsky. There are variations of this, depending on the translator. This was also a cited reference in Michel Foucault's book *History of Madness*.

moral degenerate and irresponsible. "Lips that touch liquor shall never touch mine!" was a common refrain.

Alcoholism was a term coined near 1852 by a Swedish physician, Magnus Huss (1807-1890). He was the first person to view chronic drunkenness as a pseudo-medical concern. The new name he chose for chronic alcohol consumption was alcoholism and for the consumer, the relapsing drunk was an alcoholic. The terms were not in common use in North America until near 1870. But even with the new medical-sounding labels, Protestant-American society still viewed drinking, to any degree, as a moral failure. So, alcohol consumption, alcoholism, and the alcoholic, according to that Protestant-Christian view, was a sinner's lifestyle of corrupt morality. Consumers of alcohol were "bad" Christians.

The Protestant Temperance Movement became a formal organization in the US in 1840 and preached against the moral turpitude of any alcohol use. They were principally female Protestant Christians and condemned *anyone* who drank. The Temperance Movement's goal was to eliminate alcohol drinking from society. The movement was definitely not interested in saving the individual drunkard. Society's salvation was going to be through the Protestant Christian church that would lead "us" to an alcohol-free society in the righteousness of Protestant Christianity.

The Washingtonians, a male response to the (principally female) Temperance Movement, began in Baltimore in 1840. That group, in some measure of irony and humor, focused on saving individuals from pernicious spirits and were not interested in massive cultural change. For The Washingtonians, irresponsible drunkenness was addressed by "swearing off" and taking a pledge. There was strong peer support and the Washingtonians were quite secular and not religious at all. Their approach to saving the individual drunk was successful and, in contrast to the later politics of AA, did not include God or prayer. They became a large organization, close to 400,000 members, but fell apart from their own internal strife and politics in the later 19th century. They were successful, but… their purpose of helping the individual alcoholic became lost in the conflict of political concerns, the American civil war, the abolition of slavery, suffragettes, and temperance.

It should be born in mind that The Washingtonians were quite effective in assisting the individual alcoholic *and* had a very non-religious view. Consider that this was sixty years before the advent of the automobile and forty years before the telephone; one-hundred years before the influence of medicine or psychology, and their program was very secular—it did not include prayer or any religious indoctrination. 400,000 members in the mid-1800s; rather remarkable.

The Temperance Movement, through various efforts and political maneuvering (from about 1880) became attached to and combined with, women's suffrage. Together, suffrage and temperance continued in their strong political and religious focus of cultural criticism. Christian hegemony, the disdain for alcohol and drinkers, and advocating for women's suffrage became political movements which gained influence and were supported by other political concerns. By 1916 twenty-six of the forty-eight states were 'dry.' The import, export, manufacture, sale or purchase of alcohol was illegal. There was a strong, new designation of religious moral failure: The Drinker.

This led to Prohibition (1920-1933). It is important to remember this was after a century of constant Protestant-religious persecution of drunkards. Moral failure and condemnation of drinkers were a dominate social view from about 1880 through Prohibition into the late 1940s. Alcoholism (morbid drunkenness), in the United States, became an especially serious concern, as did opiate addiction.

From about 1860 through to the depression, in the United States, there had been:

(i) cultural instability after several significant wars which had been almost continuous from 1860,

(ii) the unrelenting changes in industrialization and flourishing technology like railroads, telephones, automobiles, and airplanes,

(iii) the expanding technology of mass alcohol production and delivery, and the notable addiction of middle-class women to laudanum and other opiates,

(iv) rural, social disruption through working-class adults migrating into cities to manufacturing plants. This offered employment, a certain amount of new freedom, and a regular dollar income,

(v) drastically changing sexual values abetted by a newly-available independence and mobility—the automobile. It was a new portable bedroom. Women were much more assertive, adamant and out-spoken, with the "immoral" adoption of bare-shoulder dresses, shorter skirts which led to the shaving of legs, new facial makeup, public brazen dancing, and bobbed hair. This is partly related to women's suffrage, political activism, and independence.

(vii) the drastic change in the availability of opium—very easily available from c. 1870, then quickly restricted near 1910, and after c. 1917 not available (more later),

(viii) the exotic allure of the Jazz Age and jazz music, which embodied a new freedom of expression (drinking, dancing, socialization, sexuality) which harbored an obvious disdain and contempt for Prohibition—freedom from the constraints of Christian morality; and,

(ix) drinking, speakeasies, etc., as self-medication for post-traumatic stress disorder for veterans and stress relief from a culture in chaos.

All of this was principally situated in the large urban centers on the eastern seaboard of the US.

As regards opium... what has to be considered, and has been largely ignored, is the influence of Britain selling opium from India to Chinese merchants and opiates imported from China into the US. The opium trade and various opium wars had been going on for at least a hundred years. Chinese rulers wanted to prohibit the trade and Britain, *et al*, fought to keep trade open. Smuggling was quite evident. The Chinese war ships called Junks, used for trading in opium and in sea battles, are included in some speculation as to why heroin is called junk.

As written by James Bradley in his book *The China Mirage*, many multi-millionaires were created by the importation of opium into the US. It was on such a grand scale that prestigious universities, major railroads, the US industrial revolution, and entire industrialized cities, were built on the profits from the opium trade. Opium wealth included the making of presidents.

Near the mid-19th century, internationally, the US was second only to the British opium dealers. Together, they dominated China's economy. The opium trade governed the 19th century financial history of Shanghai. All of this opium dealing in the US was camouflaged under the innocuous name of "The China Trade." It was so pervasive that it led to the Chinese Boxer Rebellion, c. 1900, which was drastically put down to protect big-business interests. (Citation at footnote 244.) What has been unexamined, regarding its influence on alcoholism in North America, is opium.

Side Note: Cocaine, pre-1928 in the US, was identified as an ingredient in Coca-Cola. The popular drink, named Coca-Cola in 1885, was Coca from the coca leaf and Cola from a pine tree nut; actually kola. Kola nuts are from a specific evergreen tree that have a high caffeine content. Coca Cola pre 1928 was basically, water, caffeine, sugar, and cocaine. In the early years, historical levels of cocaine in Coca Cola are hard to determine. It is suggested as a general consensus that as US society became more and more aware of opium drug addiction, post-1900, the levels of cocaine in Coca Cola were gradually reduced through the years up to the 1920s. After 1925 or so it was reported to be a "miniscule" amount. For brand name licensing and patent reasons, cocaine remained in the drink until near 1928. The drink has been cocaine free since then. Now, back to opium...

Laudanum (opium + alcohol) had been readily and openly available in the US without any restriction from about 1860 up to about 1900. After 1900 laudanum was still easily available but generally obtainable by prescription. By 1917, laudanum, that had been easily available for about fifty years, became prohibited. Opiate addiction had risen to astonishing levels in the US by 1915. [235]

---

235 Laudanum (various formulas—approximately 90% alcohol and 10% powdered opium by weight) was from Paracelsus' formulae c. 1530 CE. It was then modified/improved in England c. 1676, by Dr. Thomas Sydenham. Laudanum was _very_ popular, widely recommended, and easily available. In the American civil war 10 million opium pills and 2.8 million ounces of opium powders were distributed to the Union soldiers alone. That doesn't include consumption by civilians or Confederate soldiers. Laudanum was sold without restriction in a wide range of retail outlets from grocery and clothing stores to pubs and hotels. Estimates of the total US population (est. 101 million c. 1915) have been about eight to ten percent of the entire population were addicted to opium; (very approximate) nine million opium addicts. The other estimate, offered by a few people, is sixty percent of opium addicts were middle-class women (about 5.4 million women opium addicts). Heroin was advertised as a cough remedy (1898). Side Note: even if that's inaccurate by twenty percent, that's still a seriously remarkable number. Many laudanum "home remedy" books were published. In our modern mindset think "take an aspirin," it was

Laudanum had been principally used by women. Some reports suggest near nine or ten percent of the general population were addicted to opium, and in the US, nation-wide, sixty percent of all opium addicts were women. It is worthy of note that these opium-addiction numbers don't include any alcohol use, which would be an additional, significant portion of the general adult population. After fifty years of easy availability, by 1917, laudanum became unavailable by federal legislation. So... A significant influence on the increase of alcohol consumption c. 1917 would have been laudanum being unavailable to opium addicts. From then, through to the present day, this has created a strongly criminalized sub-culture called junkies. (After about 1920 through to 1930, the principle opium user changed from middle-class women to lower class urban males—but that's another story.) Today, the moral majority still sees junkies as a "nasty collection of despicable social deviants" who became the target of political persecution, prominent after 1973. (More later)

Let's back up... After 1920, illegal speakeasies, which ran twenty-four hours a day, every day, unexpectedly filled with large numbers of women who soon became upwards of thirty or forty percent of speakeasy patrons. This has been described as a drastic, unexpected change in the drinking population; where did all the women drinkers come from? It is a very plausible connection that the est. 5.4 million opium-addicted women, mostly in the large urban centers who could no longer obtain opium, ended up in speakeasies. That was certainly a factor in the significant increase in women drinkers. (Addiction substitution.) When about nine million drug addicted people in the US cannot get their opium, they will turn to drinking. And, as is well known, drinking alters morality. After 1920 or-so, the new availability of portable bedrooms (the mobility and privacy of enclosed vehicles) contributed to a major shift in the culture's sexual expression.

Federal regulations prohibiting laudanum, general cultural instability, post-war trauma, technology, and Prohibition brought on by The Temperance Movement, altogether caused a drastic increase in the drunkenness problem c. 1920. Thus, religious, righteous morality contributed to creating a problem larger than the one they had been trying to solve *and* encouraged social changes they hadn't anticipated. There was a new, much less restricted expression of sexual values for a mobile, alcohol-dependent society. (The drastic change in sexual values and social defiance of the 1920s was later reflected in the "hippie culture" of the later 1960s. Repression breeds contempt and rebellion, but that's another story.)

---

that common. It was especially recommended for women and children and the accepted solution for female "hysteria," the "vapors," menstrual cramps, diarrhea, pain, headaches, colicky or upset children, nervous conditions, and commonly given to infants who were teething. By 1900, in larger urban centers, opium dens for smoking were numerous and popular. Canada, Britain, and the USA had initiated restrictions and drug label requirements and by 1917 laudanum was largely unavailable. In the US: Where do 5.4 million opium-addicted women and 3.6 million opium-addicted men go? To speakeasies and alcohol. (More at Appendix III.)

Near the 1920s... The fundamentalist, temperance, Protestant-Christian perspective of life was: "Suffering-Sinner-Guilt-God-Forgiveness." That allowed for a proposed evangelical-religious solution to cultural depravity offered by the Lutheran minister, Frank Buchman (1878-1961). An American-Lutheran in England, Mr. Buchman reported his own sudden Christian conversion experience in Keswick, England in 1908. He was attending a service given by an English evangelist, Jessie Penn-Lewis. Mr. Buchman's evangel was that repentant sinners could claim salvation through a Christian-Lutheran God for all "moral failures," i.e. prostitutes, criminals, drug addicts, liars, cheats, unmarried mothers, grifters, adulterers, pick-pockets, homosexuals, alcoholics, wife-beaters... in a Protestant-Christian world untrammeled by sin. Frank Buchman began preaching his evangel in England and his meetings began to collect members. Within a few years he brought his vision to America. [236]

In 1933 the US Federal government repealed Prohibition. There were four principle reasons for this, with many side issues. (i) The significant expense and impossibility of enforcement—social defiance, contempt, and illegal drinking were rampant in the general population. (ii) The obvious rise of violence in organized crime and gangsters, and the difficulty of their apprehension because of general social collusion. (iii) The 1932, yearly projected loss of about 500 million dollars in tax revenue from liquor sales. That's about 9 billion dollars a year in 2020. (iv) Because of the depression, tens-of-thousands of people could now find work in breweries and distilleries with (a) income for the unemployed to boost the economy, (b) a reduction in the financial drain of fewer people needing social services; and (c), more personal income tax revenue. Prohibition was repealed. Now, to the later 1930s...

The dominate Protestant-Christian view of alcohol use was it was a sin and drinkers were condemned. That view had been present for the previous one-hundred years and was carried into the 1930s. Then, Frank Buchman's Oxford Group had emerged, in the later 1920s mainly in the North East of the US. He was organizing a semi-underground, evangelical Christian movement. The Oxford Group attempted, through small group meetings, to correct the general, increasing social problems of violence, gangsters, alcohol consumption, drunkenness, drug addiction, prostitution, poverty, adultery, crime, and the general failure of society to be governed by Christian morality. Anyone who was sincere but on the "wrong side" of Christian morality (sinners in general) were welcome in the Oxford Groups.

---

236 From 1908 to 1920 Buchman's group had no official name but gained influence and membership in small areas in England. In 1921 the movement was named A First Century Christian Fellowship. In 1929 they changed to The Oxford Group until 1938. Their publication *What is the Oxford Group?* by The Layman With A Notebook, was published in 1933. In 1938 they renamed themselves Moral Rearmament. In 2001 their name was changed yet again to Initiatives of Change. Today it operates under that name with a strongly Christian focus.

With Henrietta Seiberling, Bill Wilson originally attended an Oxford Group and through that met Bob Smith (co-founders of AA). Those two, and friends, c. 1937, combined information from their personal insights into drinking and their struggles to stop, from medicine (Dr. Silkworth), from psychology (Dr. Jung), from philosophy (William James) and religion (The Oxford Groups). They made a proposal that had not been heard before—recovery from the social malfeasance of alcoholism. Mr. Wilson authored *Alcoholics Anonymous*, pub. 1939, with some guidance from other male-Christian AA members. Their success eventually began to shift the Temperance Movement's view of drunkenness from being a hopeless moral plague to a treatable malady. Treatable is the operative word here. A society free of general sin was still the agenda for the evangelical Oxford Group, but the sins of morbid drunkenness might now be stopped through AA. In that, Bill Wilson saw the wisdom in backing away from the strong evangelical focus of the Oxford group and offering a less militant version of God. It was still certainly Christian, but much milder and gentler. (See YouTube: Bill Wilson Kips Bay Group 1950)

From the time of Dr. Huss, c. 1860s, alcoholism had been seen as an illness of some vague medical concern attached to an American religious view of moral corruption, but with no offer of solution. Mr. Wilson and company now offered a somewhat credible solution: sobriety, God, forgiveness, contrition, and the twelve steps. This was a bold and strange diversion from the religious view of hopeless moral degeneracy which had been around for about a hundred years. (Hopeless is the operative word here.)

So... In 1939 there was now something called AA, with their own published book. AA offered hope for treatment for moral corruption—which was really conversion from a miserable sinner (irredeemable deviance) into a stalwart, sober God-believer, seeking forgiveness and Christian-social respectability. What was presented in Alcoholics Anonymous was certainly "acceptable" to temperance and Christian hegemony; however, African Americans, homosexuals, junkies, women, and atheists were certainly "not welcome," but hard-core, older drunken white men were.

The early AA groups and their book *Alcoholics Anonymous* offered a new, tentative but verifiable solution that irresponsible drunkenness (alcoholism) was a treatable issue. Recovery with social approval became somewhat believable. This acquired faint medical credibility from Dr. Silkworth (1939, general medicine) and in 1944 from Dr. Tiebout, Psychiatry (cited at footnote 87). Granted, at that time, there was only a small percentage of success, but it was working. [237] The

---

237 Illness is a word in disfavor in modern recovery. Disease is in common usage since about 1990. There are very subtle reasons for this shift that started near 1985. Disease makes this "medically credible" and financially lucrative for medical doctors. Disease is more dramatic. Illness has shades of mental health attached to it. Bill Wilson, as late as 1961, presented that illness or malady were the more accurate terms to use for alcoholism. (See Disease or Illness in Chapter 2.)

literature of AA began the shift of social perception from irresponsible, hopeless sinner to social (Protestant) respectability, called recovery. Early sobriety success rates from AA, granted with some reservations, were credible. However, in one way, that only lasted about thirty years. [238]

With this new perception of there being a solution to drunkenness, the historical-social view of "irresponsible, moral failure and Protestant sinner," had a new possibility: being a recovered God believer. Drunks just might, maybe, perhaps and possibly, have a solution to their irresponsible moral deviance. They could redeem themselves in the eyes of 1939 society and the church: stay sober, pray to God, seek forgiveness, complete the steps, and be socially responsible. That is quite evident throughout the book *Alcoholics Anonymous*.

Morbid drinkers, whether called drunks or alcoholics, or labelled as having a malady or illness, could "recover," but that recovery required forgiveness for their sin of being an irresponsible, moral degenerate (from the shadows of temperance). They had to find God, were forgiven by God, *and* had to eventually forgive themselves and others. This stands against the recent, stronger presentation of disease rather than illness. Medicine tells us God isn't the solution to disease. (More later.)

Here's a necessary shift in perception: Albert Einstein advised: No problem can be solved at the same level of consciousness that created it. True enough. [239]

The five-point fundamentalist Protestant-Christian view of life was suffering-sinner-guilt-God-forgiveness. The "problem" of drinking—whether alcoholism or not; those morally degenerate drinkers, and the "depraved" culture that harbored them, that problem (if it was in fact a problem) was increased by the Christian mind-set of the Temperance Movement and religious condemnation. Any consumption of alcohol and the claimed general, moral degeneracy of society from the Temperance Movement, suffrage, and political clout, led to Prohibition. The increased social problem of alcoholism after 1920 (escalated by the influx of frustrated opium addicts) and the solution offered by AA in 1939 were created in the same era and by the same level of consciousness that contributed to their creation. The 1939 style of "AA" worked because it was part-and-parcel of that society.

---

238 Being drunk was categorized as a moral problem but being drunk and driving was a crime (public danger). In the United Kingdom being drunk while in charge of carts, carriages, cattle, and horses, became a minor crime in 1872. In 1925 in the UK it became an offence to be in charge of any mechanical vehicle while drunk. In the United States it was New Jersey in 1906, New York in 1910, and in California shortly after that. In Canada, federal legislation against drunk driving appeared in 1921. Dr. Harger (Indiana, USA), invented the first breathalyzer called a Drunkometer (patented in 1936). After 1933 it was again legal to drink in the US, just don't drive. What changed everything was The War on Drugs.

239 If you create problems in any relationship by anger and secrecy then a new level of openness and honesty are the level they must be solved at. See Chapter 6 on Applied Problem Solving. Actually, nothing is ever resolved by anger.

That society of 1939 is gone. After about 1970 it began to lose effectiveness and, after 2000, success has been dismal. That religious influence and their morality is greatly reduced. The values of modern culture, the decrease in religious influence, new social consciousness, and social addictions have changed everything. The faces of addiction are much more complex. The demographics changed in addiction preference, gender ratio, social categories, cultural heritage, religious and atheist views, and age. And, this culture is severely dislocated, much differently than in 1939.

Then, in 1973, the blatant labeling of drug addicts as criminals, and the politics of having a newly-created social enemy in The War on Drugs, and the Drug Enforcement Administration, permitted a legal level of persecution and the long-term erosion of civil rights with more stress and social dislocation. The purview of the DEA is a reflection of the Revenue-Prohibition agents of the 1920s—a specially appointed government police force against citizens in general where both federal police forces—Prohibition Agents and the DEA—are enforcers of an imposed religious morality. Side note: Prohibition Agents made no money for the government. The DEA and local police forces make billions from the unreasonable seizure of cash and assets.

All of this, including the significant presence of abstinence not-available addictions, the rise of atheism, and misunderstandings in the treatment of addiction, are extreme changes from the situation of 1939. Abstinence not-available addictions (like shopping, sex, celebrity worship, television, exercise, relationships, etc.) cannot take advantage of the 1939 abstinence-required solution for alcohol consumption. Alcoholics Anonymous, into the later 1950s, worked well for that era. (It may be helpful to review footnotes 11 and 13.) Today, we cannot address the addiction problem based on a 1939 abstinence model. It is necessary to go to a different level of consciousness. Here are several reasons why the original AA (and other similar twelve-step groups) and our present focus of treatment cannot reduce or even begin to resolve the addiction issues of 2020:

(i) The 180-year-old view of a morally degenerate alcoholic still strongly persists in social consciousness, as does the drug addict being a criminal. Neither label, "degenerate" or "criminal," can embrace a mindset of illness treatment. These social views are being changed (granted much too slowly) and so must treatment change.

(ii) The 1939 twelve-step solution was offered within a culture of Protestant-Christian moral dominance and white-male privilege. That culture no longer exists.

(iii) The original AA was a reflection of religious values that actually contributed to the problem. Those religious values, although still obvious in many parts of society and programs, have significantly less moral authority. Atheism is notably increasing. Treatment or recovery cannot suggest that participants must return to a 1939 mindset. The "find-God-forgiveness model" may have worked for some people then. Recall the information regarding the success of the Washingtonians with their 400,000 members and their absence of God and prayer.

(iii) Society in the 1920s definitely contributed to the alcohol/drug addiction problem of that era. Society and culture in 2020 definitely contributes to the global, multi-addiction problem present today. Recovery must be changed to reflect this new, larger wave of addictions. Abstinence is not available for many of them and so "sobriety" will not be available. We must begin to understand successful restraint.

(iv) The socially xenophobic twelve-step groups of the 1940s—no homosexuals, no sex addicts, no drug addicts, no people of colour, no Muslims, very few woman (the white, over 35 hard drinkers men-only club) was strongly reflected in the writing of very early AA, and to some degree, persists today. The groups and membership have changed; the writings used have not. The original AA program was created out of that middle-class white-male mindset and should not even be suggested in treatment today.

(v) Abstinence not-available addictions are the dominate type of addiction after 2000. These addictions cannot embrace the abstinence-available model presented for alcoholism or drug addiction. We must learn how to incorporate and establish successful restraint for this new arena of addiction.

(vi) Remember from Graph II: Group B addicts manage society, have given themselves permission to be addicts, and they persecute Groups C and D. Getting addicts to shift out of C and D into Group B is ineffective at best. That makes long-term abstinence, outside of residential treatment, a setup for failure: Please quit this addiction then go live with addicts of a different stripe. This is why residential treatment in a controlled environment appears so successful during residence but demonstrates such a high failure rate outside of residence. Addiction substitution is not recovery. Without proper education about the true nature of addiction and culture "we" can only expect a modicum of achievement. And, finally...

(vii) The 1960s and '70s style of recovery counselor was principally someone who was sober for a while and could explain well the AA recovery program— paid twelve-step work. Addiction has become terribly complicated and varied in its presentation. Now, counsellors must have a very well-developed base of knowledge about society, history, psychology, poly-addiction, relationships, and well-established skills in intervention. This is seldom the case and people willing to seek recovery are often-times bewildered by not getting the specialized help they need.

Cultural Focus Regarding Addictions - Graph II [240]

---

240 At Appendix I, Prof. Hackler advised this perspective was originally discovered in relation to alcohol use as far back as 1972 by Canadian researchers. He saw a similar pattern in family violence and reported that in his discussion paper, c. 1987. I have recast it back into addictions. Prof. Hackler cites credits at Appendix I.

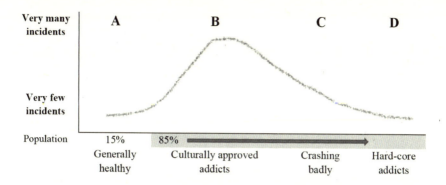

We must neutralize the still-present myth of the war on drugs (see below) and examine our significant cultural culpability. Out of that examination, we have to create an intimate, personal psychology for the resolution of addiction because it is so personal and unique to each person (review footnote 46). At its initiation, treatment must present a solution that exists outside of religious or political interference. That is why The Washingtonians were so successful, so fast—they sidestepped religious influences and social condemnation. Their efforts were kept to personal responsibility and support. The Washingtonians didn't condemn or embrace religious views. Any personal views (of religion) just weren't important to what they wanted to accomplish. Recall Mr. Einstein's observation that a problem cannot be solved at the level it was created.

The Washingtonians did not include religion or prayer, which was automatically at a level removed from the protestant religious persecution that contributed to the problem. To the Washingtonians, religion or prayer, or not, was a personal choice outside of sobriety and recovery. They didn't blame, preach or accuse, they just supported each other in not drinking and were quite successful.

In the introduction I offered this: Addictions are an epidemic, worse than any plague in the dark ages. I said I would offer an explanation in Chapter 8 and here we are. What makes addictions "worse" than the plague in the 14th century which killed about thirty percent of the population? That's a matter of perspective which I will explain.

During the plagues of the middle ages people got sick, the disease ran its course, many people died, others got sick and recovered, some didn't get sick at all, and it disappeared. About thirty percent of the population didn't get sick at all. [241] The Black Plague was a short-term illness (yes, very painful) that often ended in death. It created a superstitious view of illness, in a comparatively

---

241 The numbers are thought to be, in any plague as in the late middle ages, about thirty percent get sick and die. Forty percent or-so get sick and recover. About thirty percent don't get sick at all. See *Guns, Germs, and Steel* by Jared Diamond, 1997.

primitive society, that was generally illiterate and very ignorant of science and medicine. Death came on rapidly; it was over quickly, and life went on.

In 2020, addictions don't affect thirty percent of the population, it's more like eighty to eighty-five percent in varying degrees. That eighty-five percent, on the right of the graph (groups B, C, D) altogether have a painful, recurring negative influence on everyone, including Group A. The negative effect on everyone in society is through medical costs, violence, premature death, institutional cost (prisons, hospitals, treatment), unsuccessful treatment (repetitive inadequacy), divorce, court proceedings, adultery, poverty, extended illnesses, sexually trans-mitted diseases, welfare, incomplete education, unemployment, absenteeism, greed, debt, dishonesty, government encouragement (endorsed by big pharma-business and advertising), bankruptcy, crime enforcement, and irresponsibility. Addicts don't die within a few days, as with the plague, nor is it gone in a year or so. Addicts live for decades, constantly and repetitively inflicting pain and chaos on everyone and everything, including the environment. It's an invasive, expensive, insidious condition where eighty-five percent of the population affects one-hundred percent of the population in perpetuity. The emotional, social, and financial cost is extreme and never-ending.

Cultures, businesses, and politicians of the middle ages never encouraged the plague. Nobody in 1350 approved of the plague. Not only do we approve of addiction in 2020, we promote it. This culture encourages addiction. In twisted ways, this society is quite proud of our commerce, greed, righteousness, spend-ing, TV shopping channels, sports violence, the internet, fitness obsessions, fascination with technology, shiny things, debt, power, pointless travel, privilege, celebrity worship, superficial sex, and affluence. We categorize these as signs of success, and they aren't. These all feed and increase socially approved addiction and socially approved addiction harms the planet. [242]

A bumper sticker, from years ago, read: "There is no Them there is only us." This is subtle. We don't "openly" encourage street junkies and hard-core alcoholics in Groups C and D. The addicted power brokers of Group B, with their socially approved addictions, have created the perception that they are not them. Groups C and D addicts are abandoned to a slow death and acute despair and suffering by government "harm reduction." They warrant less entitlement to respect and care because they are viewed as moral failures and criminals. Culture essentially endorses and encourages (actually requires) addiction in Group B, which is called "social success," who then lament the horror of Group D. By

---

242   The resistance culture demonstrates to resolving the destruction of the environment is directly related to the global presence of Group B addiction—greed, wealth, pointless/meaningless travel, technology, power, privilege, convenience, exotic food, glitter and glamour, celebrity worship, shiny things, entitlement, and conspicuous consumption. These addictions require ne-glect of responsibility and destruction of the planet's ecology. That's why there has been so little progress in saving the earth. Until we educate people about addiction and drastically reduce it in Group B the environment will stay destroyed.

not examining Group B we enable Groups C and D. And almost finally, Group B addiction affects the entire world population, not just one geographic area. Altogether, addiction, today, is worse than The Black Death. There is no Them there is only us.

The War on Drugs

In association with the 1939-AA concept of recovery being a way to resolve moral corruption, limited as that view was, over the next three decades that gained credibility. The success of Alcoholics Anonymous in establishing sobriety and some degree of religious and social respectability created a new idea that morbid drunkenness was treatable.

Drug addiction had always been kept separate from drunkenness, but AA's success had a long-range palliative effect as regards drug addiction. The illness-recovery idea for alcoholism was adopted by drug addicts. AA style recovery expanded into the drug culture around 1950. Drug addiction, always generally segregated from alcoholism, became viewed as treatable through Narcotics Anonymous. [243] Physicians would still have nothing to do with formal treatment of drug addicts or alcoholics but did endorse detoxification with lectures on morality and defiance: "Go home and smarten up."

In the culture of the 1930s, the illness perspective of alcoholism was always subtly attached to the alcoholic as a bad person. It was an illness of the morally corrupt. To the credit of AA, over the next thirty-five years the illness-treatment idea gained favor. By 1970-71 AA had thirty-three years and Narcotics Anonymous had almost twenty years of success. But, in the early 1970s, as an outcome of the political demonizing of drugs, our cultural focus was grossly misdirected. American politicians created another myth: The War on Drugs.

Beginning in the late 1960s, for various political reasons (only briefly mentioned here) there was created a myth. It was the myth of the danger and horrors of drugs—LSD, cannabis in any form, and opiates. This was tied into the exaggerated reports that drug-addicted veterans returning from Vietnam were a horrible social menace, as was the social defiance of "drug-smoking hippies," the rebellious popularity of rock-and-roll music, and the sexual freedom offered by birth control and penicillin. A general social defiance was linked to drugs. This was accompanied by a great social insubordination of young adults in the

---

243 Narcotics Anonymous, NA, was organized in the very early 1950s and chartered in 1953 in the Los Angeles area of California. Jimmy Kinnon, and others, were founders. Originally NA was quite separate from the AA program. NA's growth and success in helping individual drug addicts was duly noted by society. From the success of NA in its own right, and from the then established fifteen-year success of AA, the illness concept of alcohol or drug addiction as being treatable became believable.

US—opponents to the Vietnam war *and* the legitimate and active demands for peace, gender equality, and civil rights.

All of that combined and exaggerated, led former US President Richard Nixon to vilify drugs and justify social repression. He created the Drug Enforcement Administration in 1973. Politicians promoted the horrors of drugs, the evil of addicts, the menace of social disobedience, and the immorality of drug-addicted pacifists and war protestors (all by inference, exaggeration, and innuendo). It is certainly much more complex than this, but that is the sense of it. [244]

It was a perfect confluence of issues for political abuse and erosion of legal rights. Politicians, who are terrified of losing power, or their abuses of privilege being exposed, could easily exaggerate the problem and legitimize the DEA, The War on Drugs, increased police powers of search and arrest, and justify draconian court punishment.

We cannot justify a war against good guys. War, in any country, is always justified as "necessary violence" against some form of evil. Politicians had to have an enemy to legitimize their war on drugs (which eventually was extremely lucrative for Nixon and law enforcement). Politicians needed a new enemy: drug-addict criminals. Drugs became evil and drug users an enemy of culture.

The political rhetoric was drug users were, by definition and implication, corrupting morals, luring children into depravity, irresponsible, involved in prostitution, committing welfare fraud, spreading infectious diseases, responsible for petty crime, socially unstable, and lazy. They were presented as "destroying our culture" and on the wrong side of this new war. Ordinary folks were duped into a perception of drugs and their users as being a huge and nasty corruption in society. This attitude is painfully evident today when communities band together to prevent treatment facilities in their neighborhood. Fear and dread. No one ever objects to a new children's hospital or cancer clinic.

The War on Drugs had historical, mirrored parallels of righteousness that were in The Temperance movement one-hundred-and-forty years earlier. In 1973 American politicians presented us with a variation of the Christian-historical view of alcoholics being morally corrupt from as far back as 1840 and again in Prohibition in 1920. The religious-cultural view of alcoholics being some form of social depravity had been firmly recreated in 1973 against drug addicts.

What the war on drugs did for drug-addiction recovery was take the newly established, promising view of drug addiction as a treatable illness, that started in Narcotics Anonymous around 1953 in California, and shift that view of drug

---

244 See Bruce Alexander's books, *Peaceful Measures* and *The Globalization of Addiction*. His website <www.brucealexander.com> is worth a careful read. Also see *Empire of Illusion, The End of Literacy*, by Chris Hedges, 2009. These speak to modernity. There are also these important books: Caroline Jean Acker's *Creating the American Junkie*, and James Bradley's *The China Mirage*, regarding opium. See also the documentary film *The Culture High*, Produced by Score G, BKS-Crew, and Sophia Ent. directed by Brett Harvey. The PBS documentary *Prohibition* is particularly interesting and informative, narrated by Peter Coyote.

addict + treatment to evil cultural criminal. This, in essence, destroyed the illness concept that had been gaining favor and pushed the growing success of intervention back forty years. Alcoholics were exempt from this war-enemy classification. Alcoholics remained only "morally bad" as long as they didn't drive, but drug addicts became both morally bad *and* criminal enemies (like arsonists and communists).

Two things are still apparent. The first is drug users are still on the wrong side of a political-social "war" and so they have been, and are, the target of intense criminal law enforcement. In an environment of "evil criminal," illness evaporates. In the politics of persecution, the DEA became the morality police for Christian righteousness in US drug enforcement units. Drug squads were formed all over North America. Canada jumped on the band wagon of persecution.

Prior to this, drug enforcement in local police departments was typically a small section within a larger Morality Unit. They chased prostitutes, closed brothels, nabbed bootleggers and gamblers, harassed homosexuals, arrested dope smokers, and hassled grifters. In 1973 drug enforcement was instantly elevated to being elite units (stress elite)—bigger guns, special search and seizure powers, big-time wire-tapping, clandestine undercover agents, secret surveillance units (with cameras!). Drug Squads became secret saviors of morality. There was often a glamor competition between the formerly elite unit, Homicide Squad, and these newer street-wise drug officers.

The DEA, and all other local drug squads, became the political-police soldiers fighting the "righteous war" against evil drug addicts. Mr. Nixon and his DEA were enforcers of Christian morality. An entirely demonized criminal subculture was established that affected all levels of society. [A side note: This legal enforcement of morality isn't much different from those geographical areas that made interracial marriage or homosexuality illegal for consenting adults.] The War on Drugs was a parallel to Prohibition—a political war, with a federal political police force (Prohibition Agents or the DEA; pick one). Collectively, politicians were accumulating power, punishing civil disobedience, guaranteeing that church-and-state were not separated, and erasing civil rights. This has gone unchecked for near fifty years.

The second thing that happened, around 1973, was the segregation between alcohol and drugs was significantly reinforced, as it had been in the 1940s. "Sick" people like alcoholics didn't want to associate with "known criminals" like addicts. Alcoholics were at least legal, morally corrupt maybe, but legal as long as they didn't drive. Drug addicts were lawbreaking criminals, driving or not. In the 1970s this re-established the elitist view of the AA meetings of the 1940s—drug addicts are not welcome here. This attitude is still prevalent in many AA meetings today regardless of the addiction: "Alcoholism is ours, other addicts: Keep Out!" Many recovery groups share this intolerant attitude; a kind of xenophobic pecking-order in the hierarchy of addiction recovery.

Recovery segregation persists. Gender specific recovery groups (Women vs. Men) are prolific and susceptible to an array of problems that entrench isolation.

Gamblers are ignored—nobody knows what to do with them. [Actually, no one has to do anything with anyone—acceptance and compassion are what needs to be "done."] Homosexuals meet "over there somewhere" don't be here. Food addicts aren't real addicts, just get a grip and go on a diet. Sex addicts are oftentimes subjected to the strange perception of having the good fortune to get laid a lot—what's to complain? But real sex addicts are icky, wash your hands. Relationship addicts are just complaining they didn't get their own way. Atheists are a threat—we don't like you; you can visit but just be quiet about it. We are back to Us and Them, but there is no them.

All of this, in a thousand variations, is partly from the various manifestations of addiction, partly from shame and fear, and partly from ignorance about addiction; ignorance and prejudice in religion, politics, and culture. All of this isolation is a reflection of unresolved relationship concerns. Running away is easier than any hard-work understood alternatives. Some addictions are unique unto themselves. There's the religious demonizing of addiction and sex, huge misunderstandings and failings in gender politics and civil rights, and the catastrophe of social dislocation. It's all very complicated.

With the psychological subtext of alienation in all addiction (Mr. Wilson called alcoholism a cave of loneliness and isolation), emotional identification between any of these groups is almost impossible. There is a *serious* ignorance of addiction, cultural complicity, and avoidance of responsibility. Dislocation and violence are significant, loneliness is prolific, relationships are transitory, exercise, privilege, and spending addictions are encouraged, alcoholics are tolerated (provided they don't drive), drug addicts are condemned nasty criminals, gamblers are generally bad, and sex addicts are really, *really* sick. People who are fanatics about religion aren't addicted to self-righteousness, they're just a little too passionate. This leads us to the subtle racist-hubris of "our kind only." Recovery xenophobia. From 1939, alcoholics were worthy of help, providing they sought forgiveness for being morally bad. After 1973 drug addicts were worthy of persecution.

A deep segregation was created and exists in addressing addiction. This is evident in treatment, in medicine, in religion, in politics, in gender concerns, in sexual orientation, and in twelve-step programs. Segregation is apparent in how many people are insistent and fussy in belonging to groups of my-kind-only or refer to themselves as just alcoholics. Others insist on being just drug addicts which carries a certain increased level of notoriety (criminality) and social drama that alcoholic doesn't. Gamblers usually can't join in recovery, and sex addicts rarely try to belong anywhere—they anticipate rejection and just stay away, forgoing the inevitable. All of this is judgment and evaluation, fatal to a spiritual recovery.

Criminalization and the related moral condemnation are two reasons for the rapid increase in recovery houses, especially for drug addiction. These centers, whether effective or not, are a reaction to persecution. They try to meet the needs of addicts in a society that doesn't approve of their illness or their presence.

The demonizing of addicts from the war on drugs took them out of society into private recovery to care for each other; nobody else would. The sick and lame of addiction are helping each other in the face of punishment and rejection. As I said, notice the negative community reaction and protest to a recovery house being in anyone's neighborhood. [245]

As an aside to all of this, for anyone seeking recovery, what sits next to the illness concept; what is still present and tangible in culture and should not be forgotten is the Christian insinuation alcoholic-addicts are sick in a morally corrupt way—sinners requiring forgiveness. Without exception, all of the addict-alcoholics I have worked with in Groups C and D have one thing in common. They have adopted a deeply ingrained view of themselves that corresponds with the imposed religious political doctrine: they are bad. They feel guilty and ashamed for being a social failure and a trouble-maker. Interesting, too, that all of the socially-approved addicts I have worked with from Group B are appalled and defensive that they might, possibly be addicts contributing to the horrors of "those really bad ones" over there and invariably claim it's not me it's Them.

As has been discussed elsewhere, being morally bad is an imposed religious perception that stands opposed to the illness-disease model. No one need seek forgiveness or the resolution of guilt for cancer or Alzheimer's or diabetes. No one seeks forgiveness for smoking. Quit—yes; forgiveness—no. Why seek forgiveness or guilt resolution for the illness of addiction? The subtle confusion is professionals and treatment centers, including most twelve-step programs, abetted by almost everyone, preach illness or disease but indoctrinate sick people into a structure of forgiveness. Every person, and I include every addict in treatment, has to resolve this unexamined conundrum. Attached to that is the mind-set of addict-is-criminal from the political war on drugs.

This leaves everyone, especially addicts themselves, with a noticeable, deep fear and dread of addicts or alcoholics because they are subtly viewed as nasty criminals, violent, or morally corrupt. This view of moral corruption, very evident in the early literature and most twelve-step programs, is quite negative and must be avoided, through education, in developing new programs.

There's anxiety and strong distancing from this immoral, suspicious gang in our midst (groups C and D), never mind that about sixty percent of society are addicted and denying it. This is subtle: In the medical version of "addiction-is-disease," that immediately excludes Group B from the problem. No one can convince anyone in Group B they have an illness, let alone a disease. But, in the spiritual version, Group B is the major contributor to the problem. An uneducated population will believe this social manipulation as they eat sugar, watch porn, surf television channels seven hours a day, spend hundreds on a shopping

---

245   There are similar parallels between all of this and our view of mental illness, especially from the mid-17th to early-20h century. Old, cold, stone prisons and big institutional-type buildings became insane asylums. The writing of Michel Foucault describes this well. See his *History of Madness*. It's a detailed 750 pages; not for the faint of heart.

channel, hunt for lovers on dating sites, harm themselves in obsessive fitness, are fixated on beauty, grossly irresponsible in pharmacology, or spend themselves into a bankrupt stupor.

Gamblers as addicts have recently gained some credibility but will remain marginalized; businesses and government will not tamper with the profit from gambling. The next group that society will have to come to terms with will be sex addicts. That will be a big one because of the religious strangle-hold on morality.

We urgently need a new educational effort to understand that addiction is an illness with definite cultural collusion. As was said earlier regarding the parental rejection of unruly children, parental frustration and rejection are often a significant part of the problem. Addiction is always a subtle issue of relationships and self-destructive addicts are rejected by society. How much of the problem is the actual addiction, how much is ineffective treatment, and how much is the rejection and disavowal by a culture that subsidizes the problem?

Diabetes patients are not given sugar and cancer patients are not given tobacco. Schizophrenics are not soaked in ice water (they were in 1910). Post-Traumatic Stress Disorder patients are not beaten with sticks. Eating disorders are not treated with chocolate cake. The chronic advertising of alcohol or giving opiates to drug addicts ("harm reduction" [sic] in Canada) makes corrupt and preposterous the social-medical-political claims that addictions are a disease. The absence of compassion in scapegoating addicts is obvious.

Governments and enforcement agencies, especially around opiate and designer chemical drugs, are very rejecting of the addiction-is-illness perspective. We continue with war, persecution, and accusations of moral failure. Violence and tyranny suit the government's purpose more than treatment.

There is considerable social hypocrisy and cruelty to be explored in the shallowness of how we use the word disease or explain harm reduction as regards addiction. Free needles and dispensed opiates in an old building in a slum district is not harm reduction. That's more at indifferent cruelty, regardless of how it is justified. Harm reduction to addicts would be respectful treatment, in a compassionate environment, with wise guidance, and the long-term establishment of acceptance in relationship. In Portugal, with notable, verified success, all drugs were decriminalized. Education is the only thing that can accomplish this.

Cultural Dislocation and Stress

Alcoholics Anonymous, the book, brought insight and relief to many and has, more or less, stood the test of eighty-five years. Always bear in mind, however, that a 1915 Christian moral righteousness helped create the problem that 1939 AA responded to, and within AA over the last sixty years the God-thing has pushed many people away from recovery (review footnotes 30 and 60). Within the writing of AA, it states that more would be revealed over time, and old ideas must be abandoned if recovery efforts are to advance. Much has been revealed about addiction and society, and it is time to abandon old ideas about treatment.

Increasing addiction problems across the decades, beginning with alcoholism and progressing to drug addiction (more prominent after 1940), with the now over-riding general cultural addictions of Group B is where we sit. It is almost the case that this culture is altogether a manifest personality disorder. And, as society changes, there exists a complex philosophical contradiction—the label of disease within a society that still holds it as a moral failure.

There's a major, social cognitive dissonance. Capitalism and financial "success" are necessary in North America but that "success" is significantly responsible for the drastic increase in pharmaceutical-drug and abstinence not-available addiction. Today we are trying to fix a problem that culture is complicit in creating while attempting to deny any responsibility for that complicity. [246]

Since 1939 there is a new and drastically different social structure. This is evident everywhere—in employment, disparity in privilege and wealth, in education, parenting, and sexual expression. Some drugs are legal for tax revenue, designer chemicals and opiates aren't. Pharmaceutical drug addiction and hypochondria are encouraged, and transient relationships are standard. There's socially approved addiction, abstinence not-available addiction, family disintegration, increased social violence, and global religious violence as political statements. There's the loss of tens-of-thousands of small and medium size companies through mega-corporations, pension plan frauds, and slave wages everywhere—the globalization of manufacturing and business. Government indifference threads through it all.

Altogether, there's significantly higher levels of stress, chaos, poverty, and biological toxicity. Complex health concerns like Alzheimer's, autism, diabetes, dementia, undifferentiated loneliness, cancers, depression, street drug use, harmful medical prescriptions, alcohol consumption, sex addiction, obesity, strokes, and suicides are increasing. Inadequate housing, homelessness, and violent crime are "up." All of this is more prevalent than twenty years ago.

---

246 In a related spiritual point of view, Albert Schweitzer, winner of the 1952 Nobel Peace Prize, said, "Example is not the main thing in influencing others. It is the only thing." This culture and the society that inhabits it are largely bereft of spiritual endeavor and therefore absent of example.

Governments kill people over gasoline. Political terrorism of the 1960s has become religious terrorism of 2015. There's no end in sight. Hopeless isolation.

There's the influential voice of minorities, increased immigration, and more awareness of prejudice, sexual abuse and religious corruption. A technology that denies emotional responsibility is insidious. Exposure to different religions, religious terrorism brought on by politics, the definite increase of atheism, the necessary changes to gender equality, personal choice, and civil rights cannot be addressed as quickly as is necessary. Power-brokers, government, law enforcement, the military, big-business, and the Christian religious conglomerate resists and defies any effort to water-down their privileges. In recovery meetings the age, presenting addiction, male-female demographics, and the influence of religion, have drastically changed. In recovery, there is a backlash reaction from the older moral majority. And last but not least, overall, it appears there is a much higher level of education with a lower level of literacy.

All of that contributes to a cultural situation that has never been experienced before. One of the unspoken-of consequences to mass media and instant information through the internet is that people are subjected to information and change faster than it can be assimilated. This creates anxiety and a definite sense of being constantly overwhelmed. That precipitates a retreat from responsibility. That retreat can be in front of the television seven hours a day, a retreat into sex and addiction, or exorbitant debt and exotic travel, or into isolation and depression—hiding from an unmanageable, hostile society. Group C and D addicts in short-term treatment, who are fragile for the first three or four years, are discharged from a controlled environment back into that chaos.

Altogether, these create an extraordinarily different recovery population and different treatment needs than in the 1940s. All of these are major contributing factors to the rise in addiction. In my view, these demand a very sophisticated approach to personal recovery/treatment, more than saying prayers and superficial step work without education. Before we can figure out where we have to go, we have to recognize where we are. What do we do about this as regards addiction?

Two observations: The treatment of addiction is the healing of an entire personality. The study of addiction must include the study of culture.

These observations are made to point out how personal and professional recovery programs, counsellors, treatment, the public, governments, doctors, and twelve-step programs must incorporate all of this into their offerings of assistance. They cannot, with any success, demand of this society, compliance with the former Christian-God-forgiveness model from 1939. To insist on that style of AA-God recovery is to guarantee diminished returns for investment. This is obvious in the est. ninety-five percent relapse rate. It is also apparent that spirituality and humility, essential to recovery, are held in suspicion as religious dogma by many. [247] Modern culture encourages all this dislocation and shame. It

---

247 Forgiveness is definitely optional, which is dependent on a person's perspective of illness. I

routinely demands participation in unspiritual behaviour and imposes punishment and guilt for anyone not compliant. Punishment for non-compliance and the imposition of guilt has always been a dynamic of religion and culture. The insecurity of the majority.

These are the foundation of modern culture. Nevertheless, from history and society, addiction is still seen as a rebellious moral deficit. It is as much the moral deficit of society as the individual; one is reflected in the other. That is why society has unconsciously created the A-B-C-D social groups. People in Group A, the generally healthy ones, are just plain weird. Group B are the majority, cooperating with their own rules of approved addictions. They view themselves with myopic thinking that they are embodied success. Groups C and D, our friends and relatives, are the rejected failures that warrant blame.

We must now educate ourselves out of this mind-set. Abandon any idea that the Christian-God-forgiveness model is necessary for everyone. Religious morality should never be imposed. [248] Compassion in education towards an insightful awareness for the mess we have all created is essential. It's time to move to a personal, spiritual psychology for resolution that exists underneath culture, happens outside of drastically changing religious views, and avoids the encouragement of approved social addictions. We cannot reduce the addiction crisis within the model of God-forgiveness and, as insurmountable as it seems, it cannot be reduced until we challenge this addicted culture and the society that inhabits it. This begins with educating "addicts" in addiction recovery for they are the most invested in learning it.

Political Tyranny

How close are we all to being disenfranchised rats? (footnote 253)

The cruelty of creating political and social enemies has become obvious from the end of the Second World War. Greed needs a victim and all politicians in our xenophobic, global war-culture always need a bad guy. They used and use parallelism to create new enemies (leap-frogging from bad guy to bad guy). Enemies went from Russian Communists (the cold war), to Chinese Communist types (i.e. Red China and Vietnam), to drugs (built on an exaggerated concern of returning veterans), which quickly attached itself to those "belligerent" drug-smoking, draft-card burning, rock-and-roll peacenik hippies. That soon included

---

know this will generate controversy with some people, but it has proven viable (briefly outlined later in this chapter). See 'Contracts and Forgiveness" in *Spiritual Transformation, Third Edition*, beginning at p. 332.

248 As many of us have read and seen over recent decades, many people are aware of a moral corruption and abuse in religion, with mounting evidence to support that. Religions are a righteousness of opinion that cannot provide guidance in the resolution of addiction.

those socially disobedient women who wanted equal pay, and those "subversive" activists for civil rights, even though there was nothing subversive about any of it. They were all nasty radical types and enemies of good social order (meaning white patriarchy). From there it easily went to drug suppliers (suspicious foreigners who spoke Spanish), to drugs and drug dealers (but never to include big-pharma companies), and drug users (but not to include adults who drank a lot or swallowed valium by the pound). [249]

Each of these groups, and anyone associated with them, were portrayed, at various times and to different degrees, as evil, destroying families, being horrible parents, criminals, lazy, spreading disease, a threat to good social order, morally corrupt, a threat to children, vicious, lazy, undermining democracy and proper religious order, culturally dangerous, and worthy of being repressed. Of course, in a very few isolated situations some were valid concerns, but generally grossly exaggerated to justify the accumulation of political power and judicial bullying.

With drugs, this is to create social fear; to more easily manipulate an anxious, poorly informed, fearful population, and to justify the erosion of civil rights and privacy. Finding vaguely weak connections in the creation of enemy demonstrates a false parallelism. It's easy to claim similarity in thirty-second sound bites and flashing television pictures of depravity and aggression when the politicians, business conglomerates, and religious officials remain unexamined. This leaves modern culture in chaos, people living with fear, dread, and major stress, believing lies, and a government that too easily defends its violence. If it can't defend its violence or privileges suddenly it becomes an official secret. Political tyranny. Within this cultural deterioration, there's a significant rise in addiction.

Why put this here, isn't this about recovery? As was said earlier, people with addictions have to know their enemy. Successful treatment or recovery is much more than just reducing the five social symptoms. It is also dependent on knowing the enemy. I wrote that the Temperance Movement and Prohibition helped create a massive cultural problem with alcoholism. With political clout, they imposed their strongly held religious beliefs of moral depravity on an entire culture. Since 1973, the politician's war on drugs and criminal persecution of drug users (but not alcoholics) has done the same thing.

Mass media misrepresentation and political tyranny are significant contributors to the brutality of our culture. Drug addicts are actually political criminals. This is fear-mongering and persecution. No addict should ever be classed as a defiant trouble-maker, meaning socially disobedient to the mandate of hypocrisy in the moral majority. All of this creates the ineffective clumsiness of treatment and the rising death rates of addicts.

---

249 Earlier I wrote of the common availability of laudanum pre-1915, principally used by middle-class women. Most of us are aware of the nasty addictions from decades of easily available benzodiazepines from c. 1960—valium junkies, principally prescribed to woman. Comparing 1915 and 1965, there is a parallel, similar, gender delineation between mood altering drugs for women. Opium to valium. Humm…

It's impossible to resolve or harmonize the disparity between what's necessary in addiction treatment and what's presently available in this society, today. What's needed is éducation (of probably everyone) acceptance that there is no Them, there is only us, relationship integrity, and sincere support in personal choice. Imposing the status of moral failure or criminal, or the need for God-beliefs, can never be classed as acceptance. Compassion and developing the complex issues of relationship health are essential. This is quite impossible for the spiritually unregenerate. What we actually have is medical interference motivated by greed, social-emotional relationship conflict, cultural dislocation, political/criminal persecution, and an attitude of addiction being moral corruption with the subtle religious condemnation of sinner.

There's punitive political and religious violence just about everywhere. All the righteous types are right, ask them, they'll tell you you're wrong. Atheism should not be criticized or demeaned. The no-god alternatives are a valid and a generally non-aggressive personal opinion for at least thirty-five percent of society. There are no reports of agnostics arrested in a plot to blow up a synagogue. News Flash: Atheist Arrested for Shooting a Physician at a Family-Planning Clinic. News Flash: Agnostic Blows Up Subway Station. Look to religions for those.

In the last four decades this has been made worse by modernity. Modernity, very briefly, is the clamoring for a global market and the destruction of small businesses and communities. It is the lack of stability, increased greed, celebrity worship, glamour and status, impression management, fractured family relationships, too much mobility and relocation in unstable employment, the conflict of technology vs. emotional responsibility, people alienated from each other, drug companies creating cultural hypochondria, religious terrorism, and racism in all corners of the world. There's a loss of personal identity in this nasty spectacle, and a mass media that advertises all of this constantly. [250]

It's bigger and more complex than that, but that's the sense of it. In a very generic overview, remember that we have probably 5,000 years of traditional, small-community lifestyles and mutual social-family support (about 170 generations) destroyed in 150 years (five generations) of industrial revolution, political irresponsibility, international wars, technology, and corporate greed.

This domineering industrial-global marketplace upsets the traditional, stable economic system of small industry. It creates a very transient work force both in tenure and geography. Employment cannot be depended upon, even with exceptional ability and extensive education. Moving entire corporations to another country for tax breaks and a minor increase in profit is common, which means

---

250 Celebrity worship, impression management, and status are entrenched in the recovery community's need to participate in massive world conventions which, at a spiritual level, are actually a harmful spectacle (spectacle: from Latin, a 'public show'). Holding hands to say a prayer, whether 50 at a meeting or 60,000 at a convention, is a spectacle. The larger the group the less spiritual it is. Spectacles bestow bragging rights: look how special we are, wow! What humility is there in public displays and showing off?

that for the first time in history unemployment is caused by avoiding taxes and embracing greed not business failure. The gross disparity of wealth, the cruel indifference of politicians to hardship, general financial instability, the necessity of debt, religious and secular violence, the destruction of the planet, and failure to respond to social need, are all consequences of Group B addiction. Whatever former stability was available is now broken. The dislocation is real and a principle cause in the rise of addiction and illness.

This relates back, in an obscure way, to the ego structures of addicted relationships described in Chapter 4. The reality of an entire population being forced to accept government neglect and mishandling (of their rights and their money) creates a deep dislocation and an emptiness to a meaning of life. There can be no stability in identity and no sense of truly belonging. There is a permanent and personal sense of being overwhelmed, feeling isolated, and loneliness as a part of this human condition. (Review Loneliness in Chapter 4.) This creates a desperate search for relationship and feeds "dating sites" and the recent recovery-meeting claims that exaggerate the importance of fellowship. Casual sexual encounters, debt spending, notoriety, flamboyance, aimless travel, escape in exotic fantasy, celebrity worship, and glitter and glamour are pursued. These are socially approved and have been increasing since the early 1950s. [251] All of this is (mostly) for combatting loneliness and social dislocation.

Relationship addictions are drastically increasing. In Chapter 2, I discussed that addiction is not a family illness. You can now understand that it's a cultural issue that is only reflected in family. After all, it's easier to chastise a family than it is to condemn a culture. In the introduction I wrote we have to recover from this culture as much as anything else.

What's more is, modern treatment interventions are designed to get people from unacceptable addictions like drugs, alcohol, pornography, and gambling back into society. Admirable at one level, but society and culture are an ocean of active addiction. Again: We are pulling people out of a fire, treating their burns, and sending them to live in a burning building. Treatment is to manage symptoms in addicts in Groups C and D in order to push them back into the subtle addictions of Group B. North America is undertaking addictions management not addiction treatment. (See Appendix III) It is quite the same with civil rights and violence; manage the recurring injustice, but don't make the effort to eliminate the root causes.

And now it becomes a little more complex. Along with all of this is the undeniable stress associated with extended illness, an aging population with limited access to proper medical aid, and limited support in dying with dignity. There's stress with substandard food products, limited access to clean water, addiction to medication (lucrative and convenient for some doctors and pharma

---

251 This is remarkably well-predicted in James Jones' novel, *Go To The Widow-maker*, wherein two characters, Al Bonham and Lucky Grant, discuss the new cultural phenomenon of glitter and privilege. A brief excerpt from his book is quoted at Appendix II.

corporations), destruction of the environment (briefly spoken of at footnote 242), poverty, inadequate housing, emotional isolation, racism, religious terrorism, violence, and double-dealing indifferent politicians (endorsed by big business).

There is also significant stress and loneliness related to the disparity in longevity—women living eight or ten years longer than men. Near 1920 life expectancy was approximately equal at sixty-one years. Stress related to cancer, c. 2018, was one in two woman and one in three men will experience at least one episode of cancer in their lifetime. In the 1920s, when five times as many people smoked, one in eleven people contracted cancer. These changes in three generations are very significant. There is a decided lack of human connection that embodies integrity and little stability in caring that we can depend on, unless you are rich.

Since the industrial revolution, cultural dislocation as in *dukkha* described in Chapter 2, has gotten continuously worse. It is now global and certainly out of control. We are crushed by modernity. This is a significant cause of the proliferation of addiction, especially to the socially approved abstinence not-available ones.

From all of this, one of the greatest sources for anxiety is that we subconsciously somehow sense, but cannot articulate, that people have become disposable. We are disposable like broken toasters or outdated cell phones: Throw them away. Treatment: Sure, we care—$30,000 for thirty days then go away. Huge corporate layoffs and relocation: We are disposable. Get a divorce: My own subtle addictions make my spouse disposable. Pension plan frauds: My greed is more important. People are disposable. Integrity and compassion are only camouflage to conceal self-centered indifference. No one really cares when it interferes with selfishness. [252]

This marries up well with the subtle but abusive justifications for (opiate) harm reduction. Addicts are the enemy from the war on drugs. It's easier to dispose of them and less expensive, rather than to sincerely look after them. People have become disposable. All of this creates a drastic increase in stress and loneliness, and about that, there is much to be said. The only way I know to begin to shift any of this is through the education of addicts, for they are the ones invested in learning this. [253]

---

252 Modernity. The destruction of small industry, the resulting lack of a sense of personal worth, the clash of technology against emotional responsibility, alienation from each other, religious terrorism in most corners of the world, and a loss of personal identity. It's bigger and more complex than that, but that's the sense of it. Bruce Alexander's books, cited earlier, discuss this in some detail.

253 The HBO Documentary, *One Nation Under Stress*, by Dr. Sanjay Gupta (released early 2019) is well worth watching, at least twice. There are too many important observations and comments in the film to be listed here. The end result is suicides, anxiety, depression, disease, addiction, loneliness, food disorders, illness, cancers, are all rising. Stress and illness rates are increasing. We may be living longer but are sicker while doing that. Also see the documentary film *Rat Park*, a Crave Original Documentary from Vice Studios Canada, directed by Shawney Cohen. Rats in

Richard W. Clark

Is Forgiveness a Contradiction in Recovery?

We have all been laid low by illness and injury: flus, colds, accidents, cancers, headaches, diarrhea, broken bones, scrapes, heart attacks, bruises, and depression; such is life. Often, when we experience these, we are sometimes incapacitated and depend on others to make an extra effort to help for the few days or weeks while we are laid low. We would like to receive help as we would help others we care about when they are ill or banged up. We call that a supportive relationship. Fair enough.

In the personal transaction of forgiveness, i.e. "I forgive you for your bad behaviour," before you can forgive anyone for some insult or misdemeanor two things happen that are never spoken of. The first is you have judged their behaviour as mean or nasty and the person as "bad" for doing whatever they did. The second is, you have unilaterally decided they owe you something for their nasty behaviour. You have created a debt—they owe you. You are now entitled to one I'm sorry, a week of doing dishes, theater tickets, or a winter condo in Mexico. But, and it is a big but, because you are so magnanimous and kind and spiritual and very generous you forgive them the debt that you have decided they owe you.

In other words, they have been judged (by you), found guilty of bad behavior (by you) for being human, judged (by you) that they owe you something, and sentenced to pay some arbitrary debt you assessed that they owe you. But just wait... wait for it... you suspend the debt that you assigned—you forgive their debt to you. How noble, "But don't let it happen again."

Here's the forgiveness transaction. It begins with their offense-insult (against you), your judgment for that behaviour against them they are bad or mean—critical and unaccepting for sure and absent of humility. Your condemnation of them, with a certain righteousness assumed by you with your perception of the offender as a bad person. Appropriate punishment is authorized by the judge (you) with an assigned level of debt (what they owe you for their offense) but here it is... wait for it... how magnanimous that you forgive their debt to you. It is completely absent of acceptance (forgiving a debt that you arbitrarily assigned contains neither compassion nor humility). There you have it: Forgiveness.

Forgiveness is principally a western religious construct orchestrated by the church. It is symbolically identical to what I described above. Here it is translated into church doctrine.

Forgiveness appears to have a vigorous presence in church doctrine in the 16th century, which is coincidental to the rise in wealth of small kingdoms spread across Europe. The pope wanted money and the numerous wealthy landlords and

---

a crowded, hostile environment invariably chose liquid morphine over water and food. Rats in a large, safe, rat-friendly environment frequently chose water over liquid morphine. How close are we all to being disenfranchised rats? We cannot understand addiction or treat it effectively until we understand stress and environment beyond family.

royalty had gold and jewels. It was decided, by the pope, that offenses or insult against arbitrary church doctrine (meaning the church's assessment that God would also be offended) required forgiveness.

It was judgment against you by the priests. Critical and unaccepting for sure, absent of humility, with condemnation of you by them on behalf of their opinion of God. Assumed righteousness by church officials gave them the right to categorize you as a bad person for some variation of sinning. The priest's estimate of an appropriate punishment with an assigned debt-owed (what you owe the church for your offense). Was it a contrite apology? Two Hail Mary's? Three acts of contrition? One gold candle stick? Pay for repairs to the chapel? If you agreed and paid the fine you could get back in. How magnanimous that God unilaterally agrees with the church. God's satisfied, the church gets paid, and you're less guilty. This soon led to the pope creating "purgatory" which kept the money flowing in, but that's another story.

Church forgiveness is completely absent of acceptance or compassion. The Church patriarchs themselves decided, on behalf of their self-proclaimed opinion of God, that you sinned, you are responsible, and therefore you owe a debt to the Church-and-God (whichever it was assumed you offended first) who then condemned you. Ask: Were you condemned by God and now the church gets cash, or condemned by the priest and now God is offended...? Don't worry, forgiveness is available if you do what the church wants.

Forgiveness is one of the ways the Christian church allowed parishioners continuous membership. After all, if everyone was kicked out for sinning in a few months there'd be nobody there, including priests. Forgiveness and the remission of sin became a significant fundraiser for Pope Leo X in the 16th century (Indulgences and Purgatory). Forgiveness has a long and complex history of punishment serving the church and manipulating the laity.

In personal relationships, don't worry, forgiveness is available if you pay the fine that I have assigned for your misdemeanour. Whether religious or personal, this is your contractual agreement with externally imposed guilt, discussed in the third stage of childhood development, and in society claiming that addicts are just irresponsible trouble-makers. There is no compassion, acceptance, or humility in these transactions.

The pious, religious rhetoric from the 1840s was that drinking alcohol was a moral failure; a sin. In the 1920s drinkers were subject to criminal prosecution—social criminals and sinners, not "ill." What the religious people did was ignore their own participation in creating the problem, ignore their grand-scale righteousness of condemning an entire culture, and not challenge their own abusive morality.

The Women's Christian Temperance Movement and the Temperance League altogether had near to 375,000 members by 1885. That small minority, about 3.3 percent of the entire US population c. 1920, had enough religious clout to control 96.7 percent of 105 million people. Of course, that was closely linked with suffrage and voting rights which were valid and necessary. Temperance being attached to the legitimacy of voting rights was the umbrella that gave it some credibility. In the US, drinking became a national moral failure according to religious Protestants and forgiveness for this sin was a necessity.

Here's a scenario: A close friend contracts a blood infection. They are admitted to hospital for intravenous therapy for a few days; they recover, and all is well. You helped them out for a week or two. Fair enough. How would you respond to your friend standing on your doorstep a few days later asking, "Could you please forgive me for having that infection? I am so terribly guilty and bad for being sick." They are asking for forgiveness for being sick. Sounds strange, doesn't it?

If we are sick, we are sick. I understand that most people don't wander around the community wanting to be a dead-end drunk or a hard-core junkie. No one chooses, in addiction, to be a nasty, lying scoundrel; remember they are symptoms. In the normal course of human affairs no one wants to get diabetes or cancer. These, and other illnesses and broken bones, are a considered and inescapable aspect of life. Next comes a thoughtful change in point of view.

Understand that self-harm, lying, selfishness, arrogance, irresponsibility and the like, are the visible symptomatic behaviours of addiction. Symptoms are not optional. Symptoms are a requirement of illness (or disease) and demonstrate a person is legitimately ill with an identifiable condition. "I had pneumonia, please forgive me for having a fever." "I have narcolepsy, please forgive me for falling asleep." "Ah shucks, I am so sorry I had a heart attack will you forgive me for taking pills?" No one discharged from a cancer clinic is told to go home and seek forgiveness from their family.

What abusive hubris would suggest the need for seeking forgiveness for being sick? What need is there for forgiveness? "I am an alcoholic (an illness with definable symptoms) but I am also a morally bad trouble-maker (apparently a sin), can you forgive me for being ill?" "I am a drug addict (an illness) and therefore a morally corrupt criminal who is deliberately cruel and irresponsible. Can you forgive me for having an illness?"

Next: Compare those to this, "I have committed adultery can you forgive me?" Religious people seek forgiveness for sins of moral turpitude (like adultery or kidnapping). As I understand it, religious types don't seek forgiveness for contracting diarrhea or malaria, they receive compassion. To solicit or expect forgiveness for addiction is clear evidence that it is still seen as a moral failure (the 1939 opinion) not an illness. That is evident when people in treatment or meetings are told they have to forgive themselves, which means they have agreed with the imposed religious-social condemnation they are bad. Having addiction is an illness and forgiveness should not and need not be sought [254]

Acceptance is understanding, without judgement or blame, that good things and bad things happen all over the place, and people have different, personal ways of expressing their humanity. Illness is required as a part of life, so are flooded basements, flat tires, and broken arms. Forgiveness does not have to be

---

254 This is also explained in *Spiritual Transformation, Third Edition*, beginning at p. 332.

sought for a condition of life, such as going bald or heart attacks or having an addiction. I do appreciate the difference when discussing deliberate criminal behaviour like fraud, or deliberate breach of contract like adultery, or elsewhere where a deliberate choice to abuse was made (think kidnapping).

Does addiction, in its identifiable symptoms, fall into the moral degenerate category? No, but it appears that way because the five social symptoms are viewed as social defiance. If addiction is moral turpitude like adultery then be "punished" and seek forgiveness. If it is an illness, forgiveness must neither be sought nor demanded. Certainly, and yes, responsibility must be taken for abuses and misdemeanors within any addiction. Forgiveness should not be any part of the recovery equation.

Acceptance and compassion that addiction is one of many awkward situations inherent in life, as are car accidents, death, and earth-quakes, is the spiritual position to aspire to. There is something vicious in a society that's a major culprit in creating addictions and then condemning those who have them.

Of course, there will be disagreement with this based on the AA literature. That 1939 model was a significant modification of The Oxford Group and Mr. Buchman's effort to increase Christian social dominance. At that time, near 1940, the perception of moral turpitude and sin as regards drunkenness had been inherent in US culture for about one-hundred years. Neither the AA co-founders nor the professionals who supported them had any awareness of the major religious or cultural-historical influences at play in the creation of the huge alcoholism problem they faced in the 1930s. For them, there was no possibility of understanding addiction or recovery as it related to society, temperance, industrialization, opium, or psychology, and no awareness of social anomie. Causes went far beyond anything they could conceive of. The offering in *Alcoholics Anonymous* was limited and narrow of focus: recovery from morbid alcohol consumption for white males over thirty with a Christian religious affiliation.

In North America, at that time, Christian morality was dominate. The Ku Klux Clan was prominent. Morally "bad" behaviour, c. 1920, included sex when not married, single-women pregnancies (consequence: shame and banishment), social defiance (consequence: censure and punishment), atheism (consequence: exclusion), masturbation (consequence: labeled shamefully perverted), being a pacifist (consequence: prison), homosexuality (consequence: aberrantly sick and prison), racial intermixing (consequence: ostracism, death, prison), drinking alcohol (consequence: moral failure and sinner), and in the faint background, drug addiction (consequence: criminal). Yes, it sounds unbelievably outrageous today, but in 1920 these were the realities of Christian and political dogma.

Early Alcoholics Anonymous members believed that alcoholism recovery had to include some watered-down version of temperance religion, which was the culture they were raised in. Bill Wilson was born in 1895 and Bob Smith in 1879, at the very height of the Suffragette and Temperance movements. That meant total abstinence, praying, and sinners seeking forgiveness. *Alcoholics Anonymous*, the book, presented a moderately acceptable view of morbid drunkenness as a malady with bad behaviour which, if there were sobriety and forgiveness in that recovery, it would meet with social, Christian approval. "Yes, you may have an alcoholic illness, but you must seek forgiveness for morally irresponsible behaviour." The philosophies of moral corruption and religious forgiveness are at odds with any perception of legitimate illness.

Bill Wilson's 1939 version of "illness" was more akin to moral malady. It met with Protestant-Christian approval because there was an indirect admission of forgiveness required (for moral failure) included in it. Self-proclaimed moral turpitude catered to religious righteousness. Illness would not be taken seriously by the establishment for decades, and in most quarters, it still isn't in 2020.

As pointed out by Caroline Jean Acker, in her book *Creating the American Junkie,* doctors wouldn't treat addicts a hundred years ago, and were clearly aware of their medical collusion with opium addiction. Doctors would dry out "drunks" in sanitariums—detox only, but "treatment" was not something they participated in. What happened near 1980 was the coopting of addictions treatment by the medical community; harvesting the medical cash crop of billions that was available from treatment. With that, the label switched from illness (pseudo-psychiatric/spiritual) to disease (medical). Addiction "treatment" is lucrative, even if it really isn't treatment.

What we have now is doctors, counsellors, concerned citizens, and most addicts claiming it's a disease, but seeking forgiveness for being bad. "Treatment" has become more social indoctrination than actual treatment, with fear, dread and moral suspicion from the larger uninformed public hovering in the foreground. The professionals are making billions and the relapse rate is hovering at 95 percent.

Side Note: 1: Credible research (see "Does Alcoholics Anonymous Work?" Harvard University and Stanford University, YouTube) advises the more traditional AA-style of self-help for only alcohol addiction has a better recovery rate than behavioral or psychological interventions—est. 20 to 60 percent better. Fair enough. Consider that if the usual failure/relapse rate for therapies and recovery houses is near 90 percent, that means only 10 percent of people get and stay recovered out of formal treatment—10 out of 100. If we increase that by the better recovery statistics from research into AA, it increases 20 to 60 percent. That means that rather than 10 out of 100, it is now 12 – 16 people out 100. Still abjectly dismal. (Review footnote 13 for 1939 relevant AA statistics.)

Side Note 2: I have examined the reported statistics for recovery at three treatment centers who claimed a thirty or forty percent success rate. They followed up with less than half of the people who completed treatment and reported that this less-than-half group stayed sober for seven days post discharge. Seven days sober, for under 50 percent of discharged clients, at $25,000.00 dollars a month for treatment. Can you imagine a team of medical researchers seeking approval for a surgery or a drug that had a ninety-five percent failure rate and that failure almost guaranteed more harm and possible death? It wouldn't get anywhere.

What Mr. Wilson did accomplish was great—the foundation of a process that would enable recovery from alcoholism. Originally, that was a personal effort directed towards daily sobriety and compliance with Christian-religious beliefs. Fair enough, but that opened the door to better alternatives. The related psychology of personal change was, of course, hidden underneath the religious rhetoric in vogue in the 1930s. With the subsequent, drastic changes in society and the modern intrusion of politics, government, medicine, atheism, financial profit, and the misunderstanding between treating the symptoms and treating the addiction, two things are apparent:

(i) Recovery meetings have fizzled into badly managed social-dating-therapy groups. They lack direction and are confused about purpose, process, and end result. This has placed twelve-step groups on a path of political associations, outside influence, and shallow commitment.

(ii) Most treatment is some thinly veiled indoctrination into Christian opinions; OR, it's a shallow attempt to convert addicts into compliant taxpayers. (See Appendix III)

The future is in serious doubt. If you want to change your world, change yourself first. Alcoholism isn't sinning, its illness. Forgiveness? Not required.

Negative Capability

John Keats (1795 – 1821) was an English poet of some renown. His poetry is still read and studied. Keats' poetry is not why I include him in *The Addiction Recovery Handbook*. He offered us an idea in relation to poetry that is insightful and important to recovery and spiritual transformation.

In a letter to his brothers in December 1817 Mr. Keats wrote: "*...and at once it struck me... which Shakespeare possessed so enormously—I mean Negative Capability, that is when man is capable of being in uncertainties, Mysteries, doubts, without any irritable reaching after fact and reason... remaining content with half knowledge. ...the sense of Beauty overcomes every other consideration...*" [255]

What he means by this is, in the creation of beauty through literature and poetry; in trying to create something rare and meaningful, the author is always in some measure of uncertainty. There are always many doubts. Will the final poem capture what the poet intended? Will it present the ideas the author wants? Will it be good enough? Is the effort to create it, and all the uncertainty, worth it? Can the writer really convey a sense of meaning to their writing and offer this to readers? Mr. Keats was referring to literature and poetry. I include it in all sincere creative endeavor.

The artist or writer, dancer, musician, must be willing to abandon all social considerations to achieve a work of art that is worthy. They never know anything

---

255 John Keats, as reported in *Keats's Poetry and Prose*, Edited by Jeffrey N. Cox, Norton Critical Editions, 2009, p. 109.

for certain while creating it, with no facts or reason to guide them, and must be content with very little knowledge during its creation. What's more is, they create out of the unknown without any reassuring comfort from fact because there is no fact available to guarantee results in an undefinable future.

If the artist or writer is capable of enduring this doubt and uncertainty with poise, they have a *negative capability*. They are capable of forging ahead to create something good or beautiful in the face of uncertainty and doubt, without facts or reason beforehand. There is always the influence of an unknown future in this. Negative capability: the ability to rise above anxiety towards an unknown result with poise and conviction during the effort, never knowing either the facts that motivated the creation of art or the end result before-hand.

This is exactly what's required in the transformation from addiction to a spiritual lifestyle. Negative Capability. There is significant ignorance about addiction. There are doubts about what is or will be required, fears and terrors around rigorous honesty, concerns about complete responsibility, and no knowledge of where a person will end up before they get to "wherever" they don't know they might be going. Through the process of becoming spiritual and anticipating its rewards, nothing can be known beforehand. The realization of the end result is always unpredictable. To undertake this journey governed by principle and to act with confidence and grace is *negative capability*.

All that can be done by any person in recovery is to persevere through this and venture into the unknown. Attempt to ignore your doubts and fears with a relaxed acceptance and patience. Have some slim measure of confidence in yourself and your own effort. Calmly move towards a dim and vague goal of principled living that it will come out alright.

Being spiritual is always a one-person game, never shared. It is not a collective, group experience. Doing "group step-work" and "fellowship" are a complicating avoidance of what you alone need to do, which creates more repetitive inadequacy. "Group work" always indoctrinates you into the needs of the group (most important) and your needs (least important). Success is always the defined by the limitations of the group and not by you.

Nothing about a truly spiritual life can be shared or known beforehand. Even if three sponsors, two therapists, and four people you trust say recovery and spiritual transformation will be worth it, it is still, and the future result will always be uncertain. Realizing some assumed and better reward is usually abandoned for what is good enough. Deeper spiritual benefits can only be known long after they are achieved.

In spiritual endeavor, a person can only hope and speculate where they want to go but they will never end up there. It's always approximately close, but not really. A person will never know if the effort required will be worth the "hoped for" end result because the end is never known *and* there is never an end to principled, spiritual endeavor. The deeper path into spirituality is burdened with uncertainty and doubt. As with Mr. Keats the poet, so it is with true spiritual discipline. It demands a negative capability.

"For if there is a sin against life, it consists perhaps not so much in despairing of life as in hoping for another life and in that eluding the implacable grandeur of this life."

Albert Camus, *Summer in Algiers*

Epilogue

A Final Post-Script

If you have read this from the beginning, you have covered a lot of ground with me. Some of it may have been annoying, but hopefully it brought some understanding or relief to the confusion or fear you had when you started this. Thank you for wandering through this with me.

> *I shall be telling this with a sigh*
> *Somewhere ages and ages hence:*
> *Two roads diverged in a wood, and I—*
> *I took the one less traveled by,*
> *And that has made all the difference.* [256]

I propose here, the road less travelled.

The paths of love and fear are so close together you can change from one to the other and go nowhere. Traversing that very short emotional distance from fear to love and compassion, which harbors acceptance, will then render forgiveness unnecessary. In the realm of human relationships, it is a very important emotional truth there is no compassion in forgiveness. It is very difficult to go from fear and addicted thinking to forgiveness, and then much more difficult to go from condemning and judgement to acceptance and compassion. Addiction recovery is more recovery from a corrupt human condition as anything else. This is the road less travelled.

The truth for me is there is healing only in relationships that embrace compassion, respect, and acceptance. Only that creates the environment that allows personal recovery to endure. In the introduction I wrote that we must recover from this culture. Social compliance is spiritual death. We must stand against culture to be spiritual.

You will have worked hard and challenged yourself a great deal. You will have lived with anxiety and trusted your sense that your journey was worth it. To accomplish this, you haven't travelled anywhere. The world around you will be

---

256 "The Road Not Taken," *The Poetry of Robert Frost*, Robert Frost; Edited By Edward Connery Lathem, Holt, Rinehart and Winston, 1969, p. 105.

quite the same and only you are different. All you have done is forced yourself to change your mind.

I believe at the end of each day it comes down to the truth that we are each, in our own way, guardians of the human spirit, especially to care for those who have yet to learn how this is done. We cannot be guardians of what we do not understand; we cannot protect what we don't have. Safeguarding our soulful spirit—whatever it is that sits at the core of our humanity, is a lost art and requires a principled life. Sincere discussion and contemplation of spiritual ethics in how we treat each other will eventually allow for compassion and wisdom in relationship.

Remember: You are a sexual being, in a physical body, trying to be a spiritual entity, in a human context, within a limited but unknown segment of eternity. Even without dysfunction and abuse, or addiction and a destructively oriented personality, it's incredibly complicated.

As an addicted person moving towards this strange lifestyle, somehow realize within yourself that nothing will guarantee your remaining spiritual except being spiritual on a moment to moment basis. Knowledge is not the solution. In its broadest sense, authentic living governed by spiritual principles is the solution.

Live intimately with trusted loved ones. Develop compassion and acceptance. Maintain an intimate, long relationship with a spiritually oriented mentor or therapist you trust where there is mutual respect. In all of this, hold equality, veracity, humility, compassion, charity, and personal responsibility as your highest values. Labor with devotion and patience only to this end: Through the maintenance steps, be governed in all endeavor by spiritual principles. You will eventually appreciate some peaceful consciousness that you are recovered, but only in hindsight, and only by continuing to embrace your ever-present frailties. This will not put you into a utopian existence, but will offer freedom from the annoyances, ailments and misdemeanors of life. There is no longer a seemingly hopeless state of mind and body.

Some might call you wise and many will resent you. You'll be able to smile gently because, for you alone, it will be sufficient to quietly repose in the safety of knowing that the mysterious machinations of the universe are beautiful.

Words cannot describe everything.
The heart's message cannot be delivered in words.
If one receives words literally, they will be lost.
If one tries to explain with words, they will not
attain enlightenment in this life. [257]

---

257 *Zen Flesh, Zen Bones, A Collection of Pre-Zen Writings*, complied by Paul Reps, Anchor Books, 1989, p. 120 (with minor editing of pronouns).

<u>*As for myself...*</u>

As I negotiate through the eternity between my own birth and death, I am forever encased in the being alive of my own existence. I must frequently remind myself that, regardless of my efforts and accomplishments, I unfold into only a minor, temporary, supporting role. At my own last exit, I will face alone my own final curtain, the closing of which always comes before the end of the play. As for encores, if there are any... probably none that I'll remember.

Richard Clark
White Rock, British Columbia
April 2020.

About the Author

www.greenroomlectures.ca

Richard Clark was born in Ontario, Canada. He wandered through the 1960s and college in a manner of 'protest and experimentation' and traveled widely throughout North America. He was known to lean heavily on a line from a William Blake poem: *"The road of excess leads to the palace of wisdom."* [258] Certainly, there was a lot of excess, but some people might question where that excess led him.

He's been a construction worker, miner, soldier, military policeman, security consultant, driving instructor, police officer, seniors' social worker, church chaplain, teacher, artist, musician, therapist, counsellor, seminar leader, health consultant, writer/author, and business owner. Richard began addressing his own addiction(s) in 1980 and has lived in monasteries, Christian and Buddhist, for extended periods.

Richard trained in addictions treatment and many of the issues related to addictions at several colleges and private training centres. He's a certified addiction counsellor (CAC II) through the Canadian Council of Professional Certification and trained in several energy healing modalities. He's offered seminars and lectures to about ninety-thousand people on topics that include

---

258 This William Blake quote comes from his poem *Proverbs of Hell*, which begins: *"In seed time learn, in harvest teach, in winter enjoy. / Drive your cart and your plow over the bones of the dead. / The road of excess leads to the palace of wisdom. / Prudence is a rich, ugly old maid courted by Incapacity. / He who desires but acts not, breeds pestilence…"* From: *The Portable Blake*, Edited by Alfred Kazin, Viking Portable Library, p. 252.

244

addictions, sexuality, violence, relationships, change, stress, trauma, religion, culture, spirituality, Buddhism, atheism, applied problem solving, gender issues, therapy and counseling, life skills, body energy healing, interpersonal communications, twelve step programs, and residential treatment.

As a therapist and educator, Richard has maintained a private counselling practice since 1985, taught in colleges, First Nations' communities in Canada, private industry, and prisons in Canada and the US. He has worked for non-profit agencies, recovery houses, and treatment centres. He's offered seminars and lectures in Canada, the United States, Israel, China, Ukraine, England, and Russia.

At the time of this publication Richard lives near Vancouver, BC.

The Next Project

Recovery for Agnostics and Atheists
Buddhism and the responsibility of transformation.

The manner of serenity in the human spirit.
(working title – hopefully available 2021)

The avenues to a spiritual life for agnostics, atheists and non-religious Buddhists will be detailed. There are advantages to being agnostic which may, in the long term, be a better option for many people in recovery from addiction. In line with what is thought to be original Buddhism (pre-350 BCE), there will be practical explanations of the fundamentals of Buddhism, its origins, and doctrine as it might be applied today. There will be descriptions of elementary Buddhist principle for addiction recovery in modern culture. Parts of the original addiction recovery textbooks will be recast into agnostic/humanist terms.

Appendix I

I had the opportunity to study adult education at the University of Alberta (Edmonton) in the mid-late 1980s. While there, I was fortunate to receive a copy of a research paper by Prof. Jim Hackler of the Department of Criminology. His report *The Reduction of Violent Crime and Equality for Women, Discussion Paper 18*, over the years, has proven invaluable to my work. I received generous and kind permission from Prof. Hackler, now at the University of BC in Victoria, Sara Dorow, Chair of the Department of Sociology, and Lesley Cormack, Dean, Faculty of Arts, both from University of Alberta (Edmonton) to reprint *Discussion Paper 18* in full.

University of Alberta - Centre for Criminological Research

THE REDUCTION OF VIOLENT CRIME AND EQUALITY FOR WOMEN

Jim Hackler

Department of Sociology
University of Alberta

DISCUSSION PAPER 18

ABSTRACT

It is not unusual for people to express an interest in the reduction of violent crime without recognizing a link with equal rights for women. This paper suggests links between the equality of women and the reduction of violent crime in the future. Central to the logic of this argument is the nature of the distribution of violent acts.

Most people assume that the distribution of the frequency of violent crime is described by a <u>bi-modal</u> curve which allows us to distinguish between minor, unimportant offenders and a distinct group of serious offenders. Thus, the target for many policies is the serious offender who falls under the smaller hump on the violent end of the continuum. In fact, this bi-modal distribution does not exist therefore, policies based on it will not be fruitful. The larger group of minor offenders who represent the greatest number of violent acts is basically ignored.

The distribution of violence is better described as a <u>continuous</u> skewed curve. Further, the <u>shape</u> of this curve remains constant and an effective policy to reduce violence would have to shift the <u>entire</u> curve to the left.

A more profitable strategy recognized the desirability of reducing the more numerous acts of lesser violence rather than concentrating on the rarer cases of extreme violence. Since much of this violence is nurtured in family settings, policies that decrease stress in family settings would have a meaningful impact on violence in the future. This paper will argue that a number of issues relating to the equality of women are related to family violence and thus would have a long-term impact on violent crime.

Acknowledgements

The author would like to thank Nanci Wilson, Meda Chesny-Lind, Nicole Hahn Rafter, Murray Straus, Barbara Price, Leslie Kennedy and many others who provided ideas for this paper. The interpretations, however, are those of the author. I would like to acknowledge support from the Ministry of the Solicitor General of Canada through their contributions grant.

THE REDUCTION OF VIOLENT CRIME
AND EQUALITY FOR WOMEN

LINKING VIOLENCE WITH EQUALITY FOR WOMEN

The expression of concern for the amount of violent crime in modern society is widespread. However, many who favour programs that would due violence do not see a connection with equal rights for women. When policy makers are faced with programs for reducing violent crime, suggestions for raising the family allowance or providing greater economic equality are viewed as changing the subject, as irrelevant to the issue at hand. The majority of people do not see a clear link between providing financial support for mothers, economic equality for women, and the reduction of violent crime. This paper tries to trace such a link and argues that policies directed toward economic equality would ha a long-range impact on violence.

There is little debate on the evidence that a great deal of violence occurs in a family setting. The argument to be made takes the findings from research on family violence as a point of departure (Walker, 1984: Kincaid, 1985; Pagelow, 1984; Straus, Gelles, and Steinmetz, 1980; Fleming, 1979; Schechter, 1982). There are some disagreements regarding the impact of family violence on the behaviour of children raised in such families, but it is not necessary to resolve these minor debates in order to pursue the logic presented here. Nor will much time be spent debating the link between financially troubled families and the likelihood of family violence. Elliott Currie (1985: Ch. 4) and others deal with these questions quite effectively showing that economically disadvantaged families are more likely to produce children who will contribute to violent crimes. My argument is with the response to these findings. The economic factors are frequently treated as "minor" problems which do not require an urgent response. We can appreciate the long-range implications of the decrease in social support for families (Currie, 1987: 11-12), but those in policy making positions are under more pressure to respond immediately to dramatic forms of adult violence.

One can respond to violence with two types of policy decisions: the first focuses directly on serious violent crime. The second strategy concentrates on factors that might lead to violent crime in the future. Policy makers are frequently preoccupied with attempts that do something to offenders. Unfortunately, these efforts rarely have much positive impact on violence. In fact, the consequences may be negative. At the same time policy makers neglect changes that, in the long run, would yield a greater return for the efforts and resources provided. There is a tendency to focus on those *persons* who commit violent acts rather than on the *conditions* that give rise to violence. This paper argues that it is difficult to legislate against violent crime, but structural changes that would decrease conditions leading to violence are more amenable to legislative change.

Before we can discuss appropriate policies, we must first examine the distribution of violent crime and ask where changes would have the greatest impact.

THE DISTRIBUTION OF VIOLENCE

A fundamental assumption in the following argument is that less serious crimes are more frequent than more serious crimes. This is fairly obvious to most people, and it has also been documented systematically for a variety of offenses, such as self-reported delinquency (Elmhorn, 1965). The various ways of measuring crime will influence the recorded distribution, but Uniform Crime Reports, victim reports, and self-report surveys show considerable agreement that serious offenses are less common than minor ones (O'Brien, 1985). Nettler (1984) summarizes crime patterns by noting that "behaviours guided by social norms tend to describe a unimodal (one-humped) graph that looks like a 'J' or an 'L' depending on how it is drawn (p. 82). This type of distribution is shown by the curve in Figure 1 indicated by the solid line.

While empirical evidence for the greater frequency of less serious crimes is plentiful, less attention had been paid to the way society responds to rare events in contrast to common events. We tend to respond more vigorously to rare extreme cases than ordinary less serious events. Even though our jails are more likely to be crowded with the poor who have committed minor property offenses, the public outcry is more likely directed toward the Clifford Olsens who are rare.

Figure 1: The frequency of violent acts committed by the total population charted against the seriousness of each violent act. *

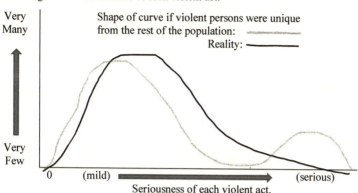

Seriousness of each violent act.

*Basic Idea from Whitehead and Smart (1972)

The exact shape of the curve depicted by the solid line in Figure 1 could be somewhat different for different types of crime and still be compatible with the argument presented here. The exact shape of the curve to the left of the hump of the solid line is unimportant for our purpose. It does not matter if there are a few people who are "almost perfect," which would mean the curve drops as shown in Figure 1, or if the left of the curve simply represents minor offenses with the curve continuing upward on the left side of the graph. Our interest is in the steady decline toward right side of the graph. What is important is that crime does not take on a bi-modal distribution which has a second hump on the right, as shown by the dotted line in Figure 1. Violent crime does not increase in frequency as it increases in severity.

The recognition of these distributions and their implications for policy should be credited to those doing alcohol and drug research. The logic for the argument presented here is borrowed primarily from empirical work done by Canadian alcohol and drug researchers who note some previous work that has been done in France (Popham, Schmidt, and deLint, 1976: Schmidt and Popham, 1978: Whitehead and Smart, 1972). They noted that drug use fit the pattern described above. Minor offenders were common. As the drug abuse became more serious, offenders were less frequent. If we lump all sorts of drug use together, it seems that many people drink coffee and ingest the occasional substance that is not very healthy. Relatively few, however, are hooked on heroin, alcohol, or smoke six packs of cigarettes a day. While the news media calls attention to different substances from time to time, the general phenomenon of drug abuse remains fairly stable: minor abusers are more common than serious abusers. However, we respond more to the serious abusers and tend to ignore the minor abusers.

While this seems reasonable at first glance, a better policy might be to respond uniformly to all substance abuse. Let us apply this logic to violent crime.

CHOOSING THE APPROPRIATE TARGET

First, who are the logical targets of our efforts to bring about change? Typically, we assume that the problem lies with a particular group of bad people. These violent individuals require our immediate attention. The rest of the population commit minor acts of violence from time to time, but because their acts are less serious, they can be conveniently ignored. In general, this large number of people who are "typical" is not seen as a serious problem. Their wrongs are numerous, but each individual act is seen as being of little consequence. Instead, public outrage is directed toward that special group of extreme individuals who omit serious crimes. We direct programs and laws against the *minority of serious* trouble makers rather than toward the *majority of minor* offenders. The central theme of this paper is that concentrating on the small number of people who represent the serious cases will not be as effective as attempting to achieve more modest changes among a larger population.

The curve with two humps.

In figure 1, I have attempted to diagram the frequency of violent acts committed by the total population charted against the seriousness of each violent act. As one can see, the horizontal axis goes from "not serious at all" to "very serious". On the vertical axis, we have the number of people who are in that particular category of violent behaviour. If we look at the solid line, we see that the single hump of the curve is toward the left where a large number of people commit minor acts of violence. Most people occasionally spank their children; many children get into minor fights. There are relatively few completely non-violent people on the extreme left of the chart. People who do not step on insects and do not kick vending machines when they lose their money are rare. Most of us fit under the large hump. As we move out toward the right of the curve, we have people who are more violent in a variety of ways. The main point is that the curve tapers off to the right with the more extreme behaviour being much less frequent.

If one looks at the *dotted line* in the figure, instead of the solid line, the shape of this curve might describe reality *if* those individuals who commit serious wrongs, that is the truly violent individuals, are unique and are truly different from the rest of us. The dotted line describes a curve which has two peaks, one on the right side of the chart in addition to the one on the left. Belief in this bi-modal curve can lead to a certain world-view. Most of us have no trouble with the peak on the left. The paragons of virtue are rare and most of us commit indiscretions that are not truly serious. The large group of people representing the hump on the left are not viewed as a problem. The real problem is with those who are more dangerous. They are the ones who need special handling. This particular world-view assumes that we can tolerate the hump on the left, but we must somehow cut off that second hump to the right by some dramatic action. The basic flaw in this argument is with the shape of the curve and with the assumption that one can eliminate part of the curve without affecting the rest. Actually, the true curve is more likely to be represented by the solid line in the figure. *The implications if using one curve or the other.*

Since there is no distinct and unique population of serious offenders who can be delineated as a logical target for a particular program, the Canadian alcohol and drug researchers mentioned above argued that drug policies were inappropriate because they were based on the two-humped curve. Programs designed to change the extreme drug abuser were common, but an effective policy would have to alter the *entire* curve. Thus, programs that would reduce the consumption of tobacco and alcohol among the majority would move the entire curve to the left. In other words, if one assumes the shape of the curve remains the same, efforts to change the behaviour of *large numbers* of people make more sense than efforts to change smaller select groups.

In the case of drugs, such changes may have taken place in parts of North America in recent years. Smoking has decreased in many areas. The light smoker may have contributed more to the change in smoking patterns than the heavy smoker. One could argue that this has move the entire drug using curve to the left. The recent concern about smoking is related to more general concerns for good health. In addition, recent reductions in alcohol consumption seem to fit this general argument. Substance abuse may be seen as interconnected with general conditions influencing more than one specific behaviour.

I wish to utilize the same logic regarding links between family stresses and crime. Modest changes for man types of minor forms of violence would eventually influence the extreme behaviour of the few. The extreme and dangerous behaviours would be influenced by the conditions that influence violent behaviour in general.

Applying the same logic to crime, we should recognize that there is no distinct target population; serious offenders are simply at one end of a *smooth* continuum. We could cut the curve at some arbitrary point and make those people the target of some anti-violence strategy. However, there is good reason to believe that the *shape* of the curve would remain constant, and efforts on that small population on the right of the curve will have little impact on the entire curve. In other words, the only way to reduce violence on the right side of the curve is to more the entire curve to the left.

The use of seatbelts offers a useful analogy. Clearly, seat belt usage saves lives, but it also reduces minor injuries as well. The entire injury curve has been moved to the left. In this case, the serious injury was the target and the minor injuries the bi product, but the important point is that increasing seat belt usage from 20% to 70% has a universal impact on injury.

Unfortunately, our public policies conceive of the violence problem in terms of the curve with two humps represented by the dotted line. We tend to ignore the group under the hump on the left had side of the chart and focus instead on a theoretical distinct group on the right-hand side of the graph. The incorrect assumption behind this second line of reasoning is assuming that we can deal with a small portion of the population while ignoring the rest. It may be possible to move the curve to the right or to the left, but there is no small, special population that can be treated in a unique manner while the rest of us continue going about our business as usual.

This is the logic I wish to apply to family violence. Instead of concentrating on extreme cases, my hope is to emphasize conditions that influence the entire curve. According to a number of researchers, some feminist issues are related to family violence. (Tong, 1984; Atkins and Hoggett, 1984; Brophy and Smart, 1985). This research identifies specific situations which lead to violence, but my point is that the wide range of these issues taken together contribute to a wide range and considerable volume of violent crime. The evidence for some of the specific links suggested in the literature can be debated, but there is general agreement that feminist issues deal with areas related to stress and violence in the family.

FAMILY VIOLENCE AND FUTURE CRIMINALITY

Evidence that physical violence in families can influence subsequent criminal careers has been approached cautiously. White and Straus (1981) argue that this topic has been neglected for two reasons: First, the family is an institution which should provide love, supportiveness, and moral training. This makes it hard to view the family as an institution which teaches violence (Steinmetz and Straus, 1974). Second, most family violence is seeing as legitimate, as in parental use of physical punishment or the high rate of pushing, shoving, slapping, and throwing things that occurs between spouses (Gelles and Straus, 1979). The acceptance of this violence tends to blind us to the possibility that it cannot only train children to be violent but can also contribute to criminal behaviour.

White and Straus also explore the various mechanisms by which children are socialized into violent behaviour (1981). They conclude that such behaviour is transferrable from one setting to another. Child abuse, then, especially when it is a part of an erratic punishment pattern, teaches the victim that the world is not predictable or controllable. A child might learn that terror tactics and the invincibility of the bully are transferrable to other settings. Violence in the family becomes a training ground for violence outside the home. Let us examine some of the evidence related to these claims. First, we should, distinguish between parents hitting each other and parents hitting their children.

The consequences of parents hitting children.

The juvenile learns that violent behaviour is transferable from one setting to another partially because the rules transfer as well. The family is the setting where rules are first leaned and reinforced. The rule that a marriage license is also a hitting license and the rule that members of the family can be physically punished "if they deserve it" are common. These rules are understood as norms of behaviour and can be applied to other social settings. In their national study of family violence, Straus, Gelles, and Stinmetz (1980) found that the more the husbands and wives they studied were hit as children, the greater the rate of both mild and severe violence toward their own spouses. According to Lincoln and Straus (1985 Ch.10) the more children are hit by their parents, the higher the rate at which such children hit their brothers and sisters and their parents. It has been argued that such learning is not a general prescription for violence and would not necessarily lead to violence outside the family. However, Lincoln and Straus point to evidence that shows a clear link between being hit by one's parents and assaults on people outside the family, particularly for boys. One Canadian study produces similar findings (Jaffe, et al., 1985)

It is more difficult to show a direct causal relationship between violence in the family and future criminal behaviour, but the work by Joan McCord, in her analysis of the subsequent careers and life experiences of participants in the Cambridge-Somerville Youth Study is strongly suggestive (1979, 198). She compared the assessment of home atmosphere with official records of subsequent criminal convictions. She found a clear relationship between the home atmosphere and subsequent serious criminality. In Canada, Ross found that children who had been beaten were more likely to injure themselves (1980).

Others have argued that the evidence is less convincing (Pagelow, 1984). In a recent review of the literature on early child abuse, neglect, and violent crime, Widon (1986) notes that:

> While a number of researchers have suggested that aggression is a common outcome, other evidence indicates that withdrawal may be related to early abusive experiences. Most of the existing work in this area examines delinquent behaviour generally; few studies focus specifically on adult violent criminal behaviour. Of those studies which examine violent behaviour the findings are contradictory. Some studies found more violent offenses committed by the abused delinquents, whereas others found no differences. (p. 16).

The consequence of parents hitting each other and violence outside the family.

Lincoln and Straus (1985) also report findings showing that boys growing up in families where there is physical fighting between parents were much more likely to be assaultive outside the family. Similarly, such boys were more likely to have higher rates of vandalism and higher overall delinquency scores. However, for girls there was no significant link between family violence and non-family delinquency.

It was somewhat surprising to find that adults who used violence against children were not more likely to be arrested for outside offenses. However, there was an association between a high rate of serious marital violence and the adults being arrested, particularly the wives. Lincoln and Straus use a victimization explanation to bring some of these findings together.

The unjust victim hypothesis.

The role model of violent parents is probably a factor leading to violent crime, but why does it also lead the theft, vandalism, and non-violent delinquency as well? Is there a link between being a victim and committing crime? Teenagers who have been assaulted by parents exhibit high rates of crime outside the family but the parents who carried out the assaults do not appear to be more criminal. In addition, Lincoln and Straus note that it is the wives in violent marriages, rather than the husbands, who have higher crime rates outside the family. Since the wives are the predominant victims of marital violence, even when they are violent toward their husbands, this is consistent with the victimization hypothesis. Victimization can lead to crime because it tends to undermine faith in the efficacy and fairness of the world that supports confirming behaviour. They have learned that the world is not a just place to live.

The link between violence in the family and violence as adults is not the main thrust of this paper. Rather, family violence represents a broad portion of the curve described in Figure 1. Even the disagreements on specifics, a modest reduction in all family violence could have a broad reaching impact. The growing research in this area may force policy makers to recognize the importance of reducing family violence as a possible means of influencing other types of violence in the society, but it is less clear just how one can proceed.

In Canada, as in most countries of the world, serious violent crime is frequently a chance outcome from many situations with a potential for violence (Hackler and Gauld, 1981). The reduction of potentially violent situations should influence specific acts of violence. Instead of treating an imaginary hump on the right of our hypothetical violence curve, we would do better to concentrate on the single large hump on the left. In other words, small changes in the larger population would lead to shifting this skewed curve to the left, thereby reducing the number of serious cases on the right. Efforts to help those with severe problems are still necessary, but changes which help many people a little might provide a better overall return. Directing attention to the large number of potentially dangerous situations may in fact be the most effective way of reducing the severe cases of violence. Decreasing the dominance of men over women will

be used as an illustration of a strategy which could lessen some of the strains which lead to family violence.

White and Straus (1981) and many others offer a number of strategies for rehabilitation. The danger, however, is that policy makers could utilize research on family violence in a manner that would not yield the best results. It is tempting to focus efforts on changing those families that have already been identified as being severe problems. In other words, one could use the model of the world which fits the curve with two humps as described in Figure 1. One could concentrate on prosecuting men who are severe wife batterers. While this may be appropriate in the specific situation, it should not distract us from focusing on economic factors, for example, conditions that make it difficult for women to leave a family situation that is under stress.

GOVERNMENT ATTITUDES TOWARD FAMILY VIOLENCE

Before proceeding with my final argument, we need to examine the way policy makers respond to family violence. When Margaret Mitchell, Member of Parliament in Canada, told the House of Commons that one out of 10 men regularly beats his wife, there were guffaws from some of the male members. Obviously, an initial task is convincing our predominantly male dominated policy making bodies that a problem exists. Beyond this there is the tendency to treat wife beating in isolation. The battered wife becomes the focus of attention. The wife beating problem becomes increasingly "medicalized," professionalized, individualized, and de-politicized (Conrad, 1975; Conrad and Schneider, 1980). The battered woman is given "therapy" and shown how to "identify tensions in the marriage relationship" (Tierney, 1982), as if she were the problem rather than the larger male-oriented values which influence social inequality.

Another element in this strategy, perhaps unintended, is that militant feminist groups which emphasize basic changes in society can be "cooled out" by sympathetic social agencies and government projects that are willing to sponsor those programs which focus on a specific identifiable problem. Clearly, feminist movements need to rely on traditional institutions to keep specific programs operating, such as shelters for battered women; however, Tierney (1982) point out that these traditional institutions have political structures and goals that may be antithetical to the larger, more militant movements.

The way in which governments respond to problems is a complex process and understanding how problems are "discovered" and identified will influence the official response. Pfohl has pointed out that the discovery of child abuse was not attributable to an escalation of abuse itself (1977). Rather, there were organizational advantages to the medical profession which set I motion a process for labeling child abuse as deviant and in need of legislation. Similarly, there are advantages for different groups in the way certain family issues are labeled. A variety of social agencies have a vested interest in specific programs. My concern is that the dynamics of identifying problems and drafting legislation will lead to the selection of strategies that satisfy the needs of certain groups, many of which have very honorable intentions. Traditional social service strategies may focus only on a portion of the problem. This may be a meaningful contribution, but there is the danger that it would detract from the larger feminist movement that could move the entire violence curve to the left.

At this point I would like to shift the argument to various issues concerned with economic equality for women. There is little disagreement with the work that has been done in this area, but some recommendations would impinge on the skewed curve in different ways. My argument is for breadth rather than for a sharper focus

WOMEN'S LIB AND MOVING THE SKEWED CURVE TO THE LEFT

The Canadian family allowance.

Broad based programs which have a very small return for any individual family, may, in fact, be very significant for moving the entire crime curve to the left. The modest impact on many families may eventually have a meaningful impact on the most serious problems. Let me use the family allowance in Canada as an illustration of a nationwide strategy which helps a little in many situations. In Canada, a family allowance is paid to mothers of young children. It is a universal plan which does not have a means test. Wealthy mothers receive a family allowance as well as poor mothers. While this amount must be added to their taxable income, one must admit that many families receive the allowance when they do not need it. On the other hand, the universality of the plan prevents some needy families from getting lost in the shuffle. One could also argue that some mothers buy booze instead of food for their children. While this may be true in some cases, there seems to be considerable evidence that the money is used to help children in the majority of cases. One could also argue that I some families the father is the more appropriate person to receive the family allowance. This is probably true, but statistically the mother is more likely to be the person caring for the children. The question of whether or not the mother is married is not relevant. The goal of the program is to provide universal support, admittedly at a low level, for children. This type of program makes a modest contribution toward the financial independence of women which may in turn decrease strains in families, make some women somewhat less dependent on their husbands, and decrease the likelihood that some women in a marginal position would have to go on welfare.

The Canadian family allowance is an illustration of an overall policy which attempts to avoid problems in advance. In the United States, there may be a tendency for families to struggle on their own, and after the family has failed, a variety of aid programs will come to the rescue. Currie argues that during the

1980s the United States had done poorly in helping marginal families nurture children and predicts more future crime as a result (1987: 11-12).

My argument would be that programs which wait for the problem to appear before taking action follow the logic of the curve with two humps. We spate the world into those who need help and those who do not. The attempt to draw a line between these two populations is unwise. Modest gains achieved from supporting families who are struggling, but not yet in great difficulty, could have an important payoff for society. The main theme of this paper is that one thrust of the women's lib movement involves the economic needs of women and children, which in turn is related to a variety of stresses in the family.

Recent data from an Alberta survey of wife battering is consistent with this agreement (Kennedy and Dutton, 1987). This Alberta study showed that wife battering occurred about twice as frequently among the 18 to 34 age category compared to the older categories. While the study has not yet analyzed the data on these young couples, it is likely that young people with young children face more economic problems than those who are more established.

The Alberta study also showed that among those families earning less than $6000 per year wife battering reached 55%, however there were only 9 cases in that category. The 3 categories with incomes between $6000 and $45000 did not show much difference in the percentage of wife battering (13.8%, 14.7%, and 13.8%), but those couples earning over $45,000 showed an incidence of wife battering of 7.5%. While the economic data are not overwhelming, financial support probably plays a role and thus provides some guidelines for policy. Are there ways to ease some of the strains that lead to family violence by providing funds in a judicious manner?

Using child support payments to move the curve to the left.

The question of child support can be used to illustrate the same argument. In the family courts, we continually see cases where a mother is there because the husband has failed to make payments for the care of his children. Sometimes the husband is unemployed, but whatever the reason, the judge is frequently faced with the situation of trying to get money for child support when the father is facing financial difficulties as well. The needs of the children are not paramount in this whole process. Rather, it is sometimes a contest between two uncooperative individuals who are suffering in a variety of ways. Although a number of studies have targeted the laws in several countries as part of the problem (Atkins and Hogget, 1984; Brophy and Smart, 1985), the very fact that families must use the courts to solve problems adds pain to the situation. If instead the state took on the task of paying child support and then collected it from the husband, the situation would be quite different. For example, if a divorce settlement included child support payments, and the main concern of the court was the adequacy of the payments in terms of the needs of the children, instead of the ability of the husband to pay, the size of the payments might be different from the ones which are awarded today. Once awarded, the state could guarantee that those payments would be made on a monthly basis.

The other side of the coin would be collecting those payments from the father. It is possible that an unemployed father would have difficulty making payments. But I would argue that this should be a contest between the court and the father, not between the mother and the father. Admittedly, there are those who argue that the state should not be involved in such family affairs. It is the obligation of the parents, and for those with a traditional orientation, the father in particular, to provide for the children; but in fact, we do not follow that logic. When the needs are great enough, welfare comes in and helps the family in trouble. My point is that we create stresses by waiting for the family to get into trouble. Situations such as divorces already involve tremendous amounts of stress. If this society is interested in minimizing the negative impact on the children, it would be desirable to make the mother of young children as independent as possible. Chasing a former husband through the courts in order to recover overdue child support payments is not the best way for a divorced mother to use her time or finances.

Such conditions also create the conditions for violence. A man wishes to see his children, but the mother says he isn't making payments, so she denies access. Friction can potentially lead to violence. If payments were guaranteed, an ex-wife might even be sympathetic toward the plight of a former husband who is unemployed.

Policy makers sometimes claim that such practices would be impossible to legislate, but other countries have developed more reasonable strategies for dealing with this problem (Bridge, 1985: 23-27). Several Scandinavian countries have developed public maintenance advance systems that take into account salaries of parents and needs of the child, but the major point is that the child is somewhat protected from economic problems faced by the parents.

Our present situation penalized the weakest people. Mothers of small children are the most vulnerable. Economic factors frequently make it difficult for a woman to leave a potentially violent situation. Whether it is during a marriage or afterwards, society has a vested interest in enabling women to act independently and avoid stressful conditions.

TEACHING EQUALITY AND REDUCING AGGRESSION

In trying to relate the women's' liberation movement to crime, I am attempting to link many different steps. The last two decades have produced a variety of information on aggression against females (Davidson, 1978; Lacerte-Lamontagne and Mamontagne, 1980; Sunday and Tobach, 1985; Borkowski, Murch, and Walker, 1983; Bowker, 1983; Schechter, 1982; Fleming, 1979). There can be specific debates over many aspects of this research, but my argument is that some broader strategies relating to economic equality between men and women could be used to change some of the conditions that foster violence. These conditions become chronic and persist for long periods of time. While crash programs are appropriate at times, long term intervention is needed for many behaviour patterns. To illustrate, let us look at some of the evidence on aggression.

Huesmann, et al, (1984) point out that 8-year olds who were more aggressive at the beginning of one study were also the more aggressive 30-year olds at the end of the study. Thus, aggressiveness seems to be a rather stable characteristic and is predictive of criminal behaviour, spouse abuse, and self-reported physical aggression. Eron (1980) argues that to reduce the level of aggression boys should be exposed to the same training that girls have traditionally received in our society and that they be encouraged to develop similar kinds of socially positive, tender, cooperative and sensitive qualities. In other words, if we treat boys more like girls they may be less aggressive. While Eron and his fellow psychologists are talking about specific socializing practices, they are consistent with a larger world-view and social policies that reduce the present dominance of men over women.

Girls who learn that mothers are unequal in a variety of ways may also accept unequal relationships in their dealings with father, uncles, brothers and males in general. The vulnerability of girls seems to contribute to their delinquency. Learning to "be a girl" has its negative side. Chesny-Lind (1983) points to research indicating that many young women who find their way into the juvenile justice system are actually victims of physical and sexual abuse. She summarizes the argument rather well by presenting evidence that:

> Possession of some traditionally masculine traits lowers female delinquency potential [and] possession of some traditionally female traits lowers the likelihood that males will engage in delinquency, particularly aggressive delinquency. Contrary to popular mythology, freeing the sexes from the confines of narrow, stereotyped roles may actually prove to be an effective approach to delinquency prevention (1983: 39).

At other times feminists themselves can contribute to unwise policies by taking stands that are "anti-male". For example, Leslie Kennedy, in reporting on the Alberta study of wife battering mentioned above, points out that researchers are reluctant to report findings that point to the woman as the initiator of violence. The initiation of family violence comes from the female almost as frequently as it does from the male, but there is some pressure to blame males and ignore certain aspects of female behaviour. The consequences of family violence, of course, ae much more devastating for women with the result being that women need protection. However, simply punishing men who batter wives is also a policy which follows the logic of the mythical curve with two humps. It focuses on extreme individuals when the reality is that couples, not just men, are frequently the source of the problem. Attempts to change violent men living in problem families usually requires long term intervention. Short term intervention may be required but should not be viewed as leading to basic change. The point is that finding someone to blame may be less effective in the long run than striving for laws that enable women to be independent.

Economic equality and the reduction of family stress.

It is difficult to provide clear and specific evidence for the broad argument I am trying to make. Economic equality is something that can be influenced by policy makers, and it would influence a broader world view about how men and women relate to each other. When women marry, or live with a man, and bear children, they frequently lose economic power and independence (Atkins and Hogget, 1984: Chap 1). The state could do more to balance that power, for example, by requiring that a portion of a breadwinner's salary is controlled by the homemaker. At present, housewives to not automatically have financial "worth." Obviously, the state cannot dictate how families handle their money, but tax incentives could be used to give women more financial independence.

The details of these policies are not the issue in this paper. Rather, changes that would diminish economic differences between men and women and reduce the differences in socialization practices between boys and girls would also alter the balance of power and increase the ability of the woman to negotiate. This would increase the possibility of avoiding some situations that could be achieved among many families, this would also have an impact on the number of families who are on the extreme right of the continuum which produce violence.

CONCLUSION

Some authors have argued that women's' liberation has been accompanied by greater female involvement in traditional crime, including violence (Alder, 197). The debate concerning changing female roles and their involvement in crime should not be confused with the ideas presented here. I am concerned with that aspect of the feminist movement which enables women to leave conflict producing situations and remove children from such circumstances. The link between the women's' liberation movement and the reduction of violence follows a sequence of steps. First, the connection between violence in the family and future criminality, including violent behaviour, has been supported by several research studies. A few have been noted earlier. A conventional response to this finding, however, could be to focus on those families who seem to be unique, those currently displaying violence. However, these families do not represent a distinct group which can be clearly identified. Instead we are faced with a continuum of family violence with obvious illustrations as well as with many who are marginal. The pattern is like that represented by the skewed curve. Since the target group is unclear, the only truly effective strategy would include many who are viewed as marginal. Because of the volume represented by the more typical family, which faces minor stresses and experiences minor violence, universal plans which have a minor impact on many families would eventually reduce the number of families with severe problems.

Many women's' issues deal with the financial independence of women, especially women who are raising small children either without a husband or with a husband who is not supportive in a variety of ways. The general public usually overlooks the criminogenic aspects of family situations which are the product of this lack of resources in the hands of women. By simply providing the means to move away, a number of situations conducive to violence might be altered.

It is possible that some of these changes are already occurring in North America. When Straus and Gelles (1986) reported a decrease in child abuse and wife abuse between 1975 and 1985, there was a mixed response from official agencies who claimed that they had been receiving in increase in cases of this nature. The survey results did not coincide with the experience of many agencies. One possible interpretation is that a broad-based social concern leading to a variety of programs could have an impact. Such programs might make women seek help instead of enduring beatings. This should not be used as an excuse for complacency. Rather, it suggests that when a society mobilizes, there is the possibility of a positive impact. That principle could be generalized to broad based programs that make seemingly modest contributions to the quality of family life for many families in addition to the type of intervention that takes place for those few who are clearly identified as having problems. Much of this help could be provided by modest changes in legislation, in the way we deliver legal services, and in the support systems in social services and education. It may also reduce violent crime in the next generation.

Jim Hackler, Department of Sociology
University of Alberts (Edmonton)
(c. 1987)

References

- Alder, Freda. 1985 Sisters in Crime, New York: McGraw-Hill.
- Atkins, Susan and Brenda Hoggett. 1974. Women and the Law. Oxford: Basil Blackwell.
- Borkowski, Margaret, Mervyn Murch, and Val Walker, 1983, Marital Violence. London: Tavistock.
- Bowker, Lee. 1983. Beating Wife-Beating. Lexington: D.C. Heath.
- Bridge, Karen L. 1985. An International Survey of Private and Public Law Maintenance and Single-Parent Families: Summary and Recommendations. Ottawa: Status of Women Canada.
- Brophy, Julia and Carol Smart (eds.) 1985. Women-In-Law. London: Routledge ad Kegan Paul.
- Browne, Angela. 1987. When Battered Women Kill. New York: Free Press.
- Chesny-Lind, Meda. 1983. "Girls and Violence: An Exploration of the Gender Gap in Serious Delinquent Behaviour." Report No. 285, Youth Development Research Center, University of Hawaii at Manoa.
- Conrad, Peter. 1975. "The discovery of hyper kinesis: notes on the medicalization of deviant behaviour." Social Problems 23 (Oct):12-21.
- Conrad, Peter and Joseph W. Schneider. 1980. Deviance and Medicalization: From Badness to Sickness. St. Louis: C.V. Mosby.
- Currie, Elliot. 1987. What Kind of Future? Violence and Public Safety in the Year 2000. San Francisco: National Council on Crime and Delinquency.
- Currie, Elliott. 1985. Confronting crime. New York: Pantheon.
- Davidson, Terry. 1978. Conjugal Crime. New York: Hawthorn.
- Elmhorn, K. 1965. "Self-reported delinquency among school children in Stockholm." In K.O. Christiansen (ed.), Scandinavian Studies in Criminology (Vol.1). London: Tavistock.
- Eron, Leonard. 1980. Prescription for reduction of aggression." American Psychologist 55(3):244-252.
- Fleming, Jennifer Baker. 1979. Stopping Wife Abuse. New York: Anchor.
- Gelles, R.J. and Murray Straus. 1979. "Determinants of violence I the family: toward a theoretical integration." In W. Burr, R. Hill, F.I. Nye, and I Reiss (eds.), Contemporary Theories about the Family. New York: Free Press.
- Huesmann, L. Rowell, Leonard Eron and Munroe Lefkowitz. 1984. "Stability of aggression over time and generations." Developmental Psychology 20(6):1120-1134.
- Hackler, James C. and Laurel Gauld. 1981. "Policies toward violent crime: Alberta as a case study." Canadian Journal of Criminology 23 (July):313-329.

- Jaffe, Peter, David Wolfe, Susan Wilson, and Lydia Zak. 1985. "Critical issues in the assessment of children's adjustment to witnessing family violence." Canada's Mental Health 33:15-19.
- Kennedy, Leslie W. and Donald G Dutton. 1987. "The Incidence of Wife Assault in Alberta." Report No.53, Edmonton Area Series. Edmonton: Population Research Laboratory, University of Alberta.
- Kincaid, Pat J. 1985. The Omitted Reality: Husband-Wife Violence in Ontario Land Policy Implications for Education. Concord, Ontario: Belsten.
- Lacerte-Lamontagne, Celyne and Yves Lamontagne. 1980. Le Viol: Acte de Pouvoir et de Colere. Montreal: La Presse.
- Pfohl, Stephen J. 1977. "The 'discovery' of child abuse." Social Problems 24:10-323
- Lincoln, Alan J. and Murray Straus. 1984. Crime and the Family. Springfield, Ill: C.C. Thomas.
- MacLeod, Linda and Andree Cadieux. 1980. Wife-battering in Canada: the Vicious Circle. Hull: Minister of Supply and Services, Canada.
- McCord, Joan. 1981. "Consideration of some effects of a counseling program." In Susan Martin, Lee Sechrest, and Robin Redner (eds.) New Directions in the Rehabilitation of Criminal Offenders. Washington: National Academy Press.
- O'Brien, Robert M. 1985. Crime and Violence Data. Beverly Hills: Sage.
- Pagelow, Mildred. 198. Family Violence. New York: Praeger..
- Popham, Robert E., Wolfgang Schmidt, and Jan de Lint. 1976. "The prevention of hazardous drinking: implications for research on the effects of government control measures. In J.A. Edwing and B.A. Rouse (eds.), Drinking. Chicago: Nelson-Hall.
- Ross, Robert. 1980. "Violence in, violence out: child abuse and self-mutilation in adolescent offenders." Canadian Journal of Criminology 22 (July):273-287.
- Russell, Diana, E.H. 1982. Rape in Marriage. New York: MacMillan.
- Schechter, Susan. 1982. Women and male Violence. Boston: South End Press.
- Schmidt, Wolfgang and Robert E. Popham. 1978. "The single distribution theory of alcohol consumption." Journal of Studies on Alcohol 39 (March):400-419.
- Steinmetz, Suzanne and Murray Straus. 1974. Violence in the Family. New York: Harper and Row.
- Straus, Murray and Richard Gelles. 1986. "Societal change and change in family violence from 1975 to 198 as revealed by two national surveys." Journal of Marriage and the Family 48:465-479.
- Straus, Murray, Richard Gelles, and Suzanne Steinmetz. 1980. Behind Closed Doors: Violence in the American Family. Garden City, NY: Doubleday/Anchor.
- Sunday, Suzanne R. and Ethel Tobach (eds.). 16985. Violence Against Women. New York: Gordian.
- Tierney, Kathleen. 1982. "The battered women movement and the wife beating problem." Social Problems 29 (Feb.):207-220.
- Tong, Rosemarie. 1984. Women, Sex, and the Law. Totowa, NJ: Rowman and Allanheld.
- Walker, Lenore E. 1984. The Battered Wife Syndrome. New York: Springer.

- White, Susan O. and Murray Straus. 1981. "The implications of family violence for rehabilitation strategies." In Susan Martin, Lee Sechrest, and Robin Redner (eds.), New Directions in the Rehabilitation of Criminal Offenders. Washington: National Academy Press.
- Whitehead Paul and Reginal Smart. 1972. "Epidemiological aspects of drug use and implications for the prevention of drug abuse." Pp.369-374 in Craig Boydell, Carl Grindstaff, and Paul Whitehead (eds), Deviant Behaviour and Societal Reaction. Toronto: Holt, Rinehart, and Winston.
- Widom, Cathy Spatz. 1986. "Early child abuse, neglect, and later violent criminal behaviour." Paper presented at the Society for Life History Research Conference, Palm Springs, California.

Appendix II

I have always been a serious admirer of the writing of James Jones, American author (1921- 1977). Two of my favorite reads are his books *Some Came Running* and *Go To The Widow-maker*. He is the author of *From Here To Eternity*. [I had, and still have, the same fascination with the work of Fyodor Dostoyevsky and Frederic Nietzsche, as with Mr. Jones, since I was about fourteen.]

In Mr. Jones' book *Go To The Widowmaker* is a passage of particular note that was a foreshadowing of the mess we are in today, prescient and prophetic to say the least. An unstated backdrop in *Go to the Widowmaker* is the author's view of the drastically changing North American culture after World War II. What I have written about in this book regarding glitter, glamor, and celebrity worship, Mr. Jones indirectly implied in his book—the growing fascination and desire for glamour, status, and celebrity that is so much a problem today.

There is a conversation between two characters, Al Bonham and Lucky Grant. Al Bonham, a skin/scuba diver in the Bahamas, caters to the wealthy. He is planning a business venture that will take advantage of the early 1950s social fascination with privilege and glamour. Lucky Grant's husband, Ron Grant, is a famous playwright. Ron is considering investing in Al Bonham's business of pleasure diving cruises that cater to the want-to-be rich and famous. The book is set principally in the Caribbean a few years after the second world war. In my 1967 first edition the passage begins at page 364.

"*My theory is what I call the Chosen Ones,*" [said Al Bonham to Lucky Grant] "*or the New Aristocracy. The Chosen Ones simply means celebrity hood... you and Ron qualify. In our own time this celebrity-hood jazz has become worldwide due to technological advances begun in World War II and expanded enormously since then. Lumped together these advances are called Mass Communications. Whatever the process, a Chosen One, once arrived, once 'chosen', becomes different from other people, actually lives by other laws almost. They are protected by everybody, they get better service, are treated with deference, are given better deals on everything, live off the fat of the land... They become protected symbols of what everybody would like to be.*

"*Now the other phenomenon that has grown out of the technological advances begun in World War II is Mass Cheap Travel. In this age of 'You-must-work-forty-hours-a-week-government-required', the carrot under the nose of 'Citizen' or a 'Comrade' is that for two weeks every year (or a month if you're an executive) he can live like a Chosen One lives all the time. Not really of course, but enough to make the pretense digestible. If he saves his money the other 48 or 50 weeks of the year, he can go just about anywhere in the world, be catered to, be treated as if he really were a Chosen One. This is known as the Tourist Industry. All the exotic places, the faraway romantic names, he can now visit and pretend (for a while) he is one of the New Aristocracy he has helped to choose, and preserve... It's an entirely new field. The Tourist Trade... being 'Pioneered' by people who want to live like the Chosen Ones live all the time. And the Chosen Ones, the real Chosen Ones, are the kings of and key to it all.*

"Where the Chosen Ones go the unchosen ones want to go... Soon the big advertising will start..."

James Jones (1921-1977)
Go To The Widow-maker
Delacorte Press, 1967

Appendix III

Political Indoctrination is not Treatment

The opium consumed in the US, referred to in Chapter 8, was principally imported from China. Several American millionaires neatly camouflaged the importation of opium under the innocuous name of "The China Trade." There are several YouTube presentations regarding this—search author James Bradley who speaks to his book, *The China Mirage – The Hidden History of the American Disaster in China*. Mr. Bradley also has a section of time in the documentary film *The Coming War on China*, from Dartmouth Films by journalist John Pilger. Mr. Bradley's appearance in the film; his exposition on the opium trade and 19th century American millionaires, is near the 40-minute mark of the film. These are available on YouTube. Mr. Pilger's documentary film is well worth watching. These are very revealing of racism and xenophobia within the US against the Chinese and leads to the distinct possibility of another world war, instigated by the US with China.

The American purchase of opium was so pervasive and destructive to the Chinese of that era, that it led to the Chinese Boxer Rebellion, c. 1900. What the Chinese wanted then, among other things, was to stop the opium trade and reclaim some independence from foreign economic dominance. That rebellion was vigorously put down by the American military protecting American big-business (opium) interests.

I refer now to Caroline Jean Acker's book, *Creating the American Junkie*, Johns Hopkins University Press, 2002. Some of my references come from her seminal work on drug addiction in the US. Her book describes the unregulated sale of opiates and morphine pre-1910, used principally by older, upper middle-class women, for their self-diagnosed physical or emotional discomfort. Opium sales were so common and uncontrolled that around 1898, heroin was socially marketed as a cough remedy. Laudanum was regularly used for female "hysteria," depression, and given to colicky children. Doctors distributed morphine "as requested" by their patients. It was so egregious that iatrogenic addiction (addiction from doctor's prescriptions) led to rapidly increased restrictions, product labelling, and government control. The post-1910 restrictions and prohibition of opiates led to a social change in users. By the later 1920s or so, opiate users changed from upper middle-class women to lower class urban males. This is far more complex than I can explain here. Caroline Acker's book explains it well.

By 1910, Protestant religious morality as a social movement had become well organized. Within a decade, it stood against prostitution (brothels) which had been silently, socially tolerated, against tobacco, against new Jazz-age uninhibited dances, against gambling, against drinking (its original cause), and by the early 1940s encouraged the persecution of homosexuals as deviants. Through a convoluted path, which was partly outlined earlier that ended with the war on drugs, drug addicts became criminals and were seen as irredeemable deviants. All of this leads to this observation... Alcoholics and opium-heroin-cannabis addicts had become compelling, negative smears of shame on how Christian society viewed itself **and what it** wanted to accomplish—Christian, moral purity.

Psychology has it that we conceal our own shame and reject the people we are ashamed of. Alcoholics and addicts, prostitutes, etc., from 1920, were rejected by Christian society and alienated by law. Addiction "treatment" by doctors was non-existent and addiction was pushed to the shadowy areas of society. The only "treatment" for drug addiction was to give them drugs and doctors refused to do that; a refusal that was related to the issue of iatrogenic addiction noted above. This carries many sinister shadows for what we now call harm reduction in culture.

The view was that addicts were abnormal—an "inversion of normal" (from Caroline Acker's book, *Creating the American Junkie*). Addicts were seen as socially deviant and "backwards" to what American Christians defined as normal. If addicts are "inverted from normal" what this inherently implies is that successful "treatment" is to get addicts to become normal—socially acceptable law-abiding citizens obedient to government-regulated Christian morality. That is not soulful or spiritual, but it is normal according to society. That leads to...

When doctors encroached into addiction treatment, c. 1980, the label shifted from illness to disease. It all shifted from individual recovery to assembly-line treatment centers. That's where the money is. The intrusion of doctors, politics, and funded agencies caused a significant shift in the views of treatment and recovery. The purpose of treatment became quite different from personal recovery pre-1975-ish. Before then, it very generally meant some established level of spiritual responsibility and a more reserved or quieter lifestyle.

Addiction treatment today has come to mean two things: (i) establish some measure of sobriety; **and** (ii), become a good tax-paying citizen-consumer. Get back to cultural-normal. This is the now-established position relative to the 1940s view of addicts being an inversion of normal. Modern treatment is designed to switch addicts from the inversion-of-normal back to socially normal and culturally cooperative. That isn't spiritual but it is normal. It's quite difficult to recover from a group C or D addiction and then be pushed into living a group B addicted lifestyle, but that's what "normal" is.

This takes us directly into two reasons for the very high relapse rate. (1) We are trying to teach Groups C and D addicts to adopt a Group B-addicted lifestyle. That's addiction substitution not recovery. (2) In the socially approved addictions of Group B, there is very little authentic, compassionate, relationship honesty, harmony or respect. That absence sits at the core of all relapse. These guarantee an ineffectiveness in treatment, which was explained back in Chapter 4: The Probability of Ineffectiveness.

Being sincerely spiritual, which stands against our cultural values of consumerism, approved addiction, glitter and spending, status, and religious dogma, has gone by the wayside. Treatment has become an effort at political indoctrination—become a good citizen, cooperate quietly in socially approved addictions like celebrity worship, disposable relationships, and shiny things, pay taxes as required, and don't be rebellious or irresponsible.

These are far removed from any authentic spiritual lifestyle. Under the euphemism of "treatment," recovery now means successful indoctrination into a seriously dislocated culture—participation at a social level of acceptable addiction. What we see as "hard-core" Group C and D addicts cannot live in an addiction-approved Group B lifestyle. This is now the benchmark for addiction treatment—political indoctrination into socially-approved addiction. This is not treatment and will not engender spiritual success.

Index

Printed in Canada